D1624978

The
Weatherford Collection

Donated by the family
of
Heiskell Weatherford

MANY DIMENSIONAL MAN

This book has been published
with the aid of a Bicentennial Grant
from the Phi Beta Kappa Society

MANY DIMENSIONAL MAN

Decentralizing Self, Society, and the Sacred

James Ogilvy

NEW YORK
OXFORD UNIVERSITY PRESS
1977

Copyright © 1977 by Oxford University Press, Inc.

Library of Congress Cataloging in Publication Data

Ogilvy, James
   Many dimensional man.

   Includes bibliographical references .
   1.   Man.   2.   Civilization, Modern—1950–
I.   Title.
BD450.O367   128   76–57273
ISBN 0–19–502231–9

Printed in the United States of America

For my teachers
For the lessons
   not all academic

For my wife
For the passions
   not all romantic

For my parents
For the support
   not all economic

For my friends
For the good times
   not all comic

Preface

Every explorer needs provisions. One does not forge into the wilderness alone. Yet few ever hear about the base camps, the bearers, the incredible logistics involved in mounting an expedition. We admire the courage of the few who reach the summit, but we forget that the privilege of courage presupposes the preparation that distinguishes courage from foolish bravado.

This book is an exploration, a series of log entries based on adventures in some little known lands of the intellect. Of course there are those who have gone before. But it is worth noting at the outset that these scribblings make no claims to be definitive maps, only sketches drawn by a pen moving all too quickly before cold or storm forced a retreat to the safety of more familiar thoughts. Once the less familiar has become more familiar, others will doubtless find it both necessary and possible to improve upon these primitive charts.

As for provisions, references will be found in footnotes. Many follow like humble bearers behind the main body of the text. Some of the footnote numbers have asterisks attached, e.g.[27*]. The notes so designated are less humble than the rest. They sometimes make substantive additions to the text, additions that were better tucked into notes because their contents were too technical or too arcane for the general reader.

In addition to noted debts to other authors there are of course the countless debts to students, teachers, friends, editors, typists and readers. The list is so long it would be folly to begin. Nor would an enumeration express the uniqueness of the many contributions. Yet there is one contribution without which all the rest might never have come together. The entire expedition drew sustenance from the generous and gratefully acknowledged support of a Phi Beta Kappa Bicentennial Fellowship.

J.O.

Williamstown
May 1977

Contents

MANY DIMENSIONAL MAN

Prologue

Social philosophy traditionally begins with the question: How does man mediate his relationship with nature? Politics and technology provide answers to the traditional question. Technology masters physical nature; politics manages human nature. Because the traditional point of departure for social philosophy assumes a hostile nature, politics and technology appear as useful tools for attaining domination over hostile environments, both physical and human. But social philosophy needs a new foundation for the simple reason that nature is no longer the hostile environment. A gradual but fundamental shift has brought us to a point where the traditional solutions have now become the problem: politics and technology have replaced nature in the role of alien environment. The new problem: How to carve out livable spaces within the political-technological wasteland?

Simply to see the migration made by politics and technology from the role of solution to the role of problem should be sufficient for finding new foundations. But like old paradigms, old questions die hard. Convinced of the need to dominate the environment, we retain a

3

compulsion to seek a better politics, a better technology. We are reluctant to grant that these man-made tools have taken on lives of their
own. If we could tinker a little more with Frankenstein's innards we
might tame him, or so we like to think. Despite our by now platitudi-
nous alienation from the political-technological environment we are
nonetheless reluctant to regard it as truly alien. It is as if alienation
were *our* problem, one to be overcome by some sort of shift of attitude
or psyche. But as the best of the alienists have seen, psychic distance
from society is itself a social product.[1] So the radical therapist turns
from the task of adjusting the "sick" consciousness to the sick society
and tries instead a political solution to the illness. He and she become
politicized. But this radicalism cannot reach the root (*radix*). It is
insufficiently radical. Politics repeats itself as if the fundamental
question of social philosophy were still the problem of mediating our
relationship with nature. The attempt at political solutions perpetuates the illusion that politics is a tool still in our control.

Similarly, the problems caused by technology are thought to
be solvable by a better technology. If only we can iron out the kinks,
develop a new technology of purification for cleaning up the mess of
the old technology then everything will be all right. More technology
is the answer advanced to take care of an already reckless technology.
Old paradigms die hard. We are reluctant to cut our losses and grant
the need for a new beginning.

Nor can we start utterly afresh. No return to Eden is possible.
We can no more turn our backs on politics and technology than earlier
we could turn our backs on nature. The return to nature may be an option for a very few but civilization cannot occupy the hills of northern
New Mexico. Many of those who fled to the mountains merely played
out another move in the dialectic of over-conversions. First, the radi-
calization of the therapist leaves him fighting an obsolete battle he
cannot win. Second, his subsequent flight after the failure of his forays into politics leaves him in a similarly one-sided condition. Now
he stands on the opposite side from whence he began—with nature as
opposed to man.

But all this movement remains confined to that now outmoded spectrum on which politics and technology span the distance between man and nature. This radicalism misses the root of the present problem, namely the shift of players in the role of alien environment. Like the ascetic who, as Hegel showed, defines and determines his existence by the very niceties he intends to escape, their absence now becoming "precisely the most important consideration," so the political ascetic, "by giving the enemy a fixedness of being and of meaning, instead of getting rid of him, really never gets away from him, and finds itself constantly defiled."[2] Even in his flight into nature the political ascetic, the abstainer from politics, perpetuates the problem by giving a fixedness of being to its terms: man-politics-nature.

What are the new terms: man-?-politics; man-?-technology? What will fill in the blank left by the migration of politics and technology from the role of solution to the role of alien environment? And with the shift of players in the role of alien environment is there a corresponding shift on the other side of the spectrum? Is man the same? These are the questions with which to found a new social philosophy. Nothing less radical will do. The mediation between the new man and the new alien environment must be as global a strategy toward politics and technology as politics and technology were toward nature—a tall order. Yet the outline of that strategy is already at hand, as it must be if social philosophy is to defend itself against the charge of mere utopianism, idle speculation about what would be nice if only. . . .

The outline is at hand in the practice of many who yet lack the means to articulate what they are doing because their actions do not fit the old paradigms. Not only do they lack the means to understand their practice, but social theorists as well are at a loss for words to make sense of their actions. Neither 'revolution' nor 'protest' nor 'apathy' are quite adequate to describe those patterns that prefigure the yet to be developed social philosophy. Nor is 'anarchism' appropriate, though it comes closer than most. New words are called for, even if only to name the problem rather than solve it.

A paradigm case of the new practice is the spread of para-professionalism. Like the more general systems of politics and technology the particular professions have become unwieldy. The increased technology of medical practice creates a demand for increased specialization on the part of professionals. As each doctor learns more and more about less and less, the problems of everyday family health care become ever more remote from most doctors' concerns. Enter the paraprofessional whose interest is not more and better medicine in the sense of research breakthroughs to new and exotic cures; instead the paraprofessional sees the kid with the cold and the pregnant mother. The paraprofessional mediates between those who need care and an increasingly esoteric system of medicine that seems increasingly unable to help. The paraprofessional does not create new tools; he provides access to already available tools. *The Whole Earth Catalog* is subtitled "Access to Tools." *The Whole Earth Catalog* is an example of what we might call, to coin a new and necessary word, paratechnology.

What about parapolitics? The ratio, patient-paraprofessional-professional to man-?-politics suggests at least the linguistic appropriateness of 'parapolitics' as the name for the social practice mediating between man and the new alien environment. The prefix "para-" connotes both "beside" and "against". What theory defines the practice so named? Surely not the theory of anarchism, more an antipolitics than a parapolitics. The stance of the anarchist is too close to that of the political ascetic, too reminiscent of the will to turn one's back on the alien environment rather than work both beside and against it. Yet the anarchist remains more likely than others to see the sense in which the tools of politics will turn on their modern manipulators and tie them more tightly into the knots they wished to escape.

To complete the preliminaries, the naming of the problems prior to their attempted solutions, what of the new man? What sort of person will flourish in those parapolitical enclaves carved out of the political-technological wilderness? Both the professional's practice and the theory to be developed show him to be a many dimensional man, pluralized and multi-selved. A decentralized parapolitics calls for decentralized people.

The hierarchical organization of politics in advanced industrial society demands one-dimensional, narrow individuals to fill increasingly specialized slots. A rigid sense of self-identity receives reinforcement from a bureaucratized social hierarchy—a proper place for each and each in his proper place. A pattern of mutual reinforcement binds the centralized self and the centralized society. This tight knot is the target of Marcuse's *One Dimensional Man*. All talk of social decentralization seems vacuous where the social system absorbs each and every dissenting group into a yet wider pattern of repressive tolerance. Even the so-called deviant cannot break out of the circle of mutual reinforcement when the label 'deviant' defines one more of its functionally specialized arcs.

In order to break out of the circle of narrow centralization both parapolitics and many dimensional people complement one another. The concept of critical mass is helpful here: only when enough radioactive isotopes are brought together will their mutual interaction set off a nuclear reaction. So with many dimensional people: only with a critical mass is parapolitics possible. But once that mass is reached then the reaction sets up a new circle of mutual reinforcement between the decentralized society and the decentralized self.

The structural relationships between self and society, the patterns of mutual reinforcement, render certain debates of the late sixties and early seventies both obsolete and basically misleading. The argument over whether social change follows from changes in consciousness *or* changes in political structure obscures the fact that *both* must change if an alteration in either is to survive.

Because there is no axiomatic primacy of consciousness to politics, no center to a decentralized system, the very notion of a new *starting point* of social philosophy comes into question once the new question has been asked. The nature of the question casts doubt upon the kind of technological rationality that starts with axioms and proceeds in linear fashion toward deductively argued conclusions. In asking how the new man will mediate his relationship to the new alien environment we open the possibility of a new man whose mode of rationality is itself less hypothetico-deductive, less internally bureau-

cratized, less linear. Many dimensional man exhibits paraconsciousness, a mode of thought more appropriate to the content of decentralization. Paraconsciousness complements the rationality of the Enlightenment with symbolic consciousness, intuition, and affective sensitivity. In place of an intellect whose only functions are analysis and
judgment subsuming analytic elements under higher unities, the richer rationality of paraconsciousness both allows and demands more
varied modes for presenting a reasonable case: not only argument
from evidence but also aphorisms built on analogy; not only analysis
into parts but synthesis into wholes; not only theoretical explanations
but exemplary stories.

The book's division into three parts therefore reflects a movement appropriate to the subject matter. Part One begins from *present*
actualities that are ill-understood according to current concepts of
power, freedom and subjectivity. Part Two uses stories from the *past*
as exemplary contents for illustrating the structures achieved by Part
One's *abstraction* from the present. Part Three returns to the *concrete*
present and future with tools honed by Part One's abstraction and Part
Two's exemplification.

The case for many dimensional man fits neatly on no available
methodological or conceptual foundations. Nor is its thought so new
that it might hover in the fresh air of total novelty. Instead the foundations are messily eclectic, a cornerstone here, a piling there, a sewer
pipe at some distance from either. Consequently what might have
been a short book bulges with pages putting the prefabricated pieces
in order—e.g., existentialism, Marxism, structuralism, hermeneutics, psychohistory and cybernetic information theory. Since none of
these traditions is alone quite adequate to the task, since each has
staked out claims not to be ignored, the best course is to show how
each of these ostensibly separate traditions joins a group portrait re-
vealing their significance as a family. By the simple fact of their simultaneous existence and broad family resemblances these seemingly
separate traditions demonstrate as well as contribute to the emergence
of a kind of thinking whose timeliness, growing universality and es-

sential simplicity are often obscured by the sometimes arcane and sectarian developments of similar ideas.

The simplest title for this complex portrait might be *relational thought*. Its interrelated axioms and exemplary applications run very briefly as follows. (1) To be is to be related; e.g. to be a human being is not only to contain certain biological components but also to maintain human relationships with other human beings. (2) Relations of *difference* prefigure resultant identities; e.g. we do not enter our relations with others with our identities already intact. Instead our identities are progressively shaped by whatever and whomever we take to be other or different. (3) The most important identities for social philosophy are identities of *structure;* e.g. political structure is more significant for social diagnosis than differences among the personalities who successively occupy the structure; and conversely, structural changes should not be obscured by the fact that successive politicians fill positions retaining the same names. (4) Under conditions sometimes described as causal we are entitled to call one structure of difference a *transform* of another structure of difference; e.g. the difference between many dimensional man and the new alien environment is a transform of the difference between earlier humanity and nature. The language of causality describes the historical succession poorly because causality connotes singular agencies rather than sequences of relational structures. (5) Because the terms of relations are determined by structures of relations, *context* is significant for determining content; e.g. the meaning of the presidency in a parapolitical context will differ from its meaning in a traditionally political context.

The structure of the following chapters both fills in and follows from the demands of Relational Thought. Political power, once plausibly analyzed in terms of singular sources of causality, now receives a relational analysis in terms of a structure of multiple constraints. Freedom, once regarded as a simple lack of causality, now requires an analysis in terms of alternative transforms of difference. Subjectivity, once plausibly analyzed as a singular source of freedom, now requires explication in terms of alternative contexts for the exercise of agencies as multiply diffused in persons as power is diffused in nations.

The three chapters of Part One sketch the relational structure of power, freedom and subjectivity in turn. Part Two introduces exemplary content to the abstract structures developed in Part One. The polytheistic pantheon of Greek gods and the multiplex personalities of Nietzsche's Zarathustra serve as parallel organizing principles to illustrate in concrete and dramatic terms the abstract argument of Part One. Part Three draws together the several themes and arguments of the first two parts as they bear on the psychology and theology of transcendence and immanence, ecstasy and instancy, ascension to the white light and descent into the secular city of contemporary reality. To seek out the poles of one's soul and in those whitened wastes to chase the secrets of one's dark tropics—that is the love of wisdom, philosophy.

PART
ONE
STRUCTURES OF
AGENCY

I The Structure of Power

The contemporary American's experience of the President of the United States is very much like the ancient Athenian's experience of Zeus. The ancient Athenian counted on Zeus and sometimes blamed him. The ancient Athenian performed certain rituals much as we perform elections, and with about the same return on his investment of time and energy. The ancient Greeks never actually saw Zeus. Just as the Athenians heard about the decisions of the gods through priests like the oracle at Delphi, so we hear of certain equally efficacious decisions from media pundits like Eric Sevareid, and with about the same sense of seriousness. Symbols of authority breed both reverence and whimsy. We wish and we do not wish our lives to be under control. Both the presidency and the Greek pantheon are symbols of control. Both are focuses for fantasies about power and its machinations. Both reflect their believers' ideas about the way human life ought to be organized.

Both the presidency and the Greek pantheon share socially functional similarities. Yet common sense thinks them different.

13

"Unlike the Greek gods," sounds the objection, "the presidents actually exist." But what about the more abstract role, the presidency? If we have learned anything from theology it must be that existence with respect to fantasy figures has less to do with being locatable in space and time than with the beliefs of those who worship. Countless factors from the mortality of some presidents to the acts of others have strained belief in the presidency—to the point that a presidential candidate could come to the White House by playing on the declining belief in precisely the office he would occupy. Fantasy life is rich in ironies. Witness religious belief's role in perpetrating a political atheism in order to gain the political power that supposedly replaces religious authority.

The presidency is dead. The sentence has the terminal impact of an older more familiar cadence: God is dead. Surely neither the presidency nor God dies like a dog. The invocation of death is metaphorical. But the glancing glow of metaphor can reveal more than the glare of the literal.

Nietzsche's announcement of the death of God clarified the shift from religious to secular consciousness. His attitude toward that shift was justifiably ambivalent. On the one hand the God of European Christianity had to die. He was a god grown old and weak and pitying, a castrated god, a god to whom only the weak could kneel. On the other hand the act of killing God left man in a flatland of secularism, a dull plain of spiritual exhaustion where none of the passion of Raphael's vertical ascensions and damnations remained. Nietzsche's portrait of the man who killed God falls under the title, "The Ugliest Man." Nietzsche's announcement and mourning of the death of God shed light on both the fact and the threat of modern nihilism.

The announcement of the death of the presidency sheds light in a similar way. We are no longer living in a unified nation. However strong the vestigial will to political monotheism, no single figure can satisfy that will because the office he would occupy has lost credibility and belief is the stuff of imperial power.

Because neither god nor the presidency dies like a dog, because it is quite impossible to take a literal pulse before pronouncing death, it behooves the undertaker to attend to less literal signs of life before proceeding with the burial. The "house of God," for example, still stands. The countryside is dotted with churches; coffers clink with the loose change of millions. Yet who among the literate needs to be convinced of the modest claim that the church is no longer at the center of society? The modern political system is most often distinguished from the premodern precisely by the separation of church and state, by the legitimation of authority in secular terms.

Now the political papacy is under attack. We face a Reformation in the realm of politics. The rituals will persist. The buildings will remain standing. Washington will not disappear behind clouds like the peak of Olympus, nor will the Pentagon levitate. But for many the nation no longer commands the patriotic zeal that once replaced religious zeal. It is as if we could now replace 'politicians' for 'gods' in Hegel's description of "the bitter pain which finds expression in the cruel words, 'God is dead.'" He continues: "Trust in the eternal laws of the Gods is likewise silenced, just as the oracles are dumb, who pretended to know what to do in particular cases. The statues set up are now corpses in stone whence the animating soul has flown, while the hymns of praise are words from which all belief has gone. The tables of the gods are bereft of spiritual food and drink, and from his games and festivals man no more receives the joyful sense of his unity with the divine Being."[1] Flowery but accurate, at least for a significant number. There will always be throwbacks to earlier ages, men whose spirits dwell for better or worse in centuries long past.

Common sense, the residue of centuries, will protest that our faith in politics is not the entire stuff of its existence. Just as the religious believer takes comfort in the idea that come the day of judgment his god will damn the heathen to hell-fire precisely because they lack faith, so the politically minded will persist in claiming that power functions quite independently of belief. Obviously the power of the Internal Revenue Service will not evaporate when one among millions ceases to believe. He will soon find the shape of his daily life quite different behind bars. In testing the will of the political gods so brashly and independently he tempts their immediate wrath, or so it will seem. But similar tests could be devised to prove the persistence of a religious order in the universe: break all ten commandments in a week and the "wrath of God" will soon descend, or so it will seem. Extreme tests will always provoke a response extreme enough to allow a simple interpretation in terms of a simple source of power, whether divine or political. But extreme tests tell us nothing about the subtler aspects of supposedly religious and political life. Despite the language of life and death Hegel and Nietzsche were making a subtler point about God. A subtler point remains to be made about our political superstitions.

In announcing that God had died they admitted that God had lived. God was neither an eternal verity nor, as simpleminded atheists would have it, a mere fiction. God is an *historical* fact. Religious consciousness truly lived in a world-over-which-God-presided. But that world is a thing of the past. Its passing was not only a function of declining religious belief. A complex interplay of political, cultural and economic determinants generated a new world where politics replaced religion as the arena in which authority received legitimation. Similarly complex factors now conspire to replace politics with parapolitics as the tool mediating man's relationship with his new environment. Political affairs are no longer at the theoretical center of mediation between man and environment. Instead politics now migrates toward the environmental periphery once occupied by nature.

Can the meaning of 'politics' migrate from solution to problem? Some theoreticians support common sense's superstition that it cannot. But their claims for the permanence of politics depend on shuffling definitions of 'politics' that are so flexible and all-encompassing the term 'politics' becomes meaningless. For example, Talcott Parsons claims, "Political affairs are the center of integration of all analytical elements of the social system, and not one of these particular elements."[2] If Parsons intends his remark as a definition rather than as an observation, then clearly it cannot be falsified. Whatever plays the role of "center of integration" will go under the name of politics however much it may differ from politics as we know it. By defining politics formally as the "center of integration," a theoretician assures that the world-over-which-politics-presides cannot pass. Yet the contents that come to satisfy the definition may not satisfy our common sense concepts used in recognizing what we now call politics, e.g., systems of representation, legislation, voting and so on.

The theoretician has a choice in defining 'politics' either formally or according to the specific contents we now recognize as political. Though either option is open, some social scientists wish to have it both ways. Most claim that politics is at the center of society in a sense that is factual rather than definitional; yet further, politics *must* remain at the center. Curiously enough the necessity of the 'must' is more definitional than factual. Thus Daniel Bell: "Though the weights of the class system may shift, the nature of the political system, as the arena where interests are mediated, will not."[3] We could agree that there will always be an arena where interests are mediated. But Bell has something far more specific and falsifiable in mind when he claims, "It is not the technocrat who ultimately holds power, but the politician."[4]

Who holds the power? Who governs? These are the questions that command the imagination of political scientists, viz,., the very title of Robert Dahl's influential *Who Governs?* The shape of the question determines the range of answers that qualify as mainstream social theory. In fact mainstream social theory has taken a few twists and turns before reaching the pluralized delta yet to be described. A brief trip upstream will review the course of that dialectical debate whose latest stages reflect but ought not to be confused with the earlier.

The dialectic of power
in mainstream social science

Without troubling to seek the spring-fed sources or map every sand bar of this theoretical Mississippi a hasty geographical survey will reveal three major watersheds in the mainstream's course. The first two are familiar. The third is that more recently created delta where the power of politics dissolves into a proliferation of tidal basins quite different from the plurality of tributaries upstream.

The first pits conservative against liberal in a debate that is primarily normative: *should* there be strong central power? On one side was the consensus among many political thinkers early in this century that liberal democracy was superior to both laissez-faire and charismatic politics. Against laissez-faire the liberal consensus admitted the possibility of improving on nature. Their strong belief in progress and culture issued in a politics that assumed the improvability of man through social and political cultivation according to the higher lights of enlightenment rationality. The Apollonian ideal of crystal clear intellect figured in the rejection of charismatic leadership. The very idea of charisma stood as an offense to a world view devoid of hazy shadows and glowing auras. The early consensus for liberal democracy embodied a philosophy of total consciousness. "Where id was let ego be. Where unconscious forces lurk let the light of conscious intellect shine. Then will there dawn a new day with a new deal," or so the story goes.[5]

Still within the first watershed, the conservative critique of liberalism stresses the danger of totalitarianism. "The less government the better because, whoever governs, the phenomena of public and private life both good and especially evil are so dark and complex that conscious intellect cannot hope to comprehend them much less map their future course according to elaborately administered plans. Man is not perfectible, inequality is the natural condition." The conservative critique continues toward filling in a position that masks itself as metaphysics but more often than not serves as a rationalization for greed.

In the terms of this crude geography, C. Wright Mills opens the second watershed of the mainstream's continuing course. Though exhibiting some of the old liberal norms, his attack on the "power elite" cuts across the first debate. He unmasks the conservative support for laissez-faire politics by showing how the preference for no controls permits increasing concentrations of control in the hands of a very few. He describes a pernicious concentration of power and thereby chastens the hopes of those who labor under the liberal illusion that concentration of power in the hands of the government leads to progress in the realization of egalitarian ideals.

Within the second watershed there are those who criticize Mills neither by harping on albeit chastened hopes for more benevolent central administration nor by holding the frayed mask of laissez-faire conservatism even higher in the face of the embarrassing facts of economic concentration. Instead the new debate departs from the *normative* stance still evident in Mills and takes up a more *descriptive* attitude. Mills's own departure from the earlier debate depends partly on a turn toward description. To those arguing over whether big government is good or bad he protests that they have missed the more important point that the most dangerous concentration of power is economic rather than strictly political. While refusing to ally himself with orthodox Marxists he presses an essentially Marxist argument in his attempt to show the uselessness of quibbling over the virtues and vices of big government *in principle* when a description of the facts shows a greater concentration of power in big business. Yet his "description" of the "facts" is so colored by his interest in championing the cause of the downtrodden that even those sympathetic to his cause are forced to admit, "Mills' positive argument for the power elite, as opposed to his pointed critique of areas of analysis omitted from consideration in pluralist theory, is marked by unsupported gaps covered by rhetorical flourish."[6]

Mills's critics therefore question not the virtues or vices of a power elite, whether governmental or economic, but the very existence of any unified elite. They point instead to countervailing constituencies arranged in a pattern Robert Dahl calls polyarchy. This second watershed pluralism is significantly different from the first watershed laissez-faire conservatism, both in its liberal support of emancipatory interests and in its denial of a top-down dynamic of social change according to which benefits to the upper classes purportedly "filter down" to the lower. Nevertheless, Dahl's critics identify him with the reactionary tendency toward cloaking socially combustible issues beneath a bogus consensus. The elites of the various interest groups have been coopted by the government to such a point that the interests of the various elites are supported against the interests of their betrayed constituencies.[7] Despite appearances, the power is once again located if not "at the top" then at least "at the center." So the story goes as the mainstream wends its way through the second watershed during the fifties and sixties.[8]

Before forging further on this fast-moving tour the weary traveler may wish to catch his breath and ask not only, "Where have we been?" but also, "What does it matter? Why can't we have a look at where we are going and leave it at that?" Answer: the metaphorical tour covered the pros and cons of two different debates: first, among conservatives and liberals over the *virtue* or *vice* of centralized political power; second, among more recent political theorists over the *fact* or *fiction* of a power elite. These two debates with their four respective pros and cons call for a quick review for two reasons.

First, further discoveries in social theory ought not be confused with earlier positions. Though the term 'parapolitics' will be used to descibe a strategy of decentralization, its rationale and practice ought not be confused with either first watershed conservatism or second watershed pluralism. Parapolitics differs from both, and that difference derives from different historical and theoretical origins.

Second, the need for a sense of the origins of parapolitics requires the foregoing review of mainstream social theory. The point of departure for parapolitics follows from an analogy derived from its origins. Just as second watershed social theory follows from a challenge to the basic question of the first watershed debate, so the rationale for parapolitics follows from a challenge to the basic question of the second watershed debate. Conservatism offered a negative answer to the question, *should* power be centralized. Second watershed pluralism offers neither a negative nor a positive answer to that question. Instead both Mills and Dahl offer different answers to the question, *is* power centralized in a power elite or diffused in polyarchy? Just as the second debate takes its point of departure from an undercutting of the first watershed question, so parapolitics takes its point of departure from an undercutting of the second watershed question. *The social theory of parapolitics challenges the assumption that power remains constant in a system whether that fixed amount of power be centralized or diffused.* Perhaps power is not the sort of thing that retains a constant quantity while shifting from hand to hand.

While political scientists ask, "Who governs?" and interpret the question as, "Who has The Power?" social philosophy asks instead, "What is power?" Does power obey some law analogous to the physical law of conservation of energy? Or is it not possible that power might pass away? What kind of thing could power be such that it could come to be and pass away?

The next section will analyze the concept of power to expose the confusion involved in Dahl's assumptions. He assumes that the absence of a power elite constitutes an argument for the presence of power elsewhere in the society. Following an analysis of the way the energistic concept of power figures in the explanations of political scientists, the central sections of this chapter will review some accounts showing the decentralization of advanced industrial society. Without the assumption of an energistic concept of power, however, those accounts do nothing to justify polyarchy—the theory that The Power is shared among many different interest groups. On the contrary, those accounts will show the sense in which political explanations in general, and the office of the presidency in particular, fail to provide satisfactory accounts for the current phenomena of decentralization.

Power and intention

Forces make things happen. Power makes things happen according to an intention. We speak of the "forces of nature." A hurricane happens, it is not done. Of course we also speak of powerful winds, horse-power and the like, and who is to say, as some have said, that certain uses of 'power' are metaphorical while others are not?[9] It seems safer to admit that a stipulative element is bound to enter into any hard and fast definition of power. Any narrow definition will render some uses metaphorical and virtually any use can be declared metaphorical under some plausible definition of 'power'. The point is to settle on a few reasonably clear distinctions and then retain as much syntactic consistency and semantic plausibility as possible in generating a coherent theory from the manifestly incoherent maze of uses found in ordinary language.

To stipulate, then, with a semantic plausibility that remains to be argued: power is to be distinguished from force by the intentionality of the former and the nonintentionality of the latter.

If this bone-dry stipulation has any basis in the best entrenched uses of 'power' and 'force' then the corresponding concepts of power and force can be used to cut through the soggy marshland of many a confusion in contemporary political theory. E.g. we need not take sides in the same old way on whether there is a power elite. We may sympathize with the intent without entirely agreeing with the substance of Charles Reich's remark: "Of course a power elite does exist and is made rich by the system, but the elite are no longer in control, they are now merely taking advantage of forces that have a life of their own."[10] His point is well taken as far as describing forces with a life of their own, but to the extent that the elite lack control over those forces they are no longer a *power* elite. An opportunistic elite exists. A rich elite exists. But a power elite no longer exists because power assumes the realization of intention and the elite, most particularly and symbolically the presidency, is no longer able to effect intentions of its own design in any politically meaningful way. Of course the rich can maintain their riches, at least for a while. As for controlling advanced industrial society, however, mere crisis management cannot count. Whatever the visibility of our crisis managers they no more determine the quality of day to day life among the people than a traffic cop determines the destinations of drivers. Nor is it clear that those in Washington can avert collisions as well as the traffic cop. Even the "best and the brightest" could not find their way out of the "quagmire" in Viet-Nam.[11]

The study of *politics*, political science narrowly conceived, naturally tends to obscure this most important *historical* point: that power, the currency of politics, is passing away—and with it the condition for the possibility of politics, the context for our concept of the presidency. Dahl grants a spectrum of opinions between those political scientists who "postulate that power relations are one feature of politics among a number of others" and those for whom "power distinguishes 'politics' from other human activity." But most important for the present argument is the presupposition of the following claim: "In either case the analyst takes it for granted that differences between political systems, or profound changes in the same society, can often be interpreted as differences in the way power is distributed among individuals, groups, or other units. Power may be relatively concentrated or diffused; and the share of power held by different individuals, strata, classes, professional groups, ethnic, racial or religious groups, etc., may be relatively great or small."[12] Dahl's language presupposes power as subject to the law of the conservation of energy: since its quantity must remain the same it will be "distributed" in different ways. It may be "concentrated or diffused." One has a "*share* of power."

Given an energistic picture of power it will be natural to assume that if those on the periphery feel impotent then those at the center must be powerful. But empirical studies of perceptions of power in corporate structures reveal just the opposite: when those in lower management feel powerless, more often than not those who are supposedly in control feel powerless as well. When top management reports a sense of power, others in the organization often perceive their own roles as powerful. If parts of complex organizations are beyond the control of the people tending those parts, then chances are the system as a whole is beyond the control of anyone. Everyone then perceives the system as being controlled by someone else and the hallowed institution of buck-passing sets in. At least part of this dynamic is the result of false beliefs about the nature of power, namely those energistic beliefs hallowed by those political scientists who can hardly afford to entertain the notion that the currency of their domain could be passing away.

The energistic concept of power not only obscures the distinction between power and force but follows from a definition that explicitly conflates the two.[13] Hence, "The closest equivalent to the power relation is the causal relation." And with this result the analyst can consider himself liberated from the lure of messy considerations about human intentions.[14] Instead he has found the firm foundation supplied by a science of causes.

Explanation and political "science"

Pious theologians used to say that half a philosophy led one away from God and a full philosophy back toward Him. Similarly to-

day, half a science leads one away from man and a full science back
toward him. For the political scientists are only halfway toward a full
science: far enough away from man to want to abandon the concept of
human intention yet not far enough to have mastered more than a
crassly Newtonian concept of science.

Dahl unabashedly admits the oddity of social scientists' unwillingness to abandon causal language when their honored and emu-
lated colleagues in the natural sciences have long since ceased talking in causal language.[15] Yet he records the so-called "Newtonian
criterion" most frequently used to measure political power, "On the
analogy of the measurement of force in classical mechanics."[16] Despite Newton's status as a great scientist the point remains that
science has come a long way since 1704. Though debates among
scientists and philosophers of science have hardly issued in unanimous opinions on the concepts of cause and explanation, yet another
brief survey of the much broader terrain of scientific explanation will
reveal three realms whose borders are as ambiguous as their internal
partitions. Though 'realm' will serve as a cue connoting types of explanation while 'watershed' will continue to connote types of political
theory, the geographical metaphor remains apposite because the first,
second and third realms of explanation contain the first, second and
third watershed political theories among their respective internal divisions.

To the simple question, Why do things happen as they do?
residents of the first realm answer: because they were meant to be that
way. Or: because it is for the best. Or, in particular cases like an
acorn's aging into an oak: because the nature of the acorn is to strive
toward its *final cause* or *telos*, namely an oak tree. Let this first vast
area be labeled the land of *teleological* explanation. Foremost among
its citizens was Aristotle.

The second realm is in some ways a mirror-image of the first
for in denying the usefulness of explanation by final causes its foremost citizens did not challenge the principle of explanation of *single*
events by *single* causes. Rather, they substituted efficient causes for
final causes, pushes for pulls. The explanatory cause for a house is its

builder rather than the protection of its eventual inhabitants. Such an explanation seems more intellectually satisfying to inhabitants of this second land, among whose citizens names like Newton and Spinoza are revered. Contemporary common sense lives mostly in this second realm and some of our leading scientists have not left it.[17]

Third realm rationality differs from both first and second in several ways, but most significantly in its departure from the passion for identifying *single* causes for singular effects. Cybernetics borrows from mathematical probability theory a mode of explanation that asks not why one particular thing happened but instead why everything else did not happen. Rather than appeal to positive causes supposedly emanating from singular substances, the relational thought of third realm rationality appeals to networks of negative restraints.[18]

Cybernetic explanation, rather than rendering explanations that are unconvincing to the causally oriented first glance, actually renders the greatest justice to an intensely Newtonian view of a world in which everything is interrelated, everything connected in countless ways with everything else. Some connections are simply stronger than others—or should we not rather say things are only weakly connected to most others save a few.

Man's efforts at natural science have naturally enough begun with the relatively easy problems where all constraints were weak save one or two. From thence we derived the concept of monolinear causality. It did not help that the British empiricists were billiards players. Nor was the invention of elaborate though mechanically linear clockworks a negligible influence upon the continental rationalists' concepts of causality. Having once fashioned the concept of causality we then forget that it is the product of an abstraction. We then return to less simple contexts than those investigated and isolated by the natural scientists and in our forgetfulness expect that we can locate *the cause* of the First World War, where a moment's reflection on the concept of causality as an idealized abstraction from complex contexts of restraints would show the question of *the* cause of the First World War to be about as misguided as the question of the cause of mankind.

Explanation by negative constraints does not *deny* causality. Rather it comprehends so-called causal phenomena as a special case—quite as more comprehensive theories often do with their predecessors. In fact the description of natural laws in simple causal terms often involves a fudging of phenomena precisely equivalent to the differentiation of causal explanation from cybernetic explanation: classical mechanics speaks of bodies falling in a "perfect vacuum," of "perfectly elastic" bodies bouncing off one another in reaction, and so on. Cybernetic explanation grants the infinite multiplicity of intervening variables that must be ruled out to render the ideal or limiting case of a single cause generating a single effect. Single cause explanation, then, is an idealized abstraction.

The laboratory experiment is *designed* precisely as an effort to screen out all the additional factors whose equilibrium or slight imbalance normally accounts for the behavior under study. Multi-factor analysis is only slightly less abstract when each "factor" is conceived as a cause. The most truly comprehensive explanation is one that considers all possible factors and grades their degree of relevance from close to perfectly causal (as with, say, billiards where the table is *designed* to offer minimal restraint on its surface and predictable restraints at its cushions) down to the negligible (as with, say, the position of the moon for the running of the Belmont stakes).

The quest for a single source of power, whether in the office of the presidency or in an economic sub-structure, whether before or after an event, reflects a continued attachment to taking singular substances as prior to relations.[19] To those who reason in the third realm, structures of relations are not secondary. The concluding sections of this chapter will return to a more detailed account of relational thought. That account will serve not only the third watershed social theory but also the psychology and theology of later chapters. For now, however, the meaning of the metaphorical death of the presidency is the point at issue. Can we *explain* very much in advanced industrial society by reference to the office of the presidency? Do very many of our decisions derive from a hierarchical political structure with the presidency at its peak? Of course the presidency still exists

in a literal sense. The metaphor of death might nevertheless illumi-
nate a shift from the appropriateness of second realm explanations to
the greater appropriateness of third realm explanations.

What would serve as a sign of such a shift? Since cybernetic
explanations seek no simple cause, no single sign is likely to signify
the shift. Rather the reading of society will have to proceed on a subtler course, a more complex questioning of the assumptions of second
watershed social theory and its proclivity toward second realm explanations. Before pronouncing the death of the presidency it behooves
the undertaker to achieve a reading that shows the irrelevance of the
second watershed assumption that a proliferation of social groupings
goes hand in hand with a decentralization of political power. The following sections suggest a reading of advanced industrial society as
splintered into a vast array of social groupings, no one of which has
appreciable political power.

Power, cause and the Kapellmeister

As an analysis of contemporary political economy showing the
differences between power relations in the second and third watersheds, J. K. Galbraith's *New Industrial State* is in many ways made to
order. Galbraith argues that we have entered a phase of economic history for which the categories of Keynesian, much less classical Ri-
cardian economics are no longer adequate. The entrepreneurial phase
in which ownership and management coincided has given way to the
new industrial society in which owners—stockholders—have very little say in the decision-making process. Nor does so-called top management have a great deal of say on most decisions. Rather what Galbraith calls the *technostructure* determines just about everything from
petty cash flow to major policy.

Since most of the decisions made in advanced technological systems call for the processing of immense amounts of sometimes highly technical data, committees of specialists filter out relevant information from the noise. Decisions then follow first from calculations based on that information and second from values that stress growth and stability above the narrowly conceived traditional motivation of individual profit. Since the committee members are *not* likely to be rewarded for additional profits but *are* likely to be jeopardized by a failure following a bold but ultimately ill-advised risk, they have everything to lose and nothing to gain from alterations of even a minimally profitable status quo.[20] By the time their "decisions" reach the desk of the top executive they are covered with a mantle of epistemic authority far more "powerful" than the now symbolic authority vested in the role of "top executive." Yet the decisions of the technocrats are not powerful in the sense of power one associates with the earlier entrepreneurs. Galbraith misses this point and it is precisely the weak spot in his otherwise impressive analysis of industrial society.

What is the difference between the power of the entrepreneur and the "power" of the technocrats? Most briefly it is the difference between the power of the yes and the "power" of the no. To some this will seem a petty point, a piece of formalistic chicanery utterly devoid of significant content—like arguing over whether a glass is half empty or half full. Not so, for the entire dynamics of decision making—as well as an accurate appraisal of that dynamic—hinges on this distinction. It is a well known fact that committees tend to be conservative if indeed they are committees and not hired yes-men. For every inspired suggestion there is sure to be a negative response from someone, for every affirmation a corresponding negation. Committees consequently and almost inevitably reach the "least objectionable," the "safest," the "only possible" choice by a "process of elimination." So functions the "power" of the no.

The model for the positive power of the entrepreneur, the model that informs our use of the term 'power' in political contexts, is something like that of an organist at a keyboard with tracker action.

Reading from the notes on the score of his intentions he pushes the appropriate keys thereby setting in motion a series of direct mechanical pushes and pulls whose final effect is to release the force of proletarian bellows in precisely the right pipes at the right instants. Assuming those pipes have been tuned correctly and that all is in order in the elaborate mechanics of the keys, pedals, levers and pulleys that make up the bureaucracy of the State, the intentions of the single-voiced Kapellmeister will issue in a rich polyphony sufficient to delight all those humble folk who have taken part in the ceremony.

Such a model is utterly inadequate to the modern State, yet its push-pull mechanical essentials continue to inform most thinking about power. We now elect frauds to wave their fingers over the keyboards of a player organ as its own mechanism spins out tunes not of their "players'" making. The modern concert in the political arena is the pseudoevent of the press conference where a president contrives to appear in command by recalling relevant briefings.[21] The president's "power" consists chiefly in the veto, the no, the ability to push one of the *stops* to *prevent* a given set of pipes from sounding. Surely this is a species of influence but one that is importantly different from that of the old Kapellmeister who, like the classical entrepreneur or chief magistrate, could pull out all the stops and fill the Cathedral of the State with his own music.

"Who," it will then be asked, "cuts the roll for the modern mighty Wurlitzer? Who programs the State? Surely they have The Power!" But here again the same dynamic that restricts the president to the "power" of the veto also restrains the technostructure. Rather than single programmers setting their intentions to the role of the player organ we find committees where once again the "power" of the no determines the outcome. In short the entire system is a system of negative restraints rather than positive causes.

Galbraith's analysis sustains the metaphor of the mechanical Wurlitzer with one exception: he insists on speaking of the *power* of the technocrats.[22] His critics have faulted him for the wrong reasons, but there is a grain of unharvested truth in their objections to Galbraith's insistence on the power the technocrats have to manipulate consumers' needs and wants. The usual critic, faithful to the ideology of individual freedom in the market society, protests that he is not like some child whose desires can be manipulated by mendacious advertising. But Galbraith anticipates the predictable resentment of those who insist their choices are their own. Again and again he repeats that *aggregate* demand is the object of advertising. It is not essential that John Doe of Dubuque buy a Ford. It is essential that in a given year a predictable number of John Does buy either Fords or Chevrolets or Cadillacs, etc.[23]

Galbraith's critics, even if wrong in their contention that the technostructure has no influence over buying patterns, are nevertheless right to sense *something* wrong in Galbraith's insistence on the *power* of the technocracy. For it is not power as classically conceived after the manner of the Kapellmeister. Rather the technostructure and its minions in the media exercise a vast network of *constraints*. Even on Galbraith's own analysis advertising does not force *specific* decisions. Rather the point is to render some general possibilities virtually inconceivable, e.g., *no* life insurance, no car, no armory of electric appliances. But this again is negative restraint rather than positive and specific monolinear cause.

Maintaining consumerism is not the work of some single power conceived on the model of mechanical pushes and pulls. Consumerism is instead the air we breathe, the very atmosphere maintained by and maintaining our economy. An ecological metaphor is far more adequate than the magisterial. But in that case the language of power is inappropriate, the logic of cybernetics more germane.

We no longer live in a pyramid of top-down power relations. Instead, the socioeconomic context of advanced industrial society is a highly intricate network of interlocking constraints, an ecological system. The attempt to locate a single source of power in contemporary society is as pointless as a corresponding attempt in nature: the project is reminiscent of the earliest religious impulse to account for thunder as the wrath of God. Granted the difficulty of fixing on any one set of singly negligible relata in an ecological system, one must start an account somewhere. So with full consciousness that each separate instance *could* be taken care of on the old model of power, consider now some exploratory reports which, once synthesized, render the old model of power less parsimonious than the new.

Statuspheres, situses and other splinterings

Is Tom Wolfe a credible sociologist or simply an enfant terrible of the new journalism? Can one trust the maps of an explorer who raves and interrupts his written reports with so many exclamation points? The question raises yet another instance of the issue in question, namely whether the literary quadrant of the old hierarchy remains intact or whether a certain disorder in the literary world does not reflect in both form and content a corresponding crumbling of the political pyramid. In an essay on what he interestingly prefers to call "parajournalism," Wolfe notes that in the old order journalists were job-work hacks in a realm where novelists were princes and responsible academics were kings. Parajournalism and the nonfiction novel have ruptured the line between journalism and the novel, and both "novelists" and "journalists" alike are venturing into the world of ideas. Like so many lumpenproles these interlopers, with "their low-life legwork, their 'digging,' their hustling, their damnable Locker Room Genre reporting," are "helping themselves to the insights of the men of letters while they're at it." In short, "they're ignoring literary class lines that have been almost a century in the making."[24]

Having now allowed explorer Wolfe to defend his credentials before the court academics—and he needs some defense for his personal and literary appearance is hardly the garb of your usual explorer—let us let this dandy relate his diggings, his new empirical finds. For to refuse to hear him on the grounds that he does not present the proper literary class credentials would be to beg the very question at issue—the credibility of "credentials," the abiding coherence of our system of legitimation.

What has this dapper scout to tell us about the territory he has surveyed? His *Pump House Gang* is more than a series of unconnected sketches. In his introduction to the separate essays he ventures a few generalizations on their significance taken as a whole. Essentially the point is a flat-out rejection of the dour Marcusian vision that ours is a one-dimensional homogeneous society. Instead Wolfe finds a welter of separate "statuspheres"—from motorcycle gangs to *nouveau riche* art buffs, from teeny-boppers to naked lunchers (not the Burroughs variety but those who frequent tables served by topless waitresses). Whether or not Wolfe intends a touch of irony in his portrait of Hugh Hefner as modern hero, champion of all those who wish to *"split* from communitas" and start their own leagues, clearly there is something to his attack on the nostalgic vision of community with which Marxists used to hark back to *Gemeinschaft* in their condemnations of the frivolous products of *Gesellschaft*:[24] "Every night, in this vision, the family would gather around the hearth and listen to Dad read from John Strachey or Mayakovksy while WQXR droned in the background. The high point of the week would be Saturday afternoon, when Dad would put on his electric-blue suit—slightly gauche, you understand, but neat and clean and pressed, 'touching,' as it were— and the whole family would hold hands and walk up to the Culture Center to watch the shock Workers of the Dance do a ballet called 'Factory.' "[25]

Wolfe suggests, "Community status systems have been games with few winners and many who feel like losers."[26] No wonder they opt out and with the aid of even limited affluence and some technology set up tribes without chieftains, gangs without leaders, networks without centers. Even where the alternative groups reproduce the hierarchy of the old game, which often happens, the simple fact of a plurality of hierarchies inhibits the hold of the old order. "People are now reaching the top without quite knowing what on earth they have reached the top of. They don't know whether they have reached *The Top* or whether they have just had a wonderful fast ride up the service elevator."[27]

Lest we scorn this scout's fable for its wit alone let us turn to the less frivolous, the Harvard sociologist Daniel Bell whose credentials allow him to mount expeditions at the court's own expense. Bell reaches conclusions remarkably similar to Wolfe's in some important respects: "The older bureaucratic models of hierarchically organized centralized organizations functioning through an intensive division of labor clearly will be replaced by new forms of organization."[28] In a stab toward defining what those new forms may be Bell follows Wolfe in envisioning an alternative to status. Where Wolfe coins the term "statusphere" to denote a dissociation from the horizontal striations of society, Bell falls back on "this unfamiliar sociological word *situses* to emphasize the fact that in day-to-day activities the actual play and conflict of interests exist between the organizations to which men belong, rather than the more diffuse status identity and ethos."[29] A situs system differs from a status system in that it divides society by a series of vertical cuts rather than horizontal layers. Where a status system subordinates some layers to others, a situs system would slice society in such a way that the language of a vertical hierarchy is inappropriate for describing the relations among different situses. As Wolfe puts it, ascent to "the top" of a statusphere (= situs) is hardly arrival at "The Top" since "The Top" exists only within a hierarchical status system.

Bell confirms Wolfe's claim for the social significance of statuspheres/situses. As one of two major historical turns in the last quarter century Bell notes, "The second, and structurally more pervasive, shift is that in post-industrial society the *situses* rather than the *statuses* would be the major political-interest units in the society."[30] For the first fundamental turn Bell points to "the subordination of the economic function to the political order."[31] But one seeks in vain for the meaning of 'political order' once the traditional hierarchical model has, by Bell's own account, given way to a plurality of *situses*.[32]

What are some of the statuspheres or situses whose splinterings articulate modern industrial society? What are some of the groupings whose loyalties outweigh the political abstractions of class consciousness or party affiliation? Consider for a mere start the following five groups, the loyalties of whose members may obviously overlap.

(1) ETHNIC GROUPS: The past twenty years have witnessed a significant change in the theory and practice of American society as a melting pot. A growing literature records an increasing refusal to accept homogenization into a universalist culture whose customs represent the unacknowledged imposition of Wasp values in the name of universalism.[33] The price of Americanization is then the adoption of an individualist ethic of autonomy girded by strong internal restraints rather than external bonds of brotherhood with one's group on whose customs, however parochial, one can depend for guidance. Michael Novak notes the difference between the Protestant respect for "strength of character" and the Catholic respect for what is perceived as quite natural "human weaknesses." In Catholic countries, "Forgiveness and compassion are values highly prized; persons easily offended by the sins of others are widely considered guilty themselves of 'spiritual pride.' Isn't the 'laxness' of Catholic morals a scandal to the Protestant world? It is, instead, a quite different set of morals."[34]

The new ethnicity renders difference respectable. Blacks, Jews, middle Europeans are no longer so eager to hide their origins like some dirty little secret. Some are opening the sealed trunks of their traditions, the baggage from the old country we carry in the complex chemistry of our most immediate reactions, our very gestures. "Emotions, instincts, memory, imagination, passion, and ways of perceiving are passed on to us in ways we do not choose, and in ways so thick with life that they lie far beyond the power of consciousness (let alone of analytic and verbal reason) thoroughly to master, totally to alter."[35] These stored treasures are the different resources denied us by a universalism that would leave us rootless.

(2) GENERATIONAL IDENTIFICATION: Among the most obvious splits of the sixties was the generation gap, a phrase now so trite that no one dares mention it in print. Yet the phenomenon not only continues but proliferates, the lines being drawn in more detail than the simple cleaver stroke at age thirty. The students of the seventies, the new careerists and protoprofessionals, take care to differentiate themselves from the students of the sixties while at the same time denying their likeness with the apathetic breed of the fifties. At the other end of the life cycle the Gray Panthers show their perceptiveness of the advantages of solidarity with a group that cuts across both ethnic and conventional political affiliations.

(3) GENDER CONSCIOUSNESS: Who needs to be reminded of the breadth and depth, the cataclysmic cultural significance of the women's liberation movement? The very meaning of "chauvinism," derived from the military-political enthusiasms of one Nicholas Chauvin in his admiration for Napoleon, now drifts in a way that shows our attitudes toward gender to be more in need of a vocabulary of militancy than our attitudes toward politics.

(4) REGIONALISM: The financial crisis of New York City signifies not only the ills of urban centralization but also the decline of the Northeast as the center of American power and culture. Nor is it clear that any other area can take its place as the center from which it all began hundreds of years ago. Instead there is a new sense that the educated of the South and West need not send their children to the Northeast for schooling. The Ivy League schools whose founding relieved earlier generations of the need to go to the old universities of England and Europe now find themselves similarly challenged as new generations of locally endowed universities offset the prestige of the Ivy League. The understated snobbery of the Yale man is no longer the gracefulness of noblesse oblige but the anachronistic affectation of an endan-

gered species in our cultural ecology. Grab for the laurel of an Ivy League diploma and life is liable to pass you by. The action is elsewhere—in Austin, San Francisco, Ann Arbor and countless other localities that no longer languish in the shadow of the Big Apple and its educated hard core. Towns that were satellites are now suns radiating their own light. The constellation of American culture lacks a center.[36]

Nor can Washington claim to be much more than a symbolic center for the international intercourse between Americans and the citizens of other countries. At the Mershon Center in Columbus, Ohio, Chadwick Alger and his associates have been assembling data indicating the large extent to which foreign relations bypass the bottleneck of Washington bureaucracy. Direct exchanges of people, money, information and goods give the lie to a simple model of cities depending on their national centers of trade for their relations with the people of other nations.[37] Though Alger does not deign to mention what might be one of his best examples, Tom Wolfe is quick to note, "Columbus is the world capital of the motorcycle life."[38]

(5) ALOCALITY: Just as the diffusions of culture and commerce to multiple centers undercuts the significance of politically conceived boundaries, so does the direct transcendence of national boundaries by the new breed of multinational corporations. Precisely in their lack of local homes the multinationals largely escape the web of political constraints imposed by any single country upon its local corporations. According to Myra Wilkins their structure comes to replicate in the economic arena the cultural diffusion just described. In *The Maturing of Multinational Enterprise: American Business Abroad from 1919 to 1970* she describes "a sequence of multinational organizations, evolving from a 'monocentric' to a 'polycentric' form, in which the planets disengage themselves from the parent sun and wander about the economic universe on their own . . . ,"[39] free, that is, from the power of political authority.

The decline of political power

The list of situses, statuspheres and other splinterings could continue to include the anti- or quasi-political influence of the media, the unions and heaven knows how many other factions influencing the lived shape of contemporary society. The five just described recommend themselves by the fact that all—the new ethnicity, generational identification, gender consciousness, regionalism and the alocality of the multinationals—are relatively recent additions to the overlapping striations of society. Taken separately any of these countervailing forces old or new can fit easily into a model of society whose central institution is a political hierarchy and whose primary explanatory principle will be political power conceived as a Newtonian force. Taken together they render that simple model hopelessly inadequate. Life in the delta cannot be explained by a causal analysis of what happened upstream. Instead one needs a relational analysis of what Ronnie Dugger has nicely named The Simultaneum, "our common life, the simultaneous circumambient continuum in which, bombarded by events from everywhere in it, we live."[40] The water level in one stream of the delta cannot be predicted by a calculation based on rains upriver alone. Rather the flow in each stream is a function of constraints in all the others—factors over which the dwellers on one stream have no control. A backup in one branch floods others; dredge one branch and others go dry.

Clearly we are not completely helpless, though the wave of recent preoccupation with power testifies to nothing if not a growing sense of impotence.[41] Clearly we retain some capacity to influence our immediate environment. But politics in its grosser dimensions is no longer the tool. Big-time politics has passed what Ivan Illich calls—conveniently for our dominant metaphor—the second watershed. Illich describes two watersheds through which growing institutional tools may pass: the first contains their progress as they expand and centralize needed services; the second contains their growth to gargantuan proportions, increasing professionalization and decreasing returns until finally they become counterproductive. He claims that education has already passed through its second watershed and that the vast increase of iatrogenic (doctor caused) disease indicates that medicine is well on its way. Curiously he has not seen that politics too is a prime candidate for his categories. Consequently he calls in vain for politicians to cure the ills of the other professionals.[42] Some European theorists have not failed to notice politics' own passing through the second watershed.

Giovanni Sartori addresses not only the situation in France but politics in all advanced industrial societies when he comments: "Whether we ask if parliament controls the government, or the parties control parliament, or a presidential system is needed, the fact remains that essential sectors and entire spheres of power escape all control; the fact is that the very size of the object to be controlled threatens to overwhelm the controller, and that the bureaucratic state's elephantinism escapes the control of the democratic state more and more by virtue of its dimensions."[43] In Germany Bohm argues, in a manner not unlike Galbraith's argument transformed from the economic into the political dimension, that like the corporate executive the mechanics of representative democracy only *endorse* decisions prepared and foreordained by the political middle management.[44]

The most sustained attack on the mythology of politics is Jacques Ellul's *Political Illusion*, a book he describes in his preface to the English translation as "typically French." But it is a book that is nonetheless as important to Americans as his earlier and better known *Technological Society*. Though filled with typically French polemics, *Political Illusion* is essentially correct in its estimate that "political disputes today are what disputes between Christians were in the sixteenth century."[45]

Ellul's insight has not escaped American scholars altogether. Robert Nisbet notes, "From about the sixteenth century the national state became much the same kind of haven for man that the Church had been from the time of the fall of Rome in the West."[46] Having noticed the coincidence of the decline of one system of legitimation with the ascendancy of another, Nisbet is then keenly aware of the fact that politics is not, as social scientists from Parsons to Bell take it to be, the necessary and permanent arena for the mediation of conflicts. Rather he speaks of the "twilight of politics" and adds: "The erosion of confidence in the political state is rooted in some degree in the recrudescence of ethnicity, religion, locality and kinship."[47]

Nor have American observers failed to notice the dimension of propaganda and illusion in the selling of the President. Dan Nimmo concludes his work, *Political Persuaders*, with a metaphor from Plato's *Republic*: "The impact of the new technology may be to recast symbolic participation in a new guise, as para-social play that provides a more subtle illusion, but still not the substance of transferring power from voters to attractive, trustworthy leaders. The shadows on the cave wall will be more precisely focussed, but they will remain shadows."[48] Similarly, Murray Edleman remains sensitive to the largely symbolic impact of supposedly substantive political issues.[49] But beneath these latter studies there lingers an abiding faith that the clouds of illusion can be dispelled and politics restored to the status of a working tool. The same impulse toward a political counterreformation is evident in the increasingly mountainous literature on political "participation" whose sheer volume alone, like a stepped up campaign in apologetics, is a sure sign that people, being not dumb, are leaving the faith.[50]

The rituals will persist. People for the most part need a faith, a sense that someone, if not God then at least the president, has his hands on The Controls and can if necessary avert disaster. But The Controls, the tools of national politics, are no longer subject to anyone's control, at least not in the sense of the positive exercise of power as it is traditionally conceived. The Presidency is dead. The role of the political Kapellmeister has been taken over by a vast network of simultaneously interacting statuspheres, some rational, some less so. But the system as a whole, believe it or not, has a certain rationality, a pattern of coherence marvelous to behold.

To appreciate the patterns of coherence in contemporary society is not to endorse all the components of advanced industrial society. But how can one alter anything in a system whose structure one does not understand? The following section returns to a more detailed description of a third realm rationality adequate to the third watershed social theory.

Relational thought

First a word of caution for the well informed and a word of encouragement for the less informed. The following paragraphs are unavoidably abstract and compact. Rather than introducing facts easily assimilable into our old ways of thinking, they introduce a new way of thinking: the cognitive dimension of paraconsciousness, on which more later. This "new way of thinking" is not entirely new. Theorists from several traditions have devoted decades of research to its emergence. A separate book could synthesize and distinguish the contributions from relativistic physics, structuralist linguistics, cybernetic information theory, and hermeneutics (the theory of interpretation). In this chapter, however, only structuralism and cybernetics will serve as backgrounds for relational thought, and the wellread will feel themselves riding rough-shod over the finer distinctions between even these two traditions. Those who are innocent of either tradition deserve a brief introduction to some basic concepts without their more arcane ramifications. Further, the less informed as well as the wellread deserve this word of encouragement: the abstractions introduced in the following paragraphs will gain concrete filling in the following chapters. Even the conclusion to this chapter will include applications of relational thinking to the issues of power.

Prior to the stage of their familiarity and acceptance, new ways of thinking necessarily suffer a certain awkward age: we have seen that the old ways of thinking, e.g., about power, are no longer appropriate, yet new ways of thinking will seem obscure precisely because they are new and unfamiliar. Nor will concrete examples from everyday life be sufficient to introduce new ways of thinking because our everyday life takes its recognizable form from our old ways of thinking; hence the necessity of an abstract introduction followed by a reinterpretation of everyday life within the new context. The next chapter will begin with an account of the awkwardness inevitable for attempts at conceptual revision. But now it is time to take some gangling steps into the abstract.

Gregory Bateson distinguishes between the kind of science the political scientists take as their model—the science of "impacts, forces, and so forth"—and the science of information theory where "you leave behind that whole world in which effects are brought about by forces and impacts and energy exchange. You enter a world in which 'effects'—and I am not sure one should still use the same word—are brought about by *differences.*"[51] What is a difference? ". . . the sort of thing that gets onto the map from the territory. This is a difference." In other words the *least* change in the territory that must show up in the map in order that the map be an adequate map, the least change in sound that renders one syllable *different* from another and not just a regional variant of the *same,* will qualify as a difference.

The cybernetic definition of *information* as a difference that makes a difference closely resembles the structural linguists' definition of the *phoneme*: the minimal unit for conveying linguistic meaning. Like the "bit" of information, the phoneme is a difference that makes a difference. A difference of pronunciation of the same phoneme, a stutter for example, would not change the meaning of the word being pronounced. Cybernetics uses the term "noise" to describe those differences that make no informational difference.

For both cybernetics and structural linguistics *context* is crucial to the question of whether a given sound is to be taken as a phoneme or mere noise. Structures of contextual constraints therefore substitute for the substantive notion of particular stimuli acting as singular causes. "The positivist notion of the linguistic *fact* has been replaced by that of *relationship*. Instead of considering each element by itself and seeking for the 'cause' in an earlier stage, it is envisioned as part of a synchronic totality; 'atomism' gives way to 'structuralism'."[52]

Just as the linguists surrendered the idea of the isolated linguistic fact for the less atomic, more molecular model of a relational structure of significance, so information theory stresses *context* as crucial to the meaning of a given difference. Both Bateson and the structural linguists see the significance of the *part* as determined by the *whole*. Hence Bateson's interest in and contributions to thought about ecology—the *logos* of the environmental context.

Atomistic or substance-oriented thought considers the individual organism as the unit of survival. But just as relational thought in linguistics shows that the unit of meaning is not the single word related to an atomic fact but rather the sentence plus its entire linguistic environment, so relational thought in ecology shows the necessity of taking organism plus environment as the unit of survival.

Just as the notion of the singular cause gives way to emphasis on a structure of relationships, so the corresponding concept of the singular effect proves obsolete. Recall Bateson's doubts: "You enter a world in which 'effects'—and I am not sure one should still use the same word—are brought about by *differences*." As if in response to both Bateson's misgivings about 'effects' as well as his emphasis on difference, Jacques Derrida coins the terms 'trace' and *'differance'* (*sic*). The suggestion of a gerund in the substitution of an *a* for an *e* connotes *a differentiating that precedes or generates distinction*. In place of distinctions purporting to name differences among atomic facts, the process of *differance* transforms the undifferentiated into the different.[53]

For both structuralism and cybernetics the concept of *transformation* is crucial. In his book on structuralism Jean Piaget describes its method as an effort to look at its objects—whether a text, a

tribe or a psyche—always as "a self-regulating system of transformations."[54] Bateson describes transformation, as does his follower R.
D. Laing, in terms of mapping: "These *mappings* or transformations
may be very complex, e.g., where the output of some machine is regarded as a transform of the input; or they may be very simple, e.g.,
where the rotation of a shaft at a given point along its length is regarded as a transform (albeit identical) of its rotation at some previous
point."[55]

To summarize and slightly recast the contributions of cybernetics and structuralism, consider three tools that will fashion much
of what follows: the first tool is *marginal* or *differential* analysis; the
second, *dimensional* analysis; the third, *transformation* or the *map/
territory* relationship.

The three concepts of marginal difference, dimensionality and
transformation are theoretical correlatives. Each can be defined in
terms of the other two; none is primary; together they define a matrix
in terms of which other concepts can be more easily understood. A
marginal difference—say between the more objective and less objective—determines a *dimension,* in this case the dimension between
subjectivity and objectivity. But 'between' is the wrong word to use
here, however habitually we may think of The Subject and The Object as poles *between* which experiences are strung like so many
clothes on a back-alley line. To appreciate the relation between marginal differences and dimensions the mathematical analogue of an
imaginary axis is a better model than a laundry line. An axis needs no
pulleys or poles to keep it from falling into useless disarray. An axis
need not stretch between already determinate extremes. On the contrary an axis defining a coordinate system is usually extendable without limit. A direction or dimension is determined, not a destination.
A given *differance* defines a direction of difference while a given *dimension,* once determined, serves to define a matrix for the measurement of that difference relative to other differences in the same dimension.

Take from economics the dimension of profitability. It measure the *difference* between income and costs. That difference can be either "positive" showing a profit or "negative" showing a loss. Because difference differentiates, two terms rather than one come to be associated with each dimension, e.g., 'profit' and 'loss'. But only one dimension is involved, and one that may lack any limiting poles such as The Profit and The Loss. Of course some dimensions *may* have determinate extremes, e.g., colors and sounds; but who has ever heard absolute silence or seen absolute blackness? Differentiations among the colors *between* white and black, differentiations among the sounds between silence and . . . what?—define dimensions whose extremes *may* be determinate but, at least as far as our experience is concerned, are as fictional as the more obviously absurd limits of The Up and The Down.

If the model of a mathematical or geometrical axis more accurately captures the difference between profit and loss or up and down , then perhaps some other differences often conceived in terms of substantive opposites might make more sense when described as differences on a dimension *without* extreme limits, e.g., The Subject and The Object, those philosophical holy grails that have provoked more than a few futile crusades.

Still the felt need for substantive opposites intrudes with the question—But what is a given difference a difference *of*? How are we to define a difference apart from that *towards which* or that away from which it differs? From thence emanates the temptation to fix some first dimension by naming its poles—a double error, both in the priority of the poles to the dimension and in the priority of one dimension to others. At this point the concept of *transformation* combats the temptation to name the poles of a primary dimension whose poles would ostensibly determine what some "first" difference is a difference *of*.

In its mathematical employment the concept of transformation serves to map one set of axes onto another. Rather than regard one point on a shaft as an (identical) transform of another, one can "rotate" axes as well. One set of axes can define another set as, say, a forty-five degree rotation of the first set. A curve whose coordinates are mapped on the first set of axes can be mapped on the second by applying as an "operator" the "transformation equation" that maps expressions in terms of the first set of coordinates, say x and y, onto expressions in terms of the second set, say p and q. But most important: just as a second set of *axes* are describable as equations mapped on a first set of axes, so the first set of axes are describable as equations mapped on the second set.[56] The dimensions that had served as "fundamental parameters" are describable in terms of their own rotated transformation now taken as a new set of "fundamental parameters." As far as descriptive range or scope is concerned neither set of axes is *first*, neither *primary* in any absolute sense. What is more, a single or "first" difference need not be depended on to define a dimension without poles. The temptation to reify poles for purposes of defining what a difference is a difference *of* now has an answer other than a set of primordial poles: each dimension is describable not only in terms of marginal differences along its own axis; those marginal differences can be described in turn as *transforms* of differences along other axes. Or, each dimension is describable not only in terms of differences defining its own direction but also as a rotation or transform of other dimensions.

Later chapters will recall the concepts of transformation and rotation of axes as a model for showing the sense in which the political, psychological and religious dimensions allow transforms of a given concept—say, monotheism—from the religious dimension onto the psychological and political dimensions. The political transform of monotheism is monarchy, or the presidency conceived as a singular locus of imperial power. The psychological transform of monotheism is the imperial ego, the self as a hierarchical ordering of impulses according to a singular self-identity. The usefulness of the concept of transformation consists in the fact that, unlike the more familiar notion of analogy, transformation permits the more radical move toward taking the basic parameters themselves—the political, psychological and religious dimensions—as transforms of one another. Unlike symbolism and analogy, which tend to assume a basic or literal foundation on which an analogy is built or a symbol drawn, the concept of transformation assumes no fundamental dimension.

If not only the particular concepts in given dimensions but the dimensions themselves are transforms of one another, then reductionism—a hallmark of second realm rationality—is not possible. If no one dimension is fundamental then it makes no sense to say, for example, that the gods are *merely* psychological projections. Nor does it make sense to argue the priority of theology to politics. What does make sense is the effort to comprehend the hold of certain concepts on our imaginations by examining their several transforms in several dimensions.

The strategy of this book is therefore organized around the idea that we will never understand the death of the presidency and its parapolitical alternative unless we have also understood the demise of the singular self and the alternative of a pluralistic inner life; which in turn is a transform of the polytheistic alternative to monotheism. Of course it is equally arguable that we shall not understand the latter until we have understood the former—the awkward paradox of systematic thought. But if each part prefigures the whole, then it should be possible to catch at least a glimpse of the workings of relational thought within each of the dimensions.

The concluding section of this chapter therefore applies the concepts of relational thought to the topics of technology and political power. The point of the following section is not so much to show the one right way of looking at power and technology as to show that certain differences among theoretical approaches are differences that make no difference. That is, we gain no information from their disputes, whichever way they might be decided.

Though no information may be gained, still a lesson will be learned about syntax and semantics. 'Syntax' refers to relations among words, as when we speak of the syntax of a sentence. Syntactical definitions relate words to other words. If we define a given term syntactically then nothing in the world could change the meaning of that word—except perhaps a change in the meaning of the words in

terms of which it is defined. But even then the defined term retains
the same syntactic links to the terms defining it. In a syntactical definition those links are *necessary*. One thinks of the link between
'bachelor' and 'unmarried'.

'Semantics', on the other hand, refers to the links between
words and things. If one defines a word semantically, that is, by its
reference to a given class of things, then the meaning of that word will
change if the things change. One thinks of words like 'beauty' whose
denotations seem to drift over time and across cultures. If 'beauty' be
defined semantically by reference to the class of people fashion regards as beautiful, then the syntactic link between 'beautiful' and 'fat'
will be not necessary but *contingent* upon the fashions of the time or
place.

The theoretical distinction between syntactic and semantic
definition is of course much sharper than what we find when we look
at ordinary language and the disputes that arise from shifts in actual
uses of words. The lessons to be drawn from the following disputes relate to the arbitrariness involved in claiming some definitions as syntactic and others as semantic. Where syntactic definitions purport to
provide fixed axes for plotting semantic drift in the use of other terms,
the tools of relational thought show how terms previously subject to
semantic drift can serve as fixed axes for a matrix showing reversals
of meaning among terms previously defined syntactically. These reversals appear paradoxical to those who insist on the incorrigible
necessity of syntactic definitions. Relational thought allows an unrav-
eling of the paradoxes.

Specifically at issue is the question: are power and technology
suprapersonal agents with lives of their own, or must 'agency' be necessarily linked with 'persons'? As the title of Part One, "Structures
of Agency," might suggest, agency will emerge as a structure locatable in several different dimensions. To anticipate further, the structure of agency will emerge as a pluralized and pluralizing process
found in persons, parts of persons and among assemblages of persons. Agency has its transforms in the personal, intrapersonal, and

suprapersonal dimensions. But again, if the part prefigures the whole, it should be possible to catch a glimpse of those further horizons from the perspective of the proximate issues, power and technology.

The syntax and semantics of politics and technology

First realm rationality divides the world according to a polar distinction between The Artificial and The Natural. In accord with the belief that nature is rational and purposive, Aristotelian metaphysics takes biological development and celestial order as its natural models for artifice to imitate. Second realm rationality retains the distinction between the natural and artificial, but reverses the order of priority. Mechanical artifice replaces natural order as the dominant paradigm. Locke questions the existence of natural kinds. Hobbes assumes the hostility of nature and the need for political artifice to overcome the brutishness of life in the state of nature. Third realm rationality requires a new look at the syntactic legacy of 'politics' and 'technology' because their semantic referrents have drifted from the class of helpful tools toward the domain of hostile environment.

By a rotation that is very nearly a reversal, the artificial products of man, from politics and technology in general down to the specifics of food additives, have come to represent the alien other while the natural is increasingly sought as representing the comforts of home. This shift or reversal, what Jung and the dialectical tradition call an *enantiodromia*, becomes evident in petty paradoxes of modern life like a cosmetic company's advertising "the natural look" or a "natural food" that comes in a carton.

The political-technological creation is a *transform* of nature not in the sense that machines are physical transformations of the crude materials of nature but rather in the sense that the political-technological creation comes to play the *same role* as nature, namely that of a hostile environment out of which man must carve enclaves to make his home.

A related shift affects the meaning of power. The opposition between power and force has been *defined* in terms of the opposition between the intentional and the unintentional. Stipulative definition establishes a grammatical or *syntactic* link between power and intention on the one hand and force and lack of intention on the other. At the same time a *semantic* link ties force to nature and power to politics, technology and whatever other artificial creations man uses intentionally to overcome the forces of nature. What happens to these syntactic and semantic links when politics and technology cease to oppose nature but appear instead as a functional transform of nature in its original role of alien environment? What happens to the syntax of 'power' when its original semantic referrents take on *unintended* characteristics? According to its original syntax power was necessarily intentional. Like nature that comes in a carton, power that behaves *un*intentionally represents a reversal in the original meaning of the term, a reversal brought about by historical changes in the semantic referrents of syntactically defined terms.

The concept of transformation comes in handy here as a means of making sense of the options available for resolving the reversals of meaning in the concepts of nature and power. Different theorists have historically adopted different ways out of these paradoxes. Their different ways out, their different axial dimensions, appear to leave social theory in a shambles of disagreements. The concepts of marginal difference, dimensionality and transformation permit a comprehension of the different ways out of the paradoxes, and thus a stronger theory than those so comprehended.

The shambles in social theory can be untangled by showing how different theorists have adopted different parameters for fundamental axes on which to map social reality. The different accounts are

THE STRUCTURE OF POWER

not describing *substantial polar opposites differently*; rather they use different dimensions with different syntactic and semantic correlates derived from different historical constellations to describe what the proper transforms reveal to be *the same marginal differences*.

To take the example of the relation of technology to power: Jacques Ellul represents technology as having outgrown the status of a tool used to further man's intentions. He insists that technology now exerts its own power over man. Along with antitechnologists like Roszak and Mumford he represents technology as an autonomous agency, thus preserving the syntactic link between power and intentional agency while at the same time breaking the link that claimed intentions to be restricted to human beings alone. In the writings of the antitechnologists, purposeful behavior is once again attributed to the alien environment just as it was attributed to nature in the first realm of explanation. Technology, they claim, "has a life of its own."[57]

Apparently opposed to the antitechnologists, writers like Daniel Bell and Samuel Florman insist that power resides with the politicians. Technology they insist cannot be "personified" into a demon with a life of its own. Yet their analyses of the marginal differences in the march of modernity are structurally similar to those of their opponents. The difference lies largely in the syntax of their concepts, e.g., the conviction that intentionality is syntactically, definitionally and hence necessarily linked with uniquely *human* agency. Consequently their conceptual scheme does not allow for the possibility that intentionality might be *semantically* attributed to the nonhuman, thereby qualifying technology as some sort of agent capable of purposive behavior.

The following chapters develop the argument that subjectivity is a *structure* that may characterize complexes both larger and smaller than embodied persons. The point to be made here is that the resistance to regarding technology as an autonomous agent stems from a confusion between semantic contingency and syntactic necessity. Florman claims, "But sober thought reveals that technology is not an independent force, much less a thing, but merely one of the types of activities in which people engage."[58] His assertion makes sense if we insist on syntactical necessity for the connection between *action* and *human* agency. But the antitechnologists' argument shows in effect that the axis of intentionality has shifted and that the syntactic links based on earlier semantic entrenchments have now been broken by the semantic drift of recent history. As the artificial becomes increasingly unintentional, as the natural becomes increasingly humanized, the syntactic link between intentionality and the human can be maintained only at the price of paradox.[59]* A different syntax, which is to say a different choice of parameters—a rotation of axes that follows the semantic drift of history—allows a more coherent, less paradox-ridden account.

The concept of power exhibits a similar ambiguity according to which it is either an attribute of human politics or an autonomous agency that could be dissociated from the private intentions of individual politicians. In his *Political Power* Charles Merriam writes, "Power withdraws from its physical externals, beyond its symbols lurking somewhere behind its material defenses. It is a creature of habits, of culture patterns woven deeply into the lives of men; subjective it might well be termed."[60] Here political power is personified like technology precisely to the extent that it "withdraws" from the intentions of men. If power is to be differentiated from blind force it must be located in a structure of subjectivity with its own habits and intentions. On Merriam's reading, power is no longer something that people *have* and *exercise*. Its grammar changes. If its grammar were to remain the same, if *human* intentions were retained as a dimension on which powers were measured, then the same marginal difference—the declining efficacy of human intentions—would be described not as a *withdrawal* of power to some other agency but as the *withering* of power. As opposing social *forces* create an alien environment not unlike the hostile and purposeless nature seen by second realm rationality, power does not shift from human hands to, say, the "hands" of the personified demon of technology. Rather, according to the account that retains the link between uniquely *human* intention and power, nobody is in control: not power as some disembodied structure of agency, not technology, not a particular group of men in cahoots with one another.

So far the various views on power and technology have been represented in terms of parallel oppositions: on the one side stand those who see either power or technology as necessarily *human* tools, on the other those who see either power or technology as *autonomous agencies*. The differences in the descriptions of power and technology follow from differences in the definitions of crucial concepts in the conceptual schemes of the apparently conflicting theorists, and those differences of syntactic definition follow from differences among basic parameters or dimensions of description.

As opposed to substantive/causal thought, *relational* thinking avoids falling into the trap of maintaining that modernity is to be interpreted in terms of just *one* shift along *one* basic axis or dimension. The weakness of most accounts lies precisely where first and second realm explanations locate their strength: in the elegant simplicity of a single explanatory principle whose unity is the source of necessity. By attending to the irreducible multiplicity of explanatory principles we no doubt sacrifice some of the elegance and simplicity of reductionism. But the price may be worth paying if we can avoid some of the foolishness of one-sided accounts: if we can see that man *has* deeded over some of his power to agencies that are structures of subjectivity but that these structures are no more intentionally demoniacal than the nature they have come to replace. The lack of unity and common purpose among those structures renders *them* as incapable of carrying out *their* intentions as are men; so that the combined mess created by man *and* his several increasingly autonomous tools leaves *both* in a system of decreasing power.

In order to entertain the thought of an absolute decrease in power, the energistic-substantival concept of a constant conservation

of power must give way to the relational concept of power as capacity
to realize intentions. Bateson confirms the relational concept of power
by regarding power as a function of belief. "But the *myth* of power is,
of course, a very powerful myth and probably most people in this
world more or less believe in it. It is a myth which, if everybody believes in it, becomes to that extent self-validating . . . "[62]—very
like belief in the god who must have lived if it could be said that he
had died.

The self-validating myth of power as monolinear causality in
social contexts was sustained in recent centuries by configurations of
restraints that, like the natural scientist's laboratory, screened out
conflicting restraints. Monarchies, dictatorships and imperial presi-
dencies rest on the restraint of conflicting restraints, a double negation leaving the illusion of a single causality called political power.
However, the illusion is difficult to maintain, especially as technological development of new tools—weapons and communications—renders the reality of interrelatedness ever more difficult to screen out.
For a time these same tools were the medium for progressive concentrations of classically conceived power. But as centripetal concentrations come to conflict with one another through centrifugal spread
from the sources of classically concentrated power, the domain of
each "center" becomes crisscrossed with outward-spreading waves of
influence from all other similarly concentrated "centers." This centrifugal or third stage is like the first or precentripetal (just as the delta is superficially like the tributaries) in manifesting a certain pluralization; like the second in manifesting traces of human intentions. The
third stage is unlike the first in that the plurality of restraints are more
man-made than natural, unlike the second in that the restraints'
traces are plural rather than singular.

In order to appreciate the rationality of our splintered situses
we need to revise the paradigm of rationality itself. First and second
realm models of explanation are inadequate to contemporary existence. Yet third realm rationality is unfamiliar and unpracticed. Before returning to the cave of contemporary politics the following chap-

ters will carry out exercises in relational thought as it bears on images of self. Before we can appreciate the new pattern of rationality that at least partially informs contemporary social life, a sojourn into the self will have to question that internal presidency, the single ego whose experience informs our use of the concept of power. A sense of self as many dimensional will facilitate a return to the cave of contemporary parapolitics.

II The Structure of Freedom

Critical theory and common sense

Like 'power' and 'politics,' 'freedom' is a word whose current use sometimes virtually reverses its original meaning. When one hears the phrase 'freedom of choice' bruited about in ads for diet beverages one suspects that its meaning has been debased. Freedom of choice seems more significant when the options in question are churches rather than flavors. So much common sense tells us. But common sense will not tell us how to restore some sense to the vocabulary of social discourse.

Common sense is itself the repository of linguistic debasement. Its categories bear the imprint of all the confusion introduced as historical change scrambles the semantic links between words and their referents. Politicians were linked with power because they achieved the capacity to carry out their intentions. Once the link between politics and power has become entrenched common sense forgets the reason and then assumes that *because* certain persons are politicians they are *therefore* powerful despite whatever evidence may be introduced to show that they are incapable of carrying out their intentions.

So with freedom: we assume that as long as we have "freedom of choice" we are therefore free. Since common sense is the printout of the programming that changes the semantic links between words and their earlier referrents, common sense is incapable of criticizing the programming from which it derives.

Critical theory cannot leave common sense and its ordinary language as they are.[1] The forms of life from which ordinary language derives may be rife with antagonistic contradictions. If the only language we have is a language that labels slavish existence as "free" then the outcome of the inquiry is foreordained: newspeak will triumph. Critical theory therefore demands a term by term suspension of common sense. The project is sometimes likened to the task of rebuilding a ship at sea—plank by rotten (debased) plank. We cannot suspend the entire structure at once or we sink into the depths of inarticulateness. Nor does the historicity of human existence allow the luxury of a dry-dock where we might weld eternal verities to some keel of ageless wisdom. Instead the ordinary uses of 'freedom' call for testing against parts of the rest of our vocabulary.

How for example does 'freedom' function in contexts with the prepositions 'from' and 'to'? Does our ordinary use of 'freedom' support our freedom *from* coercive constraint? Or does the debasement of "freedom of choice" dull our sensitivity to constraints more subtle than a fate filled with nothing but root beer? Does our ordinary use of 'freedom' reflect a sensitivity to positive freedom rather than negative freedom, i.e., freedom *to* rather than freedom *from*, e.g., the freedom to improvise that comes with mastery of technique on a musical instrument? Or are we enslaved by a common sense concept of freedom from external constraint. Are we so preoccupied with liberty that only a metaphysical void could satisfy an escapist thirst for indeterminacy?

Pursuit of the presuppositions of common sense leads toward

the disclosure of an assumed if not explicit metaphysics. The stark opposition between freedom *from* and freedom *to* derives partly from the assumption of first and second realm theories of causality: if causes are singular there is a temptation to distinguish monolinear causality from freedom by the simple *presence* or *absence* of a cause. Third realm rationality admits a multiplicity of constraints relevant to every event and then distinguishes free action from determined behavior by distinguishing among *different structures* of constraints. The structure of voluntary action differs from the structure of involuntary behavior somewhat as the structure of human history differs from the structure of natural evolution, or so the later sections on language and intentionality will suggest.

The welter of issues surrounding the concept of freedom would seem to constitute a weakness for any analysis hoping to follow a simple linear course dealing with one plank at a time. Yet the wider context renders this weakness a strength. This chapter provides a systematic link between the structure of power and the structure of subjectivity. The point is to gain some insight into the patterns of reinforcement between social structure and psychic structure as both yield to historical pressures toward decentralization. Because the concept of freedom has both social and psychological roots its articulation will have both social and psychological ramifications. By emphasizing the formal *structure* of freedom the argument will abstract from the specific contents of either the social or the psychological contexts.

This process of abstraction is the critical theorist's analogue to the prophet's turning his back on his contemporaries in order to seek counsel elsewhere than in accepted common sense. The departure from common sense toward the desert of metaphysics takes place at the gate marked 'Collectivism vs. Individualism'. The return will take place at the gate marked The Structure of Subjectivity—the next chapter. These road signs forewarn the wary traveler: though the discussion of freedom takes its departure from issues in social theory, the abstract resolution of those issues will apply to questions of psychological theory.

To be prematurely specific for the sake of a guiding anticipation: the following theory of freedom finds three conditions necessary for freedom in the social context: first, resistance against deterministic forces of socialization; second, intersubjective support for that resistance lest it become blind and senseless rebellion; third, a multiplicity of well-founded interpretive schemes giving objective support to several interpretations of social interactions. As opposed to theories of freedom based on either the primacy of the individual or the primacy of an all-embracing collectivity, the structure of freedom developed here will scorn both the solitary One and the collective All in favor of the ambiguous Some as the proper locus of freedom. This social philosophy of Some discloses the rationality of a society of situses by showing how the pluralization of society need not be regarded as some degenerate stage of an essentially unified humanity. Rather the multiplicity of social groupings is a condition for the possibility of freedom for each.

The structure derived from the social theory of individuals and colletivities will find its application in a polytheistic psychology, a model of selfhood in which subjective freedom derives not from a single monotheistic ego but from a pluralized pantheon of selves together satisfying the pluralized structure of freedom. Contrary to currently debased rhetoric about authenticity and identity crises,[2] the least free persons are those whose personality is single to the point of predictability. The model for many dimensional man is therefore a model of multiple selves within each person. Each self is a source of differing interpretations of those interactions through which a single person carries its several selves.

Of course we do not ordinarily think of ourselves as so pluralized. Nor do we often think of nation-states as evanescent unifications. So short is the memory of common sense we mistake those objects of creative interpretation for permanent realities. We forget that both the self and the nation are human creations subject to human history. Caught up among the current concerns of our like-minded contemporaries we fail to notice the fact that what we take for granted as given elements of the human condition were unheard of not too many centuries ago and only very lately cast into the forms we assume as necessary.[3] Just as common sense believes someone *must* have The Power so it assumes that each of us *must* be a single agent. Little do we suspect that the sense of necessity we take to be logically grounded in the very concepts of power, nation and self is instead the result of a particular historical constellation of uniquely intense concentrations, both social and personal.

Once we internalize that sense of syntatic or definitional necessity from a historical constellation to which it is semantically appropriate, even less do we suspect that our own historical situation could be outstripping the reach of those categories we take for granted. How could we think otherwise? The old categories are our tools for thought. Only a critical theory that takes its distance from common sense can refurbish those concepts one by one to render them adequate to a new historical constellation.

Though talk of shifts of paradigm has recently become so fashionable as to court a counterrevolution in the approach to scientific revolutions, Kuhn's insights are worth recalling and strengthening with a further recollection of their Hegelian-Marxist precursors.[4*] Like ideologies, paradigms are *pervasive*. They color the way we see *everything* from our most private experiences to our most public institutions. Consequently the case for many dimensional man must wander through the welter of issues surrounding freedom for two reasons: first the disclosure of the structure of freedom has *import* for both the social theory of situses as well as the soul theory of multiple selfhood. Second, because the categories to be refurbished have the status of paradigms and are hence so pervasive that several issues bear their imprint, a challenge to a given category in one context will hardly have much success as long as the category continues to derive the strength of intellectual habit from its continued application in another context. As long as the country *must* be a unified nation with a single set of controls autonomously wielded by some single powerful agency, then what chance is there that one will be able to take the geography of the body as a land of many selves? As long as

the person must be a unified self with a single set of controls autonomously wielded by some single powerful agency, then what chance is
there that one will be *able* to take the geography of the country as a
land of many situses?

The categories of unity, autonomy, freedom, power and agency form a single paradigm through which common sense sees both
collective and individual life. To challenge the paradigm enough to
release its hold on the imagination on *either* personal or social issues,
one must challenge the paradigm on *both* fronts.

Individualism, collectivism and dialectics

'To' and 'from' connote opposite directions relative to their
speaker. The two prepositions are so closely linked in their contrariety they form an idiom, *to and fro;* for the Germans, *hin und her.* Similarly linkable if less idiomatic are the corresponding philosophies of
freedom: individualism and collectivism.

Individualism, whether in the form of Jeffersonian liberal
democratic theory or in the form of European existentialism, stresses
the individual's freedom *from* external constraints. Whether the con-
straining Other be Hegel's system (for Kierkegaard), the authority of
generally accepted opinion (Heidegger's *das Man*) or the political and
religious restraints of an alien State, the several defenses of liberty
declare the individual's independence from a socializing Other.

With varying degre metaphysical rigor the several philosophies of individual freedom all presuppose the primacy of the single individual as the building block of society. The combined All of
the social whole is the secondary result of a joining of prior units, the
pre-formed Ones who are presumably capable of making contracts *before* their social juncture is established. Philosophies of individual

liberty from the socializing Other naturally issue in either anarchism or social contract theories since both presume the possibility of a genuinely human existence in atomic form either apart from or prior to molecular congregation.

Dialectically opposed to these several philosophies of freedom *from* stand philosophies of freedom *to*. Just as the former presuppose the primacy of the individual One, so the latter presuppose the primacy of the collective All. The Marxist-Hegelian tradition argues that the individualized subjective consciousness that common sense so readily takes for granted is itself the historical result of a primordially *social* process. Mankind comes on the scene as a herd.[5] Only later, only after painful processes of domination, only after a dialectic of mastery and slavery does mankind, initially in the person of the slave, gain mastery of *thought.* And only through his interest in emancipation does the slave acquire the capacity to *reason,* to imagine and posit goals unheard of in the domain of an "understanding" limited to perceptions of historical actuality.[6]* The slave's interest in emancipation is not only a will to individual liberty. In bondage he loses not only his individual liberty but also his species-being *(Gattungswesen),* his biologically distinguishing capacity to act in consort with fellow members of the species *(Gattung)* to generate their own essence *(Wesen).* Therefore the slave's struggle for emancipation is not only a revolution aimed at freedom from an oppressor; the revolution is also a turning around from individualistic struggles of competition toward the freedom *to* of cooperation. The capacity to act in consort toward imagined goals, the capacity to reason together in order to determine historically the essence of man, is the capacity to act rather than react.

This chapter is devoted to the dialectical development of an account of freedom that does justice to demands for both freedom *to* and freedom *from*. The development is dialectical in two senses. First, the final account does not lie *between* the extremes of freedom to and freedom from; rather, the final account represents a transcendent synthesis, a "taking up" *(Aufhebung)* of the two extremes into a dimension whose marginal differences are misconstrued if regarded in terms of a polar opposition between individualism and collectivism. Second, the account is dialectical in its procedure: the pursuit of each extreme toward its own negation, its autonomous generation of the need for its own opposite.

Dialectics differ from pragmatism in this double sense: the dialectical solution to the problem of freedom follows not from theory's *concessions* to practice—as if the philosophy of individualism might concede as much to the practical exigencies of social existence as the philosophy of collectivism had to concede to the demands of individuals. Pragmatic concessions might bring about a meeting between extremes whose theoretical opposition would remain firm. But pragmatic compromise differs from dialectical synthesis precisely by the remaining difference between theory and practice. Dialectical resolution depends upon changing the very terms of the opposition. The first difference between dialectics and pragmatics—synthesis in place of concession—depends upon the second, the different appropriation of the *terms* of the opposition. Where pragmatics may grant an irreducible reality to the opposing terms, dialectics follows the development of each extreme as a "disappearing moment." By pursuing each polar theory to its extreme, dialectics would not only reduce each to absurdity but also show how its germ of truth can survive only when joined with its opposite. Yet the "joining" or "synthesis" or *Aufhebung* now appears not as a meeting between fixed poles; rather the terms of the more adequate theory represent a concrete immediacy from which the undialectical extremes now appear as falsely reified abstractions.

The abstract extremes involved in the dialectic of freedom are the isolated One prized in individualistic theories of freedom *from* and the collective All prized in theories of freedom *to*. Relying neither upon pollyannaish hopes of All for One and One for All, nor upon pragmatic concessions of All to One or One to All, the dialectical development of both extremes shows each to be a polar abstraction from the concreteness of Some. The following argument is an attempt to show that the proper locus of freedom must be a multiple subject, neither a single One nor a totally inclusive All.

Liberty as extreme individualism

Arbitrariness is the Achilles's heel of individualism. Pursued to its extreme the freedom from all determinants turns into an indeterminacy so total that one has no reason for choosing anything at all. The cost of total liberty is nihilism. If nothing constrains the will then nothing justifies the will. The fiction of total freedom from all constraints leaves one with no more volition than the rock released from the constraint of the hand that held it. Its *motion* is hardly equivalent to *action*.

Though individualism need not be pursued to absurd extremes some thinkers have had the courage to pursue their metaphysical convictions to their nihilistic conclusions. Sartre's early writings argue an existentialist ontology within which we are "condemned to freedom": "It follows that my freedom is the unique foundation of values and that nothing, absolutely nothing, justifies me in adopting this or that particular value."[7] Though Sartre pursues an important insight in his effort to show the inefficacy of past resolutions in the face of current temptations, he severs the individual subject so totally from his prior decisions that only *nothingness* remains as the core of agency. To the extent that the subject is *not* his prior decisions then of course he is free of those prior determinations. But then who *is* the subject who is free from any and all determination? He is nothing but an indeterminate cipher for whom any choice is as absurd as any other. The absurd hero falls from the nobility of an Orestes able to contest the will of the gods. His modern version is the "hero" of John Barth's *End of the Road,* Horner, whom we find paralyzed with indecisiveness.

For mere behavior or motion to count as voluntary action there must be an intention. But for there to be an intending there must be some discriminative caring. One need not contest the existentialist insight that there is no one thing essential to all men in order to make the claim that some things must be essential to each man if he is to exhibit the sort of care that generates intentions.

What are the conditions for the possibility of care? Need and hunger are not sufficient to distinguish human intentions from animal cravings. Needs motivate *behavior,* but if *action* differs from behavior precisely by virtue of the distinction between mechanical necessity and voluntary choice then needs are hardly sufficient as conditions for care and intention. Care is *noncompulsive preference.* But what are the conditions for the possibility of a preference that is noncompulsive, nonnecessary? The rock that is free of the hand is not free to return to the hand of its own volition. Socrates freed from his shackles may yet choose to return to them by denying his opportunity for escape from penalty. Whatever would possess a person to so sacrifice his liberty?

Agency and extreme collectivism.

To answer Socrates's question is to turn to the pursuit of freedom *to.* Socrates identifies himself with the laws of the polis that nurtured him. He argues that his escape would be more an act of self-betrayal than self-preservation. He cares about the laws of Athens. To violate those laws would be to violate himself. If Socrates were nothing but an assemblage of skin and bones subject to physical causes then it would make sense to preserve biological integrity by an escape from death.[8] But Socrates is more than a physical organism subject to causes. Because he identifies himself as the product of a complex network of human interactions, because he sees that his being as Socrates is the result of a particular history of commitments, he recognizes that he would preserve his biological integrity only at the price of the ontological integrity—the very *being*—of his personal identity. The body might live but the person would die if the pattern of interactions defining its identity were compromised.

Socrates's predicament is the collectivist counterpart to Patrick Henry's individualist slogan, "Give me liberty or give me death." For Socrates liberty would be equivalent to death. Or conversely, only through death can he preserve the liberties that the laws of Athens allow. If he were to break those commitments to save his own life he would condone a return to the state of nature. His escape would diminish the *being* of the pattern of rules and committments that distinguish human action and personal identity from animal behavior and biological preservation.

The ontological status of *action* depends upon the preservation of behavior patterns sufficiently regular to constitute *rules*. There is nothing wrong with going-through-a-red-light as a piece of physical behavior. The redness of the light will no more harm a traveler than would a green light. But if stopping at red lights becomes a regularity recognized as a condition for safe travel through intersections, then the violation of that regularity becomes an *action* subject not only to biological risk but also to social sanction. Considered as a piece of mere behavior there is nothing either correct or incorrect about going through a red light. Considered as an action in the context of mutually preserved rules and regularities, however, going through a red light breaks one of the rules that conditions our freedom to travel without injury.

The often cited example of the red light is but a prelude to less obvious considerations about rules, agency and freedom to. Pushed to its extreme the example of traffic laws will show the paradox involved in the concept of agency as a freedom conditioned by regularities of behavior. If action be distinguished from behavior by the intention to follow a rule then all our actions would seem to be predetermined by rules. The regularities that *condition* agency would also *condemn* agency to a juggernaut determinism of *socially* defined rules every bit as unbreakable as the natural law of gravity. If arbitrary whim is the Achilles's heel of individualistic theories of libertarian freedom from, then totalitarian determinism is the mirror absurdity of any theory that pushes the dependence on regularities to its extreme.

Because the philosophy of freedom *to* sees the individual as a social product, that philosophy tends to emphasize the primacy of the totality, the All. The State becomes the only truly autonomous individual. The truth is the whole and the totality becomes subject; it manifests a structure of subjectivity sufficient to allow Hegel to call the whole by the name of Spirit *(Geist).*[9]

However much he may have resisted the "spiritualization" of material history, Marx nevertheless admired Hegel's insights into mankind's capacity to mold its own nature through history. For both Marx and Hegel man's freedom is his collectively reasoned authorship of history. Only if members of the species reason together can they collectively posit and bring about intended ends. Only intended ends distinguish the intentional plots that make up history from the mere *events* that succeed one another in natural evolution. But neither Marx nor Hegel satisfactorily solved the problem of keeping the conditions for freedom *to* from violating freedom *from*. Since both stressed the universality of the conditions for agency, both were drawn toward the vision of One World, a dream of totality too close to the nightmare of totalitarianism.[10*]

The social philosophy of some

Having now pursued both individualism and collectivism toward absurd extremes the argument may salvage the truths of both from their respectively one-sided absurdities. The extreme libertarian must learn that reason rather than whim is the antidote to the deterministic causality of the socializing Other. The extreme collectivist must learn that liberty is the best defense against rational agency assuming the juggernaut rigidity of natural law. But how are these lessons to be learned if both the individualist and collectivist hold to their respective claims for ontological primacy of the One or the All? The individualist may concede some ground to the claims of society, but if those concessions be in the name of utility for the individual then their theoretical foundation is as suspect as the indeterminate identity of the unattached ego. How is one to know which social arrangements will best serve "the individual" when the nature of the individual is free of all specific determination? Similarly, collectivists may concede some ground to individual liberties, but if those concessions be rational actions based on regularities of social behavior, how is one to resist the charge that these so-called concessions to individual "liberty" are but necessarily determined eddies in the social stream?

If liberty is to be distinguished from a mere *absence* of constraints, freedom *from* must exhibit the *structure* of constraints known as agency. If agency is to be distinguished from natural causality then freedom *to* must preserve some of the indeterminacy of liberty. If the locus of freedom is neither the indeterminate One nor the totally determinate All but the ambiguous Some, then these apparently contradictory demands yield a coherent description of the structure of freedom.

A limited collectivity allows for the possibility of both the resistance implicit in liberty and the nonarbitrariness implicit in agency. Some can resist a socializing Other without falling into the absurdity of the individual whose rebellious isolation renders his "actions" absurd even to himself. Nor is the support of Some totalitarian. The limitation of each collectivity precludes its rule-following behavior from becoming the only available measure of rational action.

Language provides an example of rule-following behavior that is nontotalitarian. Learning a language need not determine what one says, only how one says it. Nor is one necessarily restricted to one language for *how* one says what one has to say. There are *some* languages. Not all sounds satisfy the structural criteria for a language; nor is there just one set of sounds that constitute language. Like traffic laws languages condition our freedom to. Unlike traffic laws languages are perhaps less susceptible to arguments for totalitarian universality—or so the following section will suggest.

Language and action

The distinction between action and behavior derives in part from the simple fact that an unambiguous description of physical behavior is not always sufficient to answer the question, "What are you doing?" A precisely described arc of the hand (behavior) may be a "greeting," a "goodbye," a "swat at a fly" (actions). Just as a given rock may *be* a "boundary marker," a "gravestone" or a "door jamb," so the same physical motion may *be* any of a number of actions. Just as it may be easy to give a precise physicalistic description of the size and weight of the stone while its function remains in doubt, so a precise description of behavior need not dictate the action being performed. In order to specify the action one needs to know the intention with which it was performed. But what is an intention?

The issue of intentionality is among the most controversial in contemporary philosophy. This is not the place to attempt a definitive argument resolving hotly debated issues. The best that can be hoped for is some measure of clarity about what is at stake. Without making a pretense at conclusive argument the following exposition leads toward some educated guesses on how the issues ought to be resolved if their resolution is to support the social philosophy of Some.

The rough outlines of the intentionality debate run as follows.

Granted that the grammar of action terms like 'wave' and 'swat' carry implicit reference to intentions while behavioristic descriptions do not, is it possible to further specify intentions in terms of behavior? Can the intention that would specify an action be determined from further behavior without reference to still further intentions? Can we tell what someone intends to do, and thereby interpret his behavior as a specific action, by observing further behavior? For the purposes of the social philosophy of Some the answer must be a carefully qualified "Sometimes but not always."

What are the reasons—carefully considered if not conclusive—for placing this bet against the reducibility of all intentions to descriptions of overt behavior? To continue the rough outline of what is at stake, the next issue involves nothing less than the nature of language. At least two very different pictures of language lurk in the background and sometimes leap to the foreground of talk about action and intention. One picture takes language as essentially representative. A sharp division would separate an extralinguistic reality from the language used to represent that reality. The other picture of language draws no such sharp distinction but grants that the world in which we live is already through and through linguistic.

The representative picture assumes the *givenness* of things to which words are then tied by the semantic link of ostensive reference. Re-presentation is possible because extralinguistic objects are already presented in their extralinguistic articulations as discrete entities. Surely one can point to evidence in support of this picture. Water is not fire and any language worthy of the name will have words to represent their difference. Because the differences to be represented are already articulate in the sense of being discrete in their givenness, differences among languages are finally accidental and unimportant according to the representative picture of language. One language is basically as good as another as long as its vocabulary contains enough distinctions to cover the distinctnesses of extralinguistic reality. Questions of translation and synonymy can be settled unambiguously by reference to that same extralinguistic reality.

The representative picture of language is convenient for a behaviorist theory of action. It seems obvious that intentions are in some
sense linguistic. But the behaviorist problematically presupposes a
representative theory of language. He assumes that however much an
intention may be a symbolic representation—whether consciously
formulated in language or somehow pictured in the mind's eye—the
meaning of that representation can be reduced to extralinguistic behavior. With the aid of the representative theory of language the behaviorist thinks himself safe in bypassing the intricacies of language
in favor of those unambiguous extralinguistic articulations from
which words supposedly derive their meanings. The representative
theory of language allows the behaviorist to regard the whole messy
business of language as an ultimately unnecessary detour in the description of action. Language introduces nothing essentially new. It
simply—or complexly—re-presents an already articulate extralinguistic reality with which the account of action starts and ends.

Consider now a picture of language in which the line between
the linguistic and the extralinguistic is not so sharply drawn. Take,
for example, La Rochefoucauld's observation that we would not *experience* love as we do had we not learned to talk of love.[11] The implication is that the world we experince is anything but extralinguistic. Rather the terms with which we frame the intentions distinguishing our actions from mere behavior are themselves partly responsible
for carving out distinctions that are by no means fully articulated pri-
or to their presentation in language. Parts of our experience derive
their structure from the language used to present (not re-present)
them. Which parts? And how does this linguistic structuring bear on
the account of action and intention?

The two questions are closely related, for the parts of our experience most susceptible to linguistic structuring are precisely those
parts having to do with action and intention. The representative picture of language draws support from examples having to do with physical descriptions of natural phenomena whose articulations have little
if anything to do with human intention.[12]* Linguistic relativists may

point out that Eskimos have many words for different kinds of snow and hence *experience* snow differently than we do. Similarly with Arabs and sand. Another favorite example draws on the several ways different languages carve up the color spectrum at different intervals.[13] But each of these examples drawn from physicalistic description plays straight into the hands of the behaviorist. A rose by any other name is still a rose, and so with snow, sand and colors. Natural evolution has achieved a certain articulation among things that only the most avid idealist would attribute to human intention. Those differences we find among languages in the way they carve up *nature* are clearly explicable in terms of the *behavior* of language users, some of whom behave among sand dunes, others among drifts of snow. As for colors the availability of quantitative spectrographic measurement assures us that it is *the same* extralinguistic hue that one language groups with green, another with blue.

But what about differences among languages where the objects of description are not natural but man-made? What about those parts of our experience that have to do not with the articulations achieved by natural evolution but by human history? Where is the analogue to the spectrograph that would tell us that the romantics were writing about *the same* phenomena as Masters and Johnson? Where the very phenomena in question are human creations, the language used in formulating the creators' intentions plays a constitutive role in the process of creation. 'Love', 'power', 'freedom', 'self' and 'history' itself are historical terms in the sense that their meanings are not *given* by nature but are instead successively constituted and altered by the ways they are used.

A rose is a rose is a rose but success is not success is not success. The criteria for satisfying some intentions are not reducible to ahistorical descriptions of natural phenomena. A "success" in the eyes of some is a "sell-out" in the eyes of others. The action performed with a given bit of behavior is very much a function of its place in a historical context of other actions suggesting appropriate interpretations of still other behavior. One has but to think of a quite different example often drawn from the snowy tundra: the Eskimo's offer of his wife to the weary traveler. Must she commit an "act of adultery"? Has her husband been "cuckolded"?

The previous discussion adumbrates protracted arguments and utterly ignores a good many issues that must be joined to achieve anything like a convincing argument. Nonetheless the hasty review points toward some implications that remain undeveloped in the literature of linguistics and action theory. Most important for the social philosophy of Some is the simple observation that the term 'language' represents an abstraction from the deceptively obvious existence of many languages. No one speaks *Language*. One speaks French or German or English and so on. And within each language there are many language games: describing, threatening, joking, lying, promising and so on.

Recollection of the obvious is necessary only because the fantasy of unity has such a strong hold on the theoretical imagination—as if differences among languages were somehow accidental; as if the structure of Language had to be everywhere the same at some level sufficiently deep beneath surface differences. The fantasy of necessary unity is at play in the refusal to acknowledge the possibility that *historical differentiations* run every bit as deep as structural similarities among different languages. Yet the fact of historical differentiation (and thus its possibility) is evidence (and condition) for a *freedom that is neither arbitrary nor totalitarian.*

Recall that the conditions for freedom call for both the resistance of a socializing other implicit in liberty *and* the intelligibility derived from rule-following behavior implicit in agency. Individualism answers the libertarian demand for freedom *from* but at the risk of loss of intelligibility. If the individual breaks totally from others then he has no shared categories in terms of which to articulate his behavior as action. The linguistic correlate to liberty is an utterly private language. But the concept of a private language is incoherent.[14] A sound is a word only if it plays a fixed role in discourse among a multiplicity of speakers who collectively act as arbiters of *correct* usage. If an individual invents a word and tells no one else its meaning, how is he to know when even he has used the word correctly? Because he set up a fixed rule for its use? But how is he to know whether he has correctly followed the rule? Perhaps his new usages *change* the rule or *reinvent* the word. Without other users this private language is like a game of solitaire with no rules at all—an aimless shuffling of "signs" that lack the criteria of correctness necessary for them to signify anything. In short, a "private language" is not a language at all.

Now to come to the point of the previous reflections on the relations between language, action and history: it appears that the concept of an utterly public, totally universal Language may be as mistaken as the notion of a private language. Such a universal language would be the linguistic correlate of a collectivist theory of freedom just as private language is the correlate of individualism. The absence of a universal Language provides evidence against the collectivist theory of universal agency just as the incoherence of private language supports the critique of individualism. How might that highly suggestive if obvious piece of evidence fit into an argument that is more than merely suggestive?

Among the most important premises would be the distinction between nature and human history. For after all, is not the distinction between voluntary action and mechanical behavior another version of the distinction between human freedom and natural necessity? History is precisely the record of our escape from natural necessity. History is the chronicle of *actions*, intentional plots with beginnings, middles and ends. To compress an already compact adumbration of arguments so that they will fit through the needle's eye of novelty: if the freedom of voluntary action requires intention and intention requires language and language requires a multiplicity of language users, then the free actions constituting the historical transcendence of natural necessity would seem to court all mankind toward a collective authorship of history. But then the moment of libertarian resistance would be lost. The crucial element of liberty is regained and preserved with the observation that the multiplicity of languages is no accident. The distinction between history and nature is important precisely for the fact that the uniformity of natural laws sustains a multiplicity of histories much as a single bit of physical behavior may be interpreted as any of a number of actions. The ambiguity of behavior with respect to action is a microcosmic analogue to the diverse potentialities of the natural world with respect to macrocosmic history. The crucial middle term that maintains the plausibility of this analogy is language.

If a single language mediates between a bit of behavior and how it is meant as an action, then a multiplicity of languages is likely to spawn a multiplicity of histories; and conversely, that multiplicity of histories will reinforce—beside and against the uniformity of nature—a multiplicity of languages. So construed, the pattern of interrelationships among language, action, behavior, history and nature render a theoretical foundation to the claim that the locus of freedom is necessarily a limited collectivity: not One, not All, but Some.

Some offer *enough* intersubjectivity to keep agency from falling into the criterialessness of a private language. Some avoid arbitrariness by having each other as standard bearers for the *correctness* of their behavior. At the same time the difference between Some and All is sufficient to resist the collectivist temptation toward considering the entire species of mankind as the true locus of freedom. By logically limiting the locus of freedom the social philosophy of Some enables each and every collectivity to maintain its liberty from assimilation by others.

Racism, elitism and marginalism

Only the limited Some can satisfy the conditions for both agency and liberty. The locus for the structure of freedom is therefore a limited collectivity. Lest this pronouncement be mistaken as an endorsement of racism let it be clear that the premises on which the present argument is based prohibit a racist interpretation. Precisely because the patterns that distinguish action from behavior are man-made and not natural, neither biological similarities nor differences are sufficient to define either the brotherhood or the disparateness of human beings. Natural evolution conditions the possibility of certain types of *behavior*—whether a member of a certain species can fly; human history conditions the possibility of certain types of *action*—whether one can sign a binding contract. But unlike nature, history is neither uniform nor universal.

The term 'history' is as much of an abstraction as 'mankind'. Who has ever seen "mankind"? "Mankind" comes on the scene not as a herd but in herds, tribes, limited collectivities. The social genesis of individuals derives not from the entire species but from particular groups. The concrete origins of subjectivity are everywhere limited by specific customs and specific regularities that may extend beyond the whims of individuals without encompassing all *Homo sapiens.* However much the *ideal* of universality functions as a condition for rational agency—on which more below—the *actual* range of the regularities conditioning rules rarely if ever extends to encompass all human beings.

As with the abstraction "mankind" so with the abstraction "history": while it may be possible to offer a biological definition that extends to all men at all times, their suprabiological humanity is everywhere conditioned by different histories, not by one common History. Hence the terms in which the members of any Some cast their intentions are not as universal as the parameters for describing natural events. The logic of the concepts of space, time and mass is significantly different from the logic of concepts like success, honor and duty. Granting an *implicit* universality to the latter as well as to the former—all these concepts presuppose the contextual location of the particular within the general—still the *explicit* range of the "universality" of concepts like success and honor is limited by the fact that their presupposed contexts are *non*-natural. The inventions of reason transcend the uniform regularities of the natural laws comprehended by understanding. The same freedom that differentiates rational agency from natural behavior also encourages differences among the historical inventions of reason. So while racism represents a pseudospeciation of humanity, differences based on different *histories* are not so lightly dismissed as "pseudo."

However innocent of racism the social philosophy of Some may emerge, the taint of elitism remains. Even if the limited collectivities that serve as loci for the structure of freedom are historical rather than natural in origin, their multiplicity would seem to spell doom to all hopes for universal brotherhood. Does the advocacy of devotion to Some necessitate a sense of "we precious few"? Must loyalty toward a few mean snobbery toward the many?

Neither a naturalistically based racism nor a historically based nepotism will survive a reference back to the premises of the argument for a social philosophy of Some. Where the refutation of racism refers back to the importance of the distinction between the natural and the historical, the refutation of elitism refers back to both (a) the ecological argument for organism-plus-environment as the unit of survival and (b) the historical claim that we are entering a period where situses rather than statuses mark the striations of advanced industrial society.

Because (a) each Some is dependent upon its relations with others for its survival, *no* limited collectivity can afford to let others become so desperate that the variegated structure of the whole is threatened by any one group. However false the reification of One and All, the concrete reality of each Some does not preclude consciousness of a *differance* mediating individuality and universality. Relational thought about social issues need not posit The World as one pole of concern in order to avoid the smug comfort of isolationism. Precisely because a locus of freedom is defined in terms of its relation to the socializing other, preservation of the other is essential to its existence. Resistance is hardly equivalent to elimination or indifference. The difference between resistance and total conquest will emerge in greater detail as later chapters develop the difference between monotheism and polytheism in general, and more specifically the difference between a power-mad Zeus and Ares the Warrior. Those personalized symbols of quasi-universal syndromes will reflect back on the social philosophy of Some.

Because (b) the social philosophy of Some takes its departure from the phenomena noted in chapter one, namely the splintering of a centralized, hierarchical status-system into a multiplicity of situses, no special Some can justifiably claim the status of an *elite* at the pinnacle of a crumbling pyramid. Rather each limited collectivity becomes *marginal* relative to all others. If decentralization means that "the center is everywhere," so too are the margins. The logic of marginality in place of superiority will likewise take on greater detail as later chapters fill in the locus of selfhood with a structure of multiplicity that challenges the centrality of the ego and the superiority of the superego.

Even if the social philosophy of Some can be vindicated from the charges of racism and elitism—perhaps the most unjust and contemptible species of the genus, parochialism—still the passions inspired by residual provincialism threaten to consign the social philosophy of Some to the dustbin of barbarian politics. Tribalism has no place in civilized society. The Enlightenment taught us to transcend our petty differences toward the unity and equality of all men. The belief in universal brotherhood extends to the claim that no one is free until we are all free. Yet the social philosophy of Some would seem to move toward a lifeboat ethics in which the freedom of a few is possible precisely as a result of their resistance against the rising tide of unfreedom swelling from the many.

In order to forestall misinterpretation and misapplication of the social philosophy of Some, recall yet another of the departure points: the emphasis upon structure. No specific content, no specific liberties hold the status of incorrigible first principles. Rather the stress upon structure leaves open the possibility that different groups will wish to defend different liberties against encroachments and assimilation by a socializing other. Consequently, though the locus for freedom is inevitably a limited collectivity, every One may be a member of a Some that is free.

The logical structure of this defense of freedom is not as simple as libertarian individualism or universalist collectivism. The ambiguous Some lacks the attractive elegance of both One and All. Yet we have seen the shortcomings of reliance on either extreme, so now it is time to take the trouble to comprehend a more complex equality, a more complex universal brotherhood than that found in the childish faith in the one Father.

Our equality lies not in some equal gift of a universal "nature of man." If anything defines us universally it is our historical transcendence of nature. But precisely the freedom inherent in the exercise of reason guarantees that the contents of our several transcendences, our several histories, are bound to differ in significant respects. Granting also those significant respects in which we are the same—for we never transcend the uniformity of nature entirely—still the exercise of freedom and reason has brought us to a state in which our equality lies not so much in our universal inclusion in one family as in our universal marginality. We are each part of a marginal Some resisting others; relative to some others we are each the Other.

The 'Some' in 'social philosophy of Some' does not refer to any specific group—much less to an elite or a race. Instead, membership-in-a-Some is a structural role that any may play. The complexity inherent in the social philosophy of Some sacrifices the elegance of One and All in order to protect the freedoms of liberty and agency without falling into the one-sided absurdities of extreme individualism and extreme collectivism. In order to clarify this necessary complexity and lend the elegance of metaphor to abstract argument some final reflections on languages will summarize the meaning of both the equality and the differences among Somes.

Levels of language vs.
dimensions of interpretation

Like 'Mankind' and 'History', 'Reality' is a noun that does not
refer to a single, univocal totality, but to a *role* played by many realities, just as many different worlds play the role of The World for different peoples. This relativizing of 'reality' according to intersubjectively reinforced interpretive schemes does not reduce to subjective
relativism—the view that anything goes for me so long as I believe it
to be so, and similarly for you.

One of the strongest bulwarks for the belief in a single univocal reality is the certainty that subjective relativism is absurd. But
subjective relativism is not the only alternative to a belief in The-
World-that-is-the-same-for-all. Subjective relativism *is* absurd because a single subject can generate no intersubjective criteria for
what *he* regards as true and false, much less what anyone else is supposed to regard as true and false. "True for me" is an absurdity since
the concept of truth presupposes intersubjective agreement on the
rules for testing truth. The necessarily intersubjective character of
truth follows from arguments against private language.[15] Those arguments do not, however, prove the absurdity of "True for us." A Some
can constitute an intersubjective base for the intelligibility of truth.
Just as the politics of One (individualism) and the politics of All (collectivism) show the one-sided extremes of a dialectic that points toward the politics of Some, so subjective relativism on the one hand
and belief in The World with universal validity for All on the other
show the one-sided extremes of a dialectic that points toward an epistemology of Some, a *hermeneutic pluralism.*

Hermeneutics is the discipline of interpretation. The name in-
vokes Hermes, messenger of the gods. The importance of Hermeneutics to historical existence follows from the intrinsic ambiguity of the
actions that constitute history. Like an oracular text whose meaning
demands interpretation, past actions are not totally and irrevocably
determinate in their significance. Rather the future of things past

sometimes yields a revision in interpretation. E.g., however much fear of the gods may have figured in the intention and action of some ancients, we no longer interpret a particular eclipse of the sun that motivated their actions as a sign of divine wrath.

The example of *scientific* reinterpretation of eclipses cuts two ways: while serving as an example of reinterpretation, it also demonstrates a tendency in second realm explanation that would eliminate "mere interpretations" in favor of universal truths appropriate to the uniformity of nature. The successes of physicalistic explanation lead toward a literalism that ignores the distinction between nature and history. Just as fundamentalism forecloses interpretive possibilities for the fundamentalist, so the force of physicalism on our thought is so strong that it alters our capacity to imagine a metaphor according to which physicalism itself is but one interpretation among several. With respect to the "texts" of social histories, centuries of scientism have made fundamentalists of us all. But surely fundamentalism is *one* among many approaches to the Bible. And just as the attempt at literalism is but one interpretation of the Bible, so physicalism is one interpretation of human experience.

To see the force of physicalism on our understanding of interpretation one need only consider the intellectual habits bred by considering physical objects in space as paradigms for objectivity in general. Euclidean space has three and only three dimensions. Consequently the perspectives necessary for viewing the entire exterior of a cube are limited in principle. If one circles a cube, looks at each side, its back, its top, its bottom, one knows from the nature of space that one has completely exhausted the perspectives necessary in order to view its entire exterior. Not so with a text. How could one ever know, either with a text or with history, that one had exhausted the perspectival stances one might take up in order to make sense of such objects? Yet the habits of scientism, bred by the observation of objects in space, carry over into the humanities where they encourage misreadings in the name of definitive readings.

Scientistic literalism makes nondialectical concessions to the "human sciences" in the form of the spatial metaphor of different *levels* to which different explanatory *languages* are appropriate. One speaks of the physical level, the psychological level, the social level, the spiritual level and so on till all the various explanatory schemes have been granted a level on which to operate. One wonders, however, how the metaphor of levels is to be taken. No doubt it is convenient, but it is also misleading to the extent that it leaves the door wide open to reductionism while at the same time contributing to a picture of human existence as inexplicably severed into separate domains. The language of levels seems able to maintain a distinction only by fixing what is distinguished in separate substrata: each level (stratum) underlies (sub-) part of what is distinguished.

Just as our atmosphere separates into different levels so our spirituality ostensibly occupies only the rarified air of the upper levels of our existence. Just as our dwellings have different levels so our psyches are ostensibly separated so that our sexuality inhabits the dark cellar of our existence.[16] Once our multidimensional, solid existence has been separated into two-dimensional layers then the way is open to a process of ontological distillation according to which all *other* layers are reduced to the status of being shadows of the one layer that a given theoretician takes as Reality. The metaphor of levels contributes to the plausibility of reductionism because it is easy for us to imagine one two-dimensional picture that is congruent with or structurally isomorphic to another level so that it is then easy to imagine one level as an image or shadow of another level. The mapping relationships between one level and another needn't be precisely one to one any more than different languages need be precisely translatable into one another. Nevertheless the basic idea remains: just as '*rot*' means "red," so one can find correspondence rules among the various explanatory schemes describing different levels: a thought-of-sugar (mental level) corresponds to firing-of-x-, y-, and z-neurones (physiological level).

Once we accept the analogy between levels of existence and different languages (as many contemporary theorists have),[17] then we fall prey to the natural temptation to find among the levels of existence something corresponding to The World that different languages ostensibly describe. Since no one is so provincial as to claim his national language as the one true language approximated by others, the analogy between languages and theoretical levels *should* lead to the antireductionistic picture of a multiplicity of equally well-confirmed theoretical world views. Instead the passion for a single foundation dominates recent handlings of both sides of the analogy between languages and theoretical world views, thus allowing the analogy to be preserved to the falsification of both semantics *and* philosophy of science.

In semantics the passion for a single foundation first took the form of the myth of the ideal language whose propositions were imperfectly represented by the *sentences* of natural languages. Now that only a scattering of logicians and other idiosyncratic vestiges of the Vienna circle wish to hold out for the ideal language projected in Wittgenstein's *Tractatus*, the passion for a single foundation has taken the form of a semantics of ordinary language according to which "extralinguistic Reality" is expected to play the role of sure foundation. Of course this stance begs the question of reduction since it is simply assumed that such a Reality must be univocal. Nor is it clear how we are to converse with the single voice of this Reality if not linguistically, but then are we any longer dealing with the extralinguistic?

The passion for a single foundation in philosophy of science takes the form of classical reductionism: all the terms of alternative theoretical schemes correspond to, and can therefore be reduced to, configurations of the basic elements of the One True Theory. The language of levels, especially as interpreted on an analogy with levels of languages related to a single, foundational level, contributes to the belief in the reducibility of some theories to other theories, and the history of science adds support to the belief in reducibility. But just because reduction is possible in some instances, it does not follow that all world views *must* be reducible to one.

To dampen the passion for a single foundation it will be sufficient to understand that passion's truth and to release that truth from the seductive falsehood of the language of levels. First the truth, then the falsehood: the passion for a single foundation derives from the logic of universality displayed by each of the alternative explanatory world views. To be an explanatory world view is to purport to explain *everything*; naturally, then, everything must be accessible to the theory professed. If the theory is physicalistic, then so-called mental phenomena must be reduced to correspondent physical phenomena for physicalism to retain the universality its theoretical status demands. Now to turn to the falsity of the language of levels: if the mental be conceived as a *separate level* from the physical, then the physical level must be conceived as a foundational level on an analogy with extra-linguistic Reality. The separation of levels implicit in the metaphor of levels together with the demand for *universality* on each level encourages the second realm theoretician to collapse all levels into one level so that universality can be maintained.

As a modest proposal for resisting the seductive pressure of the language of levels consider the simple substitution of *dimensions* for *levels*. Dimensions are total but overlapping. Height is everywhere, depth is everywhere, breadth is everywhere. Every point in an *n*-dimensional space has some value in each of the *n* dimensions. Dimensions are not separate from one another. The universality of one dimension does not preclude the universality of others. Consequently determinations and descriptions in one dimension do not call for the reduction of other dimensions to that one.

Just as hermeneutics appeals to an irreducible multiplicity of dimensions conditioning a single individual, so does it secure a multiplicity of communities of interpretation for each dimension. Unlike the idealized object of classical science whose univocal determinacy allows only *one* correct interpretation—which is therefore not an interpretation at all but a literal representation—the hermeneutical object supports a multiplicity of interpretations: alternative psychologies, alternative religions, alternative aesthetics, etc. Consequently, resistance to socialization into one set of interpretations is not necessarily equivalent to resistance in the face of The Truth. Yet some truth claims must be possible for resistance to count as a genuine alternative. Not just any wild hypothesis will do. Nor will a simple negation. Only a community of interpreters can generate the intersubjective basis for a set of criteria that might validate the truth claims forming a coherent interpretation. The moment of truth is saved from a subjective relativism that renders the very idea of truth absurd.

Only *some* interpretations make sense. Their sensibleness is a function of their satisfying certain rules for good interpretation, rules that in some cases are no different from the rules for good science, e.g., elegance and simplicity, freedom from subjective bias. But the rules for good interpretation no more secure the convergence of all interpretations toward one literal representation than the rules for football secure the convergence of all games of football toward one perfect game.[18]* The fantasy of convergence is but one interpretation, certainly a very seductive interpretation given the paradigm of description and ever more accurate measurement of spatiotemporal objects, but nevertheless, one interpretation.

Once free of the paradigm of the univocally determinate object towards which all descriptions converge like ever more accurate measurements, one can see how the social philosophy of Some represents a dialectical structure of freedom and not merely a pessimistic concession of Mankind's inability to realize unity in universality. Since interpretations need not converge, naturally there will be *resistance* to socialization into *one* interpretation. Second, even though the plurality of interpretations shows the idea of Truth-as-target-of-convergence as a mistaken theory of truth, a mistaken extrapolation from a limited paradigm, still the moment of truth must be preserved. Consequently the critique of literalism demands communities of like-minded interpreters as an alternative source of grounding truth and intelligibiliity. Communities of like-minded interpreters are necessary for truths to be possible. A multiplicity of communities will be actual wherever interpretation is possible. To sum up the modal options that tie together the critique of reductionism and literalism with the three aspects of the formal structure of freedom: the critique (1) accounts for the *actuality* of different interpretations resisting one another, (2) requires the *necessity* of community for interpretive validity, and (3) shows the *possibility* of multiple dimensions of interpretation. The first point finds reinforcement in the multiplicity of languages. The second is confirmed by the arguments against private language. The third follows from the distinction between historical and natural objects of knowledge and the ambiguity inherent in the actions that constitute history.

This chapter began with the legacies of common sense that led to a dialectical development of libertarian freedom *from* and collectivist freedom *to*. The problem to be solved: how to make sense of freedom without falling into the absurd extremes of the utterly indeterminate One or the totally determinate All? The solution: the locus of freedom is a pluralized Some. This chapter's outcome therefore complements the last chapter's historical accounts of advanced industrial society. The last chapter showed how advanced industrial society is disintegrating into a plurality of situses and statuspheres. This chapter supports the claim that the social ecology of proliferating cultures manifests a rationality invisible to second realm rationality and second watershed social theory.

The sections on hermeneutics, languages, levels and dimensions contribute to an account vindicating Hegel's claim that the actual is the rational and the rational is the actual.[19] Where the last chapter offered a portrait of actual plurality, this chapter argues the rationality of plurality as the locus of freedom. Taken together these two chapters show the *rationality* of a society of multiple situses, and the *actuality* of third realm rationality. The issues of both chapters are transforms of one another: universal grammar is the linguistic transform of the uniform homogeneous state. Second realm rationality sees an ordered hierarchy of levels wherever it looks: class status in society, levels of language in scientific and linguistic theory. Relational thought denies the finality or fundamentality of a hierarchical ordering of levels, both in society and among languages. A statusphere or situs is the social transform of a language among languages, and vice versa. Using the model of an ecological system of constraints, the relational thought of third realm rationality allows us to see how hermeneutical interpretation among languages and statuspheres can substitute for second realm procedures of universal translation into one fundamental language.

The pretension of acccess to a fundamental, universal language threatens freedom. The pretense to universality becomes the justification for theoretical reduction, whose social transform is the subordination of Some under the universally socializing Other. The rationality and freedom of statuspheres rest upon both resistance against the socializing Other and upon the support for the resistance that Some can give better than an isolated One.

As the following chapter's section on hermeneutics will argue, the resistance of Some against a socializing Other can take the form of resistance against the pretense of translating the *experience* of the Some into the purportedly universal language of the socializing Other. The thematic thread of cultural pluralism and freedom will be woven with other themes: the loss of *experience* in the public language of information about behavior, the retrieval of experience in the opaque language of *stories,* and the irreducibility of the left-handed intuitive intellect used in interpreting stories. But prior to further weaving, a problem threatens to cut the threads already woven. The structure of freedom courts a paradox wrapped in a dilemma: either individuals alone cannot be free, or, if the individual be a pluralized Some unto himself, then the argument leads toward an infinite regress of selves within selves within selves. The following chapter grasps the second horn of the dilemma and unravels the apparent paradox by a further appeal to relational thought.

III The Structure of Subjectivity

Situses are limited collectivities differentiated from one another not by "horizontal" status demarcations within a hierarchy but by "vertical" divisions marking each Some as marginal to all others. The structure of freedom discloses the rationality of a society of situses by showing that each locus of freedom must itself be internally pluralized yet nonuniversal—neither One nor All. The pluralization of groups and histories therefore reflects reason's interpretive freedom, not reason's failure to realize some single ideal. The proliferation of human tribes and languages marks freedom's triumph over the uniformity of nature, not reason's fall from uniform grace.

The disclosure of the structure of freedom nevertheless raises another problem as it answers the question of the rationality of a pluralized society. How to do justice to intuitions claiming the freedom of the solitary individual? The argument of the last chapter would seem to have the counterintuitive result that since the Some is the locus of freedom, only groups qualify as subjects while individuals, as mere *parts* of these group subjects, cannot by themselves be free.

In keeping with a plank by plank testing of common sense there is something to be said for accepting this counterintuitive result as it stands . . . but not enough. In favor of accepting this counterintuitive implication as a surprising *discovery*, one might point to collectivist considerations suggesting the extent to which individual identity is the result of group identification. One is who he is by virtue of his relations: his associations, the values he internalizes from others, the traditions. Therefore the "free" decisions of the individual are arguably the decisions of a relevant collectivity merely manifested through the mouthpiece of the individual.

As arguable as the collectivist case may be, still it does not do justice to equally arguable existential-individualist considerations. Not often, but often enough there seem to be individuals for whom one is hard pressed to find a collectivity that would reinforce those revolutionary actions that nevertheless turn out to have been intelligible to the individual all along. Most of our manifestations of freedom take the form of breaks with one pattern of predictable behavior in favor of another pattern, the break itself being predictable according to neither pattern. Most of our breaks may be interpreted as border skirmishes among collectivities—say, parents and peers—between which we may be caught for brief moments of confusion before our anomalous behavior is rendered intelligible as action by the collectivity that eventually wins. But for some, for those who go into the desert alone either literally or figuratively, there seem to be breaks that are neither arbitrary nor accountable by reference to any known collectivity. How is this possible according to the disclosure of Some as the locus of freedom?

This chapter's answer appeals to the *structural* features of the last. The *structure* of freedom requires plurality, but the *terms* of that structure may be several: some persons, some parts of persons, some assemblages of persons. The *structure of subjectivity* compounds structures of freedom: a society is free when it mediates among some collectivities without allowing the totalitarian mastery by any one collectivity over others; a collectivity is free when it mediates among some persons without allowing the totalitarian mastery of any one person over others; a person is free when he mediates among some parts of himself without allowing the totalitarian mastery of any one part over others.

The structure of subjectivity compounds the structure of freedom but does it not tempt a regress toward parts of parts of parts that are progressively simpler, less compounded and therefore less capable of satisfying the pluralized structure of freedom? The structure of subjectivity avoids the regress toward progressively simpler and more deterministic homunculi within the self by once again resisting a misleading spatial metaphor: the language of *containment*. The parts of the self mediated by free persons are themselves the complex projections of free societies. Consequently societies are "in" selves as much as selves are "in" societies. The grammar of inclusion for the structure of subjectivity does not follow the logic of inclusion for Euclidean space where larger boxes will not fit in smaller boxes. The structure of subjectivity is not an architecture of boxes; rather it is an order of mediations, a "circular" order in the sense that the series of successive mediations bends back upon itself so that the "smallest" parts of the self mediate among the projections of the "largest" collectivities. How is this possible? What models do we have for such a curious structure? How does this abstract topology make sense of ordinary life?

This chapter begins to answer the above questions as they relate to three arcs in the circular structure of subjectivity: the personal, the intrapersonal, and the transpersonal. The three corresponding parts of the chapter have a double strategy: each tries to show why common sense now resists locating subjectivity elsewhere than in the individual, and second, how it makes sense nonetheless to see selves within selves within selves and so on throughout a circular structure of subjectivity.

We begin with the personal, move to the intrapersonal, and end with the transpersonal. Since most of us are quite ready to find subjectivity in persons alone, the first section will stress the reasons for prying the structure of subjectivity loose from individuals alone. Dionysus, god of fusion (One into All) and dismemberment (One into Some) will be our guide. A brief history of the rejection of Dionysus will record common sense's reasons for locating subjectivity only among individuals. Then a contemplation on the meaning of the return of Dionysus will prepare the way for the second section's anatomy of dismemberment and the third's account of fusion.

1. Dionysus and self-identity

"Who am I?" We pose the question as if in answer to the Delphic oracle's injunction, Know thyself. Socrates, proclaimed by that same Delphic oracle to be the wisest man in Athens, declared the unexamined life not worth living. But the oracle's injunction, like all oracular sayings, is less than perfectly clear. Were Socrates alive today would he declare the overexamined life not worth living? Our passion to plumb the depths of our private psyches and our rage to affix our personal identities run the risk of generating false identities in the process of asking and too eagerly answering the question, "Who am I?"

Could it be that we are not the autonomous individuals we take ourselves to be? Could it be that we are, in our dispersion into privatism, symptoms of a sickness in the history of man, victims of an illusion? Could our passion to find "personal identity" be like the paranoiac's need to identify "the enemy"? If so the question, "Who am I," can only deepen the sickness, at least until it leads to the further question, "Who are we?"

But then who, crudely speaking, are we to include among the group specified by 'we'? Before saying anything about this group, before defining its identity in terms of issues and problems, how to draw the lines defining the extension of the group we are talking about? Are *we* the philosophers? Are *we* the writer and readers of this document? Are *we* all Americans? Are *we* all humans? The answer to the question quite obviously depends on how the question is intended. The asking of the question will determine its answer.

Yet this circularity infects even the Socratic posing of the question, for he who for the first time takes seriously the issue of self-knowledge undergoes the change from a non-self-reflective being to a self-reflective being. The self to be known after the posing of the question is in an important way different from the self to be known before the posing of the question. It is as if the mere asking of the question allowed one to lift oneself by the philosophical bootstraps, even though one had only intended to strap one's boots to gain a firmer footing.

According to Nietzsche it was Socrates who, in an effort to gain a firmer footing, toppled man off his feet. Having turned man's gaze inward he changed man from a creature of immediacy to a mediated self-reflection. The ideal of Apollonian order replaced Dionysian ecstasy, only neither god could be well served without their fraternal union. For Nietzsche, the young student of philology, the birth of tragedy in Athens marked a brief union of Dionysus with Apollo, a moment in history when the Dionysian spirit of music could be held and savored without being destroyed, neither by itself in an orgy of dismemberment, nor by nurturing hands that held it and squeezed it too tightly like a child overcome with adoration for a young pet. The delicate balance between reason and passion, individuating order and fusion, lasted only briefly until Socrates and his favorite playwright, Euripides, tipped the scale ever so slightly toward Apollo the individuator. Ever since then, certainly until Nietzsche, we have suffered the disease of too much order in our politics and in ourselves.

Surely we have had too much disorder as well. Dionysus, once exiled from the city of wholeness, leaves that city behind him worse for his absence. He returns as an unknown warrior to destroy that city however he can. No easy task to make peace with Dionysus once he has been exiled . . . or repressed. There are certain dues to be paid, and not through a delicate process of negotiations at the gate.

Nietzsche lamented the exile of Dionysus and wished to welcome him back into the fold. If more had done so perhaps we shouldn't have had to pay with Auschwitz, but instead Nietzsche got blamed. The gatekeeper's son was whipped for the return of the prodigal son, who would have surely climbed the gate anyway if Nietzsche had not flung it wide.

During the 1960s we heard that Dionysus had returned and was alive and well in California. Certainly the signs were right—good vineyards (Dionysus might easily be confused with Bacchus, the God of wine and drunkenness . . . and mushrooms?), plenty of music, plenty of killings. And how would we welcome him? We held a festival at the gate, but now the Fillmore is past. Bill Graham was the gatekeeper and he got sick of it, Woodstock and all the mess. Is Bill Graham our reluctant Nietzsche? Or perhaps, less reluctantly, Alan Freed, who first coined the term 'Rock and Roll', who used to defend his music and his show in little sermons sandwiched between "Earth Angel" and Elvis Presley? Somehow there seems to have been a debasement represented in the comparison between Alan Freed and Friedrich Nietzsche, perhaps further dues for keeping Dionysus waiting yet longer at the gates of our culture.

Or have we domesticated Dionysus? Is the decline a result of our having achieved the greatest cooptation yet? Has Caliban been educated? Has the wild beast been tamed, dressed in coat and tie and put to work selling soap? The very idea is enough to elicit the demonic laughter, another trademark of the satyr Dionysus. And if laughter is the result, if that mix of pessimism and irrepressible joy is the result of the unlikely appearance of Dionysus in apron strings, can we be sure he has been entirely domesticated?

We who wish to know who we are and wish to find out by facing this question of the proper welcome for Dionysus, what do we feel about his return to the city? For he challenges our carefully cherished sense of individuation. Dionysus, who left our culture when Socrates

blinded him with the glare of Apollonian ordering insight, challenges
the sense of order that would let us bask in the comfort of a securely
fixed identity. Dionysus thrives on fusion and flux, in the destruction
of those neatly drawn boundaries erected in order to answer the question, Who am I? Dionysus represents a threat to the Apollonian cult of
self-identity. Therefore the prospect of his return into our culture demands a rethinking—and a refeeling—of our sense of selfhood; unless, that is, we wish to keep him waiting at the gates yet longer, letting the price we pay for his return rise still higher. But that would be
madness.

Yet madness is precisely what we must contemplate in entertaining the return of Dionysus. It is madness to reject him, yet to accept him is to accept madness. For Dionysus is the god of madness.
The exile of Dionysus and the rejection of madness as having a place
in human society are one and the same thing. The history of attitudes
toward madness is therefore a helpful guild for the cultural biography
of Dionysus. In developing the history of Dionysian satyrs we should
not be surprised to find stories that are less strange to our most
contemporary ears than they may have seemed to the historians
themselves.

Herodotus, one of the very first of the historians, recounts as
if from some cultural distance his knowledge of a Thracian cult. "The
Satrae, so far as our knowledge goes, have never yet been brought under any one, but continue to this day a free and unconquered people,
unlike the other Thracians. They dwell amid lofty mountains clothed
with forests of different trees and capped with snow, and are very val-
iant in fight. They are Thracians who have an oracle of Bacchus in
their country, which is situated upon their highest mountain-range.
The Bessi, a Satrian race, deliver the oracles; but the prophet, as at
Delphi, is a woman; and her answers are not harder to read."[1]

Are these people mere savages? Ten or twenty years ago we of
the provincial West might have been more inclined to think so; but
now, more familiar with Tibetan Buddhism, more drawn to the
heights of the mountains of New Mexico or Colorado or Big Sur, more

inclined to listen to the voices of our women, we wonder. Is it such a mystery that these worshippers of Bacchus-Dionysus were free people? Now that we are more familiar with the structuralism of Levi-Strauss, who has shown us that so-called "primitive" cultures are built on structures as complex and sophisticated as ours, we wonder whether their freedom is not the result of a cultivation of spiritual capacities that we have dismissed as signs of madness. With respect to madness our culture is more simple, more primitive, than theirs. Just as they knew nothing of the forces of electricity, so we know little of the forces of Dionysus. We prefer to order our lives in (at least temporarily) safer and more predictable ways. Science, as the sum total of laws of prediction, is a religion of the commonplace rather than a religion of the extraordinary, the ecstatic. The extraordinary is anathema to science. While playing a certain role in the pathway of discovery, counterexamples and exceptions are to be eliminated, just as madness is to be done away with, healed. (Apollo is also the god of healing.)

To the Greeks on the contrary, madness "comes not from mortal weakness or disease, but from a divine banishment of the commonplace."[2] Plato knew about *mania*. His description of the ascent out of the cave begins with a radical turn away from what is commonplace, the shadows on the wall. Given the technology at his disposal, his description of the usual run of men staring day after day at a play of images on the wall of the cave bears an uncanny resemblance to a description of contemporaries watching television. Merely turning away from the images is not enough, for one's vision will take time and exercise to get accustomed to a different set of objects and a brighter light. Moreover the ascent does not stop with real physical things that cast shadows. Nor does the ascent cease with science and mathematics.

The highest level of Platonic inquiry, dialectics, is symbolized by the sunlit world outside of the cave and by the sun itself, likened by Plato to the Idea of the Good. The symbol of the sun stands both for what is highest and for what is most dangerous: one must approach the Good, but with caution, for there is danger of blindness if one looks straight into the sun too quickly or for too long a time. Once one has finally become accustomed to its power he will not find it easy to return to the realm of shadows: "if he should be required to contend with these perpetual prisoners in 'evaluating' these shadows while his vision was still dim and before his eyes were accustomed to the dark—and this time required for habituation would not be very short—would he not provoke laughter, and would it not be said of him that he had returned from his journey aloft with his eyes ruined and that it was not worth while even to attempt the ascent? And if it were possible to lay hands on and to kill the man who tried to release them and lead them up, would they not kill him?"[3] Or at least have him committed to an asylum?

If we ever believed that the ascent out of the cave would take us up to the fundamental formulas of a unified field theory as the ultimate key to the universe, then Plato's description of the trials of descent seemed somewhat overdrawn. But if we are prepared to accept both the spiritual truth and social terror inspired by madness, more of us may be ready to read Plato's description of the ascent from the cave as something other than a purely intellectual odyssey.[4]

Through our own experiences and through cultural and intellectual developments of the sixties we are just beginning to be able to understand phenomena that were seemingly incomprehensible to scholars of earlier generations. Even Erwin Rohde, Nietzsche's close friend, now appears to have been unwilling to accept much of his findings regarding the cult of Dionysus in ancient Greece. He speaks with at least as much cultural distance from the phenomena he describes as that which separated Herodotus from the Satrae. "The awe-inspiring darkness of night, the music, especially that of the Phrygian flute, to which the Greeks attributed the power of making its hearers 'full of the god', the vertiginous whirl of the dance—all these may very well, in suitably disposed natures, have really led to a state of visionary exaltation in which the inspired person saw all external objects in accordance with his fancy and imagination. Intoxicating drinks, to which the Thracians were addicted, may have increased the excitement; perhaps they even used the fumes derived from certain seeds, with which the Scythians and Massagetai knew how to intoxicate themselves. We all know how even today in the East the smoke of hashish may make men visionaries and excite religious raptures in which the whole of nature is transformed for the enthralled dreamer."

Despite the scholarly accuracy of descriptions that extend for pages of text and footnotes, Rohde must ask the question that will elicit a smile from every refugee of a stoned evening at the Filmore: "But, we must ask, what was the *meaning* of it all?" And given his Christianized, bowdlerized cultural background, can we blame him for answering, "The violently induced exaltation of the senses had a religious purpose, in that such enlargement and extension of his being was man's only way, as it seemed, of entering into union and relationship with the god and his spiritual attendants"?[5]

In his preface Rohde writes, "The author of the present work has renounced all attempts to cast a fitful and ambiguous light upon the venerable gloom of the subject by the help of the farthing dip of his own private imaginings."[6] Rohde's valuable work is a most excellent example of the distortions inevitably induced when the interpreter of historically distant phenomena forswears all reliance on personal experience in an effort to render the most "objective" account.

Rohde has not rendered an objective account. On the contrary he reads the structure of his own experience into the experience of the revelers. His wish to know the *meaning* of it all, to plumb the *purpose* that *must* have informed their actions, is itself a reflection of the reflective distance that characterizes his own European experience. The problem is not simply that Rohde's description is tainted with a farthing dip into his experience of European culture; the problem is further compounded by the fact that the experience whose taint is so clearly recognizable is an experience so vastly different from the Dionysian experience to be described. To put the point in its most ironic form: the very distance that Rohde assumes in order to render his account objective is a distance that renders him unable to understand the Dionysian.

Rohde exemplifies Apollonian distance, the denial of Dionysian involvement. To the Apollonian mind there must be a purpose, a meaning, for every action. But to the Dionysian spirit experience itself is self-validating apart from external ends or goals. Frenzy is its own reward. One cannot understand the cult of immediacy by regarding its rituals as mediations *toward* that which is not immediate. The cult of immediacy can be understood—if that is the right word—only experientially. But of course this experiential understanding will demand more than a "farthing dip" into Apollonian experience. Only a pound scoop into the Dionysian experiences of the 1960's allows us some understanding of the appearance of Dionysus.

From Herodotus to Rohde and beyond, interpreters of the Dionysian satyrs have been caught in a so-called "hermeneutic circle" of experiences and their interpretations. That is, the predisposition toward a particular interpretation of experience leads to interpretations that reinforce the predisposition. The circularity is salient in the question of self-identity because the asking of the question already characterizes the nature of the asked, which nature is supposedly the answer to the question. If a thorough and careful intellect like Rohde could be systematically misled in his appreciation of Dionysus, then how likely that we too will be misled? The *object* of study—the Dionysian cult—will be misinterpreted if the *subject* doing the studying is predisposed toward Apollonian assumptions of sharply individuating ego-boundaries. Yet the purpose of studying the cult of Dionysus was to examine the significance of the Exile of Dionysus and its import for overindividuated images of selfhood held by current common sense.

The hermeneutic circle involved in the Apollonian interpretation of Dionysus has the effect of rendering the non-Dionysian intellect very nearly incapable of seeing what it has lost in its effort to find it again. The exile of Dionysus is like and unlike losing one's glasses:

without glasses one's vision is blurred to the point that the sharp out-lines of one's mislaid glasses are invisible; without Dionysus one's vi-sion is sharpened to the point that blurred ego-boundaries are incon-ceivable. In either case one finds it difficult to find what one has lost because one lost the very capacity for finding what one lost. In losing Dionysus the difficulty is compounded by the fact that the clarity of Apollonian vision is likely to hide not only Dionysus but also the very fact of his loss—like a mode of "vision" whose loss induces a lapse of memory that one needed that mode in the first place.

With the aid of Nietzsche's lament for the loss of Dionysus, and second, with the example of his friend Rohde's incapacity to *see* the loss despite his looking, we should be in a position to appreciate the hermeneutic circle involved in the Apollonian-Socratic quest for self-identity. Further, to see the circle is to gain the capacity to step outside it. The next two sections step outside the circle by examining first the plausibility of individuating selves within the individual per-son—an intrapersonal dismemberment—and second, the necessity for locating freedom, agency and subjectivity in groups—transper-sonal fusion.

2. Individuating intrapersonal selves

Who are the intrapersonal selves? How do they achieve self-hood? How is it that intrapersonal selves are not just aspects or sides of a personal self? The problem as thus posed is the problem of in-dividuation: what is the principle of individuation for intrapersonal selves?

To say that a plurality of selves are intrapersonal is to say that they exist together in one body or one personal life. The body is a principle of individuation for personal selves. But in discussing intrapersonal selves we begin with the body as what these intrapersonal selves hold *in common.* The body (or the personal life) is in this context a unifying principle rather than a principle of individuation. It tells us how the several selves are the same, not how they are different. How then are the intrapersonal selves different in such a way that they deserve to be called separate selves?

The answer, quite simply: different intrapersonal selves have different *personalities. Personality* is the principle of individuation in the intrapersonal dimension; *Body,* physicality, the principle of individuation in the personal dimension. A transpersonal collectivity may individuate itself from others either physically, as by boundaries defining the *place* of a community, or by something closer to personality, e.g., a set of common interests or associations that define a geographically distributed network as a situs.

Of course it will be claimed that each person has only one personality since each person is one person. The claim is a result of the historical fact that we have taken unity as a value in our reflections about selfhood. Freudian psychology is ego psychology. Freudian psychology reflects an Enlightenment consciousness that places value in clear, unambiguous identity. It is no accident that Erikson's emphasis on identity should emerge as one of the most influential branches of neo-Freudian psychology. The value placed on unity and identity generates a suspicion of intrapersonal division: to be is to be an individual, and to be an individual is to have one personality, not several. Intrapersonal diffusion will be condemned as a sign of sickness. As long as unity and identity reign supreme there will be an effort to reject the notion that a personal self could be a mediation among a collection of individuated, relatively autonomous intrapersonal selves.

The will to unified identity is evident even among those who appreciate the sense in which a person is many selves. Using computers as a model, John Lilly sees the human project as metaprogramming the many subprograms (selves) in the direction of higher unity: "In a well-organized biocomputer, there is at least one such critical control metaprogram labeled *I* for acting on other metaprograms and labeled *me* when acted upon by other metaprograms. I say *at least one* advisedly. Most of us have several controllers, selves, self-metaprograms which divide control among them, either in time parallel or in time series in sequences of control. As I will give in detail later, one path for *self-development* is to centralize control of one's biocomputer in one self-metaprogrammer, making the others into conscious executives subordinate to the single administrator, the single superconscient self-metaprogrammer."[7]

To the parlous state of a multiplicity of small *I*s we are likely to respond: "Get it together, communicate, form a community that will not allow one *I* to haphazardly represent the whole." We call for a unifying of the several *I*s, but the form of unity we generally adopt is a monarchy of the ego. The monarch, the "single administrator," may be a tyrant or a benevolent dictator, at the very least a strong internal president. But like the external presidency, so too the internal presidency is mortal. Both are sustained by a circle of beliefs supporting unified autonomy even unto the arbitrary exercise of power in the name of "freedom." Chapter I showed how that circle of beliefs is no longer appropriate to political realities. Chapter II showed how freedom might be exercised by pluralized collectivities. Now the task is to break out of that same hermeneutic circle of syntax and belief by seeing how the phenomena of selfhood are as ready for reinterpretation in terms of a pluralized structure of freedom as are the phenomena of third watershed social structure.

Both the ascent of the imperial presidency and the emphasis on unified identity reflect the same circle of experience and belief. To grasp both the return of Dionysus and the death of the presidency is to depart from that circle of mutually reinforcing interpretations and to enter another circle whose several arcs include relational thought, parapolitics and the polytheistic psychology of many dimensional man. The immediate point of entry for this section is the intrapersonal self.

The principle of individuation for these internal personalities must be *other than* either purely physical or purely structural because, first, the physical body is the principle of individuation for persons and consequently a shared universal for the plurality of intrapersonal selves. Second, a mechanical metaprogram leads straight back into the tyranny of unity at the cost of freedom. The clear, predictable program molds an utterly predictable self, a self devoid of freedom, a self that is not mediating among a complex range of possible interpretations but *simply* determined by but *one* "interpretation."

Quotation marks are called for around 'interpretation' in this context because if the program is the only possible interpretation for behavior to follow, then strictly speaking it ceases to be an *interpretation* since the possibility implicit in what is interpret*able* in several ways retreats before the singleness of necessity. 'Only possibility' is a contradiction in terms. If a pattern of behavior is the *only* pattern possible then it is necessary, not just possible. What must be one way cannot be others.

Perpetual interpretability rests on a plurality of possibilities of interpretation. If that plurality is reduced to single necessity by modeling the intrapersonal self on a computer program, then the person will not have a plurality of *possible* selves to choose from in the self-interpretation characteristic of free action. Instead the person, in its plight of mediating among multiple programs rather than multiple selves, becomes a microcosm of a community irretrievably at odds with itself. Programs exhibiting the rigid singleness of necessity will not submit to persuasion. If programs are at odds they demand annihilation of the other, not a peaceful resolution of conflict. If the unity that individuates intrapersonal selves is the unity of a program for necessity then the person becomes a battleground in a lose-lose conflict. War is the only way out when adversaries exhibit the unthinking compulsiveness of a program. Madness is the name of intrapersonal war and winners are as rare in modern madness as in modern war. True peace—not the deathly calm following destruction but the tenuous, unstable and ever renegotiated peace of subjective mediation—grows only from the mixture of a multiplicity of noncompulsive, nonprogrammatic subjects: intrapersonal *selves* rather than programs.

At this point the argument for a plurality of intrapersonal selves recalls the argument for the pluralized structure of noncompulsive care by synthesizing the libertarian resistance of individualism with the support derivable from collectivities. Where the last chapter found too fixed a determinism in the rules of a universal homogeneous collectivity, this chapter finds a similar lack of human freedom in computer programs as models for intrapersonal selves. Nor will the addition of Turing machines (electronic random signal generators) satisfy the demand for a freedom that is nonarbitrary. Instead the freedom of the intrapersonal self must satisfy the structure of freedom found in society. The structure of freedom in the self is a transform of the structure of freedom in society. Just as a free society requires a plurality of Somes, themselves each containing enough persons to support each individual in his resistance against the socializing Other, so each individual contains a plurality of selves who must in turn manifest yet another dimension of pluralization. Just as each statussphere is a Some in a social context, so each intrapersonal self must be a Some in the personal context.

The argument appears to court an infinite regress: if each person has many selves, must each self contain still further selves, and so on *ad infinitum*? Second realm rationality would call a halt to the regress by reifying some level as *fundamental* subjectivity. Appearances of freedom or subjectivity of agency on other levels would then be *reduced* to manifestations or shadows of the one *basic* level, whether the basic level be taken as intrapersonal instincts, transpersonal economic structures or personal autonomy. Third realm rationality eschews the search for some basic level to which others may be reduced. Relieved of the quest for a lowest or highest level, relational thought can pursue the sense in which each dimension can alternate with other dimensions in playing the role of pluralized content or determining context.

The regress toward ever more internally pluralized selves leads neither toward some basic level nor toward unknowably minute selves. Instead the intrapersonal selves are best understood as different gods; that is, as different projections of different cults—Somes.

We each have our Dionysus, our Apollo, our Zeus and so on. We each possess a pantheon that is our introjected inheritance from past projections, past articulations of some groups' efforts at defining their highest values against the socializing Other. Society contains Somes; Somes consist of persons; persons contain selves; selves are constituted by the projections of social Somes. The circle of introjection and projection is infinite but not vicious, for each arc of the circular structure of subjectivity manifests readable signs that allow interpretations of other arcs as transforms. Religions are translations of the language of the soul just as psychology is a translation of the language of gods. Neither is fundamental. Both are transforms of structures of *differance* experienced in everyday life.

To demonstrate the sense in which different dimensions contain transforms of the same structures of *differance*, this section on intrapersonal selves is divided into subsections exploring widely separated fields of research: first James Hillman's development of polytheistic psychology, then a series of studies of the body as a model for unity or pluralty. The second subsection on the body is further divided into parts reviewing the Homeric body image; second, a review of recent research on the workings of the brain; third, a comparison between a model of information processing in neuro-physiology and a nearly identical model developed in political theory. The point of making these leaps from psychology to philology to neuro-physiology to political theory is precisely to show that the leaps are not that long. Instead the close juxtaposition of researches from different disciplines will add specific support to the general claim that *how* we look at a problem influences *what* we see. More specifically, what second realm rationality "sees" may not serve as evidence against relational thought once third realm rationality has had its say.

POLYTHEISTIC PSYCHOLOGY.

A theory of intrapersonal selfhood has been brilliantly expounded by a psychologist who understands the dangers of the concept of unity as well as the hold it has on our Platonic-Christian consciousness. James Hillman, a Jungian who criticizes even Jung for overemphasizing personal individuation at the expense of intrapersonal individuation, nevertheless draws on Jung for his formulation of a "polytheistic psychology" that challenges the monotheistic, monarchical conception of the personal self while at the same time allowing a characteristically human ambiguity to the personalities of minimally unified intrapersonal selves. "Jung used a polycentric description for the objective psyche. He envisioned it as a multiplicity of partial consciousnesses, like stars or sparks or luminous fishes' eyes. Psychological polytheism corresponds with this description and provides its conceptual formulation in the traditional language of our civilization, i.e. classical mythology. By providing a divine background of personages and powers for each complex, it would find place for each spark. It would aim less at gathering them into a unity and more at integrating each fragment according to its own principle, giving each God its due over that portion of consciousness, that symptom, complex, fantasy which calls for an archetypal background. It would accept the multiplicity of voices, the Babel of the anima and animus, without insisting upon unifying them into one figure, and accept too the dissolution process into diversity as equal in value to the coagulation process into unity. The pagan Gods and Goddesses would be restored to their psychological domain."[8]

Archetypes are fundamentally different from Lilly's computer programs. The Greek gods and goddesses are unpredictable. Surely they exhibit personalities. One can recognize the work of Apollo as different from the work of Dionysus. But each exhibits a full range of idiosyncrasies. The attempt to systematize their relationships in terms of a hierarchy of explanatory principles is vain. The table of elements in modern chemistry is a poor model for a pantheon of gods and goddesses whose "properties" are better portrayed by an endless and often conflicting series of *stories* ever subject to interpretation.[9]

Here of course the Apollonian consciousness of Western scientific intellect will interject: "What good is a set of explanatory principles whose vagueness precludes prediction? Even in the case of retrospective explanation one adds nothing to understanding if, when I act in a Dionysian manner, I 'explain' my actions by simply repeating—it was the Dionysus in me. We laugh at the person who excuses himself by saying, 'It was the Devil made me do it.' If an explanation is to tell us anything we don't already know, the explanans must be somehow different from the explanandum." So speaks the voice of Enlightenment and it is in many ways an impressive speech that is here adumbrated in a few short lines. It is a speech that has given us modern science. It is a speech with which man has *almost* mastered his environment, whose forces we learned to control only when we ceased interpreting them in anthropomorphic ways. But what of man? *Anthropos*? Might it not be that his form (*morphe*) *is* anthropomorphic? If it is a mistake to view the inorganic physical order in human terms, is it not equally a mistake to view man as so much matter?

The preceding questions are not entirely rhetorical. The point is not simply that science is bad and mythological interpretation good. We do not want to trade Apollo for Dionysus, Athene for Aphrodite. Only the Apollonian individuating consciousness needs to insist on this *or* that but not both. The restoration of the pagan gods and goddesses to their psychological domain requires the return of Dionysus, but only if all of the other gods and goddesses can retain their places—including Apollo, the god of unity, order and lucent reason. Do we neutralize Dionysus by "putting him in his place" in Apollonian fashion? No, because we know perfectly well when we let him in the door that he is not going to stay "in his place." We must know this, otherwise we will try to throw him out again the first time he acts up. We must know that as soon as we admit Dionysus into our pantheon of intrapersonal selves we have modified the Apollonian saying, "All things in moderation," to the self-referentially more consistent saying, "All things in moderation—including moderation." Even Apollo is truer to himself when struggling in fraternal union with Dionysus.

The fraternal union between Dionysus and Apollo will follow, as fraternal unions must, from mutual understanding of each by the other. Differences need not disappear in agreement, but an appreciation of differences derived from intimacy may allow greater mutual trust than a fear of differences based on inaccurate fantasy. In short, each must come to *know* the other. Yet this knowledge seems well nigh impossible if each remains trapped within the circle of its own beliefs. To gain an appreciation of differences accurate enough to allow trust rather than fear, *both* the Apollonian and Dionysian consciousnesses must become aware of the hermeneutic task. Otherwise each will continue to misinterpret the other as an enemy to be overcome rather than as an equal other.

The task is not impossible once its difficulties have been appreciated. The irony of the hermeneutic task lies in the fact that its failure is assured when we think it is easiest: when we are sure we see the "facts," then we are least aware of our predispositions. Therefore the strategy of showing the distortions of Dionysus by Apollonian consciousness is not designed to demonstrate the *impossibility* of knowing Dionysus. Rather the point is to appreciate the difficulties so that success will be more likely.

The remainder of this section continues that strategy through three studies of the body: first a few notes on the variability of the body-image as seen from different cultural perspectives; second, a review of the findings of some recent research into the workings of our so-called "central nervous system"; third, some speculations on the kind of rationality appropriate to what we now know about the mapping of even relatively small assemblages of neurons. The ordering of these studies of the body shows that an Apollonian appreciation of Dionysus is *possible* but *unlikely* without an appreciation for the hermeneutic task of disclosing predispositions. The several chapters of Part Two will reverse the procedure: there the philosopher of Dionysus—Nietzsche—will serve as guide for an interpretation of the articulations of selfhood. Just as the current task requires a sensitivity to Apollonian distortions of Dionysian phenomena, so there the task will require a sensitivity to Dionysian distortions of Apollonian phenomena. Just as the current strategy calls for the introduction of Dionysus into the laboratory to assure science's *explanatory* contribution to the understanding of selfhood, so there an Apollonian analysis of Nietzsche's *story* of Zarathustra will guard against misinterpretations.

THE LESSONS OF THE BODY

(1)   To proponents of singular self-identity nothing would seem simpler than the human body as clear and irrefutable evidence for locating the structure of subjectivity in persons alone: one self per body. Yet appearances can be deceiving even if, like the peels of an onion, appearances constitute the whole of so-called reality. The body is both complex and ambiguous. Even its apparently obvious unity was less than obvious to the early Greeks. Bruno Snell notes, "the early Greeks did not, either in their language or in the visual arts, grasp the body as a unit."[10] Both the use of plurals to refer to the physical nature of the body as well as the crimped joints in the early vase paintings suggest that for the early Greeks, "the physical body of man was comprehended, not as a unit but as an aggregate."[11]

Simple seeing can be deceiving, at least so it seems when others see otherwise. Our perceptions of the body as a unit are as much subject to our sense of the way we sense it *ought* to be as was the sight of homunculi subject to the sexism of those seventeenth- and eighteenth-century scientific empiricists who "asserted that they had seen exceedingly minute forms of men, with arms, heads, and legs complete, inside the spermatazoa under the microscope."[12] Their certainty in seeing men and not women was a function of their fantasy that male necessarily preceded female. Similarly our modern certainty that the body is a unity is a function of our fantasy that unity precedes plurality. Nor are these two fantasies unrelated. The Apollonian fantasy of clearly defined unity in selfhood is sustained only at the cost of a suppression of the Dionysian fantasy of dismemberment. And recall: Dionysus is a god whose original followers were women—the "raving maenads."

In his study "On Psychological Femininity," Hillman has established beyond any doubt the connection between Dionysian consciousness and hysteria, that peculiarly feminine form of madness. Instead of condemning the maenads as 'hysterics', however, he notes how the fantasy of male dominance occludes our view of Dionysus, his votaries and their rituals: "We no longer have the right maenadism, the right telestic or ritual madness, because we do not have the God. Our misogynist and Apollonic consciousness has exchanged him for a diagnosis,"[13] a verbal tool to be manipulated in the imposition of a "cure."

Hillman's scholarship, to say nothing of his sensitivity to symbols, establishes not only the invisibility of the Dionysian experience to Apollonian consciousness. Further, he shows how the fantasy of feminine mystery and darkness has colored the supposedly value-free inquiry into the "observables" of embryology and female anatomy. After recounting in carefully researched detail five separate instances from the history of embryology, he comments: "The point of these tales may be taken from Paracelsus, who said that imagination fertilizes the embryo; but imagination fertilizes also the theories of the embryo. It is important to realize how very late in history our scientific understanding of female functioning is. Not until 1827 was the human egg discovered, and not until the turn of the present century was the cyclical relation between menstruation and ovulation clearly established. . . . Feminine darkness encourages fantasy."[14]

Rather than repeat Hillman's historical research, some of which renders the above comments on Herodotus and Rohde redundant, let us examine some more contemporary studies of physiology, studies that show the obverse of the case presented so far; rather than review how the Apollonian mind obscures Dionysian data let us turn to the work of Dionysian minds at play in the Apollonian laboratory. The point of these more recent tales will be to show how the myth of unity is not so easily sustained when the body is investigated by minds that combine Apollonian precision with a Dionysian penchant for breaking boundaries.

(2)   Robert Ornstein is a research scientist at the Langley Porter

Neuropsychiatric Institute in San Francisco and a child of the Bay Area Culture of the late sixties. He received his Ph.D. at Stanford in 1968. Of course it is possible that a bright young scientist could have survived the sixties around San Francisco without ever being truly touched by the cultural upheaval going on around him. After noting that Dionysiac stirrings sometimes arise "through the influence of those narcotic potions of which all primitive races speak in their hymns," Nietzsche adds, "There are people who, either from lack of experience or out of sheer stupidity, turn away from such phenomena, and, strong in the sense of their own sanity, label them either mockingly or pityingly 'endemic diseases.' "[15]

Ornstein is not stupid, nor one would guess is he unexperienced. It is safe to say that the direction of his research is at least partially motivated by a will to understand in Apollonian fashion the Dionysian stirrings he has experienced. What have he and others working with him found?

Their research lays to rest the myth of a single mind whose functioning at its best is purely "rational" as this term comes down to us from eighteenth-century Rationalism. By a series of experiments, some involving subjects with no brain damage, others involving subjects with damage to either the right or left hemispheres of the brain and some of the most interesting involving subjects in whom the corpus callosum connecting the two halves of the brain has been severed, scientists have now shown something close to what Nietzsche suggested some years ago, namely that the Socratic-Platonic tradition's emphasis on linear deductive rationality represents a one-sided specialization of human consciousness. The other side—the "darker," more "feminine," more "intuitive" side—is not the manifestation of the whole of consciousness running somehow short of its highest potential. Instead those nonlinear holistic functions of intellect are the workings of one half of the brain whose mode of making connections is *different from* and not necessarily *less adequate* or more stupid than the linear mode that Enlightenment rationality prizes in the scientific age.

Ornstein summarizes what he regards as the significance of the split-brain research in a table that correlates its findings with differentiations in modes of consciousness explored by many others. While this neat division into two parallel columns appears to cut with a cleaver a consciousness whose specializations might be multipolar rather than simply bipolar, this first step in breaking down the myth of unity of consciousness is worth displaying in all its tentative richness.

The Two Modes of Consciousness: A Tentative Dichotomy

Who Proposed It?

Many sources	Day	Night
Blackburn	Intellect	Sensuous
Oppenheimer	Time, History	Eternity, Timelessness
Deikman	Active	Receptive
Polanyi	Explicit	Tacit
Levy, Sperry	Analytic	Gestalt
Domhoff	Right (side of body)	Left (side of body)
Many sources	Left hemisphere	Right hemisphere
Bogen	Propositional	Appositional
Lee	Lineal	Nonlineal
Luria	Sequential	Simultaneous
Semmes	Focal	Diffuse
I Ching	The Creative: heaven, masculine Yang	The Receptive: earth, feminine Yin
I Ching	Light	Dark
I Ching	Time	Space
Many sources	Verbal	Spatial
Many sources	Intellectual	Intuitive
Vedanta	Buddhi	Manas
Jung	Causal	Acausal
Bacon	Argument	Experience

From
Robert Ornstein, *The Psychology of Consciousness* (San Francisco, 1972), p. 67.

What are we to make of this highly suggestive display? Surely academia is wedded to the left-hand column under "Day." Does that mean that balance can be restored by an equally one-sided plunge into darkness? Or might the capacity for simultaneity and diffusion in left-handed right-hemisphered consciousness be precisely the necessary antidote against another one-sided specialization? Ornstein unequivocally and repeatedly affirms: "A complete human consciousness involves the polarity and integration of the two modes."[16] Appropriately, his book draws heavily on the intuitive richness of storytelling. Each chapter begins with a tale from the exploits of the wise and impish Mulla Nasrudin. To some these tales might seem to be so many distractions, so many introductory pleasantries to be endured before getting down to work. Some among the academically trained might say that Ornstein's work suffers from a "lack of focus." It would seem rather, to use the language of the academic critics, that their own criticism *begs the question.* Capacity to deal with only what has been narrowly focused is one manifestation of precisely the question at issue: whether the focused rationality of the left hemisphere is sufficient for a fully human consciousness.

(3)   The late and brilliant eclectic Warren McCulloch's contributions run from cybernetics and physiology to philosophy and poetry without pausing to balk at the usual boundaries erected in the academic curriculum. One of his earliest studies covers but five pages in the *Bulletin of Mathematical Biophysics* for 1945. It is entitled, "A Heterarchy of Values Determined by the Topology of Nervous Nets." In this brief paper McCulloch makes a leap whose arc is worth examining not so much for what is "proven" as for purposes of comparison with the arc of another leap made in the political context from logically identical premises to a dramatically different conclusion.

McCulloch shows that nets of neurons are so constituted that the "choices" achieved by patterns of stimulation and inhibition of other neurons may generate either a hierarchy of valuation or what he calls a heterarchy. For a hierarchy all that is needed is a relatively simple pattern of excitation and inhibition such that given any pattern of stimuli, "some end is preferred to all others, and another such that all are preferred to it, and that of any three if a first is preferred to a second and a second to a third, then the first is preferred to the third."[17] In short, a hierarchy is like an unambiguous pecking order. A heterarchy on the other hand has a structure like the game of paper, rock and scissors: paper covers rock, rock crushes scissors, but scissors cut paper. Scissors do not always lose. Instead they play a role analogous to what McCulloch calls a "diallel"; that is, a synaptic link that cuts across a hierarchical neural net (or "drome") to produce a heterarchical pattern of preference.

Our patterns of preference do not take the form of values arranged in a clear hierarchy. McCulloch likens hierarchical values to "magnitudes of some one kind" for which one value is clearly greater or smaller, higher or lower than another in a single dimension. "Summarily, if values were magnitudes of any one kind, the irreducible nervous net would map (without diallels) on a plane."[18] But McCulloch's research shows that there are diallels, that is, synaptic links for which it is necessary to symbolize a leap out of the simple plane in order to map the neuronal structures that account for nonhierarchical patterns of preference. E.g., "Consider the case of three choices, A or B, B or C, and A or C in which A is preferred to B, B to C, and C to A."

Oddly enough McCulloch's "drome with a diallel" turns out to be logically similar to the Voter's Paradox in political theory. A version of the Voter's Paradox was explored by Lewis Carroll, later explicated by Kenneth Arrow in a work entitled *Social Choice and Individual Values*, and most recently exploited by Robert Paul Wolff in his effort to defend anarchy. Wolff asks us to consider the ineptitude of majority rule when the preference patterns in society are like those which, for simplicity's sake, we imagine to characterize three individuals, the first of whom prefers A over B and B over C; the second, B over C and C over A; the third, C over A and A over B. "When we pair the alternatives and count the votes, we discover that there is a majority of A over B (Individuals I and III) and a majority for B over

C (Individuals I and II), but *not* therefore a majority for A over C. Quite to the contrary, Individuals II and III prefer C to A, and therefore so does the society."[19] The Voter's Paradox derives from a pattern of preference that processes information in the same way as does the drome with a diallel mapped by McCulloch.

Yet the two theoreticians, Wolff and McCulloch, do not process the information *about* those preference patterns the same way. Wolff concludes, "The result is that the group as a whole, starting from perfectly consistent individual preferences, has arrived by majority rule at an absurdly inconsistent group preference." After several refinements of the model fail, Wolff uses the Voter's Paradox as a significant link in a chain of arguments defending anarchy. McCulloch on the other hand concludes: "Circularities in preference instead of indicating inconsistencies, actually demonstrate consistency of a higher order than had been dreamed of in our philosophy. An organism possessed of this nervous system—six neurons—is sufficiently endowed to be unpredictable from any theory founded on a scale of values. It has a heterarchy of values, and is thus internectively too rich to submit to a *summum bonum.*"

Wolff is a disappointed rationalist.[20] If rationality is not perfectly hierarchical in form then utter irrationality is the only alternative: anarchy not heterarchy, no rules not different rules. The difference between Wolff and McCulloch recalls the difference between theorists of the second realm and theorists of the third. Those in the second seek *single causes* to account for manifestations of clearly locatable power, which causes once located will serve to supply unambiguous predictions. Theorists of the third realm seek *multiple restraints* whose accurate appraisal justifies certain calculations of probability, e.g., given three equal-sized branches of a delta, will a raft floating from upstream follow A or B or C?

If the probabilities are equal for each alternative, that fact provides a great deal of information about the system, information that would warrant very different behavior than if we know that the probability of one "choice" is greater than the probability of another.

Yet this information about equal probabilities in a heterarchy is ignored by disappointed theoreticians of the second realm who, if they cannot have hierarchical rationality, would prefer to throw up their hands and say the system is not a viably rational process.

There is nothing irrational about a drome with a diallel save that the second realm fantasy of rationality make it so. There is nothing irrational about the lovely flow of water save that fantasies of predictability make it so. There is nothing irrational about a system of mutual constraints in equilibrium (call them checks and balances if you like) save that a desperate need for order or control or power make it so.

The body is both a model and a concrete manifestation of third realm rationality. Because the body is both a formal model as well as part of the content it will pay to look carefully at some of its most obvious features as well as its subtle neurophysiology.

Note the plurality of so-called central systems: not only the central nervous system whose central node, the brain, turns out to be at least bipolar, but also the circulatory system and the lymphatic system. Further, the "bones," "fascia," "tendons" and other connective tissues all form a system which, when closely observed, shows no demarcations or gaps in continuity as great as is suggested by the use of different names. The anatomist will see subtle marginal differences along the continuous spectrum of that also "central" system, not sharp demarcations where "bone" becomes "tendon."

Like the heterarchical logic of nervous nets, similarly the plurality of so-called central systems demonstrates the possibility of several systems of ordering as an alternative to either one system or chaos. Granted the limitations of biological metaphors—physiological patterns neither prove nor cause similar patterns in history—still the body provides living proof that pluralized, multicentered systems of order *can* function. And once the Apollonian predisposition toward the need for singular authority suffers exposure in studies of the body, then perhaps the revelation of heterarchical ordering in that intrapersonal arc of the circle of subjectivity will suggest at least the *possibil-*

ity or viability of heterarchical ordering in the transpersonal arc of the circle of subjectivity.

Parapolitics is not the total lack of central systems desired by anarchists or the radical right. Nor is it the practice of a theory demanding a hierarchical ordering of principles descending from a single autonomous power. Parapolitics does not deny the need for economic centralization of some industries. Economics is as central as the circulatory system but no more so. Man does not live by blood alone. Nor does parapolitics deny a partial role to the old politics; the body needs a "central" nervous system (perhaps even one that is bipolar), a system of relays, information-gathering services, decision-making mechanisms, networks of communication. But again, the so-called central nervous system is not the only central system. Further, there is reason to believe that in the case of man for whom *natural history* gives way to *human history,* even the body is subject to change in a direction that renders the central nervous system even less central than its bipolarity or juxtaposition with other central systems would suggest.

If modern society is a territory that can in some senses by modeled or mapped by the body, then as the territory comes to include a technology that vastly extends the scope of the body's several central systems, so the map changes along with its territory. If the body be conceived as one's physical bounds of efficacy—and recall from Snell's observations on the Greeks that the commonsensical body image is subject to radical revision—then this bag of skin and bones need not mark the borders of the "body" any more than the range of one's literal vision limits the contents of one's mind. But as the borders of the body extend outward through the tools of technology and politics, and as those tools themselves gain a complexity such that *they* no longer exhibit the structure of a simple centralized body image, then the body (whose extensions they are) repeats in another dimension the complexification of its own structure. As territory becomes map and map becomes territory, as both come to exhibit an increasingly complex heterarchy easily confused with anarchy, then the extended though still body-bound person will experience its own organization differently . . . or become extinct through maladaptation not just of itself to its new environment but of its immediate environment to its new self.

The new self is heterarchical, many dimensional. Where the self of the first realm trusted the gods or Nature to give it its own nature, whether multiple or single, the self of the second realm took control and centralized power and authority in its Apollonian mind just as it centralized power and control in its political systems. The centralized self was appropriate to that stage of human history in which man gained a limited mastery over the nature to which he submitted in the first stage. But as that mastery pushes us into a world whose territory both extends but no longer conforms to the bodily map that was the self-image of second realm rationality, we find ourselves with the choice of holding on to that second realm image and suffering the confusions it creates with its obsolete rationality; or we can go forward. We can get in touch with our several selves and the rationality of heterarchy. And here the body, even viewed as a bag of skin and bones, still has lessons to teach.

The body is a model for the balance or harmony of many selves within the personal self—and not just a metaphor but a living, real, concrete part of the territory where one can read a heterarchical order in its physical manifestation. The body is not a straight cylinder devoid of differentiation, not a "perfect answer" to the question of balance, but a complex juxtaposition of oddly shaped, ever different yet obviously symmetrical parts that have to solve among themselves some amazing problems of physics in order to keep from falling flat on that part known as the face. Precisely *how* the body solves such problems is interestingly enough still a mystery to the science of neurophysiology.[21]* *That* the body solves them is reconfirmed every time an infant learns to walk. This humble lesson of the body should be sufficient to show second realm theoreticians that the lack of a clearly specifiable hierarchy is not equivalent to chaos; heterarchy is not equivalent to anarchy. The lack of a single and universal hierarchy of values does not entail our taking to the streets with bludgeons.

Of course there will be some who, so impressed with a projected sense of unity now introjected back into their own experience, refuse to acknowledge a heterarchy of interests in their own bodies. Believing that each of us *ought* to have a single purpose in life they would try to ignore conflicts between desire and fatigue, between hunger and revulsion at the available fare. Or to give an even simpler more patently physical example, they would ignore the competition for blood among parts of the body which can result in muscle cramps or slowness of mind after overeating. These and so many other conflicts get "balanced" by the body, usually without a cramp or a fall. Yet those who are so impressed with the second realm rationality's hope for a contradiction-free perpetual peace will not acknowledge the perpetual skirmishes going on inside them. Instead they seek a single goal toward which all can be directed, and usually end up suffering the physical symptoms of depression for their one-sidedness. Nor will it help to hear those physical symptoms described as a psychological *identity* crisis for that only exacerbates the quest for a single identity that was the problem in the first place.

The body is not just a model, not simply a good simile for the self. It *is* in one sense *one* of the selves—as in such well-known conflicts of interest as "The spirit is willing but the flesh is weak." In another sense it contains all the selves within it and serves as a mirror testifying to whether conflicts among those other selves are being dealt with or denied. In this second sense the body serves also as a model for all the other selves which also, like Anaxagorean spermata or Leibnizian monads or Jungian archetypes, contain all other selves within themselves as seen from a slightly different perspective. But here the lessons of the body anticipate later chapters where the stories of several selves will be told and Nietzsche's perspectivism rescued from its resemblance with subjective relativism.

Before leaving the structural analytic of Part One for the narrative synthesis of Part Two, the third division of this chapter remains. We have yet to see how the structure of subjectivity might manifest itself in its transpersonal arc. Once again a double strategy guides the exposition. Its first section traces some of the reasons for our reluctance to locate subjectivity in transpersonal collectivities. The second section pursues the more positive strategy of showing the plausibility of considering subjective experience whose locus is transpersonal. Where the first section traces a brief history of privatization as it has been progressively codified by a tradition of thought from Descartes to R. D. Laing, the second section draws on a little known essay on storytelling to show the lineaments of an example of transpersonal experience. Finally the third section combines both critical and positive strategies in an exposition of an important study on hermeneutics and the social sciences.

3. Privacy and the loss of experience

(1) Nietzsche's friend Rohde is certainly right to note something wrong in traditional appeals to experience: too often they represent the farthing dip into what he calls "private imaginings." The flight from experience results from the combination of a truth with a falsehood: the truth is the unreliability of private imaginings; the falsehood is the equation of privacy with experience. If all experience is private, and if private evidence is unreliable, then surely experience is an unreliable guide to truth. Here in its most naked form is the syllogism underlying much of post-Cartesian rationality even in its empiricist formulations. Both empiricism and rationalism agree on locating experience *within* the knowing subject. They differ when it comes to classifying the *contents* of this container of privacy as innate or received "from outside." Either way the link between privacy and

experience is secure. The phrase "learning from experience" presupposes the same model of subjective privacy as the supposedly opposite rubric, "innate knowledge." The empiricists who claim to learn from experience, meaning by that receiving data from outside the mind, nevertheless insist that the object of knowledge, what is learned, is the idea held (eventually) in the mind.[22]

Skepticism is the historically necessary result of locating experience in private subjectivity: the knower has no way of knowing whether his subjective experience "corresponds with the way objects really are" (quotation marks because the entire formulation is wrongheaded). The attempt to prove correspondence runs into trouble toward both ends of the subject-object *differance*. If one tries to judge the truth of an objective truth claim by testing it in the court of one's private feelings and intuitions, one must face the objection that introspective tests of clarity, distinctness and certainty may be failed by true ideas and passed by false ideas. What is clear, distinct and certain to one may not be clear, distinct and certain to another. If one then tries to judge the truth of subjective opinion by measuring it against "objective facts," in the philosophically interesting and important cases one runs into the problem of having no way of knowing which of several candidates are "the facts." The distinction between subject and object is a mediation of experience that removes the knower from immediate access to "the facts." Once experience is privatized there is no easy or direct route to a shared body of public, objective facts.[23]*

One way back from subjectivism toward shared objectivity supposes that our experience is "in the mind" and therefore conditioned by our ways of knowing, but that *all* rational beings share the *same* ways of knowing. We may not know "things-in-themselves," but what we do know will be known similarly by all. Since we all filter information through the same subjective grids, the universality of knowledge is saved not by the uniformity of objects known. Universality derives instead from the transpersonal uniformity of ways of knowing. The eighteenth-century philosopher Immanuel Kant is chiefly responsible for this so-called "transcendental turn." He saved science from the skeptics by reinterpreting objectivity as derivative from universally shared, subjective conditions for the possibility of experience. These "transcendental" conditions may be entirely subjective, but as long as they are universally shared the universality of scientific understanding is secure.

Kant's transcendental turn not only saved science from skeptics who could find no sure route from knowledge "in the mind" to external objects. Further, the transcendental turn took an irreversible step toward hermeneutics. Kant showed that the shape of experience was not simply the result of shapes given by things in themselves passively received. He demonstrated the importance of the imagination's spontaneity in working up the structures of experience according to the subjective forms and categories with which we actively constitute experience. Once the transcendental turn had been taken, philosophers of the nineteenth and twentieth centuries could then argue that the subjective conditions for experience are not universal, as Kant had supposed. In place of supposedly universal forms of cognition, theorists of different persuasions pointed in turn to a variety of less than universal conditions giving rise to varieties of hermeneutic predispositions. The evidence of history and the evidence of anthropology made it plain that different groups of men, whether in different times or in different places or in different social classes, interpret the "same" realities— e.g., love, death, soul—quite differently.

Once the claim that *all* rational beings possess the same transcendental conditions had been challenged, philosophy followed the slippery slope from all to one until it came to rest in the radical subjectivism of modern existentialism: I alone constitute my experience just as you alone constitute yours; because we have no way of knowing whether we experience things in the same way, we are ultimately invisible to one another, condemned to privacy.

R. D. Laing describes the final act in the drama of privatization: "I see you and you see me. I experience you, and you experience me. I see your behavior. You see my behavior. But I do not and never have and never will see your *experience* of me. Just as you cannot 'see' my experience of you . . . I cannot experience your experience. You cannot experience my experience. We are both invisible men. All men are invisible to one another. Experience is man's invisibility to man."[24]

Laing marks the perfectly plausible nihilistic conclusion to a path running from Descartes's subjectivist turn through the rationalists and empiricists, through Kant's transcendental turn, through the nineteenth-century relativization of the transcendental, finally ending in twentieth-century existentialism from which Laing draws much of his understanding of man. Laing's case is poignant precisely because he expresses so well the ways we deny our experience while at the same time accepting as axiomatic the wedding of privacy and experience that makes the denial of experience inevitable. "Normal men have killed perhaps 100,000,000 of their fellow normal men in the last fifty years. Our behavior is a function of our experience. We act according to the way we see things. If our experience is destroyed, our behavior will be destructive. If our experience is destroyed, we have lost our own selves."[25] But what good is the requiem if it is sung in the same key that accompanies the killing? What good is another call to private experience when we know that the farthing dip into *private* experience cannot help?

Surely Laing is right to point out the interpersonal and social games that force us to deny our own experience in favor of "normalcy." Surely he is right about our losing touch with something, and surely he is right to unmask the social games that carry our sickness. But is he right to take the historically actual wedding of privacy and experience and baptize it as a necessary axiom that experience must be private?

By radically subjectivizing experience Laing runs the risk of reinforcing the basic premise supporting the progressive loss of experience. His own theory involves a double bind: on the one hand he is intensely sensitive to intersubjective transactions, the mechanisms leading each of us to play out dramas written by others. On the other hand he so ruthlessly divorces the category of experience from the intersubjective that the writers and players of the human drama cannot communicate with one another to coordinate authorship and acting in the final production. Without a director to mediate the experience of those who "act out" roles and those who "write" them, life according to a Laingian double bind is a play virtually doomed to failure.

The source of Laing's own double bind is plain to see. Aside from whatever farthing dip he may have made into his own peculiar experience he has gone to the wrong well for a bucket of philosphical profundity. His guide is Sartre whose own subjectivism led him at least temporarily toward the absurdity of absolute freedom for the isolated subject. Had Laing plumbed another European well for the source of his philosophy, had he looked to the Frankfurt school of Marxism rather than to the Parisian brand of existentialism, he would have found a full acknowledgment of the *historical* loss of experience in privatism, but he would *not* have found that historically emergent privacy ontologized into an ahistorical feature of the human condition.[26]* Laing might have stumbled across Walter Benjamin's essay on "The Storyteller," a piece that importantly anticipates both current attention to the use of stories in religious studies and McLuhan's reflections on technology and the media.

(2) Benjamin's argument takes it departure from an acknowledgement of the fact that "the communicability of experience is decreasing."[27] Experience is not in principle incommunicable as Laing would have it, but the progressive decay of its communicability might plausibly lead one to conclude from contemporary "experience" that experience is incommunicable. Benjamin exposes the progressive loss of experience through the replacement of the story by the novel much as Foucault exposes the loss of salutary madness by a similarly "outward" sign, the replacement of leprosariums by asylums. For Benjamin the significance of the novel lies in its replacement of the intersubjectively experiential features of storytelling, which is first and foremost the *sharing* of *experiences*. The storyteller draws on his own experiences or the experiences of others to weave yet another ex-

perience for himself and his immediate hearers. Part of that weaving involves something that the hearers will take away with them, some practical advice about how to do or make something, some moral or maxim, some *counsel* whose usefulness extends beyond mere entertainment or the dissemination of information. Benjamin draws a sharp distinction between the *story*, whose *counsel* is the result of the hearers' own *interpretations* based on the mixing of their experiences with the experiences drawn on for the story, and *the report* whose data are *explained* and thereby rendered as information. The novel is neither story nor report: not a report insofar as it is fictional, not a story because "the novelist has isolated himself. The birthplace of the novel is the solitary individual, who is no longer able to express himself by giving examples of his most important concerns, is himself uncounseled, and cannot counsel others." The novelist comes to sound rather like Laing's description of the psychiatrist who, unacquainted with the experience of madness, is ill-equipped to counsel the mad.

Yet there *have* been storytellers, there *have* been counselors. The sharing of experience is not in principle impossible however improbable or difficult it may have become. What are some of the factors that Benjamin finds contributing to the demise of the storyteller? Surely the loss of experience is not the direct result of the passing of the storyteller taken as a single cause—as if intersubjective experience had been sustained by oral storytelling as its sole necessary and sufficient condition. Instead, "the art of storytelling is reaching its end because the epic side of truth, wisdom, is dying out." The demise of storytelling is "only a concomitant symptom of the secular productive forces of history, a concomitant that has quite gradually removed narrative from the realm of living speech."[29] As a concomitant symptom it joins many others in an interpretation of modernity that includes but does not entirely hinge in McLuhanesque fashion upon the significance of the technology of the printing press.

The loss of experience symptomized by the demise of the storyteller has as much to do with a disintegration of the near/far structure of human experience. As travel becomes trivial the odyssey is no longer suitable subject matter for a story. The equalization of the near and the far accomplished by high-speed transportation— which is not to be reduced to a species of communication—renders the entire phenomenon of *locality* less significant and hence less a source of sharing than it once was. When local lore gives way to the abstract grid of the real-estate developer the loss includes more than land. The very vocabulary of intersubjective experience is semantically grounded in a sense of *place* which, once destroyed, leaves the language of intersubjectivity impoverished.

(3) The need for semantic referents for intersubjective meanings figures importantly in a definitive study by Charles Taylor entitled "Interpretation and the Sciences of Man."[30] Taylor criticizes mainstream political scientists for their sharp distinction between on the one hand those objective facts not open to interpretation and on the other a subjective realm of knowledge and belief, feelings, judgments and opinions classified under the heading of "political culture." The classically empiricist classification leaves out an important domain of meanings, namely those that are neither purely objective since they derive from intepretation, nor subjective since they depend on communally shared rather than individual practices.

As his primary example of intersubjective meaning Taylor takes the practice of collective decision making. He contrasts what we call "negotiation" with the consensus system used in traditional Japanese villages. The former presupposes for its success not only a set of shared beliefs about how autonomous individuals enter into negotiations with interests on the basis of which they are willing to barter. Negotiation also presupposes an entire social order that supports the individualism brought to the bargaining table. The consensus system, not to be confused with consensus as *agreement* among individuals, presupposes an entirely different sense of community. Like the *desa* system used in Indonesian villages the consensus system presupposes a social practice simply lacking in the semantic referents needed to make sense of or directly translate our words "bargaining" or "negotiation."

Translation in the reverse direction is just as difficult: if one has not shared with others the experience of collectively arriving at a group action without reliance on the tools of voting, compromise and the mechanics of debate codified in *Robert's Rules of Order,* if one has not felt oneself as a part of a body whose cohesiveness requires that the entire body grind through the growing pains of resolving and/ or fully incorporating conflicts rather than allowing one part to resign itself to compromise with another part, if one has not experienced a totally involving group dynamic for which "decision-making procedure" is an absurdly pale description, if one has not felt an emotionally charged atmosphere in which all one's sensitivities are tuned to the progressive disclosure and elaboration of the group's and not just one's own will, if one has never spent a great deal of time with others with whom this kind of experience is possible, then it is extremely unlikely that *desa* will admit of translation into terms with semantic referents that would render them more than purely fanciful.

Because intersubjective meanings both presuppose and constitute a social reality they form arcs in a hermeneutic circle. Taylor likens intersubjective meanings to "constitutive rules" like the directions for moving the pawn in chess.[31] Such rules do not simply *describe* how the game of chess is played; they constitute part of the game of chess. Taylor does not develop the analogy, perhaps because he sees the important difference between the rules of chess and the intersubjective meanings that partially constitute different social systems. Intersubjective meanings not only require living for learning but also respond to forces for change. While the living of meanings has its analogue in the difference between a *good* chess player and one merely acquainted with the rules, the potentiality for change implicit in the self-defining capacity of man has no simple analogue in the game of chess. The closer analogue would be the frustrating ambiguity of playing a game whose rules are subject to gradual revision. A closer analogue might be a long-term human relationship. But here we find ourselves back in the hermeneutic circle of the human sciences.

Taylor does not shrink from the implications of breaking with the empiricist tradition of political science to pursue the hermeneutics of the human. In elaborating on the offense against empiricist preconceptions he confirms two of the points made earlier in this chapter and raises a third with which the chapter will conclude. The first point raises the issue exemplified by Laing's existential ontology of experience, namely the tendency to construe one's own intersubjective meanings as ahistorical *a priori* determinants for all human existence. The second concerns the *blindness* that follows from the confusion between the historical and the ahistorical. Taylor's description of both the confusion and its resultant blindness recalls Rohde's difficulties in comprehending the Dionysian festivals. Finally the third point only barely raised by Taylor: what are the alternatives to the Apollonian method of resolving disputes by bargaining among autonomous rational individuals? Given the way Taylor interrelates the first two points, a few quotations from and comments on his text will serve both to interrelate earlier arguments and to set up the problematic of the third issue of conflict resolution outside the Apollonian framework.

Not only attitudes toward negotiations but also attitudes toward labor serve as examples of how concepts and their corresponding realities may or may not be embedded in the form of intersubjective meanings: "The great interdependent matrix of labor is not just a set of ideas in people's heads but is an important aspect of the reality we live in modern society. And at the same time, these ideas are embedded in this matrix in that they are constitutive of it; that is, we wouldn't be able to live in this type of society unless we were imbued with these ideas or some others which could call forth the discipline and voluntary coordination needed to operate this kind of economy." In characterizing the difference between the civilization of labor and the peasant populations on which it has been imposed, Taylor points out the incommensurability between Dionysian existence and the Apollonian ideals imposed upon it: "They require an entirely unprecedented level of disciplined sustained, monotonous effort, long hours unpunctuated by any meaningful rhythm, such as that of seasons or festivals. In the end this way of life can only be accepted when the idea of making a living is endowed with more significance than that of just avoiding starvation; and this it is in the civilization of labor."

Political scientists are not unmindful of the role of the work ethic as supplying the cement to bind modern societies both Marxist and democratic: "The interdependent productive and negotiating society has been recognized by political science, but not as one structure of intersubjective meaning among others, rather as the inescapable background of social action as such. In this guise it no longer need be an object of study. Rather it retreats to the middle distance, where its general outline takes the role of universal framework, within which (it is hoped) actions and structures will be brute data identifiable, and this for any society at any time."

So far the brand of blindness imposed looks like no more than a selective inattention to what is taken for granted. But the problem is compounded by the particular content that is taken as eternally granted. Even when mainstream political science attends to the fundamentality of the work ethic it can do so only in terms that beg the questions to be addressed, e.g., the *value* of the secularization of which the demise of the storyteller is a concomitant symptom. "The notion is that what politics is about perennially is the adjustment of difference, or the production of symbolic and effective 'outputs' on the basis of demand and support 'inputs.' The rise of the intersubjective meaning of the civilization of work is seen as the increase of correct perception of the political process at the expense of 'ideology.'"

Just as Sartre and Laing perennialize privacy so Parsons and Bell perennialize politics. "This way of looking at the civilization of work, as resulting from the retreat of illusion before the correct perception of what politics perennially and really is, is thus closely bound up with the epistemological premises of mainstream political science and its resultant inability to recognize the historical specificity of this civilization's intersubjective meanings." Consequently those contemporary phenomena that hark back (or forward) to Dionysian culture can only appear as utterly and irredeemably irrational. Since they fall outside the grid imposed by the intersubjective meanings of the civilization of work, and secondly, since the ideologues of that civilization see themselves as so far beyond ideology that no other system of intersubjective meanings is entertainable—since the transcendence of ideology is equivalent to the elimination of the very category of intersubjective meaning—the will to realize the *we* of consensus, the collective *some* of Dionysian ecstasy, must appear as a summation of individual pathologies.

Just as Rohde must ask after the meaning of it all and must fashion an answer that conforms to the intersubjective meanings whose semantic references are secure in the Christian culture of nineteenth-century Europe, so twentieth-century social theorists like Lewis Feuer can hardly help but interpret the breakdown of the bargaining mode in terms of the bargaining mode that is breaking down: "This mainstream science hasn't the categories to explain this breakdown. It is forced to look on extremism either as a bargaining gambit of the desperate, deliberately raising the ante in order to force a hearing. Or, alternatively, it can recognize the novelty of the rebellion by accepting the hypothesis that heightened demands are being made on the system owing to a revolution of 'expectations'." If intellectuals like Feuer unwittingly come closer to more appropriate categories by discussing campus uprisings as annual reenactments of the rites of Spring they do so with a sense of frivolity betraying their incapacity to understand, not from an understanding of a fundamental need to punctuate monotony with the frivolity of a festival.

Taylor includes himself among contemporaries who cannot hope to have an adequate understanding of the radical changes through which advanced industrial society is wending its unwieldy way. But he does suggest that a hermeneutic of intersubjective meanings offers a more hopeful path toward understanding than do further applications of the very categories whose inner contradictions are now manifest as cultural chaos. In recommending hermeneutics he is careful to emphasize its differences from the dominant science of politics. While carefully establishing criteria to keep hermeneutics from falling toward the solipsistic extreme of imagining that "thinking something makes it so"[32] he takes equal care to avoid falling the other way toward a formalization of hermeneutics that would allow its integration into a science of clearly verifiable truths.

For hermeneutics the role of *insight* is inescapable. "If we have a science which has no brute data, which relies on readings, then it cannot but move in a hermeneutical circle. A given reading of the intersubjective meanings of a society, or of given institutions or practices, may seem well founded, because it makes sense of these practices or the development of that society. But the conviction that it does make sense of this history itself is founded on further related readings." For the *first* of the eventually related "readings" one needs in order to enter a foreign hermeneutic circle, a sober deduction from known data and rules of consequence will not do. Nor is it clear just what will do: "If these readings seem implausible, or even more, if they are not understood by our interlocutor, there is no verification procedure which we can fall back on. We can only continue to offer interpretations; we are in an interpretive circle."

In acknowledging not only the political scientists' difficulties in departing from their unacknowledged hermeneutic circle but also the difficulties anyone may encounter in entering a different hermeneutic circle Taylor admits: "This is a scandalous result according to the authoritative conception of science in our tradition . . . For it means that this is not a study in which anyone can engage, regardless of their level of insight; that some claims of the form: 'if you don't understand, then your intuitions are at fault, are blind or inadequate,' some claims of this form will be justified." Further, these apparently nonarbitrable differences will be more serious than disputes over the proper interpretation of a poem because when we take the society we live in as our text then the condition for a different understanding of the "text" may be a different society. "Thus, in the sciences of man insofar as they are hermeneutical there can be a valid response to 'I don't understand' which takes the form, not only 'develop your intuition,' but more radically, 'change yourself.'"

The radical imperative, "Change yourself!" raises the point reserved for the conclusion of this chapter: what models of conflict resolution are available once the radical break with the negotiations of Apollonian rationality leads one to leave the bargaining table? Does the demand for personal change as a condition for understanding justify devious means of changing another's experience so that he can enter the hermeneutic circle of one's own beliefs and experiences? Worse, does the demand for change justify forcible or violent means of changing another's experience? Part of the lure of The One True World of Enlightenment rationalism and its positivist successors lies in its ability to keep people at the bargaining table—surely with enough talk the One Truth will come to light. To proponents of monism the prospect of irreducible pluralism appears to be a step from the bargaining table toward the battlefield where might rather than right resolves disputes.

This is the riddle of pluralism: how to allow otherness without inviting war, bigotry, prejudice or other forms of strife that result from the elevation of a particular community value to a universal? Once we forswear faith in a common ground of rational interests, once we acknowledge the possibility that the interests of one community may be irreducibly different from those of another in respects that are fully as important as those respects in which some of their interests are the same, then how are those differences to be dealt with? This is the riddle of pluralism and its difficulty is sufficient to send most theorists back into the camp of monism even if only as a regulative ideal.

Summary

Taylor's appeal to hermeneutics marks more than a break with empiricist epistemology in the social sciences. Marxists have long been aware of the shortcomings of empiricism in the social sciences. The appeal to praxis amounts to the same imperative, "Change yourself!" The advantage of Taylor's appeal to hermeneutics with its explicit repudiation of scientism lies in its implicit support of *localism*. The appeal of localism remains implicit in the Marxist emphasis on praxis; but anarchists are the exceptions proving the rule that beneath the umbrella of Marxism praxis *must everywhere* reveal the single truth of the one true theory. Taylor's repudiation of scientism throws open the door to a multiplicity of hermeneutic circles: different practices support different theories and vice versa.

The hermeneutic avenue toward pluralism restores the claim of experience in each of the several ways in which experience has been lost. First, by allowing for an irreducible plurality of hermeneutic circles it reduces the totalitarian tendency toward imposing a single *theory* of praxis upon the multiple practices that are supposed to support the single theory. Second, by restoring the claim of localism hermeneutic pluralism restores the sense of locality that Benjamin shows to be crucial to the sharing of experience in storytelling. A vivid sense of the difference between near and far is a concomitant symptom of a sense of place allowing semantic entrenchment for a shared vocabulary of *experiences* in place of a universal vocabulary of *information*. Third, the restoration of the near/far structure in experience precludes a perennializing of the distortion of that structure in privatization. By locating experience in the community of shared intersubjective meanings a hermeneutic pluralism avoids the skeptical withdrawal of experience into the individualized interior where it has languished from Locke to Laing. Fourth and finally, once experience has been retrieved from the subjectivist hole into which it had fallen, then the objectivist illusion of the reducibility of experience to the behavior of individuals falls as well. Once experience is no longer conceived as private to the point of being in principle unobservable then experience (as distinct from behavior) is no longer the easy prey of those who justly argue that a difference that makes no observable difference is no difference, i.e., that there is no difference between experience and the observable behavior of individuals.

To draw the retrospective knot on the retrieval of experience even more tightly: experience has been retrieved first in the *primacy of praxis* to any monistic theory that would subvert the plurality of local experiences; second, localism supports experience against the distortion of the near/far structure by information; third, the near/far structure prevents the loss experience in privatization; fourth, nonprivatized experience is observable and therefore available as legitimate evidence against the objectivist reduction of experience to behavior.

The knot of shared praxis is a node in the circular structure of subjectivity, a pluralized Some whose intersubjective meanings are like the memories and intentions of a single individual. Just as the intention that differentiates action from behavior may take the form of a symbolic representation articulated in language when someone removes the ambiguity of his behavior by telling you what he is doing, so the intersubjective meanings of limited collectivities find symbolic representation in the gods of a given culture. Apart from all reductive considerations concerning childish needs to replace the father, the gods serve an epistemological function—that is, they play a role as transcendental conditions for the possibility of a certain kind of knowledge. Like language itself, the gods offer a vocabulary of intersubjective meanings in terms of which it is possible to differentiate the history of a collectivity from the ambiguous events that befall it. In short, theology is a "language" differentiating history from nature where ordinary language differentiates action from behavior.

Note that the role of the gods is nonetheless necessary however much we admit them to be collective *projections*—inventions of a collective imagination. Nor is their power diminished by the observation that their power over us is the result of a complementary process of *introjection* or internalization. Part Two will show how the circular process of projection and introjection exemplifies the circular structure of subjectivity. Societies project gods as symbols of the intersubjective meanings that would make sense of their social histories; then subsequent subjects—both collective and individual—introject those divine symbols as some of the selves who populate the internal pantheon of a polytheistic psychology. The strategy of Part Two consequently draws on two organizing principles for the exemplification of multiple selves: the projected pantheon on Olympus is structurally similar in articulation and function to the introjected pantheon of selves in Nietzsche's Zarathustra. If that structural similarity can be demonstrated, then the theological and psychological limits of subjectivity will have been joined in a relational identity that closes the transpersonal and intrapersonal arcs in the circle of subjectivity.

Part Two exemplifies more than the general structure of subjectivity. The structure of power finds specific content in a cultural biography of Zeus; the structure of freedom gains further specificity from Nietzsche's analysis of volition. Both the gods and the "Higher Men" of Nietzsche's internal pantheon demonstrate the viability of heterarchy against the felt need for monotheistic hierarchy. By taking an inventory of both outer and inner pantheons, and further, by showing the structural similarities of both, Part Two will instantiate the abstraction of Part One while showing the circularity of the structure of projection and introjection.

The sequence of chapters in Part Two follows the order of this chapter: where the first section on Dionysus and self-identity focused on the personal arc of the circle of subjectivity, the first chapter of Part Two—"Power, Proteus and Promising"—stresses the personal locus of subjectivity by looking at Zeus and Proteus as projected-introjected symbols of singular self-identity. Where the biography of Zeus reveals a progressive centralization of autonomy, the transformations of Proteus reveal an attempt to break the rigidity of the monotheistic ego by stringing several singular selves in succession. The price of Protean variability, however, is the capacity to keep promises. Hence the need to pluralize selfhood by a dismemberment that is simultaneous rather than successive.

Just as section two of this chapter focused on the intrapersonal arc of the circle of subjectivity, so the second chapter of Part Two will pursue the path of Dionysian dismemberment with a study of stories of death and decadence. What is the price for dismemberment, and what is the source of our fears? Finally the third chapter of part Two, like the third section of this chapter, will combine positive and negative strategies of polytheistic alternative and hermeneutic critique of monotheism. By weaving the story of Aphrodite together with an Anaxagorean critique of the Eleatic logic of the One, chapter VI discloses the logic of a collective, transpersonal unity that does not sacrifice the distinctiveness of the persons who are its components.

PART
TWO
STORIES IN
POLYTHEISM
AND PSYCHOLOGY

IV Power, Proteus and Promises

Old paradigms die hard. Like an obsolete faith in a single universal diety, an obsolete faith in the presidency will linger as long as it retains the support of correlative paradigms. The single divine father and the singular locus of political authority are transforms of singular selfhood. This chapter seeks the sources of the old paradigms in their mythological and psychological transforms.

The first section harks back to the birth of the paradigm of singular agency in projections of power onto the figure of Zeus. Once again some seemingly long leaps will lead from signs on one arc of the circle of subjectivity to readings of their transforms on other arcs. The biography of Zeus through the stages of Greek mythology will suggest a reading of modern selfhood as it situates itself in cities or suburbs. Next an appreciation and critique of the Protean archetype will lead to deliberations weighing the power of the long-range promise against the excitement of fleeting joy.

The problem, put perhaps too simply: what can psychohistory tell us about the preoccupation with control manifest in second realm

rationality? How should we mediate the *differance* symbolically represented by the opposition between Zeus's authority and Proteus's
seemingly undisciplined fickleness? Their resolution will require a
relational analysis of the different dimensions of temporality lived by
the different selves of many dimensional man.

Zeus and the superego

First among the gods on Olympus was Zeus, the father, a most
important figure for investigating the image of power and control as it
was both projected onto the divine and introjected into the human. To
look at Zeus through monotheistic Christian eyes is to risk seeing a
more powerful father than we find in Homer. The very idea of omnipotence is a later invention, one that springs more from a felt need
for power than from a sense of its reality. Zeus was strong, yes, but
hardly omnipotent. His intentions were sometimes thwarted. And if
the index of power be not only the realization of intentions but also
their manner of realization—whether by forthright or devious
means—then Zeus like most of the gods was more than once guilty of
resorting to trickery rather than potency to gain his way. To "marry"
his many mistresses he had to employ every means from his "honeyed
tongue" to transformation into a swan.

Zeus's mediations with man differ from those of the Christian
Father who univocally represents himself in the form of his "only beg-
otten son." To mankind grown unimaginative this forthright father is
more reassuring than one who is sometimes foolish to the point of bu-
foonery, sometimes enraged to the point of irresponsibility. Zeus
roared and wheedled and "wept tears of blood that fell to the ground,
for the sake of his beloved son."[1]

This Zeus is not a father to inspire confidence among God's

children. The cosmic household is not in altogether safe hands. But here lies the greatness of the ancients, that they did not need a faith in omnipotence to nourish a sense of security. They knew about hierarchy,[2] the attempt to order all differences under one higher power; but they knew equally well the folly of power unguided by wisdom. And Athena, not Zeus, was known for the gift of wisdom.

While considering Zeus as the projection of a previously introjected sense of personal power we moderns would do well to reflect on the transformation of the Trinity of Zeus, Apollo and Dionysus into their more recent mythological counterparts, the superego, ego and id. Not that some sort of literal material entities have remained identical through slight transformations of name and attribute, for Freud himself cautioned that "the hypothesis of the super-ego really describes a *structural relation* and is not merely a personification of some rash abstraction as that of conscience."[3] Nevertheless it is safe to say that Zeus personifies the same structural relation described by the superego. The point is carried by the epithet, *pater Zeus*, Zeus the father, the parent.

If the hypothesis of the superego describes a *structural relation* then perhaps it describes an instance of *differance* (Derrida's term for a differing/deferring that somehow precedes and constitutes the two different relata). Perhaps Freud intended to describe not two *entities*, the ego and the superego, but a single relation of *aspiration*. The phenomenon of aspiration, sometimes evident in an inchoate striving, need not presuppose a perfectly clear picture of that to which one aspires; nor need aspiring presuppose a perfectly clear identity in an aspirer. It is enough that the feeling alone testify to the relationship without presupposing its terms. The relationship will determine its own terms as much as the reverse. Once certain terms have been determined—Zeus and Apollo or superego and ego—the shape of those terms serves as an index to the experience of that relationship of aspiration. Within the context of this structure of relations then, Zeus and the superego play the same role as do the ego and Apollo, the *principium individuationis*.

Yet they are different. The same function is transformed. What is the transformation? E. R. Dodds describes the biography of Zeus from the amoral god of the *Iliad* to the more moral judge of later cosmologies in terms of Ruth Benedict's rubrics: from shame culture to guilt culture. The earliest descriptions of Zeus echo a sentiment little concerned with guilt and justice. Dodds finds "no indication in the narrative of the *Iliad* that Zeus is concerned with justice as such." While hardly indifferent to the woes of his favorites, while weeping tears of blood, Zeus is nonetheless prepared to accept Vonnegut's saying: ". . . so it goes." Zeus did not need a moral order in order to "make sense" of suffering. He simply suffered as did the earliest of his worshippers who would neither praise nor blame Zeus for their own joys and sufferings. The love of Zeus was regarded as "eccentric."[4] Nor did the narrator of the *Iliad* have a word for "god-fearing." In short, there was neither the first nor the second realm inclination to locate a *single* cause to account for worldly phenomena.

Only later did the more moral sentiments penetrate the vocabulary and consciousness of gods and men alike. "Man projects into the cosmos his own nascent demand for social justice; and when from the outer spaces the magnified echo of his own voice returns to him, promising punishment for the guilty, he draws from it courage and reassurance."[5] The cost of that courage and reassurance is the transition from shame culture to guilt culture. The transition demands a different divine father who will be at first more distant but finally more thoroughly internalized than ever was that humanoid hurler of thunderbolts: "In becoming the embodiment of cosmic justice Zeus lost his humanity. Hence Olympianism in its moralised form tended to become a religion of fear," a stepping stone towards the experience of sin and its internalization in the form of guilt. "The moral education of Zeus" (Dodds's phrase) tells the history of ideal man, the ego-ideal.

As Zeus loses his humanity, as he comes to embody a super-human capacity for justice, he ceases to serve what Nietzsche regarded as the foremost utility of polytheism, namely the gods' justification of human life by their own living of human lives: "The freedom granted each God with respect to other Gods gave man in the end his freedom with respect to laws and customs and neighbors. Monotheism on the other hand, that rigid consequence of the doctrine of a normal man—thus the belief in a normal god next to whom one finds only false gods—has been perhaps the greatest danger to mankind."[6]

Identity, city life and the ontology of shame

The transition from shame culture to guilt culture is the transition from the world of Agamemnon and public honor that is variously won to the world of Luther where moral rectitude is a narrower and more private affair. The transition from a polytheism of human gods toward monotheistic aspiration to the *Normalgott* of a single godlike human is nowhere more evident than in the modern preoccupation with singular identity. The preoccupation with identity has become so severe that Richard Sennett can make sense of city life in the nineteenth century and earlier twentieth century by comparing it favorably against life in contemporary suburbs where the rush toward "purified identity" creates a "purified community."[7] In the suburbs what is deemed best can dominate the human ecology like hothouse orchids. The suburbs are a slice or layer of society, not a microcosm including all parts of the ecologically richer whole.[8] Some "plants" have been designated "weeds" and relegated to the welfare roles of the abandoned inner city, the social sewer.[9]

It will seem that we have come a long way from the earliest tales of Zeus, not just historically but topically. Not so. Not for nothing is Sennett's book entitled *The Uses of Disorder: Personal Identity and City Life*. Just as theology is an index to the ideal for man, so the way we live gives witness to what we want. And the worst that can be said of social segregation is not only that it is an *injustice* to inspire *guilt* but also that it is an index of shameful spiritual poverty, a diminution of being. Why?

The difference between shame and guilt is not simply moral but ontological, i.e., a question of modes of *being.* The transition from shame culture to guilt culture marks a transition from a psychosocial constitution of the self in terms of its *relations* to a psychosocial constitution of self as autonomous *substance.* Shame depends on the Other more than guilt.[10] The physical shape of shame, the blush, is a sign to the other, and its impact upon the self is stronger because the blusher knows that the other knows. Guilt on the contrary can rankle the solitary. If Heidegger is to be believed, the capacity for guilt is almost a measure of one's finite boundedness, one's separation from the Other.[11]* Because to be is to be related, isolation from the Other is diminution of being.

Completely removed from the praise and blame of others the holy individual's authenticity is purely formal. It lacks content. The individual is authentic to *nothing.* Heidegger and Sartre retain the courage of their convictions in pursuing the ontology of the isolated individual and their steadfast course drives them straight to what some regard as the profundity rather than the absurdity of positing nothingness at the core of subjectivity. Quite correct in their denial of the pure being or affirmative substantiality of the self, they follow the dialectic to its opposite abstraction, pure nothingness. To attempt to remain true to something, to manifest a given determination, e.g., to *be* a waiter in a café, is to fall into bad faith, a perversion of subjectivity. But just as both Being and Nothing are abstractions from the richness of concrete becoming, so the core of guilty nothingness is as much an abstract extreme as a substantial subject whose shape is wholly determined by inflations of honor and dents of shame. The structure of subjectivity manifests both: a partial internalization of the Other rendering the subject capable of honor and shame, as well as resistance of the Other that is given up only at the price of guilt before oneself, a self given content by the Other.

The *becoming* of the self depends upon both the internalization and resistance of content from the Other. The other must remain Other in its relatedness. Otherwise homogeneity, whether of being or of nothing, threatens the articulation of becoming. The diminution of being reflected in the holy individual's isolation from the other has its necessary correlate in the spiritual poverty that results when the individual becomes just like the Other. How does the negation of the Other in the pursuit of loneliness turn over into its opposite?

Slater links the flight to the suburbs, that not so subtle form of segregation, together with the do-it-yourself movement in which the Apollonian ego takes not only a power-hungry Zeus but also a handy Hephaestus as its role models: "Both attempt to deny human interdependence and pursue unrealistic fantasies of self sufficiency."[12] The result is an ego not only individuated but so independent of other selves, so walled off from the Other, that each self must master all the human tasks that are divided among many in the more interdependent community. The result of this rugged individualism is an apparently paradoxical uniformity: the culture of independence with a powerful Zeus as ego-ideal allows each individual more "freedom" to "choose" his own ends than cultures of interdependence where there is greater pressure to conform to a certain role. But cultures of interdependence like the Olympian pantheon contain *greater variety* of polytheistic ideals to which one might conform. In place of this variety the unity of value implicit in the *Normalgott* of monotheism makes the freedom of the monotheistic ego turn over into its opposite: "Our society gives far more leeway to the individual to pursue his own ends, but, since *it* defines what is worthy and desirable, everyone tends, independently but monotonously, to pursue the same things in the same way."[13] Monotheism takes its toll in monotony.

Of course the alternative of polytheistic society has its drawbacks: interdependence becomes pressure to conform to some role or other; the burden of internalized guilt is put off only at the price of shame. The alternative to guilt is not "anything goes." All is *not* permitted. Shame culture pushed to *its* extreme can be extremely authoritarian. Besides, at this late date it is unlikely that we could unlearn our individuality even if we wished to. The point is that we have learned our individuality too well. By isolating the structure of subjectivity in persons alone we have lost sight of both the transpersonal and intrapersonal multiplicities that serve as conditions for the possibility of the structure of subjectivity and freedom. With a moralized and all-powerful Zeus as an ideal for the Apollonian ego, individuation takes the form of independence and isolation. Our modern mythology is poverty-stricken once Zeus claims the riches of all other gods.

As if in answer to the ascendancy of a moralized Zeus, other gods besides Dionysus have made their bids for the psychic riches hoarded by the rigidly powerful ego-ideal. The Apollonian ego, wearying of the kind of rigid identity imposed upon it by the ideal of an all-powerful and all too moral superego, now listens with eager ears to the prospect of a protean personality able to trade rigidity for more fluid transitions from one self to another. Will the addition of Proteus to the triumvirate of Zeus, Apollo and Dionysus accomplish a transition to many dimensional man? Or does the manifest seductiveness of Proteus's beckoning connote no more than a *need* for many dimensionality fallen short of its satisfaction?

Protean man

The meaning of the English word 'protean' contains a capsule description of the Greek god's character such as it was: "readily assuming *different* forms or characters; exceedingly variable." 'Protean

Man' has come to be a virtual trademark for Robert Jay Lifton's contributions to the psychology of postmodern man.[14] Proteus is with us.
Lifton's portrait of protean man—his *genesis*, his *strengths* and his
weaknesses—confirms many of the observations made here on modernity and advanced industrial society.

His *genesis* Lifton attributes to two historical developments:
first a *psychohistorical dislocation,* "the break in the sense of connection which men have long felt with the vital and nourishing symbols of
their cultural tradition"; second and closely if not causally related, a
flooding of imagery through the media. Deprived of a socially or culturally *given* identity yet generously supplied with a vast multiplicity
of albeit fragmentary images from which to fabricate an identity,
postmodern man comes to resemble Proteus, the Greek god whose
singular talent included not only prophecy but the penchant for self-
transformation.

The *strengths* of the protean personality are obvious given the
historical circumstances from which he springs: if history insists on
severing the individual from his roots by accelerating the pace of cultural change, then the individual does best who carries least in the
way of commitments to the past. Especially if gifted with a touch of
the prophet, a talent of which Lifton inexplicably makes little, the
protean personality can avoid the trauma of future shock by shocking
the future first. Leaping headlong into each new historically appropriate shape this unencumbered acrobat accomplishes a graceful flip to
land feet first in the ever liquid morrow where others flounder in vain
attempts to salvage the baggage of history. He then swims swiftly to
the next island of brief cultural solidarity, from whence he will be the
first to plunge into the next historical spasm.

He has *weaknesses* as well, most notably a necessarily im-
paired sense of *symbolic immortality* (another crucial idiom in Lifton's language for describing not only the moderns who have survived
the death of god but also the postmoderns who have survived the
death of so much more in the dreadful implications of Hiroshima).
Cut off from traditional avenues toward immortality—not only the re-

ligious but also the symbolic-secular means of biological attachments to a family for which one lastingly cares, or professional attachments to creative works that would outlast their dedicated author—protean man turns "sometimes pleasurably and sometimes desperately" to either concern for a nature that might transcend the catastrophes of human history's acceleration or to experiments in consciousness expansion whose intensity promises a transcendence of time and death themselves.

So much for the genesis, strengths and weaknesses of Protean Man. On balance Lifton finds, "However misguided many of his forays may be, protean man also carries with him an extraordinary range of possibility for man's betterment, or more important, for his survival."

Lifton is onto something important. The great success of his often reprinted essay and the deep resonances it sets off in the souls of so many readers attest to the timeliness of his discovery and the imagery with which it is portrayed. But is this discovery, together with its imagery, perhaps too timely? Has Lifton, like a protean prophet himself, appropriately foretold the present but with words that will not survive this present? Insightfully grasping the need for new images of selfhood, has he not retained too much of the preoccupation with identity? The image of Protean Man reflects an insight into a possible multiplicity of selfhood, but the arrangement of the several selves, their succession *one after another*, shows an attachment to the traditional concept of identity according to which one must be only *one self at a time*. According to this image inner contradiction remains intolerable. No wonder the image is so popular: it serves as a model for successive purifications of identity.

Lifton's data are intriguing, his examples well drawn to portray the plight of those who find it impossible to retain a single fixed identity. Those same data, those same examples, would seem to support the image of the many dimensional man as well if not better than the protean man. He cites a patient: "I have an extraordinary number of masks I can put on or take off. The question is: Is there, or should

there be, one face which should be authentic? I'm not sure that there
is one for me." The example manifests multidimensionality more than
a succession of separate identities.

Proteus and the superego

Another example taken to illustrate the image of protean man
is Jean-Paul Sartre, in whom the "image of repeated, autonomously
willed death and rebirth of the self, so central to the protean style, becomes associated with the theme of fatherlessness." Lifton quotes a
passage from Sartre's autobiography in which this manifestly multidimensional philosopher-playwright-activist reports his escape from
"the bond of paternity" by the death of his young father. Sartre concludes: "I readily subscribe to the verdict of an eminent psy-
choanalyst: I have no superego." Lifton singles out Sartre's line describing his father as "a young man who did not have time to be my
father and who could now be my son" and interprets it as suggesting
"an extension of the protean style to intimate family relationships," a
most important observation since it suggests the sheer transiency of
intimate relationships where protean personalities are involved.[15]

Lifton comments: "The judgement of the absent superego,
however, may be misleading, especially if we equate superego with
susceptibility to guilt. What has actually disappeared—in Sartre and
in protean man in general—in the *classical* superego, the internalization of clearly defined criteria of right and wrong transmitted within a
particular culture by parents to their children." Here we find a fine
articulation of an important phenomenon, the obsolescence of a re-
strictive modern mythology that would replace *pater* Zeus, Apollo,
Dionysus and the rest of the pantheon with the superego, ego and id.
But the insight falters. Instead of noting the passing of the classical

superego as an opportunity for a much needed turn from guilt culture toward shame culture, Lifton remarks that freedom from "that kind of superego" does not render protean man less guilty; "rather than being free of guilt, his guilt takes on a different form from that of his predecessors," namely, "a vague but persistent kind of self-condemnation related to the symbolic disharmonies I have described, a sense of having no outlet for his loyalties and no symbolic structure for his achievements."

No doubt this description fits many. But the same disharmonies, the same lack of a single clear superego, doubtless describes at least some others, some many dimensional men and women who have ridden the waves of recent history to further shores than Lifton in his exemplary researches has yet reached. For them the lack of a simple internalized superego is hardly an occasion for inchoate guilt or "a nagging sense of unworthiness all the more troublesome for its lack of clear origin." They have outlived the hangover of this Heideggerian angst caused as much by interiorization and privatization in general as by the internalization of a *deus absconditus*, a Nothing in the place of a Something. Instead these adventures on further shores have only partially internalized several sources of shame if not guilt. How so? What is the syndrome that joins an alternative to both the classical and the protean superego structure with a shift toward shame culture from guilt culture? And how does that syndrome arise out of precisely those phenomena to which Lifton so helpfully draws our attention?

First, for lack of a single clearly defined ego-ideal the many dimensional personality derives the initial articulations of its multiplicity by partially internalizing *several* images, not the single though ill-defined image of an absent *pater*: not *none* as Sartre would "misleadingly" have it, not *one* clear image as Freud would have it, nor one nebulous image as Lifton correcting Sartre would have it, but *some*.

Second, since the images are several and sooner or later contradictory to one another in some respects, their internalization is necessarily partial; one's Apollo is *not* one's Dionysus, one's Michelangelo is *not* one's Mick Jagger. The mode of internalization that retains externality, the comprehensive wholeness that preserves distinctiveness, is a subtle business that will receive further elucidation in Chapter VI. For now a final point to complete the initial sketch of the many dimensional personality as a closely related alternative to protean man.

Third, because several images are only *partially* internalized their separate holds on the selfhood of the entire personality are less suited to the incitement of guilt than is the iron grip of the totally internalized single superego, whether classical or ineffable. The imperatives of the single voice of the classical superego were easier to internalize totally than the often conflicting voices of a polytheistic pantheon. Even the dreadful silence of the *pater absconditus* was easier to internalize totally. This third superego structure, this multiplicity, cannot internalize totally because at an even deeper level than the dynamic of "identification with the father," as Freud calls it, there may be a fixing of pure form for what is to be identified: whether a *single* self or a *multiplicity*.

If the "choice," such as it is, is for multiplicity then the word 'internalization' lacks clear meaning for there is no longer *one* form *inside of which* a given paternal content might be *internalized*. Instead the many dimensional structure differs so far from the metaphor of containment that is *différance* outruns the way station of many volumes and continues on to the metaphor of multiple dimensions, axes that *contain* nothing but spread like open arms. A multiplicity of ego-ideals can be roughly located in terms of these dimensions but the openness of the metaphor renders the concept of total internalization meaningless on the new model. Instead the many superegos vie with one another.

Nor should the mathematical cast of the metaphor lead to a literalism according to which the multiplicity of ego-ideals might be united as a single resultant vector computed from a summation of a multiplicity of vectors. The disunity of the multidimensional self is such that the dimensions do not necessarily have a common origin.

The vector symbolizing the strength of a superego in one set of dimensions might be drawn, as it were, on a different blackboard from the vector symbolizing another ego-ideal in a different set of dimensions.

A compromise among conflicting ego-ideals would be an intrapersonal equivalent to a negotiated settlement in the transpersonal domain—better than warfare but still an internalization of the ethos of bargaining as Taylor describes it. A corresponding internalization of the consensus model trades the efficiency of the single resultant vector for the richness of a self-exploratory process aimed toward an exposure and clarification of all vectors rather than their occlusion in a secret ballot. Just as the majority need have no memory of the platform of the minority where autonomous agents negotiate, so a single superego conceived as a resultant vector of many would contain no trace of the specific ideals "averaged" in a compromise.

The superego structure most appropriate to many dimensional man must be a mediation with a memory, a Hegelian *Aufhebung* or dialectical synthesis of opposites that both negates and preserves its antithetical moments:[16] negated is the stark immediacy of their polar opposition; preserved (whether or not satisfied) is the content of each conflicting ego-ideal. Both these aspects of *Aufhebung* are satisfied through a mediation that is more apt to embellish each opposing ego-ideal with further articulation rather than assume the autonomy of already determinate interests. The internalization of consensus will not halt debate by "calling the question" in the interests of efficiency.[17]

Doubtless a multiplicity of ego-ideals makes life complicated. *Compromise* has the same appeal as Proteus: who would not occasionally trade in the old conflicts for the simplicity of a single self whose "direction" has no memory of the conflicts from which it was spawned? If conflicting *promises* could be *com*promised, if conflicting *ideals* could be leveled by a single *reality* principle (another name for the superego), then life would be much simpler. But the will to simplicity itself may be a symptom of weariness, a yawn that is the sign of an impending reductionism all in the name of "elegance" and "parsimony," those methodological correlates of procedural "efficiency."

Promises, oaths, troths and truths

Better to acknowledge and record the claims of conflicting promises than squelch deliberation with a hasty vote on some compromise. But how to acknowledge the claims of conflicting promises? What is a promise if not a pledge to be fulfilled no matter what? Does the acknowledgment of conflicting promises demand the breaking of promises? Can Protean Man even make a promise? The variability of his commitments suggests that he cannot. Promising is a problem for the multiple self, whether the multiplicity be linear *à la* Proteus or simultaneous *à la* many dimensional man.

For the Protean Man a promise is more an oath of the moment than a troth for all time. Let these two terms, 'oath' and 'troth,' stand for two kinds of promises with two kinds of temporality. Though the primary sense of 'oath' stresses the binding character of the promise made, other uses of 'oath' connote a way its pledge differs from a troth. To make an oath may also mean to curse or blaspheme. Oaths are eruptions of the moment. Troths may carry fully as much feeling but the use of 'troth' in wedding ceremonies connotes a more fully considered pledge. Granted that the limited use of these already archaic words wanders across an almost identical spectrum of promises, let us exploit their arcane color; let us stipulate that 'oath' shall refer only to that direction on the dimension of promises for which the present moment is the proper locus for finding the meaning of a pledge; 'troth' shall refer only to that other direction of *differance* for which the future is the correspondingly proper locus of validation.

Given these convenient stipulations Protean Man may be allowed a kind of promising. As he purifies himself of all past selves, as he concentrates himself into the dedication of the moment, it will be quite natural for him to make oaths. Since the strength of the Protean personality is largely its capacity to hurl itself headlong into engagements whose intensities are inhibited by the Apollonian ego's firm attachment to fixed boundaries, the Protean personality will naturally find itself pledging away its entire future as a means of expressing the measure of its involvements in the moment. Only when the intensity of his immediate engagement leads into the contract of engaged-to-be-married, only when oath becomes troth is he in trouble. For Protean Man cannot maintain a troth. His fickleness forbids it. The very idea of a troth is antithetical to the alterable essence of Protean Man.

Proteus is to troth what Protagoras is to truth, at least insofar as the Protagorean "man is the measure" be interpreted purely subjectivistically. If promises are only as universally binding as the truths of the subjective relativist are universally valid, then "I promise you" has no more meaning than "true for me."[18] Both are reports indicative of the moment, perhaps sincere and valuable in the immediate context of utterance but as worthless as foreign currency in the country called the future.

Some will deny even the ephemeral value of momentary oaths. Those who deny the value of Protean promises are probably the same as those who would find truth in the form of propositions in an ideal language. To those for whom the only function of language is a picturing of timeless facts, denoting is the only function of language. Since they feel no need for expletives to express their epiphanies, of course the Protean oath will seem a piece of sheer mendacity.

Protean personalities are experts at the game of making oaths. Whether one will allow them the game depends on whether one knows how to play. To the outsider it looks like the game of troths played poorly. Referees will come running to assure each of the players that they contradict themselves and destroy the very meaning of 'promise' when they make light of their pledges.[19] Speaking of troths the referee is surely correct. But by taking promises only as troths the referee shows his ignorance of oaths. He betrays the limitedness of his linear experience, the leveled character of his Euclidean temporality, the lack of epiphanies in his clockwork existence.[20]

Promises are a problem for the Protean personality, but the *differance* between oaths and troths allows at least a limited sense in which Protean Man can make a promise and mean it: he can express the intention of a moment whose intensity transcends time, a moment in which all past and all future fade into insignificance next to the exigency of passion. Of course such moments can be costly. But the currency of quotidian reality is as nothing when one tastes of eternity . . . and that is precisely the taste of those moments, those discontinuous peaks when the chain of linear time is broken.

For his own special reasons Kierkegaard clothed the Moment in the purple robes of religiosity. His special reasons included a pathological desire for the simplicity of the immediate, a desire that carried him beyond a mere susceptibility to the Moment.[21] The desire for immediacy begets mediated desire, a desire left unsatisfied by immediate sexual consummation. Hence the desire for the immediate looks elsewhere for the consummate. Hence God. For a Dimitri Karamozov eternity is a simpler affair, a moment in the tavern at Mokroe where he squanders all for the love of Gruchenka. Sacred or profane, the discontinuity of time is the same. But neither is available to the sober referee.

Where the maker of troths loses the momentary eternity of oaths, however, he gains time and the *being* that accrues to a node of stable relations. Like the often transient "upwardly mobile" residents of the suburbs, Protean Man suffers a diminution of being from his inability to maintain troths. In the best of all possible worlds one would both maintain troths and retain the capacity to make oaths as well. But this both/and is among the most difficult of all *Aufhebungen* to achieve.

Making oaths and keeping troths defines the problematic that leads Gurdjieff to describe man as a multiplicity of selves: "Man has no individuality. He has no single, big I. Man is divided into a multiplicity of small I's."[22] As evidence for his observation he takes the phenomenon of promising: "Each separate small I is able to call itself by the name of the Whole, to act in the name of the Whole, to agree or disagree, to give promises, to make decisions, with which another I or the Whole will have to deal." From the perspective of his awareness of the simultaneous multiplicity of selves in man, Gurdjieff adds a poignant description of the problem that promising can create for many dimensional man: "A small accidental I may promise something, not to itself, but to someone else at a certain moment simply out of vanity or for amusement. Then it disappears, but the man, that is, the whole combination of other I's who are quite innocent of this, may have to pay for it all his life. It is the tragedy of the human being that any small I has the right to sign checks and promissory notes and the man, that is, the Whole, has to meet them. Peoples' whole lives often consist in paying off the promissory notes of small accidental I's."

No wonder we have become so wary of allowing a multiplicity of *I*s. No wonder identity is critical unto literal crisis. We want to know just who is signing the promissory notes, and further, whether any others are drawing off the same account. Who would give credit to an entire group after checking the references of only one of its number?

The language of economy is altogether apposite in this context because it connotes the *systematic* character of modernity, the universal reach of the institutions of banking and politics that have allowed modern subjects to determine themselves in terms of roles whose status presupposes a stable hierarchy of power and authority. But if the argument of chapter one is correct, if the White House is now the museum-cathedral of a fading era, if the traditional systems of power and authority are now entering a period of decentralization, then the reach of the new institutions of modernity may become less universal than Weber, for one, supposed. Court cases over the Pledge of Allegiance may be as richly symbolic of a larger phenomenon as the flag itself. The context that demands such pledges as the structural supports of its systematic existence, the context that demands troths at the cost of oaths may be ebbing.

The entire phenomenon of promising appears not only in the moral context but also in a historical context.[23] Granting that both keeping troths and making oaths have much to recommend them as well as corresponding prices to be paid, granting that we do not live in the best of all possible worlds where both are possible, it behooves us to attend to just what sort of world we are living in and whether in the balance between troths and oaths we do best to continue giving all to troth as seemed necessary to the builders of the modern empire. Surely we do not want to give all to oath if the cost be the diminution of being characteristic of rootless Protean Man. But the effort to make an ahistorical taboo out of breaking a promise must be restored to the historical context in which a critic of modernity like Nietzsche properly finds it.

The second essay of Nietzsche's *Genealogy of Morals* begins with the question: "To breed an animal with the right to make promises—is not this the paradoxical problem nature has set itself with regard to man? And is it not man's true problem?" Nietzsche finds promising all the more problematic when pitted against what he calls man's faculty of oblivion, a faculty for necessary forgetfulness that sounds very like an anticipation of Freudian censorship. He remarks that pain and punishment have taught men to remember. Yet his attention to the costs of generating the condition for keeping troths does not blind him to the virtues of promising. In a remark containing an explicit rejection of the equation between morality and autonomy he stresses the command of time the troth keeper acquires: "This autonomous, more than moral individual (the terms *autonomous* and *moral* are mutually exclusive) has developed his own, independent, long-range will, which dares to make promises; he has a proud and vigorous consciousness of what he has achieved, a sense of power and freedom, of absolute accomplishment. This fully emancipated man, master of his will, who dares make promises—how should he not be aware of his superiority over those who are unable to stand security for themselves?"[24]—This from the philosopher of Dionysus who above all knows the meaning of oaths; this from the philosopher who prior to Lilly, Hillman and Gurdjieff wrote: *"My hypothesis:* The subject as multiplicity."[25]

Because Nietzsche suspected that despite his praise of the strong individual "the assumption of one single subject is perhaps unnecessary";[26] because he distinguished between the phenomenological *individual* associated with a *perceived* body and the metaphysical *subject* associated with the *concept* of matter, he was driven to ask: "Perhaps it is just as permissible to assume a multiplicity of subjects, whose interaction and struggle is the basis of our thought and our consciousness in general? A kind of aristocracy of 'cells' in which dominion resides? To be sure, an aristocracy of equals, used to ruling jointly and understanding how to command?"[27] And his answer in terms of the sovereign individuals able to make promises is as relevant to the aristocrats who are the several subjects in each individual: "It is natural to him to honor his strong and reliable peers, all those who promise like sovereigns: rarely and reluctantly."[28]

Each of the separate selves, each of the aristocrats in the society within each individual, will make troths with others only rarely and reluctantly, the better to stand security for troths made *and* leave room for the making of oaths as well. For the man who makes too many promises is as Nietzsche remarks a man "who wishes to dispose of his future."[29] No room for oaths remains in time mapped out by troths.

The temporalities of trust and joy

It is an old insight, at least as old as Aristotle who cites Solon before him, that happiness can be ascribed only to the complete life. Like 'numerous' the word 'happy' cannot modify a single moment. No more than a whole life can be embarrassing can a moment be happy. Just as "boys who are called happy are being congratulated by reason of the hopes we have for them,"[30] so a life might be embarrassing by reason of regrets held for many moments within that life. But properly speaking it is moments that may or may not be embarrassing and lives that may or may not be happy. So it is with joy and trust, the former having the moment for its locus, the latter something closer to a life.

The different temporalities of joy and trust demand different selves for their enactment, some very patient, others less so. Like the cattle tick for whom time does not exist during the years the female waits for the breath of butyric acid that will send her catapulting from her perch to the hide of a passing mammal,[31] the keeper of troths may wait years for the event that will fulfill a promise made in the distant past.

Yet is this patience? For the tick it may be argued that up to eighteen years of solar time are as nothing until the proper whiff withdraws the veil of oblivion and a dormant metabolism begins to process information. So with the selves whose scripts do not call for their entry upon the stage of consciousness until the proper cue is given: a cue planted in a promise years ago brings forth a self that lay dormant for years. Only if the stage was utterly vacant of other selves does the maker of the far-flung troth have to come forth prematurely to mumble lines it does not know while waiting patiently for the cue that will start its time. Otherwise, if other selves entertain the audience with their own acts, that self can sleep backstage and bore neither others nor himself. Given enough selves there is no call for the boredom of patience, the endless waiting.

Storytellers sometimes exploit the illusion of fullness in empty time that is therefore no time. The brief story can gain grandiosity by the insertion of a line, ". . . and he waited eighteen long years. . . ." The acute listener may wonder: what was he doing all those years? What is it to *wait?* Was he waiting while he was brushing his teeth each night? Perhaps he pined from time to time . . . as in 'pining away'. But pining too has its limits. If the self that "waits" eighteen years is as wise as the humble tick it will go into dormancy. Once perched on the twig of day to day existence that self will forget to *wait* and will assume instead the oblivion of backstage timelessness. But of course the storyteller will not pause to inform his listeners that, to the self for whom the plot of the story is relevant, time did not exist during most of those eighteen years.

To appreciate the temporality of trust and troth it will be helpful to turn once again to the researches of Robert Ornstein. His first book is a slender volume entitled *On the Experience of Time.* There he records several ingenious experiments designed to show, first, that we have no "inner clock" whose function is to keep track of something called "real time." Rather the many researchers who have attempted to discover such a biological clock in one or another of the rhythms of the body succeeded only in showing the fruitlessness of presupposing anything like a "real time" to be measured. As Ornstein remarks, to call clock time real time is like calling American money real money. The assumption resembles the pretension to a universal language. Relational thought escapes the need for a *basic* dimension of measurement, whether the *differance* to be measured be temporal, economic or linguistic. Rather than assume that our experience of time is the result of some variably "accurate" measurement of "real" or absolute time, "the approach adopted here is a relational one with antecedents in the philosophy of relativity-oriented time analysts."[32]

The second point proven by Ornstein's experiments pertains to what he calls his 'storage size' metaphor for the experience of temporal duration. He shows that the duration experienced is a function of information stored where 'information' is strictly construed according to cybernetic theory. If one codes a given array efficiently so that fewer "bits" are needed to store the information successfully, the experience of taking in that information will seem to have a shorter duration than if one codes the information inefficiently into more bits requiring greater storage capacity. Example: store the sequence one-four-nine-two-one-seven-seven-six-one-nine-eight-zero; now store the dates of America's discovery, independence, and next presidential election.

Ornstein's insights are drawn partly from work with Psylocibin, LSD and marijuana. The experience of greatly lengthened time duration on drugs is nicely explained by the storage-size metaphor: as the doors of perception are flung wide more information gets processed. Hence the sense that a great deal of time has passed while one is high—the eternity of ecstatic joy. The opposite experience, the sense of very short duration as against a relatively long segment of clock time, can be accounted for by the relationship between *interest* and coding: the class "hour" that seemed to pass quickly was one in which information was stored efficiently. The entertaining lecturer evokes laughter that is the "click" attendant to a code unlocked, a dramatic "Of course!" The bore exploits our attentiveness and fills our minds with meaningless garbage whose confusion allows no "fit." The hour drags on and on and on. If one could only go to sleep . . . which would accomplish the temporary *cessation* of that time line. "Next time," thinks the student, "I'll come stoned," which according to Ornstein's model will compensate for the professor's failure to code the information in a way that can be stored efficiently.

That which is intrinsically boring (*very* long duration because "meaningless" information is stored inefficiently) can be rendered extrinsically more interesting (relatively long duration because a great deal of information is processed) by an opening of one's sensibilities. Better still would be the coding of the lecture's information so that the escape from boredom were not a chemically induced fascination with minute differentiations in the tone of the teacher's drone. Better for both would be a clarity of articulation and energy of presentation whose expenditure is painless for both professor and student alike—a series of educational epiphanies with the contents of hours that seemed like minutes.

To return to the storyteller's hero and the humble tick, for both of whom time does not exist for eighteen "long" years: Ornstein's theory deflates the intended grandiosity of the storyteller's device. Unless the storyteller has the skill to introduce further detail that shows the story's hero as maintaining wakefulness with the self about whom the tale is told, unless he can show that the story's hero remained on stage, then his "waiting" is nothing but the dormancy of the cattle tick. His troth may be no more than a slightly discontinuous oath, like the embrace of a long lost friend with whom one never really spent that much time in the first place, just a few joyous moments. With the longer term acquaintance—not the *close* friend but the person who shared *both* joy and boredom—one is more apt to shake hands.

For this intermediate temporality, this middle ground on the spectrum between the epiphanies of joyous oaths and the happiness of troths well kept, we have the less dramatic expression, 'to enjoy'. To enjoy is not perpetually to feel the intensity expressed in 'joy', nor is it to be subject to the peace expressed in 'contentment'. One can enjoy a backrub or a visit, even a whole summer.

But what is it to enjoy if not to experience the physical pulse expressed in joy? Joy is momentary, and it does not follow that to experience joy is to experience happiness. Nor does that which gives joy give also happiness. Yet that which we enjoy can give happiness. One can enjoy one's work. 'Joy', 'enjoy' and 'happiness' express a dimension of fulfilled *nows*, each longer than the previous. Happiness refers to the contemporaneity of an entire life, as when we refer to a happy man, and as Aristotle is led to ask whether we can call a man happy before he is dead. 'Enjoy' refers to a now with less duration than an entire life, but more duration than the now of joy.

'Joy' connotes the physical more than 'enjoy', because the physical is more temporally immediate and the mental or spiritual more temporally mediated. One needs a longer time to achieve the mediation of enjoyment, and the nature of the body is such that it cannot sustain joy's long duration.

Have we a competition? Not necessarily. Just as the present is the present minute, the present hour, the present day, week, month and year, so there is no reason to insist that different sized *nows* must come in series—as if one had first to experience a minute, *then* an hour and *then* a day before beginning a week.[33] The conflict comes only among the potentialities for the *fulfillment* of those existential nows. While the passage of twenty-four hours guarantees the passage of a day, the fulfillment of moments in joy is no guarantee of enjoyment, much less happiness. Without joy there may be little likelihood of happiness, but joy alone does not accumulate as happiness because it lacks the connectivity needed for accumulation. Joy alone passes away like minutes wandering without the direction of an hour. Unconnected joy is nonetheless joy, but it might not be enjoyed. It may not hold together. And to the human being who has a need for some coherence even a multitude of the most intense joys may diffuse into a psychotic existence in which joy alternates increasingly with misery along an emotional path that oscillates wildly from one to the other with no apparent explanation.

The monotheistic tradition sometimes uses that misery to condemn joy. Preaching compromise and moderation the tradition would sacrifice joy in order to avoid misery. Because this "wisdom" lacks insight into the fact that life travels along more than one path of presents, the tradition tries to damp the oscillation by prohibiting joy.

In reaction to the traditional teaching of moderation the contemporary spirit, prodded by youth's appreciation for the immediate, strives to rescue joy from the grave. But reactions lack the truth of synthesis. A blind reaction would buy joy at the price of misery without asking for a true advance in the fulfillment of human existence.

The tradition is wrong, and the reaction is wrong. Nor does the truth 'lie between'—a cheap solution in the name of the very moderation preached by the tradition. To transcend the tradition a different awareness is needed, an awareness of the multilinearity of human time. Joy loosens its bond with misery *and* the hangman's block of moderation when joys are joined in molecular chains.

What is the valency of joy? Joys are necessarily atomic if they are to retain their immediacy—un-mediacy, no mediations, no bonds or linkages or relations. If the single strand of life be the model of human time, then joys are linked only at the price of their immediacy, which is to say at the price of their very existence as joys. The chemistry of joy must have a different adhesive for molecular construction than valency through mediation.

The answer lies not in relations between joys as such but in the multiple significances of the behaviors that produce joy. The most obvious example might be sex as both immediate pleasure and an integral part of a long-term relationship in happiness. Some acts giving joy are parts of larger structures of enjoyment and happiness, others are not. The joy is no less in the latter—therein lies the seduction. Nor is the joy necessarily greater in the former, therein lies the mendacity of the obsequious preacher who proclaims the *joys* of marriage unavailable anywhere else. But sex that is part of a grander scheme leaves less place for the misery that fills in the gaps left by the absence of a grander scheme.

The compossibility of joy and happiness—not their compromise—provides more than a model for the compossibility of oaths and troths. As with the lessons of the body whose successes are direct *evidence* of rational "decisions" reached without a rational hierarchy to adjudicate disputes among conflicting interests, so the compossibility of joy and happiness provides evidence of a multilinear temporal structure in human life. Of course there is other evidence: Ornstein cites in defense of his theory the frequently experienced phenomenon of returning from a vacation and feeling as if one had never left—as if no time had passed between leaving and returning despite the fact that, when one adopts another perspective, one feels as if the vacation lasted a long time. Like Lifton's examples, Ornstein's support the thesis of multidimensionality: the work-self "went to sleep," his timeline snipped until the reawakening with the return to work. Yet upon reawakening the worker does not interpret the time warp as evidence for multiple selves. Rather he says, "Back to Reality," or some such pseudometaphysical nonsense.

Not until the data are *interpreted* do unexplained anomalies become *evidence.* Since new theories demand refutations of rival interpretations so entrenched they seem to describe the obvious, so the theory of selves within selves demands the refutation of an equally "obvious" absolute unity to the self. The sense of necessary singleness intrudes with such unasked alacrity that of course the evidence

for multidimensionality is dismissed or noticed as only oddly intriguing. When faced with the difference between oath and troth, joy and
happiness, or Proteus and Zeus the first response will be a sense of
the necessity to ask, "Which?" Single identity demands a choice. But
both choices are unsatisfactory. A string of Protean oaths will be as
lacking in happiness as the rigid troth of a moralized Zeus is lacking
in joy. Nor will the pallid pursuit of a monolinear intermediate contentment make up for the loss of both extremes. None of these choices
works, yet we continue to regard them as exhausting the catalogue of
human potentiality.

Obviously the choice for both joy and happiness has its risks.
Troths are to be made only rarely and reluctantly, oaths sworn only
with a tacit left-handed wisdom that knows without asking when its
intensity will lead to trouble. Oaths *may* be costly; certain joys *may*
wreck the trust of a lifetime. But is the risk so great that trust in many
dimensional existence must be betrayed? The epiphantic self *can*
dwell backstage of the tedium of the day to day until his cue returns
him to his momentary time.

If the possible richness of the choice for both joy and happiness be in every case weighed against the cautious choice for one or
the other, one suspects that in most cases the many dimensional alternative would carry the day. Yet it does not. Why not? One suspects
that the alternatives are never weighed in this way. The pseudometaphysics of singleness carries the day from dawn onwards and the
prospect of many dimensionality never sees the light of day so immediate is the imposition of unambiguous singleness. The prospect of
multiple selves is literally unthinkable until one is disabused of the
pseudometaphysics of singleness, not only by abstract argument but
by experiences that undermine several of its many paradigms: the
One Self, the One World, the One God, the One Truth.

Our intellectual and cultural tradition favors the rationality
and corresponding customs of *unification*, hence the preoccupation
with single identity whether as relatively fixed (Freud), as develop-
mental (Erikson) or as sequential (Lifton). The following chapter has

two goals: first, to gain a sense of the price we pay for the affirmation of identity in the unification of self; second, to flesh out the meaning (and the price) of disunity or multiplicity. Certainly each has a price. Clearly there have been times when unambiguous identity was worth its price. But Lifton and Erikson are correct to orient their studies toward the importance of the fact that the times, they are a changin'. The question then: are their psychohistorical models of selfhood infected with a metaphysics dating from the same history they see us transcending? Are their models of selfhood not too timely in the sense that they appeal to a rationality that is very much current but altogether inadequate to the present and future fragmentation of history?

Of course these questions have little meaning until others have been raised and clarified if not solved: how has our intellectual tradition stressed unification? Can the affirmation of unity in identity be clarified by attention to its opposite—negation? What is the meaning of disunity in death? In dissonance? In decadence? The next chapter will delve into these dark shadows where Nietzsche will serve as guide in the Orphic underworld. The tour will then reemerge to pause at some of the more positive stations of the polytheistic pantheon.

So much for promises, what has been delivered? After a brief lament over the denial of Dionysus the suggestion of his return led to a reflection on the structure of subjectivity as it manifests itself not in communities, as was the argument of Chapter II; instead the plurality of community within the boundaries of the body is the subject of Chapters III and following. The metaphor of multiple programs ordered under metaprograms and a single self-metaprogrammer gave way to the process of projection and introjection of divine personalities as a model for the individuation of separate selves within the embodied self. Then followed a note on the bodily evidence for a multiplicity of personalities within the self, particularly that division known as the Apollonian/Dionysian.

Having established the fact of the ascent of the Apollonian, and further, having reviewed both the costs and the physiological evidence against allowing Apollonian dominance, the next step led into the labyrinth of internal controls: the superego. The ascent of the Apollonian ego is a function of an alteration in the ego-ideal, an alteration that can be followed in the biography of *pater* Zeus from the arbitrary father of shame culture to the increasingly monotheistic judge of justice in guilt culture.

A quickened pace of change generates psychohistorical dislocation and the flood of imagery from the media mounts into an ego-devastating tidal wave in place of the modest irrigation needed for an intrapersonal garden of delights. The question of ego management changes so radically that neither alterations in the classical Zeussian concept of the superego nor Protean substitutions of one ego-identification for another seem adequate. We are experiencing the death of the self to which the Freudian model was most germane. Protean Man is an acute but ultimately vain effort to save the paradigm. The evidence cited to defend this latest theoretical wrinkle works as well if not better in support of a new and very different theory, a theory that better accounts for a wider domain of experiences. But to explore that domain more fully, to confirm the theory of many dimensional man more completely, we must fetch a wider compass—even unto the underworld.

V Death and Decadence

Opponents of polytheism will pose the following objection: "The self," they will say, "is necessarily single just as God, if he is the true God, must be the Lord of lords and not just one god among others." Critics of religious and psychological polytheism support their objection with an argument similar to mainstream social scientists' support for a central arena of decision making. Just as Parsons and Bell insist that politics is necessarily the central organizing principle of society, so do religious and psychological monotheists insist on the necessity of the one God and the central self. "Otherwise," claim the critics in unison, "the self, the society and the sacred will disintegrate into unintelligible chaos. Without unity there will be no personhood, no polity, no divinity."

The point of this chapter is to show the true source and ultimate groundlessness of fears about disunity. Death and decadence represent two forms of disunity. By exploring their *contributions* to life this chapter will show that disunity is possible without irredeemable devolution into chaos. Following the early sections on death, pain, passion and decadence, a polemic on deception will carry on in a more appropriate tone the earlier, milder and more abstract reflections on truth and hermeneutics. Neitzsche's critique of the will to truth will support the polemic against the positivistic distinction between facts and values. His account of the will to power will appear as the personal transform of transpersonal political power relations. Finally Nietzsche's allegory of Zarathustra will answer Benjamin's exhortation to let wisdom speak through the medium of story.

While this chapter may allay some monotheistic fears, polytheistic hopes remain unjustified without further support for the pluralistic alternative. The issue of positive support is ultimately metaphysical: must anything—self, society or god—be *one* in order to *be?* This chapter postpones metaphysics in favor of a study of the psychological, religious and epistemological archetypes that represent fears about disunity. Once persuaded that there is more to fear in denying those archetypes, the monotheist may be better prepared for the following chapter where the philosophy of Anaxagoras will complete the necessary metaphysical argument for the possibility of intelligibility without unambiguous unity.

Hades and the demons

Before we proceed to other gods the demons beckon. What of the Devil, not the fellow with the cloven hooves, horns and funny ears but a figure less human in form, a figure who better evokes the fears of this age? Who is the Devil?

In trying to identify him this much can be learned from older mug-shots in the police files of human repression: he changes his form. Like Proteus he can assume any form he wishes. His disloyalty extends even into his own "self." And for precisely that reason he is difficult to identify, appearing now in one form, now in another.

The Devil's disloyalty takes other forms besides his Protean disloyalty to prior forms he himself assumes. His disloyalty takes the form of freedom. As is well known he is dishonest. He makes himself appear as something else than what he is (as well as different in appearance from what he *was* in appearance). He is, as is well known, a jailer: he deprives his victims of their freedom. How apt then that he should appear in the guise of a liberator.

The Devil's jail is death. He liberates his victims from life. The Devil negates life. Just as death is the negation of life so liberation in its demonic form presents itself as blessed release from the realities that constitute life.

Like the invention of omnipotence, the invention of everlasting life for "mortals" amounts to a denial of the necessary dialectic between life and death. Just as omnipotence turns over into its opposite, just as the aspiration toward an all-powerful ego generates the sense of impotence experienced by isolated egos unable to touch or be touched by the Other, so the aspiration to everlasting life both generates and reflects a failure to incorporate death in life, a failure whose ramifications are as follows.

First, the well-known *avoidance* of literal, biological death: no need to repeat again the many details that have recently come to light in studies of Americans' attitudes toward death as reflected in funeral practices. To select only the most poignant, take the language and content of casket ads and the very fact that people are willing to pay cash for a casket with a mattress as if the "deceased" (not the dead) were expected to enjoy a long and comfortable sleep.

To the extent that biological death is denied, merely biological life is overvalued. This second ramification of the failure to incorporate death in life emerges in sometimes absurd attitudes toward abortion and euthanasia. At the risk of tautology it is worth observing that only sacred life is sacred and that biological definitions alone are not sufficient to define the sacred. Were we to look the Devil more directly in the eye and there recognize *a part of ourselves* we would see that merely biological man is quite capable of bestiality. The defense of "sacred life" would then be a defense of the sacredness *possible* for biological life, not a defense of the *necessary* sacredness of life. The life that is sacred is the life lived in the presence of death and rebirth, not the life that simply denies the reality of death.

What is it to live in the presence of death and rebirth? The question provokes a plunge into yet a third ramification of the denial of death, namely the denial of all negativity that follows from a literalist focus on the merely biological definition of life. This third ramification of the denial of death is less discussed than the literal dimensions of funeral practices or the increasingly fashionable topics of medical ethics. Yet this third ramification of the exile of Hades from the pantheon of the gods holds more promise for penetrating some of the mysteries of medical ethics than the sometimes scholastic debates over the number of weeks required to give a fetus "life." For the question "What is it to live in the presence of death and rebirth" forces one to abandon the *abstraction* of death.

As has so often been noted one can never truly experience one's own biological death. *That* death is not the one that matters. Anxiety over one's own death—the fabled "being towards death" that figures so prominently in Heidegger's philosophy—is like so much of the rest of existentialism more an index of our age than part of some timeless human condition. Of course all humans die. But attitudes toward death do not remain the same. Some reflect a paralyzing fear of the negative in all its forms: pain and suffering, sickness and decay. Others, e.g., the early Greeks, reflect a courage to accept the concrete forms of negativity that constitute the ongoing rhythm of life culminating in the least painful of the several forms, literal death.

To turn from the risk of tautology in contemplating the sacredness of sacred life to the risk of morbidity in contemplating the less literal forms of death: how do we deny pain and suffering, decay and decadence?

On pain and passion

In one of his more prosaic passages Hegel struggles with the contradiction involved when an individual tries to comprehend the full richness of life in a purely inner way without risking negation by the Other. Hegel describes *la belle âme*, the beautiful soul who "lives in dread of staining the radiance of its inner being by action and existence."[1]

"That which remains always affirmative, is, and remains, without life. Life is built upon negation and pain. It is only by crushing out such contradiction in the crucible of fuller life and knowledge that it remains in its affirmative substance."[2]

Against Hegel's statement certain representatives of the present age would sponsor the following criticisms; first, "What a downer! Why all this pain and suffering? He must have been a Protestant." Second: "How dangerous this talk of crushing out contradictions! Could this be the intellectual backbone of less than intellectual violence?"

The objection reveals more about the present age than about Hegel, namely that the present age fears pain and sees it as a sign of sickness to be done away with. We refuse to see sickness and pain as parts of the language of the soul.[3] Rather than listen to our weaknesses as they articulate the limits of our distinct personalities we would rather erase what appears as imperfection. We would rather aspire to the monotony of monotheistic perfection.

This faith in perfection without suffering characterizes enough representatives of the present age to be almost a hallmark of modernity. Not only Messianic Marxists but mystics and mediators as well advertise uninterrupted bliss, not as a reward for anything but as the natural result of *allowing* life rather than working through it. But Hegel's point is precisely to allow life, to permit its richness even unto its depths, to admit both poles of every contradiction rather than hold on to one pole and deny the reality of the other, e.g., affirmation/ negation, pleasure/pain, life/death, heaven/hell, subject/object, fact/value, finite/infinite, good/evil, et cetera.

Agreed: the Tortured European Intellectual exhibits a syndrome that is now a tired phrase in the sentences of mankind, a phrase difficult to use again without slipping into the banal. The phrase that is the character of the solitary intellectual is a phrase that would roll deftly from the tongue of the literate speaker only to return and convict him of dealing in secondhand goods, of running no better than a pawnshop in the shoddiest neighborhood of the linguistic city. For the neighborhood of the European intellectual is by now such a well-known neighborhood, its highways and byways so well worn, that only the least adventuresome or the most linguistically deprived would content themselves to tread once more along its dark paths.

We know the basic moves for the European intellectual number: suffering, solitary, romantic, rarely capable of joy but always ready for great pain. We know these moves inside out: the individualism, the vacillation between immediate involvement and withdrawal to a critical distance, the anxiety. We know how it feels to feel the dread that plagued Kierkegaard, the unhappy Dane. We know how it tastes to drink from the cup of deep depression whose bittersweet liquid is the black coffee of intellectual life, the elixir of Descartes's "laborious wakefulness."[4] We know the separation of mind and body and the fruitlessness of trying to overcome that split while remaining entirely locked in the language of the mind.

Knowing what we do, we view the Tortured European Intellectual syndrome as a little less inevitable than in earlier days when despair seemed the only way out, the only stance of honesty and integrity. That was our "hour of great contempt" (as Nietzsche likes to put it), our hour of great loathing. But what a difference between the Nietzschean all too European loathing and *Fear and Loathing in Las Vegas*, Hunter Thompson's gonzo-journalistic trip through American madness. Now we are experiencing an upbeat barbarism that Nietzsche talked about but was disinclined to *do*. Now we know the joy of the gay science of experience and from the perspective of its immediacy (not from the perspective of 'critical distance') the effort to mediate every moment, to find meaning in every gesture, ultimate significance in every glance, purpose in life . . . the European effort looks not only fruitless but ludicrous.

No need to hold it against the solitary intellectual that he sets himself apart. Most people live lives devoid of joy. But the *way* he sets himself apart: "I say of my sorrow what the Englishman says of his house: my sorrow is my castle. . . . My melancholy is the most faithful mistress I have known; what wonder, then, that I love in return."[5] The unholier than thou posturing that extends to a literal stance of drawn up shoulders and tucked in head, the scowl, the intense walk, the tight throat that will not cry—these are unnecessary.

Agreed: the syndrome that seeks *only* the subterranean depths of Hades is to be despised.

Nevertheless Nietzsche was clearly right to protest the fear of suffering that leads to a lack of passion. Complaints about the passion of suffering manifest in Nietzsche may be more an index of our own fear of passion than a testament to our elevation or spiritual progress. We are not so "high" as to be able to look down on all of the tortures of European intellectuals. To the contrary: precisely our spiritual shortness, our lack of elevation, our failure to attain whatever height or heroism or antiheroic ideal we posit and before which we experience shame if not guilt; precisely our failure to become "realized beings" (note the Aristotelian essentialism implicit in this popular formulation); precisely our failure to attain the uninterrupted bliss that some of us suppose to be the natural condition of man, precisely this lack of bliss renders us unable to take seriously the "involuntary bliss" that beset Nietzsche more than once.[6]

He was not simply a sufferer. Occasionally he dwelt on "the Blessed Isles." But we who fear passion confirm our fear by remembering only the reports of suffering, the scribblings of "the midnight hour." We do not take seriously "the great noon" that is its contradiction, its dialectical correlate and opposite imaginary pole on the dimension that defines marginal differences quite other than the backs and forths of space and time. We forget Nietzsche's reports of the great noon because we so fear the midnight that we decline to enter the dimension of passion much less allow an increase of amplitude in our oscillations. Because we decline to enter that dimension we are radically incomplete, we moderns, we civilized men . . . even we new-age Buddhists who eschew our heritage with an enlightened rejection of the hocus-pocus of a transcendent miracle worker. The turn to the more secular teaching of desirelessness manifests an internalization of transcendence, a will to transcend our own ego-entrenching attachments, our desires. We too, we neo-Buddhists, should be ashamed (not guilty) of our lack of passion. The price we pay for power is a loss of passion. Total control is then equivalent to estrangement from the demons. Having closed the gates to the underworld we live lives devoid of death's lively representatives; and intimations of rebirth are denied us as well.

Not so for Nietzsche, whose adventures in the Orphic underworld qualify him to serve as a guide through those murky chambers. The fourth part of *Thus Spake Zarathustra* is a coda that forestalls the cadence that would complete the first three parts. That same coda forestalls the cadence that would close the gates to the underworld. The story of the fourth part, Zarathustra's further wanderings, his meetings with 'the higher men', his ecstasy and his midnight hour, will serve as a second organizing principle for the following chapters. In addition to a partial inventory of the Olympian pantheon, the tale of Zarathustra will be interpreted as an allegory for the plurality of the "single" self. Like the many dimensional man it describes, the following narrative has not only several parts but more than one organizing principle for those parts. Life is not simple.

Decadence

Decadence is rich in ambiguity. 'Decadence' connotes both the closing time of time of decay and the lack of closure in music deprived of cadence. Norman O. Brown's *Closing Time* is a purposefully dissonant etude on themes of decline and decadence from Vico and Joyce's *Finnegans Wake*. This literature of decadence is not only a lament. On the contrary, for Brown, Joyce, Spengler and Vico as well as Baudelaire, Stefan Zweig, Oscar Wilde and Apuleius, the literature of decadence represents a richer and more elaborate harmony of elements denied in the simple and sometimes insipid cadences of more classical precursors. As Jaye Miller concludes in his "Reflections on Decadence": "In forcing us to look at all of life, its births and its deaths, its good and its evil, its madness and health, its norms and its 'perversities,' the literature of decadence harbors an almost religious hope that we might have life and have it more abundantly."[7]

If cadence is a final chord struck in the tonic with terminal impact, decadence is the lack of such unambiguous closure. In life, which is similar to music in many ways, cadence is not simply death. It is as much the availability of a tonic to return to. Arnold Schoenberg, author of the twelve-tone method of avoiding a tonic, is therefore the decadent composer par excellence. Nor is it any accident that Theador Adorno, author of *Negative Dialektik* (a dialectic without closure), should have been the one to recognize Schoenberg's importance as the composer most in tune with modernity.[8]

The lack of an available tonic in decadent music of multiple tones corresponds to what Miller finds as the "central insight" of the literature of decadence: "Man is a combination of multiple selves."[9] Miller cites the conclusion of Herman Hesse's *Steppenwolf* as showing the main character "that he is all things, that his personality is a multifaceted, diamond-like gem reflecting the most divergent personality traits, experiences, and sensibilities."[10] An even richer example is the conclusion of Nietzsche's *Thus Spake Zarathustra*.

The "fourth and final" part of *Zarathustra* is a celebration of selves within selves. Even the occasion of its composition is in keeping with the contest against closure. Nietzsche had intended the third part as its completion.[11] Yet he could not rest. Just as the soothsayer returns to Zarathustra to proclaim his nihilistic weariness yet once more, so the perpetual incompleteness of his own becoming returns once more to Nietzsche in the voice of Zarathustra, a voice not so much invented as a voice that "invaded" him.[12] This voice is *one* of Nietzsche's own though not the only voice Nietzsche knew.[13] Still it is Zarathustra's voice, or Nietzsche when he hears Zarathustra, who knows best about the plurality of voices that generate a will to power. The fourth part of *Zarathustra* displays the many voices of Nietzsche-Zarathustra in a hall of mirrors called "higher men." Not only does Nietzsche decline to speak directly to his readers—for, "All that is profound loves a mask"[14]—but the very act of wearing Zarathustra as one of many masks is mirrored in the literary device of letting Zarathustra's many voices speak through other mouths with words like Zarathustra's own. These "higher men" whom Zarathustra meets on his walk through the wilderness each parrot back to him words and phrases uttered earlier by Zarathustra. But just as Nietzsche was unwilling to let his teaching stand in a state of pseudocompletion so Zarathustra is displeased with the false finality with which his words are uttered. As Zarathustra chastises each of his literal-minded hearers, warnings sound for literal-minded readers of the first three parts of *Zarathustra.* Each and every one-sided and simplistic interpretation of Nietzsche's Zarathustra receives the ridicule it deserves. As with Hegel, the truth is the whole. Only when all the higher men are gathered together in the cave symbolizing the depth of Zarathustra's soul, only then does the fullness of Zarathustra's experience burst forth at both noon and midnight.

Prior to the culmination of opposition in the juxtaposition of midnight to noon, the display of opposites so characteristic of decadence plays itself out through ordered pairs of higher men that Zarathustra meets. The pattern is unmistakable once noticed: first Zarathustra meets the soothsayer, the voice of Nietzsche's nihilism.

Despite the "Yes and Amen Song" that concluded part three the spirit of nausea and negativity returns as Nietzsche knows it must.[15] The opposition of No to Yes and Yes to No is the contradictory stuff of Zarathustra's most dialectical existence: "The psychological problem in the Zarathustra-type is: how he who to an unheard of degree both says no and does no to everything to which man has so far said Yes can be in spite of that the opposite of a nay-saying spirit."[16]

As if this first meeting between Zarathustra and the soothsayer were not a clear enough herald of the coming play of mirror opposites, his second meeting brings him face to face to face with two kings, one of whom speaks, "Nausea! Nausea! Nausea!" to which the other replies, "Your old illness is upon you." The kings are conveniently named according to another simple opposition; the king on the right and the king on the left. The king on the right announces the theme of the fourth part still more explicitly: "O Zarathustra, how well we did to go forth to see you! For your enemies showed us your image in their mirror."

Zarathustra's third encounter mirrors his own activity immediately prior to his meeting with the soothsayer, the meeting just mimicked in the relationship between the two kings. First he had made his honey sacrifice. With the honey of his happiness he cast far and wide "to see if many human fish might not learn to wriggle and writhe from my happiness until, biting at my sharp hidden hooks, they must come up to my height." Now he stumbles across a man lying beside a swamp in which he dangles his arm for leeches to come and suck his blood. The man calls himself *the conscientious in spirit* . . . and in matters of the spirit there may well be none stricter, narrower and harder." He too parrots Zarathustra's sayings back to his teacher, and just as the kings had provoked "no small temptation to mock their eagerness," so the conscientious in spirit teaches Zarathustra much about his students, but nothing that he wants to pour back into strict and literal-minded ears.

Zarathustra's fourth encounter is more serious than his previous meetings which, aside from presenting details whose richness of

symbolic content might take pages to unravel, also establish the formal framing device that renders the fourth encounter so serious. Up
to this point it has been a game that Nietzsche plays with his reader,
this display of the many selves of Zarathustra. But now, as if to test
claim, "Of all that is written I love only what a man has written with
his blood,"[17] Nietzsche allows the game to be played between himself
and Zarathustra. Does he enter the frame like a painter doing a self-
portrait? Or does he allow the frame he has fabricated to reach out
and encompass him who erected the frame? Has Nietzsche accomplished in prose something like what Valasquez accomplished in his
painting "Las Meninas," namely a representation that not only
catches the representer but the very relationship of representation
itself?[18]

    Zarathustra encounters a magician but the magician is unmis-
takably the author of *Zarathustra* himself suffering and dissembling
as only Nietzsche knew he suffered and dissembled. Zarathustra
listens for a time to his moaning and poetic groaning, to his lament for
the loss of his unknown god, to his fears and ambivalences and his
final cry, "Oh, come back, my unknown god! My *pain!* My last—
happiness!"

    "At this point however Zarathustra could no longer restrain
himself. He raised his stick and started to beat the moaning man with
all his might." Zarathustra sees through the charade and recognizes
the mockery the magician would make of Zarathustra's own ambivalences toward the death of god. So far so good. But why is Zarathustra
so much more outraged than he had been by the mockery made of his
'truths' by the earlier higher men? Why if not that this magician has
not merely disappointed Zarathustra with one-sided simplicity but
rather deceived him by his polymorphous complexity? Just as Nietzsche has deceived his most literal-minded readers by letting them
believe that the higher men he ridicules are characters quite other
than the noble Zarathustra, so the magician deceives Zarathustra with
an image of otherness. But just as Zarathustra is justifiably angry with
the magician so the reader has the right to be angry with Nietzsche.

And Nietzsche knows it, as his self-portrait in the speech of the magician shows: "O Zarathustra, I am weary of it; my art nauseates me; I am not *great*, why do I dissemble? But you know it too—I sought greatness. I wanted to represent a great human being and I persuaded many; but this lie went beyond my strength. It is breaking me. O Zarathustra, everything about me is a lie; but that I am breaking—this, my breaking, is genuine."

Far better than the frequent remarks of commentators to the effect that the fourth part is an unimportant experiment not to be considered on a plane with the rest of *Zarathustra,* these blood-stained words explain Nietzsche's extreme reticence in making the fourth part public.[19] The magician suffers from what Nietzsche, referring to himself as author of *Zarathustra,* called the *rancune,* or rancor, of what is great: "Everything great, a work, a deed, once completed then turns itself instantly against him who did it. By the very fact that he did it he is henceforth weak—he can prolong his deed no longer, he faces it no more. To have something *behind* one that one could never have willed, something in which the knot of human destiny is tied—and to have it henceforth heavy on one's shoulders . . . is very nearly crushing! The *rancune* of greatness!"[20] This Nietzsche wrote as part of a self-interpretive tract that again and again cites *Zarathustra* as his greatest work. Though the same *Ecce Homo* also includes the reference to the "third (last)" part of Zarathustra, the explanation of the *rancune* of greatness with its echo of the magician's plight gives clear testimony to the importance of the fourth part: Nietzsche needed to prolong his greatest work, to forestall closure. He needed to maintain that decadent contradiction of selves without fixing their plurality in a form that the public's hard and narrow gaze would surely reduce to one simple unity or another.

As if the message of the fourth part were pressing through the pledge to privacy *Ecce Homo* describes Zarathustra as "contradicting himself with every word, this most yea-saying of all spirits; yet in him all oppositions are bound to a new unity." In these words it is not hard to recognize a description of Nietzsche, who wrote to his friend Gast

(25 July 1882): "in many ways, body and soul, since 1876 I've been more a battlefield than a man." Of course the pain of opposition is wretched, but less to be despised than "wretched contentment."[21] Of course the disunity of opposition is difficult, but less to be condemned than the unity of premature or, as Sennett puts it, purified identity.

The new unity that Nietzsche ascribes to Zarathustra demands Hegel's categories for its description: it is a unity in disunity, identity in difference. "Such process and activity again, through which the substance becomes actual, are the estrangement *(Entfremdung)* of personality, for the immediate self, i.e., the self without estrangement and holding good as it stands, is without substantial content, and the sport of these raging elements. Its substance is thus just its relinquishment, and the relinquishment is the substance, i.e., the spiritual powers forming themselves into a coherent world and thereby securing their subsistence."[22]

The new unity, the subsistence that survives the "sport of these raging elements," is precisely that *complex* Nietzsche calls the will to power. "Willing," he writes in *Beyond Good and Evil,* "seems to me first and foremost something *complex,* something that is a unity only as a word." Very much in keeping with the structures of agency traced in Chapters I and II, Nietzsche names three factors in his phenomenology of volition: first a plurality of feelings *(Gefuhlen)* including a sense of direction *away* from—that is, a primary *differance* that secondarily leaves a sense of agency in its wake; and a feeling of *towards* whose directionality is so characteristic of *intention.* Second, *thought is* that which gives intentionality its content. "Thirdly, willing is not only a complex feeling and thinking but is above all characterized by affect: namely, the affect of command."

Neither the will to power nor willing in general has anything to do with "free will" in the sense of an unconstrained will. Of the will taken in this popular sense, of the single will that could be characterized in its autonomy as either weak or strong, Nietzsche writes to the bewilderment of those who fix too quickly on the phrase, will to power: "Weakness of the will: that is a metaphor than can prove misleading. *For there is no will,* and consequently neither a strong or a weak will. The multitude and disgregation of impulses, the lack of systematic order among them, emerges as 'weak will'; their coordination under the domination of one emerges as 'strong will'—the first case is an oscillation and lack of a center of gravity; the second a precision and clarity of direction."[23] The difference between voluntary and involuntary behavior has nothing to do with a metaphysical violation of causality; rather the difference hinges on the kinds and structures of constraints exhibited. Some structures, those with a lack of clarity, with the randomness characteristic of the concept of nature, are properly called involuntary; those with the clarity of intention characteristic of what we call mind are properly called voluntary. Neither structure depends on the presence or absence of some single substance called the will. 'Voluntary' is not a *name* for a single entity called the will but an *ascription* like 'organized' or 'happy' that can be ascribed only to certain complexes fulfilling certain criteria, namely those that Nietzsche associates with the will to power—and they are several.

Nietzsche's polemical tone testifies to his own experience of command. Only our oversimple pictures of command lead to a confusion between command and the simplicity of a 'strong will'. He for his part was perfectly clear about the *duality* implicit in command: "So far as we are at once the one commanding *and* the one obeying in a given instance, and as obeying become acquainted with the feelings of constraint, impulsion, pressure, resistance and movement that tend to arise with an act of will; so far as we have on the other hand the habit of disregarding this duality and setting in its place the synthetic concept of 'I', there follows a whole chain of erroneous conclusions about the act of willing, and further false evaluations of the will as well."[24] The polemics of command need not be restricted to one ruler. Nor were they in the contradictory characters of Nietzsche and Zarathustra. For both it remained open to offer command to each of several selves from time to time. In each case the delight of command was evidence of a will to power, and the agony of "self-overcoming" evidence of a change of command. "'Freedom of the will'—that is the expression for that multiplex pleasure of one who wills, who commands and identifies himself with the executor of an order—who so identifed enjoys the triumph over obstacles but secretly thinks that it was his will that overcame them. So it is he adds to the delight of the commander the pleasure of those useful 'underwills' or under-souls who enjoy the joy of being successful performing instruments—our body is really only a social structure of many souls."[25]

Hermes and truth

Many souls appear in the fourth part of Zarathustra, Nietzsche's census of the society of his selfhood. The magician is among the most frightening because he threatens the very visibility of those faces (or masks) that are his separate *personae*. Nor can he hear them in the darkness if they are ever deceptive. Like Dionysus who threatens the prospect of generously allowing a place for each by refusing to stay in his place, the magician threatens the proposal to allow a voice for each when he assumes all voices. Zarathustra, faithful to a courage that cannot be cautious, admits to having been deceived. But he angrily admonishes the magician: "But you—you *must* deceive: so do I know you. You must always be equi-, tri-, quatri-, quinquevocal."

The magician is Hermes the trickster, the playful impish messenger who is an agent of deception. And what a price we pay for admitting him *too* into the polytheistic pantheon. Gone is the hope of what Habermas calls communicative competence.[26]* Gone is the prospect of clear and unequivocal signals that would replace the opacity of both the self and the literal social order with a transparent statement of desires as well as a clear and technologically proficient medium for their satisfaction. No such luck! Literalism is the underside of honesty, deception the underside of ambiguity. Not all good things go together.[27] If we want total honesty then we pay with the single vision of Newton's sleep. If we accept ambiguity for the sake of the richness of perpetual interpretability then we pay with inexpungible deception.

As much as he is angered and threatened by the magician's test Zarathustra must invite him to his cave because Nietzsche knows "the will to truth" itself as hiding a deeper deception, namely the belief in a "true world" behind the appearances that supposedly deceive and are therefore to be denied. Nietzsche condemns that will to truth as a sign of weakness and unwillingness to live in the Dionysian world of flux and instability. "Man seeks 'the Truth', a world that is not self-contradictory, does not deceive, does not change, a *true* world—a world in which one does not suffer; contradiction, deception, change—causes of suffering!"[28]

In welcoming Hermes in the person of the magician—and the magician in the person of himself—Nietzsche reclaims the greatness he forswears in the speech of the magician. For precious few among Western thinkers have dared to blaspheme the monotheistic god of inquiry itself: the one true Truth. The test of inquiry has always been a willingness and ability to find the Truth *beneath* the illusion, the fruit beneath the rind. Who was there to say that the object of inquiry was more like an onion—nothing but layer upon layer of so-called illusion whose totality must therefore be taken as all that remains of so-called truth?[29]* Even the unpopular skeptics were inclined to say, or be interpreted as saying, that the rind was impenetrable: that there was such a thing as the Truth but that we mortals could not know it. The task of inquiry and the test of its success had always been the attainment of the Truth, whatever the cost (think of poor Oedipus and his hold on the deepest Freudian layers of imagination). Then comes Nietzsche who challenges not the previous winners in the contest of locating the Truth but rather the rules of the contest. Like a runner who races for the sheer delight of the occasion then waits to join hands with his follower to cross the finish line in tandem, thereby enraging the judges of a (trumpets, please) Sanctioned AAU Event,

Nietzsche challenges the deepest convictions of those who enter the chase for different reasons and with altogether different expectations about its outcome.

Nietzsche makes his challenge explicit. He condemns the victims of the will to truth of weariness with the ambiguity of *this* life, of "contempt, hatred for all that perishes, changes, varies." What kind of man seeks The Truth? "An unproductive, *suffering*, a kind weary of life."[30]

"What then was Nietzsche doing writing books?" So goes the usual response to the totally undermining, root-lifting radical attack on the age-old tree of knowledge. "How can he claim that what *he* says is true if there is no truth?" But that is not what he said.[31] *The will to* truth is the foremost object of his attack. Just as the usual picture of the will in general leads to a whole chain of false conclusions about volition, so the will to truth leads to a chain of false conclusions about the nature of truth in general. What are those false conclusions? And what does Nietzsche put in their place?

The concept of truth in general offers yet another instance of the usefulness of relational thinking and the margin of *differance*. Like the concept of objectivity, the meaning of 'truth' does not depend on a reference to a single domain at some distance beyond our subjective and sometimes errant perceptions. Just as the axis of subjectivity and objectivity is not determined by substantial poles between which a gulf of solipsism would yawn wide, just as the meaning of 'objectivity' is made manifest in countless oppositions to various kinds of subjectivity—prejudice, provincialism, privacy, bias and so on—so the axis of truth and error does not hang by some referential hook into the One True World but derives its meaning from countless differentiations between how something appeared and how it was later discovered to be, what someone said and what they were discovered to have been hiding, what one thought to be and later discovered to be an error. To make sense of these mundane margins between truth and error it is unnecessary to project The Truth as the ultimate destination of an asymptotic approach of marginal differentiations. The projection of The Truth is, as Nietzsche saw, a piece of laziness. It is as if one were tired of eating every time the margin between hunger and satiety gnawed at one's stomach and therefore eschewed mere meat and potatoes in preference for The Food that would never need to be eaten again. How Tasteless!

Truthful pluralism

To guard against the traps set by language with its nouns and its verbs—its singular agents and its doings done by agents[32]—let the modifier 'truthful' be the relational transform of 'The Truth' in substance talk. Then the task is to ask under what conditions it makes sense to ascribe the term truthful. The project is very like foregoing the search for The Will in favor of asking when it makes sense to call an action voluntary. Or, to recall the contribution of a preeminently relational thinker ahead of his time, instead of asking what Reality is, to pose the question "Under what circumstances do we think things real?"[33] Like William James, whose pragmatism shares significant affinities with the phenomenological movement,[34] when one pursues this sort of *Radical Empiricism* one arrives at *A Pluralistic Universe*. To cite the section headings of James's chapter on "The Perception of Reality" rather than the titles of his later books, one arrives at "The Various Orders of Reality" and "The Many Worlds," of which James lists no less than seven species: (1) the world of sense, (2) the world of science, (3) the world of ideal relations, (4) the world of illusions or prejudices common to the race, (5) the various supernatural worlds, (6) the various world of individual opinion and (7) the worlds of sheer madness and vagary.[35]

The spirit of positivism will doubtless retort that 'world' and 'truth' have been so construed as to render a night in which all cows are black: if *anything* can qualify as real or true then the words have no meaning and nothing is real or true. Not so. The point is simply, as Austin saw, that no single and utterly general account can be given for the many ways, the many conditions under which we attribute reality.[36] So it is with sacredness or divinity, and similarly with truthfulness as well.

At a certain time in human history the drive toward generality or conceptual unity covering phenomenal plurality clearly had its place and its importance. The difficulty Socrates experiences in getting his interlocutors to understand what he means in his attempts to find connotative rather than denotative definitions for the virtues, his sometimes tedious repetition of examples showing how to identify what different cases bearing the same name have in common demonstrate that the move toward abstract generality was extremely unfamiliar and difficult for the robust Greeks. But we monotheistic moderns have, as Nietzsche argues, learned our Socratic lessons all too well.[37] If it can be said that the prescientific savage suffers from a conceptual anarchy of utterly particularized plurality then it is equally true that we moderns suffer under a conceptual tyranny of unity.[38]

There is a way between, a parapolitics of concepts, a paraconsciousness in which the dimension of generality and particularity does not stretch between bare particulars and abstract entities called universals but grows by margins of generalization only as far as situations demand. To expose the relation between the overgeneralizing quest for the One and the way its restraint demands admitting the deceptive Hermes into the polytheistic pantheon, the present tour through the Mephistophelian underworld could hardly move ahead more eloquently than with an appropriate if rather long quotation from James:

> You reach the Mephistophelian point of view as well as the point of view of justice by treating cases as if they belonged rigorously to abstract classes. Pure rationalism, complete immunity from prejudice, consists in refusing to see that the case before one is absolutely unique. It is always possible to treat the country of one's nativity, the house of one's fathers, the bed in

which·one's mother died, nay, the mother herself if need be, on a naked
equality with all other specimens of so many respective genera. It shows
the world in a clear frosty light from which all fuliginous mists of affection,
all swamp-lights of sentimentality, are absent. Straight and immediate action becomes easy then—witness a Napoleon's or a Frederick's career. But
the question always remains, 'Are not the mists and vapors *worth* retaining?' The illogical refusal to treat certain concretes by the mere law of
their genus has made the drama of human history. The obstinate insisting
that Tweedledum is *not* Tweedledee is the bone and marrow of life. Look
at the Jews and the Scots, with their miserable factions and sectarian disputes, their loyalties and patriotisms and exclusions,—their annals now
become a classic heritage, because men of genius took part and sang in
them.[39]

The Scots know the social philosophy of some as the unar-
ticulated essence of the clan. They have found in their cold northern
spirits their various ways to temper the barbarity of Dionysian tribalism with the demands of a more Apollonian order replacing the tribe
with the clan. To have danced the Scottish dances to the drone and
wheedle of bagpipes, to have felt the warp and woof of one's own tar-
tan in its distinctness from others, is to know that the Scots accomplished a weaving of winter's chill with the warmth of summer—a
fraternal union of Dionysus and Apollo.

What has Hermes to do with this fraternal union of Dionysus
and Apollo? Hermes sets the condition for the possibility of their union as equal brothers by checking the power of Apollo, the god of
healing, the *principium individuationis.* Without Hermes the plurality
of pathologies run rampant must give way to the single ideal of perfect
health, the dull ideal of the perfect individual represented at its best
in the person of Jesus Christ. Without Hermes all men are bound to
the One True Apollonian image of what it is to be a single perfect individual.

Not to deny the depth of that image of death and resurrection
or its richness in representing the agonies of contradiction in the symbolism of the cross—think of the indignity of being nailed up on a
cross prior to an honorable precedent: pinioned between two nails as

if between contradictory right and left hands, stretched toward one side by the nail of time driven deep into the timber of existence and on the other by the nail of eternity slanted ever so carefully to exert the maximum pull against the attractions of time; or desire on the one side and desirelessness on the other; or decisiveness on the one, comprehensive wholeness on the other. (Nota bene, the nature of *this* opposition, as Kierkegaard correctly saw, is such that it can never be easily 'comprehended' without, at the very moment of successfully comprehending both sides, sacrificing the side of decisiveness, the exigency of the either/or.) Not to deny the symbolic power of the cross, pick whatever contradictions you feel to be rending your existence, then picture the crucifixion ceremony as beginning with mankind choosing one of its number to lie down on a literal piece of wood to enact or reify or make perceptually real this otherwise real contradictory character of existence . . . and suffer of it. Without denying the richness of the symbolism of Christ on the cross or the wisdom of rendering divinity fully incarnate, nevertheless: to celebrate contradiction as causing suffering is to give only a one-sided view of the contradictoriness of existence. For there is richness in existence rent with contradictions.

However human the Christ may be in comparison with the God of Abraham, nevertheless the Christian compromise between Athens and Jerusalem sacrifices the pluralism of the twelve tribes of Israel to the unity of the monotheistic God of Abraham. However much more vivid than the lacy abstractions of Platonism and its aftermath, the Christian compromise sacrifices the polytheistic pantheon of the early Greeks to the unity of the neo-Platonic One. However much Jung may find in the image of Christ as a symbol of selfhood, Hillman is nevertheless correct to criticize Jung for emphasizing the archetype of single selfhood to the detriment of his own best pluralistic impulses.[40]

Pluralism, the life of multidimensionality and many centers, cannot survive the supremacy of the principle of individuation. The point is not that there is anything particularly or irrevocably wrong with any image, Christian or otherwise, that serves in the role of model of perfection. The problem is the role itself, the very idea of one best way. To challenge the single ideal it is not enough to pretend liberality with respect to valuations in a single world of unequivocal facts. It is not enough to chant *de gustibus non disputandum* while marching under a banner of positivism with respect to facts. The attempt to admit the monism of One Truth amidst a pluralism of values cannot survive the separation of facts from values because valuation separated from facticity becomes utterly arbitrary. Anything goes. All is permitted. Nihilism of the worst kind is the result.

Why 'of the worst kind'? Because there is a nihilism that is necessary for an acknowledgment of the lack of a True World the knowledge of which would guarantee rectitude of purpose. One needs Nietzsche's nihilism of the strongest in order to acknowledge the lack of a Platonic hierarchy, unknown or otherwise. No such univocal standard awaits the moral agent to determine like Saint Peter at the gate whether he has or has not fulfilled some god-given single purpose for man. Man makes his own roles. His histories determine the ever-changing criteria for fulfillment of a plurality of possible patterns for human excellence. Contrary to that worst kind of nihilism in which it would seem that all is permitted, contrary to the simplistic conclusion that the lack of a single transcendent standard of excellence means anything goes, the histories created by humans generate their own sets of immanent standards before which men may be ashamed or exalted.

Because facts and values are not utterly distinct, because valuation draws on what is as well as what might be, a positivism of facts generating a picture of the One True World—whether or not completed in encyclopedic detail—is bound to replace the transcendent standards of a monotheistic judge with an immanent tribunal of univocal data before which all evaluations are to be measured. Because facts and values are not utterly distinct the positivistic picture of the One True World of facts cannot finally maintain its nihilistic liberalism. Taste *will* be disputed. Further, the tribunal of facts cannot finally tolerate evaluations that challenge its own deepest preju-

dice: the *value* of objectivity. Consequently, the claim to liberal tolerance turns hollow; the liberty of individualism issues in the monotony
of secular monotheism; the positivistic scientist proves himself to be a
closet Christian. In the name of the one true religion of univocal
facts, in the name of the value of objectivity, all attempts at creative
praxis appear sick (not sinful) or deviant (not devilish).[41]

A coherent pluralism can survive only when certain general
conditions are met. Of course the monism of an absolute, transcendent and single ideal means instant death to pluralism. But its opposite, the dark valley of the shadow of a nihilism in which nothing has
taken His place, where all is permitted, offers less than a fertile soil
for the growth of several ways of life. Apart from any standards at all
life cannot support itself in any determinate species or types. Arbitrary randomness reduces all to entropy. In place of the transcendent
standard of value immanent standards take root, but if immanent,
then based on the facts of history. Here Hermes makes his entrance,
for without Hermes, without the inexpungible deceptiveness of human action, pluralism will wither before the onslaught of a monism of
a single, albeit immanent, standard.

To put the point in language that the Apollonian mind might
appreciate, pluralism of values can survive only if nourished upon an
epistemological pluralism. Only if knowledge itself admits the plurality of many truths can many corresponding patterns of valuation be
confirmed. Again, this does not mean that anything anyone says is
therefore true, else 'truth' would have no meaning. Marginal differentiations between truth and error and mutual confirmations made by
communities of inquirers guarantee implicit universality to the concept of truth. But just as those marginal differentiations do not necessarily proceed toward a Reality to which they supposedly correspond,
so the several communities of inquirers need not be bound to a faith
in their ultimate coalescence in one community of agreement in order
that the concept of truth make sense.[42]*

Of course there will always be translators to insist that though
the various linguistic communities use different words they mean the
same thing. But what "mean the same thing" means in such global

contexts is less than perfectly clear. Meanwhile those of us wandering about the tower of Babel wondering at the multiplicity of tongues need not take this new tribalism as the mark of some terrible crime. On the contrary it is a reflection of one of the conditions of our freedom.

If Hermes be expelled, if the sense of what is foreign (as in foreign language) be eliminated by enlightened intellects who let the image of One True World occlude the clarity of our obvious opacity to ourselves and to one another—culturally speaking, as much if not more so than individually speaking—should there then be surprise if 'freedom' in the fully explicit environment of the One True World comes to feel curiously like one species of Sartre's ridiculous absolute freedom, namely freedom in chains? Like a false dawn the frost of artificial clarity falls on a horizon whose cows *are* all black: all 'free' in the explicit recognition of the *single* necessity of the One True World, thus all irrevocably determinate.

Hermes does not *create* the morning mist that James finds worth preserving. Hermes personifies that obvious opacity that precedes all attempts at artificial clarity. He stands for an intrinsic deceptiveness that is but another name for irreducible multidimensionality. The so-called 'same' not only *appears* differently in different dimensions. Because the different appearances, like the peels of an onion, constitute the whole, the so-called same would be the totality of *différance* . . . *would* be if it were not for the nature of *différance* always to defer the closure of premature totalization, always to leave open the hermeneutic horizon, Hermes's playground.

Breaking, lying, losing and regaining

The price of this opacity and openness is the perpetual possibility of failure. Hermes forecloses the prospect of some final proof, some magic conclusion that would once and for all unlock all the riddles of life and allow everyone to live happily ever after. To face this foreclosure on perfection Zarathustra must forswear happiness.[43] To him the *preoccupation* with happiness is a sign of the decadence of weakness, a will to deny flux by fixing on one happy Truth. Not that Nietzsche denies all happiness—he has his involuntary bliss—but the voluntary preoccupation with happiness is denied. He is willing to risk unhappiness, failure, defeat—even his own breaking under the burden of creation he cannot maintain. "I sought greatness," says the magician. "I wanted to represent a great human being and I persuaded many; but this lie went beyond my strength," says the deceptive Hermes. "It is breaking me. O Zarathustra, everything about me is a lie; but that I am breaking—this, my breaking, is genuine," writes Nietzsche, who knew the *rancune* of what is great.

By breaking the frame of his own creation, by entering the picture or allowing the picture to envelop him, Nietzsche *shows* the openness of *differance* that Derrida has difficulty *saying* without presenting it with more closure than is appropriate. In the fourth part of Zarathustra he renders incomplete what had been prematurely complete, namely the first three parts. He does so by completing the exposure of his incompleteness, his capacity for breaking, yet in such a way that the reader cannot come away with the univocal interpretation that Nietzsche was weak. Nietzsche's magic sets up an infinite oscillation between interpretations, neither of which is adequate alone, both of which contradict each other. Zarathustra says, "It does you credit that you sought greatness, but it also betrays you. You are not great. You wicked old magician, this is what is best and most honest about you, and this I honor: that you wearied of yourself and said it outright: 'I am not great.'" All the while we know that now Nietzsche is building himself up for tearing himself down—and the cycle will repeat itself infinitely.

Nietzsche's breaking of frame perfectly illustrates what Goffman observes in his *Frame Analysis:* "A self deprecator is, in a measure, just that, and in just that measure is not the self that is deprecated. He secretes a new self in the process of attesting to the appraisal he is coming to have of himself."[44] By breaking frame in exposing his own breaking Nietzsche therefore *shows* in the *form* of his dissembling artistry precisely what its *content* would *say*, namely an illustration of the perpetual oscillation among selves.

Each self is a perspective on variously interpretable experiences of the whole person. Because each self interprets differently—else it would not *be* a different self—its interpretations look like lies to at least some other selves: e.g., was that persistence courage or wasn't it really just plain stubbornness? Is this feeling love, or infatuation? What is to distinguish one self's hard-earned hope from another's foolish optimism? And so on. This intrapersonal 'lying' is Hermes's work. Without him we slide into the "single vision" of "Newton's sleep."[45]

A certain deceptiveness is essential to Aphrodite as well. Her beauty prompts Hesiod to introduce her as an appearance of "the delusion inescapable for man." Her perpetual virginity, ever restored in the ocean, is less than literal innocence. Yet Aphrodite is innocence itself. Her innocence is appearance, but appearance is her essence . . . at least in part. The following chapter expands the riddle of Aphrodite into a series of similar riddles. Aphrodite's restoration of virginity represents the riddle of distinctiveness: how can each time be the first time? Her beauty too is problematic: how to manifest one virtue without succumbing to a shallow stereotype devoid of other virtues? How to be distinctive without sacrificing wholeness?

Aphrodite's plight finds its solution in the philosophy of Anaxagoras, but the Athenians understood him even less than we understand Aphrodite. They exiled him for teachings that sound very like the circular structure of subjectivity: that the whole is in the part, the greater equal to the lesser. The next chapter tries to vindicate both Aphrodite and Anaxagoras by distinguishing their virtues from the vices of various reductionisms. Their success is then a model for distinguishing the appearance of reductionism in Nietzsche from the delusion of positivism; the appearance of nihilism in Zarathustra from the delusion of anarchism; the appearance of gods as mere projections from the delusion of atheism. Though these last riddles are prefigured in this last chapter of Part Two, their solutions will carry on into Part Three and finally back to distinguishing the appearance of parapolitics from the delusions of a dead politics.

VI Aphrodite and Anaxagoras

The several stories strung together in this second part of the book each tell a tale of selfhood. Zeus and Proteus join Apollo as variations on the theme of singular identity. Hades and Hermes join Dionysus as threats to unambiguous individuation. Finally the allegory of Zarathustra suggests the juncture of several identities within the cave of a single soul. But the juncture is problematic. Accustomed as we are to second realm rationality we are inclined to want to join the several gods and several selves by subordinating them to one Lord of lords or one Self of selves. We are inclined to think in terms of hierarchy rather than heterarchy, conquest rather than perpetual skirmishes, or at best, negotiation toward pragmatic compromise rather than dialectical consensus.

Earlier chapters have indicated something of the price we pay for our preferences. The polytheistic alternative also has its price in pain, ambiguity and uncertainty. Is the price of a polytheistic psychology worth paying? Is it even possible to maintain many in one without the supremacy of One? This chapter addresses the issue of

196

possibility. The final chapters in Part Three consider the rewards, both spiritual and mundane.

The issue of possibility raises questions of metaphysics: what can and cannot be? Our favored way of looking at issues of power and ego management has its foundations in Eleatic metaphysics. Parmenides of Elea was the first philosopher of the One. In order to think our way out of that favored tradition it is appropriate to return to its early critic, Anaxagoras. But of course we need to do more than merely *think* our way out for the right-handed, linear pattern of our thought is precisely our legacy from Elea. So in keeping with the narrative strategy of Part Two, the wisdom of Anaxagoras will speak through further stories: about Aphrodite, about Narcissus and more of the wanderings of Zarathustra.

Why just these stories? Several loose ends remain from what has gone before, and further problems can be anticipated from a rudimentary sensitivity to the times in which we live. First there remains the riddle of pluralism: how to allow differences without inviting total destruction? The metaphysics of many in one without the supremacy of One speaks to the riddle of pluralism as it is raised by the stories of Aphrodite, Narcissus and Zarathustra. Zarathustra's meeting with his shadow raises the issue of antagonism. Ares the warrior seeks his place in the pantheon. The likeness between Ares and Zarathustra's shadow recalls a second loose end: the problem of closing the arcs of the circle of subjectivity by showing a relational or structural identity between gods and selves. Anaxagorean metaphysics speaks explicitly to the identity of the "smaller" and the "larger." This chapter will question common sense concepts about space much as Chapter IV questioned assumptions about time. The form of the chapter—beginning with the gods then switching to the selves of Zarathustra—follows the content: a representation of the gods as transformational projections of selves and selves as transformational introjections of the gods.

As a final answer to the question, "Why just these stories?" a word of explanation about Aphrodite and Narcissus: ours is an age preoccupied with beauty and self. Narcissus, the god who gazes at his beautiful reflection in a pool, is a symbol for a sometimes pathological attachment to *numero uno*, the singular self. This powerful symbol calls for careful handling because, like Proteus, Narcissus is with us. Yet our historically grounded need for Narcissus, like our need for Dionysus and Proteus, leaves us in danger of misappropriating his mythical message. Cut off from the context of polytheism and its rich narratives, we see Narcissus as Freud did: not as a figure in a story of self-transformation from self-love to the white flower with the heart of gold; instead we are inclined to condemn Narcissus as an abstract principle of preoccupation with one's own singular ego. The story of Narcissus is therefore important to many dimensional man, not only because we are susceptible to narcissism, but also because the mono-theistic misunderstanding of Narcissus may distort his meaning.

On being beautiful

The very title offends if its author chooses to write in the mis-leadingly simple first person singular. For the subject is a description of the subjective experience of being beautiful, not merely in some metaphorical sense of beautiful as in the dubious beauty of The Beau-tiful Soul,[1]* but in the more literal if multiple senses of beauty as classically or romantically conceived: to have physical attributes uni-versally admired, a jaw, finely carved features in fair proportions, a full but not overfull figure. Certainly there is not just one good figure, not one set of fine features. Nor are all figures and features good. There are *some* good figures, *some* good combinations of fea-tures . . . and some that are not good. To abandon the idea of *one* perfect form is not to deny the use of the term 'good'.

There are people for whom the classical description of beauty fits. Not all people. Some. Among them some suffer from vanity. For those who do not, for those whose self-esteem does not rest on the infirm foundations of recognitions of physical beauty, for those others devoid of vanity the experience of being beautiful is nonetheless part of their experience and deserves to be described rather than repressed into the nether reaches of social unconsciousness by the censorship mechanism marked "Modesty."

Modesty is the far side of an emotion whose near side speaks as follows: "Be like others! Do not be extraordinary in any way! Evaporate into the miasma of mediocrity!" Modesty is a mixed virtue.

If one really (if rarely) sees how beautiful one is and really (if rarely) honors oneself in one's own perception, is one then more beautiful or, as modesty would teach, less? It takes a little narcissism to be loved, and therefore to love, for part of loving is allowing oneself to be loved. To remain open to a loving look that declares beauty not only in the eye of the beholder—to accept the implicit praise of love without condemning the lover of bad taste—takes at least a little narcissism. To float high—to let the relations that form one's existence weave themselves into a blanket and toss one into the sky—takes just a little narcissism.

Of course the modern age would stigmatize the Narcissus in each of us with another name: egoism. The condemnation that attaches the '-ism' to 'ego' is based on a legitimate sense of what is wrong with the way many are preoccupied with getting *enough*: enough recognition, enough love, enough money, enough attention— enough ego pats. One wants to say to them (or oneself), "Relax, it will come to you if you let it. Don't be grabby." But one will then be heard as competing ever more subtly. Egoism is a problem, but a problem less likely to gain pathological proportions in a multiselved person where the multiplicity is both cause and effect of the fact that no one self utterly excludes the rest. No single ego has claimed the sole right to say "I" for the assemblage. Narcissus is then but one of the many and his high on his own beauty is but a part of a person not at all egoistic.

Call it one's Aphrodite rather than one's Narcissus if you like, just as long as one is able to partake of that part of one's self that is the deity of beauty, of overwhelming attractiveness, sensuality. Aphrodite was not utterly innocent of her charms. Aphrodite's "magic girdle" had to be donned in self-consciousness of its effects on the eyes and genitals of its beholder whether Hephaestus, Ares or whomever. Aphrodite certainly could not have been ignorant of the effects of her magic girdle when other goddesses asked to borrow it. Yet Aphrodite was not charged with 'narcissism'. Her deity *differed* from his. Only in our day would Aphrodite's lack of innocence about her beauty be falsely identified and reviled as narcissistic.

Was she an innocent virgin? Quite the contrary? Why would she be known for *restoring* her virginity in the ocean if not for the fact that she was less a virgin than the simple nonvirgin willing to leave it at that rather than *restore* virginity. Aphrodite knew what she was doing when she donned her girdle, whose shape doubtless spoke a similarly provocative message of thinly veiled and minimal innocence.

Aphrodite was promiscuous and could gratify her promiscuity because all the gods wanted her—Hermes, Ares and Poseidon. Even Apollo once nudged Hermes as they watched naked Ares and Aphrodite struggling in the trap set by husband Hephaestus and said, "You would not mind being in Ares' position, would you, net and all?" To which Hermes replied that he would not mind even if there were three times as many nets and all the goddesses were watching with shameful disapproval.[2]

What a woman, so beautiful and knowing it, so eager to seduce. Of course she was different from Narcissus in her desire to be seen in the eyes of others rather than see herself in her own reflection, but the point is that her honored promiscuity presupposes at least a minimal reflection—enough of an image of self-as-sensuous as is required in order to *be* sensuous. Yet in our day even this much self-awareness is likely to be termed narcissistic.

But if Aphrodite is not guilty of narcissism then perhaps neither is Narcissus. That is, *who* he is, what his nature manifests, may not need to carry the stigma of an -ism unless carried to the one-sided extreme of a pathological rivetedness to the reflected image.

Aphrodite's perpetually reassumed innocence, while in some ways less innocent than the ignorance of the simple virgin, is nonetheless more innocent in that she knows she *could* draw on what she has learned in the past but nonetheless chooses not to. Instead she restores the distinctiveness of The First Time. She is the opposite of a Don Juan who wishes to reach the thousand-and-first time. And this difference is reflected not only in her lovemaking but also in her character. In the ocean she restores an identity undistorted by others' images of her. There she finds her ownmost self, innocent of the ego-enhancing lusts of her lovers. In her restoration of virginity she recalls an identity independent of others very much in the way Narcissus finds his own identity by himself as he bathes his eyes in his own watery image.

In their respective modes of self-reflection both Aphrodite and Narcissus supply to the self precisely that component that some might find lacking in many dimensional man, namely a sense of selfhood independent of others. Deceived by an oversimple dichotomy between the virtues of the inner-directed, autonomous, independent individual on the one hand and the virtues of the other-directed, heteronomous, interdependent comrade on the other, some might find that this many dimensional personality, with its capacity for shame before others and its partial internalizations of many others as ideals, lacks in something like good old integrity—a presence of self that is somehow independent of the influence of others' images of the self, whether good or bad.

Narcissus and Aphrodite possess self-presence, and the many dimensional self that includes an Aphrodite and a Narcissus among its many selves has as much of such self-presence as is needed. Integrity though peripheral is still integrity. To make the autonomous image of the self more central, to make the image of the self more autonomous, is to generate the sort of self who is justifiably worried about being narcissistic, namely a self-centered self.

Neither Narcissus nor Aphrodite had to worry about being narcissistic because both, as gods, were whole. Neither was an abstract *principle* or program. The point of personification is not necessarily the reification of some principle in sensuous form so that simple folk can have something to grasp. Personification need not be idolatry. The point of personification is rather to embed virtues in the only context in which they can be virtues rather than one-sided vices: in the context of a whole personality. Narcissus was not pathologically narcissistic, nor was Aphrodite the nymphomaniac that modern novelists might like to make her. As deities each was a positive expression of an integrated personality manifesting one particular virtue *more* than others.

The unity of the virtues and homoeomereity

To understand the combination of all virtues in each of the gods and goddesses together with the distinction of each of the deities from each other—a combination that might appear impossible to technologically tuned imaginations used to differentiating nonorganic wholes by different inventories of utterly distinct and replaceable parts—two concepts familiar to the Greeks are necessary.

The first is the concept of the unity of the virtues as that unity is explored in Plato's early dialogues. There Socrates asks after the definition of one virtue after another—courage, temperance, piety and so on until in the *Republic* he asks after the nature of justice itself which up to then had vied with temperance as a necessary condition for the possibility of exercising any of the virtues. Each of the early dialogues ends skeptically. No adequate definition for particular virtues can be found, mainly because the virtues have the annoying habit of mutually presupposing one another in such an integrative way that each virtue comes to look like all the virtues together and to that

extent just like any of the other equally integrated virtues: courage is
not foolish bravado but bravery together with knowledge, including a
knowledge of right and wrong, justice; knowledge demands courage;
piety requires knowledge of what is intrinsically lovable to the gods;
that knowledge requires a sense of justice, which in turn demands a
balancing of all the virtues, and so on.[3] The story comes to sound
something like Adelle Davis on vitamins: unless one gets all of them,
one's body lacks the means to use any of them properly. Yet there are
different vitamins. So with the virtues.

The second principle necessary for accepting differentiation
among wholes each containing all the same ingredients comes from
Anaxagoras. In order to make sense of change, the simple process of
generating something from what was *other than* the thing generated,
Anaxagoras posited so-called seeds, σπέρματα which contained a portion of everything. Nothing arose from anything that did not already
contain at least a portion of what was to be the result of change. In
addition to *spermata*, however, Anaxagoras posited a principle that
has seemed paradoxical to most mechanically minded moderns. According to his principle all the parts of a given whole are constituted
in the same proportion as the whole itself. For this second principle
he coined the term, 'homoeomerous' to describe things so constituted.

The problem: if all the parts are equally constituted, then how
can any one part as distinct from any other part give rise to a change?
Presumably a change that derives its intelligibility from its growth
from an appropriate seed rather than from nothing also presumes a
seed *not* exactly like every other seed, in short, a lack of homoeomereity.

Precisely this business of homoeomereity so boldly asserted
by Anaxagoras led Socrates and his followers toward skepticism regarding the unity and distinctness of the virtues. How was Anaxagoras able to assert the multiplicity of all in each without falling into
Socratic skepticism? Or was it Socrates's irony that smiled, like Apollo nudging Hermes, as Socrates watched analytic reason and Aphroditic virtue struggle in the iron logic of an all-too-sophistic discourse.
The ironic Socrates was not above *demonstrating* the limits of logic-

chopping sophistry by practicing sophistry himself. What is the He-
phaestian trap into which the Anaxagorean principles have fallen? Is
it possible to think again the presence of all in each *and* the distinctiveness of each without exposing this juncture to the laughter of the
gods and the shame of the goddesses? Can the bold innocence that
juncture knew in Anaxagoras's thought be restored like the virginity
of Aphrodite? Where is the analogic ocean?

Anaxagoras and the Eleatic legacy

The obstacle to Anaxagorean innocence on our parts is itself a
syndrome and not a simple 'mistake'. In returning to Anaxagoras it
should come as no surprise to find all problems in each problem and
not one elemental key. The argumentative ocean that would cleanse
the modern mind of its obstacles to joining wholeness with distinctiveness must necessarily touch the shores of virtually every issue.
Nonetheless the distinctive merit of returning to Anaxagoras rather
than to one of the other presophistic innocents lies in his suggestions
for a metaphysics that provides the preconditions for the circular
structure of subjectivity.

Anaxagoras held: "Neither is there a smallest part of what is
small, but there is always a smaller (for it is impossible that what is
should cease to be). Likewise there is always something larger than
what is large. And it is equal in respect of number to what is small,
each thing, in relation to itself, being both large and small."[4] Anaxagoras has formulated his insight as a response to Eleatic philosophy
as represented by Zeno, who wished to support the One of Parmenides by reducing pluralism to absurdity: "So if there is a plurality,"
wrote Zeno, "things must be both small and great; so small as to have
no magnitude at all, so great as to be infinite."[5] Anaxagoras's language precisely echoes Zeno's. The adversary once located, his argu-

ment need not be fully repeated to see what is at stake in Anaxagoras's response: the point is to deny the Eleatic syndrome, that way
of thinking for which (a) all is One, (b) Being and Thinking are one,
(c) nonbeing is not, (d) therefore no admixture of nonbeing is in Being, no becoming, no change, (e) therefore the appearance of change
is *mere* appearance, illusion, as is the appearance of plurality.

Not to discount the inestimable genius of any of the epoch-
making insights of the pre-Socratics, for father Parmenides too will
receive his due, this much must be said against Eleatic philosophy in
its legacy if not in its profoundest origins: the occupation of a determinate volume of an absolute space is taken as the paradigm of being.
Its eventual denial of sensuous perception is based on an absolutizing
of limited evidence drawn from Homerically vivid senses of *sight* and
touch that cry out: two things cannot be in the same place at the same
time, nor can the smaller contain the larger. So do the senses of sight
and touch proclaim their logic of Being.

Parmenides is the first great intellectualist because he is the
first to think through the sensuousness of Homeric existence to its furthest extreme where, of course, it turns over into its opposite: an in-
tellectualism that must deny the evidence of the senses. Having taken
the impenetrability of physical things as his paradigm of Being he had
to deny Being to eminently penetrable void. And having gone so far
his genius took him the further step: if there is no void there can be no
motion; ergo, no change (for sensibly evident change—motion—is, to
Parmenides, the paradigm for all change); ergo our sensuous perceptions of change are deceptive. What courage it must have taken to
draw such consequences and drive human consciousness to the point
that it could no longer take the evidence of its senses as the paradigm
for its thought.

Anaxagoras saw the next step more clearly than most do today. Eleatic philosophy illicitly extends the logic of visual-tactile per-
cepts to the logic of concepts.[6]* Consequently the contingencies of
spatial phenomena become the paradigms for all behavior: the fact
that two physical bodies cannot be in the same *place* at the same time
is carried over into a much broader principle of noncontradiction. A

and non-A cannot *be the case* at the same time—which is true enough for predicates whose meaning is genuinely founded in the logic of the visual-tactile senses, but false otherwise: a physical object cannot be both round and square in the same dimension at the same time, but it is perfectly possible to be both generous and stingy, both loving and hating, both downcast and elated in quite the same respects at the same time, viz. the experience of dramatic tragedy. Just because perceptual space knows no ambivalence it does not follow that all ambivalence is a sign of contradictions to be eradicated in the lucidity of clear vision.

Nor does it follow from noncontradiction in perceptual space that nonperceptual space knows no ambivalence. As Anaxagoras saw perhaps more clearly than anyone else, when we imaginatively extend perceptions of small and large beyond the range of what is perceptible, when we attempt to formulate *concepts* of the smallest and the largest, we cannot. The logic of the perception of smaller and larger is so intrinsically relational that anything of which 'small' or 'large' is predicable must always admit of yet a smaller and a larger. Just as there is no absolute space within which things take up their positions, so there is no absolute spectrum between a smallest and a largest. Wherever one might attempt to situate oneself on such a putative spectrum it would remain true that as many leaps toward the larger remain to be made as there are divisions to the smaller.

When we leave the perceptual space of, say, a ladder reaching from the floor (the lowest) to the ceiling (the highest), when we enter instead the *conceptual* arena where there is neither floor nor ceiling to halt the process of division or multiplication, it is rather as if the linear ladder turns into a circular treadmill: no matter where one is on what *had* been a fixed hierarchy between an absolute ceiling and an absolute floor, now one finds that no matter how much one climbs into the larger, no matter how far one descends into the smaller, not only is there always a further rung both up and down, but also the horizons over which the still longed for highest and the dreaded lowest disappear are both always equally distant. *Differance* remains, and movement in either direction—up or down, greater or smaller—but unlike the perceptual world of a room, the pursuit of supraperceptual concepts leads the thinker to acknowledge that the center is everywhere, even spatially speaking where the space involved is the conceptually ordered space of astrophysics.

The cosmological principle

Recent advances in relativity-based cosmological theory lead at least some theorists to the so-called "cosmological principle" according to which the physical universe must appear essentially the same from each and every perspective. The point is not that the shapes of the constellations would appear the same but rather that the red-shift observed in the spectra of the most distant light sources will be the same in all directions no matter where in the universe one sets one's observatory. Since greater red-shift indicates greater distance, the cosmological principle, if translated into the visual-intuitive language of absolute space as an enormous room, declares the impossibility of approaching one wall and distancing oneself from its opposite. No matter how far one moves away from what one supposed to be the center of the room, no matter how much of the universe one hoped to leave in one's wake as one approached what one expected to be its less dense fringes, one will still find the universe equally dense in all directions. The "center" of astrophysical space is everywhere, thus there is no center as ordinary perception would attempt to "visualize" it.

Bondi, Gold and Hoyle have suggested an extension of E. A. Milne's cosmological principle from space to space-time : "Minor small-scale irregularities apart, the universe by and large presents the same aspect to all observers from every space location at any time."[7]

Singh interprets: "This means that the universe does *not evolve* in time but stays put in the same steady state forever. Not that there is no change. The galaxies are born and die like human beings but the aspect of the heavens that their totality presents to any observer at any time stays the same just as the aspect of street crowds remains unchanged from generation to generation in spite of the perpetual coming and going of the individuals in the crowd." The very illustration used to describe the cosmological principle would seem to confirm the homoeomereity of the human and the 'heavenly'. One could as well use the illustration of the perpetual replacement of molecules in the metabolic succession of the "same" human body.

Whatever the outcome of current cosmological debates at least this much is clear: Anaxagorean cosmology cannot be easily dismissed on grounds of its counterintuitive offense to the perceptual logic of smaller and larger. When the most technically competent extensions of relativity theory in cosmology lead away from the perception of absolute space toward the conception of a spatiality with no simply intuitable outer limit and no single unambiguous center; when that relativity-based cosmological principle is extended toward a spatio-temporality in which every moment is equidistant from its horizons of original creativity and ultimate oblivion, then the resistance to Anaxagorean thinking can no longer appeal to an unproblematic intuition of the logic of space and time in its attempt to reject the larger "in" the less, the smaller as greater, the 'heavens' in the human. N. B.: the best of modern cosmology does not vindicate Anaxagoras by *direct proof* any more than the uncertainty principle proves "free will." The point is that one can no longer assume a simple link between what the last living hard-core positivist calls "common sense and its long arm, science."[8] The Eleaticism of common sense is no longer adequate to the furthest reaches of micro- and macrocosmic physics. However incapable of "proving" homoeomereity this modern and still controversial cosmology may be, the point remains nonetheless: the *kind of thinking* needed to grasp its counterintuitive conclusions, the kind of thinking now rendered more respectable by its quantitative context, is the kind of thinking that Anaxagoras advocated in his critique of the Eleatic emphasis on limit ($\pi\epsilon\rho\alpha\sigma$) long ago. Given this new found if not thoroughly founded respectability, this Anaxagorean thought should now be able to uncover the causes of its premature burial and see them as contingent causes rather than necessary reasons founded in Eleatic "truths." It should now be possible to resurrect Anaxagorean insight from its death at the hands of an offended Eleatic consciousness.

The exile of Anaxagoras

Anaxagorean insight can constitute an offense to our—look at the language—*highest* ideals. For what is the meaning of Anaxagoras's saying, "And when these things have been thus separated, we must know that all things are neither more nor less (for it is not possible that there should be more than all), but all things are always equal"? What was Anaxagoras saying if not that what the people took as highest, e.g., the gods, were "neither more nor less" than the least part of the self: not more, for there is as much that is greater than a god as is greater than the least part of the self; not less because there is as much that is less than the least part of the self as is less than the gods.

The insights of Anaxagoras are as close as anything in the history of Western philosophy to the structure of subjectivity. Both the fate of those insights as well as the fate of Anaxagoras bespeak the poverty of subsequent understanding of subjectivity. As for his ideas: he saw the sense in which the parts of the self are like seeds whose proportions reproduce the proportions of the cosmos. He appreciated (in some form or other) the circular dynamic of introjection and projection. As for his fate: the usual confusion between this dynamic and the one-way process of reduction—the one side of projection makes the gods look like 'mere figments of our imaginations'—led to Anaxagoras's conviction on a charge of impiety.

We are told by Diogenes Laertius "that he was prosecuted by Cleon for impiety, because he maintained that the sun was a red-hot mass of metal, and that after Pericles, his pupil, had made a speech in his defense, he was fined five talents and exiled." Whether or not they understood him properly, the Athenians knew that all this talk about the smaller and the greater was not some abstract metaphysics unconnected to the business of living. On the contrary Anaxagoras's cosmology is an esoteric presentation of a philosophy of part and whole, individual and state, self and community, one and all. That philosophy is expressed in and is expressed by the structure of one of the greatest communities in the history of man, Periclean Athens. Anaxagoras was a close friend of that greatest statesman, Pericles, who for his part wept tears before his fellow Athenians in his effort to extricate his friend and teacher from prison.[9]*

The fate of Anaxagoras and his ideas raises a problem obviously germane to the fate of any effort to reconstruct his ideas; why despite its wisdom is Anaxagorean philosophy so unpopular? Why is this philosophy experienced as a threat to human existence when in fact it articulates the most profoundly human in existence?

Idolators object to the effort at introjecting the attributes of the gods into man because they confuse introjection with reduction to a bare substratum. Because they regard the lower as absolutely and irredeemably least they regard any effort to impute its attributes to the higher as blasphemy and impiety: the problem lies in the critics' own view of the subject—whether it be the 'bare particular' of the problem of individuation in metaphysics, the 'beastly man' of transcendent theology, or the base selfishness of individuals in political theory. Lacking the experience of sacredness in the least of their own lives they then lay up their stores in transcendent idols. Their own experience of what they take to be the lower rungs of an ontological ladder is an experience of an essentially dead matter, a substratum of lifeless stuff, boring moments succeeding boring moments in monotonous, tedious existence. Because their own experience of "the subject" is of this sort, they are naturally threatened by any suggestion that the nature and structure of their idols is essentially the same as this deathly stuff. They are naturally inclined to condemn as impious any man who intimates as much. The idolators will project the poverty of their own existence onto the mundane order and any man who would attempt to introject the divine into the human they will condemn with the charge of having impiously mocked the idols by suggesting their homoeomereity with the human.

To review: the philosophy of Anaxagoras promises an answer to the riddle of Aphrodite's perpetual virginity. Less symbolically, we are seeking an understanding of how the whole can be in each part, the many in each one, *without* losing the unique distinctiveness of each part, each self, each virtue or each god. Anaxagoras suggests homoeomereity as the answer, but that answer suffers misinterpretation as long as projection and introjection are confused with reduction to a fundamental substratum of mundane existence.

Before returning to Aphrodite the following sections take up the transform of Aphrodite's riddle as it appears in the allegory of Zarathustra. Where Aphrodite runs the risk of being reduced to a sex symbol and Narcissus runs the risk of narcissism, Zarathustra comes dangerously close to atheism and anarchism. Zarathustra's story will present an alternative to reductionism, that hallmark of second realm rationality. The alternative follows from reflections on two other features of both first and second realm rationality: the belief in a basic substratum, a lowest common denominator of existence to which all else can be reduced; and second, the belief in a highest cause, whether an Aristotelian prime mover, a president or a paternal god. Nietzsche's crucial insight, a turning point in his own development, lay in seeing through the symbols of singular power and authority *without* relying on reduction to a lifeless substratum. The Nietzschean transform of Aphrodite's riddle will tie together the political, psychological and religious dimensions of monism and pluralism. By the sequence of Zarathustra's wanderings Nietzsche links the death of God with the decline of political authority. The economy of Nietzsche's symbolism ties the many thematic threads of this book so tightly the remaining chapters do little more than unravel the several significances of Zarathustra's momentary revelations.

Zarathustra's "impiety"

Zarathustra's meetings with the next two higher men after the magician illustrate the difference between the "impiety" of introjecting the divine into the human and an altogether different spirit of reductionism that sometimes infects the atheist. First he meets the retired pope whose journey is a quest for "the last pious man." The ignorant hermit whom he had sought was dead so instead he decided to seek "the most pious of those who do not believe in God"—Zarathustra.

The secret of Zarathustra's "piety" lies in the grounds for his renunciation of the old god. Zarathustra demands good taste in all things—including gods—and the old god offends good taste. Just as the biography of Zeus tells a history of theology from shame culture to guilt culture, so the biography of the god of Abraham as told by the retired pope tells a history leading to the offense against good taste. "When he was young, this god of the Orient, then he was harsh and vengeful, then he built himself a hell to amuse his favorites. But eventually he became old and soft and mellow and pitying, more like a grandfather than a father, but most like a shaky old grandmother."

So naturally Zarathustra responds, "Away with *such* a god," and the retired pope replies in turn: "Zarathustra, with such disbelief you are more pious than you believe. Some sort of god in you must have converted you to your godlessness. Is it not your very piety that no longer allows you to believe in a god?"[10]

The god in Zarathustra is that creator and redeemer who lives alongside the destroyer, the tumbler of old tablets, the redeemer and nay-sayer. The old god of the Orient wrestled with Shiva the destroyer. It is a measure of Zarathustra's respect for the old god that, among the many higher men who fill the cave of Zarathustra's contradictory soul, both the retired pope *and* the ugliest man are present. For the old god is dignified by his struggle with destruction. Zarathustra is pious in his impiety precisely because he has the capacity to destroy as well as to redeem. Yet neither of these capacities *by itself* will satisfy his taste for deity. Of the retired pope in his godless isolation even Zarathustra admits himself too weak to take *his* melancholy from his shoulders. Of the ugliest man alone we learn the following.

He lives in the valley of Snakes' Death. The symbolism would suggest that here dies not only all else that lives but wisdom as well, for Zarathustra's snake he calls "the wisest animal under the sun."[11] Here in the valley of Snakes' Death Zarathustra "fell into a black reminiscence for it seemed to him that he had stood once before in this valley." And so he had, or at least so had Nietzsche during the time that some call his positivistic period. Not that glimmers of life, creativity and redemption were ever wholly absent from his work, but in the late 1870s, around the time of *Human, All Too Human*, around the time of his fascination with Boscovich's atomism, at the time when a typical description of his state would read, "Pain, loneliness, long walks, bad weather—that is my circuit. No trace of excitement. Instead a kind of thoughtless, torpid indisposition,"[12]* during this time Nietzsche was all too familiar with the valley of death where all that remained of creativity was the distant echo of ordered motion among aimless atoms in space and time. He recognizes rancor and reductionism·as motives for the murder of god. When he meets those motives years later in the form of the ugliest man, he must write of Zarathustra, "all at once the great shame of it overcame him . . . he blushed to his white hair."

Of course, for now he knows the subtle but all-important difference between the atheism of the positivist and the polytheism of the atheist who denies the one god but lives in the immediate presence of many gods. Now he knows what it is to be inspired, filled with spirits not his own in some narrowly possessive sense but very much his own in the sense that *his* openness allows the play of their creation and destruction *through* him . . . and he is ashamed that he should have once been so closed as to believe that his "life" was nothing but the play of those Boscovichian atoms.

Yet here a curious event occurs, an interesting transition takes place. This "inexpressibly" ugly man makes a noise like a sewer slowly erupting in speech. The words he speaks pose a riddle and a warning that is itself a riddle. He asks Zarathustra to guess what revenge is appropriate against a witness, and he warns him: "I lure you back upon slippery ice. Look out lest your pride lead to a broken leg!" Nietzsche's next words transmit what seems to be his own shock of self-recognition: "When Zarathustra heard these words—what do you suppose happened to his soul? *Pity siezed him.*" The full weight of the shock is carried by a line probably lost on readers no longer in touch with the experience from which the Homeric simile draws its power: "And he sank to the ground like an oak that had long resisted a host of woodcutters—heavily, suddenly, terrifying even those who had wanted to fell it."

The primary riddle is answered almost immediately. Zarathustra rises up, his face now hard, and answers in "a voice of bronze," which is not to say brazenly; "I know you well. *You did murder God.* Let me go." Murder was the appropriate revenge against the consummate witness, of which more later. For now the more pressing question is: What of the warning? To where would Zarathustra (or Nietzsche) be lured *back*? Why is the ice so slippery there? How would he break his leg and fall with the weight of a mighty oak?

A riddle in a warning

Like his meeting with the magician, this meeting with the ugliest man provokes a response in Zarathustra much more pronounced than his responses to the other higher men. Earlier he was angry and struck out. Now, after his brief and bronzen answer to the riddle, he falls silent. He cannot speak. Again the extremity of his reaction is a key, a marker, a guide to the fact that too much is at stake here to pass by this passage on the waves of Nietzsche's rolling prose. It is not enough to accept the ugliest man's accusation against the god whose prying eyes condemned him to death. It is not enough to accept his one-sided warnings against pity though they sound so very much like Zarathustra's own. Here we are on slippery ice and in our pride as post-Nietzschean atheists we are likely to break our legs.

To pile the stakes still higher: a timely if crude analogy has been drawn between the death of god and the death of political authority as symbolized in the single seat of the presidency. It was further suggested that just as god does not die like a dog so neither does the presidency. The use of the metaphor of death demands a respect for its possible misuses, as Nietzsche well knew. As we now watch Nietzsche deal with his realization that the motives for murder are many, it will be worth pausing occasionally to consider the possible likenesses between Nietzsche's situation and our own. Who, for example, is the ugliest man in the morass of modern politics? And who the retired pope? Where is the valley called Snakes' Death, and was it revenge that killed the presidency . . . or something even less human?

For a sense of the slipperiness and the substance of this ice on which Nietzsche allows himself to be drawn it will be necessary to return to the coldest years of his greatest contempt when Nietzsche wrote the much ignored *Human, All Too Human*,[13] a book in which "one error after another is abandoned to the ice, the ideal is not refuted—*it freezes to death*. . . . Here for example 'the genius' freezes; in a further corner 'the saint'; under a huge icicle 'the hero' perishes;

in the end 'faith,' so-called 'conviction,' even 'pity' cools down considerably."[14]

The transition from shame to pity is part of this curious riddle of Zarathustra's meeting with the ugliest man. It will pay to return to this most important motif: *mitleiden,* suffering (*leiden*) with (*mit*); *das Mitleid,* pity or—etymologically more accurate though connotatively perhaps not—compassion.

Pity was Nietzsche's nemesis, his uncontrollable strength and hence his final weakness. His capacity for *feeling with* and hence *from* the most contrary perspectives gave him his insight.[15] But the cost! The price he had to pay for being the battleground for contrary passions was his final breakdown, so appropriately provoked by the sight of an old horse being beaten. No wonder then that he should have been the first among moderns to question the virtue of compassion. No wonder that during his first venture into the valley of Snakes' Death he should have observed, "there are cases where pity (*Mitleiden*) is stronger than the actual suffering (*Leiden*)," where one's love of another is so much stronger than his love of himself that one suffers more acutely at his injury than he does himself.[16] And if the sufferer goes so far as to desire pity then he does so at the cost of those who grant him compassion, a cost that Nietzsche would have good reason to resent.[17]

Nietzsche's attack on pity, begun in the frozen wasteland of his own most pitiable state, continues through his entire corpus.[18] Its major components are these: first, pity is a gift to the parasite. It perpetuates only the lowest forms of life. Second, the gift once given returns to infect the giver with the same pathology of false "virtues," the same decadence of the spirit, because where pity itself is regarded as a virtue then *guilt* is the only garland for the pitiless. Third, one finally does no favor to the receiver of actions performed out of pity for such alms are ultimately degrading; they impose upon their receiver the recognition of his pitiful condition.[19]

No brief summary of Nietzsche's polemic against pity can capture all the nuances surrounding and sustaining the insightfulness

of his attack. Suffice it to say tht his ice-cold critique left little opportunity for the fabled milk of human kindness to flow toward unfortu-
nates. Enough has been said if the sheer ruthlessness of his polemic
against pity is apparent. Enough is known to clarify the curiousness
of the sudden transition from Zarathustra's blush of shame to his experience of pity. How comes it that Zarathustra himself, the herald of
the overman, should experience pity? How horrible can this ugliest
man be to provoke not only the breaking of legs but the breaking of
what had seemed the greatest of taboos?

The dynamic is not unfamiliar: none other than the pursuit of
an extreme to its turning over into its opposite, the pitiable extreme of
the man who would deny pity altogether. Nietzsche's polemic against
pity finds its most virulent expression in the speech the ugliest man
delivers to Zarathustra, a speech in which he warns Zarathustra
against what the soothsayer had earlier declared Zarathustra's final
sin: pity.[20]

The ugliest man's explicit warning against pity comes too late
since it is he who finally provokes Zarathustra's pity. It is he, the ugliest man, who murdered god in the spirit of merciless revenge against
the witness of his deepest self-contempt. God had to die because "his
pity knew no shame: he burrowed into my dirtiest nooks." So speaks
the ugliest man, his language carefully chosen to foreshadow Zarathustra's invitation scarcely a dozen lines later: "You have warned me
against *your* way. Mine I offer to you in return. There aloft lies Zarathustra's cave. My cave is large and deep and has many nooks; there
finds the most hidden his hiding place." Nietzsche's artistry draws the
explicit parallel between the nooks of Zarathustra's cave into which
higher men are one and all invited and the nooks of the soul into
which the divine witness would crawl.

The parallel between the cave and the soul sets up a chain of
further parallels whose last links will unriddle the riddles posed earlier. First and most immediately, the ugliest man is one of the selves
to be affirmed in the many-selved chamber of Zarathustra's soul. Even
he, the most inexpressibly ugly one, must be affirmed along with the

"lovely" figure of the voluntary beggar who will be the next to receive Zarathustra's invitation. Second, the proximate parallel between Zarathustra and the ugliest man must suggest to the reader of Nietzsche's nastiest book, *Human, All Too Human*, that here he has achieved both a critique and a reconciliation with that ice-cold consciousness in which he himself very nearly perished. Third, the fullness of Zarathustra parallels a polytheism that contains but must also be contrasted with the bitter atheism of the ugliest man. Fourth and finally, that fullness finds its parallel in the political arena with a parapolitics that contains but must also be contrasted with the bitter anarchism of some very ugly men. Each of the links in this chair of parallels calls for further elaboration.

Unriddling a chain of parallels

(1) First, the affirmation of the ugliest man is doubtless difficult. Yes, he agrees with Zarathustra in acknowledging the necessity of the death of god, but the deepest disagreements come between those who agree most. Few grudges are as deep as those among formerly close friends, few feuds as severe as those among partisans of the same cause. As with the magician, the ugliest man's remarks strike close to home. He affirms the death of god . . . and yet he suffers of it. He kills god but not out of a sense of fullness or overfullness; rather from a sense of revenge, rancor, *ressentiment* against the witness of his weakness. Yes, the ugliest man disdains pity—he killed god because god's prying pity knew no shame . . . but his disdain for pity is different from Zarathustra's however much he may use Zarathustra's words in his own defense. The ugliest man's disdain places him on an order of rank only one rung above him who wishes to be pitied. Zarathustra's disdain places him above those who pity.

They are as different in their identity as active and passive voices of the same sentence, a difference that is all important to Nietzsche.[21]*

Zarathustra will nevertheless invite the ugliest man to his cave for Zarathustra has discovered what Nietzsche later boasts he was the first to discover: a formula for the *highest affirmation* born from a fullness, an overfullness; "a yea-saying without reservation, even to suffering, even guilt, even to all that is questionable and strange in existence."[22] And what is this 'formula' that would include even those indices of decadence: guilt and pity? The answer to that riddle must await the next chapter. For now a problem that leads back to the elaboration of the second link in the chain of parallels: how, if all is to be affirmed, can Zarathustra, or Nietzsche, or for that matter anyone, avoid that vapid tolerance usually confused with perspectivism? How can the affirmation of all that is questionable and strange avoid falling for that other formula: "Whatever you say! What's cool for you is cool for you and what's cool for me is cool for me . . ." and so on into the insipid?

(2) The second link in the chain of parallels worked out in the fourth part of Zarathustra is Nietzsche's own reconciliation with his earlier nastiness, his *Aufhebung* (dialectical synthesis) of his own earlier ice-cold consciousness. Put in terms of Nietzsche's image of The Three Metamorphoses (the first section of the first part of *Zarathustra*), Nietzsche's nastiness represents the stage of the lion: the beast of prey who precedes the innonce of the child and follows the indulgence of the camel willing to take all upon his back. The issue is once again the Aphroditic restoration of innocence, yet how without slipping back into the insipid? How is the yea-saying of the child different from the indiscriminate willingness of the camel?

Somewhere in his memory the child must preserve the traces of his origins in the lion's unwillingness to affirm all that the camel accepted. Somewhere in his wholehearted affirmation he affirms *both* the camel's acceptance *and* the lion's roar of denial. The child's both/and differs from the camel's indiscriminate both/and, the beast of burden's bland resignation. The margin of difference is precisely the lion's decisiveness, an either/or mentality whose essence is discrimination. The either/or mentality will look at the camel and lion and say: *either* camel *or* lion; and—at least during his hour of great contempt, during his forty days in the desert of the valley of Snakes' Death—the lion must choose for the lion alone. The camel on the other hand *says* both/and, but he is afraid of the lion so when it comes to camel and lion in the same cage of course he will affirm the camel instead of the lion: fake acceptance, false comprehensiveness, what Hegel called the bad infinite that claims to comprehend everything . . . except for precisely the finitude that represents the exigency of either/or within real and unforgiving existence.[23] Now the child: how can he comprehend *both* the both/and of the camel *and* the either/or of the lion?

Laughter is the answer—the symptom and the cause of the lighthearted dance that leads from the lion to the child. Not for nothing is the laughing lion the final symbol of Zarathustra's ripening, the sign that his children are near.[24] The lion's laughter combines both the spontaneity of the innocent child with a negativity that makes it possible to take lightly what others take seriously. The lion's laughter is a sign of an immersion in the immediacy of the innocent moment joined with traces of a memory that comprehends all that is to be despised and warred against. The lion's laughter represents the same juncture symbolized by the joining of Aphrodite, the goddess who restores her virginity, and Ares, the god of war.

Nietzsche waged war in the valley of Snakes' Death, in the time when all that had been sacred appeared as a magnified projection of what was merely human, all too human. Now that negativity has received its due in terms whose traces are for a time sufficient to forestall a return to the camel's fake indulgence, now he can afford to affirm all that is most strange in human existence. He can elevate the human as an introjection of what had been thought to be reserved for the divine. Having had the courage to face what he most feared to see—the ultimate purposelessness of human existence—he can now afford to affirm what remains without fear of self-delusion. Having questioned everything he can affirm the most questionable.

How? By having found his distrust unfounded? Is he now ready to affirm all because all is now trustworthy? The point is neither to redeem the old idols nor to attempt some *other* justification for an existence whose purposes have been irredeemably denied.[25]* Rather, as he puts it in the preface to the *Genealogy of Morals,* the point is that *morally* speaking there is *no* point but it is nonetheless worthwhile to dwell upon this pointlessness: "that nothing under the sun is more *worth* taking seriously; to which worthiness belongs the possibility, for example, that one day one might take such things *lightly*"—in short, with laughter. "On the day when we can wholeheartedly proclaim, *'On with the comedy*—with the old morals as well!' then will we have discovered a new wrinkle in the Dionysian drama of the 'destiny of spirit. . . .' "[26]

Having dwelt upon the importance of Nietzsche's most intense negativity as a preventative against the insipid, what is the value of his coming to terms with the targets of his negativity? Why is it important to *affirm* even the most questionable, even the most strange in existence? Because only by affirming it will we even see it, e.g., the awkward. But how to affirm the awkward? We do not even *see* our awkwardnesses. That is why humor so often preys upon awkwardness, humor itself so often being the sudden revelation of the awkward by virtue of the unexpected imposition (or breaking) of a frame that allows us to "see things differently." Save for slapstick, humor is *not,* as it is sometimes said, the simple introduction of the *unexpected* but the unexpected interposition of a *frame* that allows one to see what is all too expected, so usual in fact that the universality of the humor is precisely a measure of the depth of the shock of self-recognition at the otherwise invisible commonplace. Good humor is universal because it reveals layers of humanity beneath our differences. Many will see the bit, get the joke, hear the lines that let us *see* and thus affirm in laughter the little awkwardnesses we commit, the lacunae in our gracefulness, the lapses in our poise that turn into lapses of memory almost immediately as the whisk broom of repression sweeps them into the dustbag of the unconscious.

Here belongs Freud's insight that humor, like dreaming, is a golden road to the unconscious. A sense of humor is essential to self-knowledge. After all there are some things one simply cannot afford to know about oneself unless one is able to laugh about them. Is there any humorless man who gives the impression of also knowing himself? Laughter is the body's coming to terms with itself in a loud, spasmodic way altogether as vivid and important as orgasm. Who would wish to be celibate in the form of love known as laughter?[27]

But back to the point: the *affirmation* of our awkwardnesses is crucial. Otherwise they will not be seen, much less affirmed. The dynamic is illustrated by the sad case of Lenny Bruce who for a time was among the most adept at letting us see our idolatries. Then as those without humor felt their rigid sense of propriety threatened, they felt the witness of Bruce's wit burrowing its way into their dirtiest nooks. After they exiled him from city after city, he too lost the ability to *affirm* our infirmities and his act was no longer funny. Instead he became one more crusader—understandably, given the persistence of his persecutors, but nonetheless sadly given the consequent loss of humor and hence loss of vision that his humor had allowed. Bitterness became his blindfold. Negation replaced affirmation and laughter gave way to despair and death.

Q.E.D.: affirmation is essential, even of the most questionable, even of the most strange in existence. Even the arresting officer, even the prosecutor is to be affirmed, not out of some ridiculous Christian wish to turn the other cheek—the affirmation may take the form of the most stinging irony, the sharpest jab of the gadfly, or the numbing blast of the stingray[28]—but from the need to see both the "arresting officer" and "prosecutor" within each of us. And what is finally funnier than the cop whose task it is to attend Lenny's act and write down how many times he utters obvious yet absurdly bowdlerized lines like, "Please, Irma, would you suck my blank?" Or the prosecutor who insists on presenting the evidence against Bruce *not* in the form of taped performances, whose laughter preserves the frame of humor, but in the form of transcripts read in perfect dead-pan? What is funnier than the judge who forbids laughter in the courtroom? Wouldn't the wit of a Bruce have been able to tap the ab-surdity of the solemn judge in each of us to turn his persecution into a festival of humor? Has the law ever been more awkward than in its prosecution of Bruce or the pranksters of the Chicago Eight? But then who among us has the capacity to keep laughing when the pompous turn their toys against us?[29] Who has the nobility of a Zarathustra, the capacity for distance that is not a deadened indifference but an ability to leap at appropriate moments from the most intense involvement in the moment to a perspective *sub specie aeternitatis*?

(3) The first two links prefigure the third: the fullness of Zara-thustra parallels a polytheism that contains but also contrasts with the bitter atheism of the ugliest man. This polytheism contains atheism to the extent that it denies religiosity. Psychological polytheism dis-counts the *distance* implicit in a god in whom one must *have faith*. The literalism of specific *beliefs* is altogether foreign to the feeling of ambiguous intimacy with the gods. Issues of existence or nonexis-tence are altogether irrelevant to the progressive articulation of that ambiguous intimacy. To the extent that the psychological polytheist appears to deny the existence of a transcendent god whose nature has been fully articulated in orthodox theology, he would seem to join hands with the atheist. Yet part of polytheism is an epistemological pluralism, an acceptance of Hermes and hence a denial of the literal-ism that infects the atheist as well as the believer.

The atheist and the believer both take themselves to be living in the One True World. The believer sees The World as the creation of God; the atheist as an autonomous order utterly lacking in benign paternity. The believer elevates the source for the purposive order of his life to a transcendent distance from his soul. The disbeliever de-grades that source but similarly finds his own disorder in the crystal clear absurdity of a purposeless world as distant from his inner life as was god from the soul of the believer. Psychological polytheism collapses this distance by denying the positivistic division between the inner and the outer. As Hillman, the originator of psychological polytheism, puts it, "By turning to polytheism we leave behind the riddling conundrums built upon monotheism—either religion or psychology, either one or many, either theology or mythology."[30] Instead we turn directly to the business of soulmaking, to the articulation of the psyche that is the source of both psychology and, as the atheist will be quick to agree, theology as well.

Of course the conundrums of monotheism may not be easy to leave behind. If, as Jung was the first to grant, science itself derives its self-certainty from the monotheistic fantasy, and every fantasy has its legitimate claim, then the monotheistic fantasy may be every bit as difficult to integrate as the dionysiac or hermetic.[31] Just as Dionysus refuses to stay in his place once given a place, just as Hermes confuses all places as he muddles the messages that would communicate the needs and desires of the many selves, so the fantasy of monotheism if given its place will bring in its wake a science that insists on reducing all the gods to the status of *mere* fantasies of a fertile but scientifically tractable imagination. In its affirmation of the atheist along with the theist polytheism courts the very conundrums it set out to leave behind—and willingly so.

Just as Zarathustra affirms the ugliest man and thereby avoids the unrestrained willingness of the camel, just as Nietzsche comes to terms with the negativity of finding the sacred all too human and thereby allows himself to take lightly what had been an all too serious assault upon morality, so polytheism will welcome the atheist into the fold and thereby avoid any propensity toward religiosity. For one never knows when a wooden nickel may crop up. The voice of the skeptic, the bark of the wary watchdog, is a welcome addition to any well-constituted household . . . whether or not a welcome to every visitor. Just because Zarathustra welcomes all the higher men to his cave it does not follow that he welcomes *every* man to his cave. Some, one assumes, he would turn away. The bark of the wary watchdog, even the bitterness of the wary atheist, can be a welcome addition to the discriminating psyche whose psychology may be polytheistic without being omnitheistic. There are *some* gods. Not everything is sacred.

To the atheist, however, nothing is sacred. And while it may be all well and good to have a few comedians whose genius is joking till laughter brings tears and their audiences cry "Is nothing sacred?", while glimpses of their vision make these comedians good to have around, one wonders whether one would want to *be* such a comedian twenty-four hours a day. Wouldn't the lack of any frame immune to humor's out-framing create a dizziness, a vertigo of laughter? Wouldn't the lack of a single "serious" frame seriously deplete the possibilities of experience? At some point one must be able to say "I love you" and mean it. Some things are sacred. The twenty-four-hour atheist misses something—as does the "true believer."

"Convictions" were left along with "pity" to freeze to death in the valley of Snakes' Death. The opening aphorism of the ninth section of Nietzsche's nastiest book reads, *"Enemy of truth.—*Convictions are more dangerous enemies of truth than lies,"[32] because the latter can be let go more easily than the former, their error more easily exposed. Convictions on the other hand have an ironclad fixity forged so hard in the smithy of suffering that we would rather suffer further from their errors than betray the old for the new.[33] The true believer has a sense of moral justification on his side as he holds tenaciously to his convictions, even unto the glory of self-sacrifice—though not once will he entertain the surrender of self demanded by the sacrificing of his convictions. The security of certainty is higher on his order of rank than the avoidance of pain, and both rank far above the appeal of truths that might overturn the entire order in a paroxysm of self-overcoming. The twenty-four-hour true believer, wedded with a ring of convictions to the jealous wife of his single lifelong self, misses something.

Spiritual polygamy is no simple solution to the celibacy of the atheist and the monogamy of the true believer. Even polygamy can gain the status of an ossified conviction. But a polytheistic pantheon that includes Pan the playful, Hermes the Trickster, impish Eros, the impetuous Ares and Dionysus, a polytheistic pantheon composed of gods and goddesses so rich in unpredictability, would seem an unlikely support to ossified convictions. Yet the question remains: granted that both the wary atheist and the true believer miss something of the possible fullness attained by Zarathustra, granted that some sort of spiritual polygamy may be able to avoid the worst of celibacy and monogamy if the proper mates are admitted into the pantheon, still the very naming of the gods and goddesses and the fixation of their forms in epithets would seem to commit even the reluctant believer to a kind of literalism and idolatry the resident atheist cannot allow.

Need we name the gods?—a difficult question to which at least half of the following chapter will be devoted. But now no more is needed than the development of the parallel that raises the question in both its religious and secular forms: just as Zarathustra both *accepts* and *criticizes* the ugliest man, just as Nietzsche comes to terms with his ice-cold consciousness in a warmer affirmation, so polytheism makes a place for atheism without giving full way to the weight of its spirit of gravity, and so also does parapolitics make a place for anarchism without falling prey to its false presuppositions and final absurdity. The next chapter develops the third link more fully and the fourth link alone is the subject of the chapter 8. But prior to treating parapolitics alone, how does its essential structure follow from its parallelism with preceding links?

(4) Nietzsche completes the circle of higher men with a pair of opposites just a few degrees distant from the retired pope and the ugliest man. The final pair, the voluntary beggar and the shadow, reflect the opposed forms of godlessness now transformed from the religious dimension into the secular. The voluntary beggar is a benevolent, kindly old man not unlike the retired pope. The shadow, like the ugliest man, is filled with self-contempt and the odor of death: "Nothing I love is alive anymore; how should I still love myself?" The voluntary beggar, unlike the ugliest man, Zarathustra calls "lovely." To

the shadow on the other hand, Zarathustra says: "I do not like you." So the structure is established in its stark formality, an axis of opposition just slightly askew of the one just developed, close enough to be almost parallel but far enough to demand different contents to fill out its form, a transformation by rotation of axes.

To describe those contents in terms of the gross and overdrawn divisions of the academic curriculum, the final pair moves from theology to political economy. The voluntary beggar's concern is the rich and the poor. The shadow gives voice to the darkest saying of the Dostoyevskian anarchist: "Nothing is true, all is permitted." The voluntary beggar is the noble aristocrat who can no longer bestow his riches on others because "all that is base has become rebellious. . . . The hour is nigh, you know it, for the grand revolution, the long naughty protracted people's uprising." The shadow is the quintessential naughty boy, the breaker of boundary stones.[34]

But of course the crass labels of the academic curriculum are insufficient to convey the dimension of secular godlessness Nietzsche portrays in this final opposition. The whole point of displaying this final dimension in its proximity to the former might be adumbrated in the claim that the measure of godlessness is not to be taken in what lies outside the soul (as transcendent theology or social theory would have it); rather the measure of godlessness is to be taken within the soul of man himself—as *displayed* in his politics and economy perhaps, but not if that politics and economy be construed as a simple replacement for the religious dimension.

It is not enough to equate the death of god with the replacement of religion by politics as the source of legitimate authority in modernity; the deeper significance of godlessness is the prospect of *no* authority, religious, political or psychological. The modern effort to legitimate authority in enlightened secular terms is therefore intrinsically unstable: to the extent that secular authority legitimates itself by condemning all charismatic and spiritual authority as based on primitive "superstition," by the same stroke it removes the psychological basis for sustaining its own authority. Of course that psychological basis does not die easily, and politicians, to their everlasting delight, are treated as gods when they are not reviled as devils. But to the extent that political theorists attempt to ground the authority of political leaders by appeal to a system of legitimation that would wholly *replace* the religious order with political economy, they do so at the risk of throwing out the mulch with the garbage. Not that divine right is the only legitimate form of authority, but once any occupant has been tumbled from the seat of authority, the throne itself is less secure.

The psychohistorical consequences of atheism appear in Nietzsche's portrayal of the voluntary beggar and the shadow. Political economy is but an afterthought to atheism, revolution but the last echo of the crucifixion, whose final significance is now evident as the first intimation of the inevitable death of the God of Abraham. In sending his son to die he both announced and forestalled his own death, just as Abraham admits mortality in taking the knife to his son Isaac. The stories are all the same, all these fathers sacrificing their sons: Saturnine authority must eat its children to nourish its chronic hunger. Cronus, the Greek Saturn, is father time himself before whom all, even the gods, betray their mortality. Authority protects against mortality and time. Authority opposes the pyramid to the circle to keep its institutions intact. But the cost of keeping the father alive is the sacrifice of the children, a sacrifice that only forestalls the crumbling of even the mightiest pyramid—which is, after all, a monument to death despite the intention to perpetuate life.

The psychohistorical ramifications of the death of god are richer than some social theorists care to admit, for who among us wants to forge into the nether reaches of symbolic consciousness where the likes of Norman O. Brown are to be found ferreting about among the dirtiest nooks of psychosocial unconsciousness? There lies madness. To the shadow as quintessential naughty boy, Brown would add: ". . . politics as juvenile delinquency . . . The band of brothers feel the incest taboo and the lure of strange women; and adopt military organization (gang organization) for purposes of rape.

Politics as gang bang."[35] What sort of insight can such madness add
to the sober analysis of reflection on authority? Yet how better to understand the madness of a political convention, that modern answer to
the ancient fertility rite? Politics is not simply a matter of platforms
carefully summarized by the Daughters of the American Revolution.
Nor have the sons of political science quite captured its inner workings if they eschew the shadowy realm of psychosocial symbolism.

"How is the hold of a symbol to be *measured*?" the scientists
will ask. "By the most rudimentary sensitivity," must one answer,
though even that much sensitivity may be in short supply. So much
the worse for political science if its methodology forbids symbols as
data. As Max Scheler pointed out on several occasions, the notion
that important truths must be equally evident to anyone is an egalitarian prejudice reflecting a most patent ideology at the heart of our
supposedly disinterested science. When will so-called empiricism
import into its metatheory the fact that some people are irredeemably
obtuse?

At just this point the cry will rise: "Elitist! Enemy of the people!" And precisely here the speech of the voluntary beggar is germane. He fled from the poor, who would not accept his gifts, to the
cows who could teach him to chew the cud. But prior to his rejection
of the poor for their rebelliousness he had already fled the rich, "the
gilded phoneys whose fathers were pickpockets or vultures or rag-
pickers . . . mob above and mob below! What do 'poor' and 'rich'
matter today?" The voluntary beggar uses economic language to describe the source of Zarathustra's own nausea—that he has seen both
the highest and the lowest and all too little separates the one from the
other. Nietzsche's philosophy is no brief for the natural superiority of
some one class or race or granfalloon of whatever description. The
usual political divisions have very little bearing on the order of rank
that Nietzsche imposes. Does laughter know national boundaries?
Does a sense for nuance characterize the political left more than the
right? The error Nietzsche would find among political categories lies
not with any·preference of one over another, 'aristocrat' over 'popu-

list', 'rebel' over 'reactionary'. The error according to Nietzsche lies in mistaking an exclusively political vocabulary as adequate to the structures of human existence. So he will invite *both* the noblesse oblige of the voluntary beggar and the anarchism of the shadow into the depths of Zarathustra's cave, and he will criticize the one-dimensionality of each in turn.

To the giver of gifts he will speak with just a touch of gentle irony. He will note that the noblesse oblige of the rich demands an *art* of graciousness for "right giving is harder than right receiving." In response to the voluntary beggar's contempt for rich and poor alike he cautions: "You do yourself violence when you use such harsh words, you sermonizer on the mount. Your mouth was not made for such harshness, nor your eyes. Nor your stomach either it seems to me. . . ." Again Nietzsche speaks to himself, whose disposition was gentler than his polemics would imply and whose digestion was far less than perfect.

But finally the gentle irony of Nietzsche's charge is clearest in the words he puts into the mouth of noblesse oblige: the virtue of learning to chew the cud! Is this not a *reductio ad absurdum* of the dictim of Pascal (whom Nietzsche greatly admired), namely that we should all be a lot better off if more men had learned to sit quietly in their rooms? In part one, "On the Teachers of Virtue," Nietzsche's irony is evident when he makes as strong a case for quietism as can be made in Zarathustra's own language. A sage praises laughter and self-overcoming as a means to good sleep, to which Zarathustra responds: "If life had no sense and I had to choose nonsense then I too would take this as the most sensible nonsense:—to wake in order to sleep well."

Nietzsche was something of an insomniac. He could praise sleep with feeling. As a compulsive polemicist he could appreciate the peace and quiet often denied him. Yet he knew as well the one-sidedness of *quietism*. Without troubling to make an explicit transition he lets the reader draw his own conclusion from a juxtaposition between the sage of sleep and the immediately following, "On the aft-

erwordly," where we read: "Weariness that wishes to attain the ultimate with *one* fatal leap, a poor dumb weariness that does not want to
want any more: this created all gods and afterworlds . . ." and the
desire for desirelessness that would find *all* answers in the waking
sleep of meditation. Obviously: quietude has its time, but not all time
And if there are some who have *no* time for quiet they need a preacher
on the mount, a Maharishi. But the rest of us might be expected to
know better and honor the shadow.

The shadow

The shadow will disturb our quiet. His voice erupts from the
depths of the unconscious, with which he is nearly identifiable.[36] His
voice is disturbing because we do not like what it has to say. Both
what it says as well as the voice are unfamiliar, strange. The voice
and the speech are strange for the simple reason that our dislike functions as a screening mechanism to eliminate that voice from consciousness. Dislike and unfamiliarity feed each other. Not that familiarity will necessarily breed affection, but once the circle of repression and resistance has begun, *its* dynamic is self-sustaining.

Nietzsche first developed the figure and symbolism of the
shadow in the brief prologue and epilogue to the 350 aphorisms of
The Wanderer and His Shadow, the final section of *Human, All Too
Human*. The introductory dialogue opens with the shadow offering the
wanderer an opportunity to speak, to which the wanderer first expresses his surprise: "Someone speaks:—where? Who? It almost
sounds like me, as if I heard myself speak only with a weaker voice
than mine."[37] The multiplicity of one's own voices is reconfirmed in
Nietzsche's portrait of the wanderer and his shadow.

The wanderer reappears earlier in Zarathustra. In part three, in the opening section entitled "The Wanderer," Zarathustra describes himself as "a wanderer and a mountain climber." And further, "Whatever may yet come to me as destiny and experience—a wandering will be part of it, and a mountain-climb: in the end one experiences only oneself. The time is past when mere accidents could meet me; what could still befall me that is not already mine?"[38]

Here with the economy of a poetic introduction containing the whole in the homoeomerous overture Nietzsche announces the themes that link this and the following chapter: first the containment of several selves within one, second the eternal recurrence of those selves one meets again and again precisely because they are projections of one's own selves. Here lies the existential meaning of eternal recurrence, in the necessary limitedness of one's experience to a set of *some* selves one already knows.

Zarathustra's shadow is *his.* He cannot outrun it however hard he tries. Nietzsche offers an objective correlative for the opposition between the voluntary beggar and the shadow in the image of "six old fools' legs clattering along after one another," the voluntary beggar followed by Zarathustra who is in turn chased by his shadow. How much better is this image of the shadow than Heidegger's ponderous neologism, *jemeinigkeit,* ever-my-own-ness! Everybody has his own shadow. Hence its universality. Yet each one is different, each one uniquely fitted to its wearer by inescapable laws of optics and geometry working in collusion with the details of one's own figure. The correlative laws of personality theory are the principles of screening, dislike and unfamiliarity. Hence when Zarathustra gives up the chase and turns on his shadow he asks: "Who are you? What are you up to? And why do you call yourself my shadow? I do not like you."

Jung, one of Nietzsche's most careful readers, uses the symbol of the shadow as one of the fundamental archetypes. He explicitly links the shadow with the mechanism of projection: one projects on the other one's own most unwanted traits, those characteristics one does not even recognize as one's own because they have been given a life of their own in the character of the unfamiliar shadow. Because the shadow is unrecognized, the wanderer *meets* higher men who appear to be *other* than himself. "As we know, it is not the conscious subject but the unconscious which does the projecting. Hence one *meets* with projections, one does not make them."[39] Jung continues: "The effect of projection is to isolate the subject from his environment, since instead of a real relation to it there is now only an illusory one. Projections change the world into the replica of one's own unknown face." Therefore the way toward overcoming isolation is confrontation with the shadow, knowing the unknown face, and hence recognizing projections for what they are: the products of one's own fears and animosities. Confrontation with the shadow is therefore crucial to hermeneutics, for the shadow is the seat of *mis*interpretation.

This insight into the pernicious projections of the shadow, this map of an avenue toward error, can help the wary wanderer in the complex wilderness of relational thought toward at least some certainty about the *nature* of truth if not toward particular truths. Once one realizes the difference between some good interpretations and the misinterpretations foisted on consciousness by the pernicious shadow, once one has caught him in the act as it were and learned how to inch along the marginal differences that mark out the slow course of overcoming one's own self-delusions, then one no longer needs the fiction of the polar opposition between fact and fiction to make sense of truthfulness. Forswearing hard facts does not condemn us to fictions. Through confrontation with the shadow one gains another criterion of validity in interpretation, another dimension than that which supposedly stretches between Error and the One Truth.

Ferreting out our *Vorurteilen*—our forejudgments, prejudgments, *our prejudices*—is therefore the foremost task of hermeneutics as Gadamer describes it.[40] So it is natural that the shadow should appear in this political-economic transform of the dimension of religion versus atheism. "There are also of course social and collective implications of the shadow problem," writes Whitmont in his exposition of the Jungian archetype, "for here lies the roots of social, racial and national bias and discrimination. . . . Moreover, since the shadow is the archetype of the enemy, its projection is likely to involve us in the bloodiest of wars."[41]

The shadow may be Ares, god of war, Aphrodite's erstwhile lover. Just as Ares has his place in the polytheistic pantheon, so the shadow too will be invited into Zarathustra's cave. Zarathustra will come to terms with the shadow just as he came to terms with the ugliest man. He will own the secular warrior as part of himself—a limited part, a disliked part, but a part nonetheless. Confrontation with this warrior is itself a sort of warfare. If it is a true confrontation with the true shadow, some sort of violence is inevitable. The question is: What sort? How much violence and what kind?

Nietzsche's legacy has never lived down the line, "A good war hallows any cause."[42] Especially today when warfare has become so technologically demonic that it threatens the total annihilation of life on earth the prospect of a good war seems so close to a contradiction in terms as to be not worth entertaining. War and aggression have become the unholy or unholies. A whole generation of conscientious objectors who quite justifiably resisted serving in the Vietnam debacle now run the risk of raising their own children with a repression of violence as total as the Victorian repression of sexuality. No guns, no unkind words. It is as if human cubs were to avoid what is so natural to their canine counterparts whose play instinctually takes the form of tussling toward a deadly grip, teeth on jugular. The dog's weapons are his teeth. The human pup soon learns that the weapon of his species is the gun. Little wonder then that his play sometimes revolves around the pow-pow of the pointed finger if a more literal toy is taken away.

Take away the gun, exile Ares, and the one hope of minimizing violence disappears, namely the *symbolic* enactment of a confrontation with the shadow.[43] Ritual behavior need not be a rehearsal for the real thing. On the contrary ritualized play with violence can be the best method of its sublimation toward socially constructive channels.[44]* The issue is complicated because only a fine line separates rehearsal from ritual sublimation. But when the fear of crossing that line renders the ritual impossible then the result must be desublimated violence among warriors who have either forgotten or never learned how to fight and must therefore invent weapons to annihilate their adversaries.

Total warfare, genocide, is man's invention and relatively recent at that. Some would say that the capacity for genocide is an accident of our newfound technological capabilities but a glance at the "contributions" war has made to technology will quickly convince most that the connection between technology and total annihilation is hardly coincidental. We did not just happen to find ourselves capable of genocide. We got that way out of perfecting our means to annihilate the other. The question at this late date is not only how to avoid using the tools we have already perfected but also how to restrain the motives that led to their perfection: how to unlearn the will to total conquest?[45]

Could it be that the will to total conquest comes from an unwillingness to *maintain* conflict and contradiction? Could it be that the wish to eliminate the adversary—within or without—comes from weariness with the struggle? Or fear? Or both? Surely the more popular answer to the question of the genealogy of genocide has nothing to do with such mundane explanations as fear or weariness. We would rather talk of the "war to end all wars"—this as the antidote, the structurally identical antithesis, to "the final solution." Our reasons for not merely fighting with but utterly destroying the other are always of the highest caliber. Kant's essay "Perpetual Peace" is based on the Enlightenment philosophy of a world free of contradiction, a world in which dialectic is the "logic of illusion" rather than the stuff of various realities. Funny how Kantians convinced of the possibility of perpetual peace are perpetually driven by their convictions into wars of total annihilation!

The motive that leads to the will for total conquest is the monotheism of the One True World, the wish to make the entire world safe for democracy, or for communism, or for any other -ism including even pluralism if its essence is misconstrued as pluralism of values in a single world of facts.

This same motive of monotheism has its symptoms and repercussions in the self, not only in the strength of an Apollonian ego or the power of a moralized ego-ideal; the motive of monotheism *creates* the shadow who in turn creates visions of infidels and heretics who must be punished. The monotheistic ego-ideal creates the shadow by refusing to allow unwanted guests in the cave of the soul. But as each soul is a seed of the cosmos, a homoeomerous representation of the whole, such inhospitality is doomed to failure. The shadow thrives on hostility for once disowned he can do his dirty work behind the back of oblivious consciousness.

Because the shadow is in each case one's own and because Hermes guarantees that each will interpret his world slightly differently, the shadow is in each case different. Consequently no preaching about tolerance toward specific quirks can avoid the dangers the shadow holds in store. Since 'the shadow' names a formal archetype whose contents vary as widely as do dominant personalities, only the formality of relational thinking is adequate to deal with the shadow in all its forms. Any specific ethics, any content dogmatism, is bound to create yet another shadow whose projections will create yet further enemies, further wars, further visions of total conquest.

Nietzsche's "good war that hallows any cause" is precisely the war with the shadow, the confrontation that keeps *any* cause from needing to annihilate its "enemy" because it keeps any cause from oblivious ignorance of its contrary. The struggle with the shadow demands an awareness of the disquiet, the dissonance, the deep contrarities at the heart of all existence. "Peace and quiet." These are the silent harbingers of wars to end all wars. These psychological earmuffs, these meditator's delights, no doubt have their time and place somewhere behind the battleground on which the Bhagavad Gita itself unfolds. But perpetual peace is an illusion, a most dangerous fantasy whose final outcome is final conquest over whatever figure plays the role of shadow.

The shadow concludes both the tour of higher men and the chain of parallels begun with the ugliest man. He makes an appropriate conclusion for both sequences for several reasons. First, the formality of the dynamic of the shadow, the fact that *any* figure may play the role of the shadow, shows that only the aspiration toward wholeness will be adequate to defend against the dirty work of the many shadows in any community. The drive toward wholeness is the drive toward the togetherness of the several selves, the subject of the next chapter.

Second, the dynamic of the shadow is both individual and social.[46] The shadow met by Zarathustra is the sociopolitical analogue of the atheist. The fact that the dynamic of the shadow is both individual and social further corroborates homoeomereity: the part, the individual, reflects the proportions of the social whole and vice versa.

Third, the formality of the mechanism of the shadow's projections makes the specific contents of Zarathustra's shadow the most valuable diagnostic source for analyzing Nietzsche's own blindness. What was he unable to see? Where must we look to find whatever Nietzsche, for whatever reasons, could not afford to find? Precisely in the realm of the sociopolitical, precisely there we find he has no politics.[47] Nietzsche's own shadow, the naughty anarchist, the impetuous unprincipled Ares, serves as an invaluable hint: first toward the *individual's* need to maintain conflict rather than let it dissolve into the quiet calm before the storm; second and less intentionally, toward the need to look beyond Nietzsche's own perceptions of sociopolitical forms of conflict. For precisely here we are warned that Nietzsche's perceptions are at their weakest. Precisely here we are forced to acknowledge the often voiced criticism that Nietzsche never worked out the social implications of his ideas, that he was therefore partially to blame for the fascistic misuses to which they have been put.[48]*

The strategy of the following chapters will be first to follow out the drive toward wholeness by following Zarathustra's wandering through its final epiphanies, then to return to the cave of sociopolitical "realities," the realm of the day-to-day that Nietzsche seemed so assiduously to deny. This strategy raises a fourth reason for the appropriateness of concluding the tour of higher men with the shadow: the need to fathom the depths and follow Zarathustra into the heights of Nietzsche's philosophy turns out to be the need to confront the shadow of many dimensional man—Nietzsche himself. Nietzsche himself is the anarchistic individual who will finally deny life among Some for the sake of a precious One, himself. The strategy all along has been a kind of confrontation with the shadow, a reluctant recognition of his dark truths the better to recognize them as motors of projection, motives for misinterpretation. To solve the riddle of pluralism, to allow otherness without a surrender to indifference, demands that we sometimes question our deepest preferences, sometimes overcome our "convictions," sometimes overcome ourselves. Sometimes it is necessary to recognize our closest friend as our enemy, our shadow. Otherwise we continue meeting the same old enemies where we might find friends.[49]

To acknowledge Nietzsche as the shadow of many dimensional man is hardly to reject him. Quite to the contrary, just as Nietzsche shows his own need to come to terms with his own nastiness, just as Zarathustra must invite the ugliest man to his cave, just as polytheism must make a place for the atheist and parapolitics a place for the anarchist, so many dimensional man must confront the nether reaches of his soul through which Nietzsche will be his most faithful guide—faithful even to the point of a necessary faithlessness, an unforgivable infidelity, a breaking of frame in which he enters his own creation only to deprecate himself. Who would follow such a self-deprecator? Who would break frame to admit that the creature he had "created" was greater than he could maintain and hence an enemy to his peace of mind?

A backward glance

How can Aphrodite restore her virginity? How can Narcissus avoid narcissism? How can the whole be distinctive, the homoeomerous be everywhere unique? How can the smaller contain the greater, the moment contain eternity? To the Eleatic tradition these questions pose paradoxes at best; at worst they are contradictions to be avoided at all cost. Anaxagorean logic allows a comprehension of these so-called paradoxes but, alas, that logic must be *lived* in a synthesis of wholeness rather than looked at in an analysis of parts. By its own partiality, by its implicit invitation to quiet armchair reflection, the written word is not suited to an introduction to Anaxagorean logic. That logic needs the activity of Pericles or the art of a Nietzsche to overcome the fixed framing that words alone invite.

The fourth part of Zarathustra explores the interiority of a many-selved soul through the symbolism of wanderings in an exterior wilderness. As Zarathustra meets each of his projections, as Nietzsche turns his soul inside out, he anticipates the sensibility of a century he did not live to see. Nietzsche's words are to writing what Schoenberg's tone-row is to music and Escher's pictures to visual art. All three delight in breaking the frames of "normal" perception. Just as Escher paints the hand that is painting the hand, just as he paints stairways on which "the way up is the way down,"[50] so Nietzsche descends toward an ascension. Just as Schoenberg denies the closure of a single tonality so Nietzsche refuses the simplicity of a single self but seeks in the depths of his own decadence the artful dissonance that is his own beauty. His own. For the optics of the shadow are such as to fit each of us with our own. Nietzsche's beauty is not to be borrowed or imitated—but experienced. Therein lies the lesson of the fourth part of Zarathustra. Each of those who parrot Zarathustra's sayings is mocked. So Nietzsche shows the need for perpetual renewal, each time a first time and not a repetition of what has gone before. Yet at the same time each time is a comprehension of *all* that has gone before, a redemption. Just as each Anaxagorean seed contains all, so the Moment may contain eternity, each self contain all others, and the way down to the truths of the shadow reveal the way up toward the truths of the light.

Each of the questions of this chapter reveals a similar logic of whole in part, a distinctiveness of parts, and hence a distinctiveness of wholes. Homoeomereity has its temporal, spatial, cosmological and characterological transforms. If one is possible then all are possible. An experience of the actuality of any supports the possibility of others against the claims of Eleatic logic. The experience of Nietzsche's words breaking frame and containing their author as greater in lesser yet the lesser as greater because of the break, Nietzsche's artful evocation of the ambiguities of frame in the structure of multiple selfhood, serves as an actual example to support the parallel possibilities of the Moment containing eternity, each god and goddess containing all others, each seed containing all, each person containing a pantheon.

The answer to the puzzle of homoeomereity—how can one seed generate a distinctive change if each seed similarly contains the whole—is the same as the answer to the riddle of the symbolism of Aphrodite's restored virginity, the perpetual distinctiveness of her confrontation with Ares: each part is distinctive in its reflection of the proportions of "the whole" because "the whole" is not describable as contained within an unambiguous greatest limit. Like Leibniz's monads each part is a perspective on all others, yet the 'all' of 'all others' alters its meaning with new interpretations from each perspective. "The Whole" is like that—ever self-differentiating along countless different dimensions of *differance*, ever-redeeming itself by transfiguration, a refiguring of the same differently. As each seed represents the ever different whole, each seed will exhibit a distinctiveness whose proportions of sameness and difference reproduce the proportions of sameness and difference in the whole.

The Anaxagorean logic of sameness and difference differs point for point with Eleatic logic. Where the hierarchy of Eleatic forms finds a lowest foundation in an indeterminate substratum, where difference appears as spatial separation of material (or logical) atoms, Anaxagorean logic finds a very different subject of predication: a structure of subjectivity that has no lowest limit. Just as the microscope reveals as much *information* as the telescope so the so-

called substratum is every bit as *formal* as the forms supposedly in-
forming it. The notion that division will at some point come to an end
in least indivisible atoms—whether physical, logical, linguistic or
personal—is a fantasy bred of the mutually reinforcing circle joining
Eleatic logic, bureaucratic atomization of experience and a deadened
existence whose sluggish weight is projected as the concept of matter.

Of course the Eleatic logician will object to this characterization of the logic of atomism on the grounds that the characterization is
guilty of psychologism. But the sharp distinction between the logical
and the psychological is itself part of the fantasy that the purely formal can be completely separated from the material content in which it
is found.

In the relative *differance* between formal and material *roles*,
one structure plays the *role* of content for another structure's formation. Eleatic logic reifies this relative *differance* into the fixed poles of
form and matter.

In Anaxagorean logic the quest for the subject leads not toward an undifferentiated substratum utterly different from formalizing
consciousness. Rather the "lower" reaches of subjectivity reveal a
shadow of the higher. Here the different "poles" are the same in
structure, homogeneous or homoeomerous rather than heterogeneous.

What of the forms? In the point for point difference between
Eleatic and Anaxagorean logic how do the predicates exhibit a different logic of sameness and difference? Since Eleatic logic gains formality by abstraction from content, since the pure form of circularity
abstracts from all differences among particular circles, the form of
Eleatic forms must itself abstract from all difference toward an undifferentiated unity—in-formation that tells nothing about everything.

In Anaxagorean logic, form is the totalization of differences
from a given perspective rather than an abstraction from differences
to a "formalism free of perspective." The form of each self in the
multiple structure of subjectivity will not be a dimensionless point to
which all differences are tied, but the process of formation itself,[51]

the evolving personality that exists only in its perpetually self-confirming interpretations of all selves from its own perspective. Form is not abstraction *from* differences but an ordering *of* differences. Different orderings are different forms—like the days of the week and the dates of a month. The concept of order does not require the ultimacy of *one* order for others to make sense.

PART THREE
THE SACRED AND
THE PROFANE

VII Ascension

The chain of parallels uncoiled in the last chapter has further links as yet uncoiled: Zarathustra's meeting with the ugliest man made it clear that the atheist would retain a place in the depths of Zarathustra's cave yet the ecstasy of something like religious revelation would not be ignored. This chapter explores that third transform in the chain of parallels, the next chapter the fourth, the equally ginger appropriation of anarchism.

The specific question postponed for this chapter concerned the naming of the gods. Ecstasy is notoriously ineffable. If the sacred speaks its name, if speech intrudes upon the ecstatic silence, then the divine has been defiled with human determination. So speaks a long tradition of negative theology from the mystics to Karl Barth. Yet polytheism particularly calls for some articulation of the divine, else the many meld into the indeterminate One. Zarathustra's ecstasies at noon and midnight are dramatic events in a story whose interpretation provides an answer to the questions of negative theology in the polytheistic context. To interpret these events properly their significance will be set against approaches to the absolute in the monotheistic context. Finally the fruits of Nietzsche's lessons turn ripe in the context of current efforts to name the gods using the polytheistic pantheon of astrology and the pluralistic analyses of the *I Ching*.

The events

After Zarathustra had left his shadow with words well spoken to those enamored with Nietzsche's challenges; after he had warned his shadow, "Look out lest some narrow faith trap you in the end, some delusion of hardness and strength. For you are likely lured and seduced by whatever is narrow and firm";[1] after having thus cautioned against precisely what is worst in most Nietzsche enthusiasts, Zarathustra left the last of the higher men. But not really, for when he was alone, "he found himself yet again and again," for he had been meeting his several selves all along. Now, however, now that each of the several has had his say, now that each has been confronted rather than fled, invited rather than refused, now Nietzsche is ready to cease *naming* the gods and, with a silence woven among different words, to *show* that those several selves were gods he had named, not merely men, much less the mere parts of his soul. For after the cycle of their inventory is complete, then does Zarathustra's soul "take flight"—or whatever. At this point words fail, or so say most words from the mystic tradition. Words are at best a set of tracks left in the wake of an experience that transcends the differences from which words derive their meaning.

Yet the tracks left by even the most reluctant mystics are so much the same. One often finds the footprint of eternity, the heavy mark of time that stopped, the stamp of perfection, completeness, joy . . . and often too the dark night of the soul that has seen the beatific vision and been denied its duration. The reports are all so similar even in their symbolism and in their silences. So it is with Nietzsche as well, most reluctant mystic of them all.

Zarathusra lies down at noon. Time stops. The world is perfect. He tastes eternity, sees the golden round ball, awakes "and behold, the sun still stood straight over his head." It hadn't taken any time at all. The same old story. The same old ecstasy.

What does it take to paint this patently experienced, often repeated story in words? Anyone who has been there will recognize what one is talking about immediately and will also know that words are inadequate to describe it to anyone who has not been there. Nor will words take one there, even though they may untangle other words that keep one away.

So that, perhaps, is Nietzsche's intention in his addition to the familiar list of "mystic experiences." Perhaps he is untangling some of the mystifications about the mysteries. Perhaps like Hegel he would like an opportunity to point out what is wrong with both the scientific insight of the Enlightenment *and* the belief of superstition. To the rationalist he would point out that such experiences do in fact occur, as much as to say, "Yes, ye true believers in so-called science, ye sober conscientious ones, the soul does take flight on occasion, does leave the body, does travel after a fashion, and to perspectives from which all of these day-to-day worries and cares seem both incredibly inconsequential and at the same time terribly beautiful. Yes, it does happen." Probably some rare physiological condition, thinks the scientist of the Enlightenment. "Yes, certainly that," would answer Nietzsche who knew if anyone did the importance of physiology.[2]

"You know he did a lot of drugs,"[3] cautions the conscientious voice of science, which still insists that if an event can be causally correlated with some physical alteration then it is *nothing but* that physical alteration—as if their own words were *nothing but* vibrations in the air, configurations of high and low density photon reflections off intricately printed pulp called paper. Of course they are right too. And what the scientists see is itself a thing of beauty. But not all of it.

And the superstitious: to them Nietzsche so much as says, "You true believers. You have named the gods, and done so poorly. You have left out some and others you have clothed in pretty costumes that do not become them. And worst of all you have narrowed your sights to one whose hold over you forbids you from seeing the others; one whose hold forbids you from experiencing their fullness, from undergoing their contradictions and hence from overcoming their contradictions. Both this single god and the style of your worship prevent you from precisely the *experiences* whose tracks are traced all over your own religious writings. Here," says Nietzsche, "I've had one of your so-called mystical religious experiences, but only after considerable tolerance to parts of myself that you would condemn as 'unworthy'; only after an extended tour through what you call the underworld of hell but I regard as very much a part of this experience here on the surface of earth." Nietzsche says to the superstitious, the believers in good works and Christian Love, that their love of the enemy is a fraud,[4] that they do not *love* their enemies because in exhorting one another to love their enemies they admit they have enemies, those they do not love—yet they exhort one another to love because they have not accepted the hatred that burns in the nether nooks of their souls. So the hatred does its work in darkness, beneath the cover of unconsciousness, making enemies one must love rather than confront lest one find there the parts of oneself one hates. What a silly way to live, loving everyone like that!

Nietzsche says as much by writing a worship in the *grand stile* of satire—a last supper that is a festival to an ass, a worship with laughter, foolishness in the face of piety like a turd in the priory. It stinks! What a rotten trick to play on Christians who almost wanted to "believe in" Zarathustra, to leave them choking on his exit line from the ass festival: "And should ye do this celebration again, this ass festival, do it for fun, and do it for me. And in remembrance of *me*!"

ASCENSION 249

What a travesty on the holy communion, pure foolishness bordering on bad taste.

The Eastern traditions have a name for this sort of thing. They call it *lila*, which loosely translates as 'holy play', as in the young "perfect master's" perfect motorcycle wheelies that wheeled round Rennie Davis from his career as a new left politico to his equally one-sided career as an apostle;[5] *lila* as in the outrageous behavior of the illustrious Trungpa Rimpoche who shows he knows what he is talking about by, aside from less mentionables, arriving sometimes at so-called important occasions "drunk on his ass."[6] This same *lila*, this playfulness is present in Nietzsche's approach to the experience of godhood. In his playfulness he places a plague on the houses of both the Enlightenment and superstition, those opposing literalisms who "take in each other's wash."[7]

His holy play in the priory declares that nothing shall be permanently prior. Nothing shall be utterly immune to impiety, least of all that which purports to consume one's entire life. Passion yes, but not the one-sided hurling of an entire life in a single direction either sacred or profane, either enlightened or superstitious. This spiritual professionalism that prohibits the richness of existence, this specialization of the soul, is clearly wrong, even where the specialty in question is a special bliss.

The context

Nietzsche indicates the dialectic of perfection very differently from Hegel and Plato but the logic of their appropriations of the Absolute is fundamentally the same. For each it is necessary to complete the circuit of forms of consciousness before the experience of absolute knowledge is available. For each the circuit is much more than the appropriation of different *objects* of knowledge by a consciousness that remains essentially the same. For Plato the divided line marks off not only four different kinds of objects of knowledge but also four kinds of consciousness corresponding to those objects. For Hegel too the path toward absolute knowledge is an experiential "highway of despair" marked by cataclysmic "conversions of consciousness" between the various forms of consciousness (*Gestalten des Bewusstseins*).[8] For Nietzsche the several forms of consciousness are represented by the several selves of the Higher Men, each an entire personality—a form of consciousness—each in its one-sidedness inadequate to absolute knowledge, yet each necessary to complete the many-sided absolute.

In the context of a comparison with Plato and Hegel on the dialectic of the absolute, Nietzsche's strategy in *Zarathustra* IV becomes clear. The problem is just this: must the mention of completeness or perfection mark an *end*, a cessation, death? The problem arises in Plato as the question, Why must the enlightened one return into the depths of the cave? So formulated the question is the same as the issue separating Hinayana from Mahayana Buddhism: is it possible for a single soul to attain enlightenment or must one stop short of the final goal and return as a bodhisattva so that all will attain enlightenment together? In the Hegelian tradition the same issue appears in a slightly different guise: does the attainment of absolute knowledge presuppose the end of history?[9]

Each of these traditions exercised in its own time and its own place a salutary rounding influence. By lifting their hearers out of a one-sided concern with whatever immediate convictions held them prisoners, each of these traditions liberated a significant number for the experience of totality—a perfection that includes imperfection, an absolute that includes the relative, an overcoming of all contradictions without a one-sided opting for either side. Because the Buddhist and Platonic traditions have their origins among peoples whose lives were tied to the earth, to an experience of intense immanence, the salutary myths of those traditions were necessarily myths of transcendence. Hegel culminates the myths of transcendence with the prospect of a transcendence of history (the human world become temporal and dynamic rather than spatial and static). Yet Hegel's culmination also marks a turn, for the attainment of absolute knowledge follows not from a transcendence of wordly experience—the veil of maya or illusion whose escape figures so prominently in both the exoteric Platonic and Buddhist Way.[10] Instead the vision of perfection follows only from a completion of *that very experience.* Hegel marks a return to immanence necessitated by a Western tradition that had become too otherwordly. Yet Hegel's handling of the dialectic of perfection, culminating and transitional as it is, remains not only obscure but fundamentally ambiguous.[11]

Less so Nietzsche, who enjoins us always to remain true to the earth. Nietzsche leaves the necessarily fleeting character of beatific vision unambiguously clear by subjecting Zarathustra to a song of melancholy even after his vision, then plunging Zarathustra into a black trance at midnight. Zarathustra's further wanderings demonstrate the difference between demonic escape and divine transfiguration. Recall that it is the devil's trick to offer liberation, a death whose description is almost indistinguishable from a divine release from the commonplace—which words echo Plato's description of madness.[12]

All these lures look so similar. How are we fish to know the difference, to avoid the barb of demonic death and madness when swallowing what appears to be final enlightenement? How are we to know that this "revelation" is not just another name for going over the brink, for giving up and taking a simple way out, a walking suicide that does not bother about the biological processes' continuation? How are we to distinguish between heaven on earth and a soporific, some absurd distortion that simplifies everything to leave us smiling through the apocalypse while our friends mumble among themselves about our going mad? These are the questions whose answers are demonstrated by Zarathustra's further wanderings.

They are good questions. They raise the issue of the false prophet and how to recognize him. They are work for the residual atheist, a task of identifying wooden nickels. For what is the difference between the detachment of the bodhisattva and the detachment of schizophrenic dissociation? Their descriptions are the same.[13] R. D. Laing describes the false self-structure in terms of a withdrawal to a stance of *watching* rather than genuinely *participating in* the activity of the person whose body then houses at least two selves divided by a schism of withdrawal.[14] Baba Ram Dass describes a state of enlightenment in which it is as if one were standing on a bridge watching one's experiences go by. Rather than being dragged under by a depression, one is then able to say appreciatively from the bridge's elevation, "Oh, *look* at that depression!"[15]

But so situated on that inner bridge does one then experience joy . . . or that which *would* be joy if one were participating in it rather than watching it? Agreed: a capacity for withdrawal to a perspective *sub specie aeternitatis* can be very helpful when one is suffering *momentary* pain. But if that capacity be overworked, if one finds oneself stranded on the time line of eternity alone, and if one is then unable to experience the now of immediacy with all its petty cares and woes, if one is *only* sublime, then what has been gained in this Moment of revelation? What has been won with a transcending of all difference that leaves one facing a light so bright one is blinded? What has been lost in a total light whose effects are indistinguishable from total darkness? What has perished in a life indistinguishable (except biologically) from death? What exists in Being that is indistinguishable from Nothing?

Hegel had in mind not some abstruse issue of abstract logic when he began the great *Science of Logic* with the observation that Absolute Being and Absolute Nothing are indistinguishable, that one *must* therefore begin with Becoming. All those thinkers who have questioned the necessity of the "transition" from Being and Nothing to Becoming—many have questioned Hegel on this point[16]—have misunderstood to a man what is at stake in this move that is not a *formal* logical consequence at all but an existential dialectical necessity: to be—to exist in a way that is differentiable from death—is to become. To enter the logic of life is to confess oneself fallen into the self-divisive process of becoming, the perpetual repetition of negation and negation again before the affirmation of *Aufhebugn*—transcendence, sublation, elevation, ascension. By beginning in Becoming the *Science of Logic* adumbrates the entire *Phenomenology*, which is working through the *phenomena* of becoming toward the discovery that the totality of those phenomena constitutes all there is—there isn't any more: no truth, no noumena *behind* the phenomena—only in, among, beside and sometimes against the appearances. By working through every possible escape route that consciousness takes in its attempt to assert a Being *behind* the becoming of phenomena, by totalizing and (less successfully) ordering the ways in which consciousness attempts to assert an unambiguous difference between Being and Nothing, Life and Death, Revelation and Madness, Beauty and Ugliness, War and Peace, Insight and Superstition and so on; by showing in every case how consciousness itself comes to discover the difference it thought to be *given* to be a difference of its own making, Hegel reaches the point in the *Phenomenology* that allows him to adumbrate at the beginning of the *Logic:* now we know that all these polar distinctions—of which Being/Nothing is perhaps the barest—designate no real and substantial poles but are the products of a process of *differance,* the process that is life.[17]

To refuse this process, to fix the distinctions in determinate and lifeless opposition, is to deny the perpetual repetition of the process of *differance,* the process that is life. To affirm a fixed and obvious distinction between life and death is already to deny life. So we are always and ever *becoming,* always faced with *making* differentiations where they are not to be unambiguously *found.* That is where the *Phenomenology* ends—with an absolute knowledge that describes the total commitment to becoming in terms of a recognition of self-consciousness, the discovery that what we thought was a knowledge of the other was really a knowledge of self—though let us add quickly, before Marxists hurtle in with the epithet 'idealist', that 'self' in this context comes to designate all there is, all the history and culture and war and peace and politics and everything else the Marxists claim as the Being (*Sein*) that determines consciousness (*Bewusstsein*).[18]

With the ending of the *Phenomenology*, with the recognition of absolute self-consciousness that is a confession of becoming, the *Logic* begins. So this "transition" from Being and Nothing to Becoming is no more questionable than the relationship of the *Phenomenology* to the *Logic*. But then scholars have had trouble on that score, too.[19] They find him answering rather than dissolving Hamlet's question, To be or not be be? They read the *Phenomenology* as a completion of Being rather than as a confession of the perpetuity of becoming. And if the *Phenomenology* be read as such a completion, then of course the transition from Being to becoming remains a mystery, an apparently unnecessary regression. The exigency of Hamlet's question dissolves in the necessity of being. So is Hegel sometimes misread, and so is he somewhat to blame for the ambiguities of his culminating and transitional answer to the age-old question: Is there an Answer, a condition of completion after which all anxieties will wither before the radiant Being of the perfect Absolute?

The young Nietzsche and the context

Nietzsche has a few interesting things to say about Hamlet's question, a few things that reflect on the interpretation of Zarathustra's further wanderings which, it has been promised, will demonstrate the answers to those several questions—life or death, etc.—that are abbreviated in the blessedly brief, To be or not to be? In his very first book, *The Birth of Tragedy*, a book at which he will later glance back critically, he says that Hamlet hesitates to act not for any great surfeit of possibilities whose lures leave him indecisive in his reflection; rather, having looked deeply if briefly into the heart of

things, having *seen* truthfully if ecstatically, both Dionysian man and
Hamlet are loath to return to a quotidian reality whose petty differentiations they view with horror. "Knowledge kills action, for action requires the veil of illusion."[20] Here Apollo becomes crucial for the
young Nietzsche—to weave a veil of illusion through his mastery of
image making. Apollo saves the ecstatic from despair by forging illusions to fill the darkness after the revelation.

The young Nietzsche succumbs to the inevitability of nausea.
"In the consciousness of this once glanced truth man sees everywhere
only the dreadfulness or absurdity of being (*Seins*), he now understands the symbolism in the fate of Ophelia, now recognizes the wisdom of the woodsprite Silenus: it nauseates him." Only an aesthetic
justification, the product of Apollo's plastic art, will give metaphysical solace to Solon's or Silenus's or Midas's misery, which in each of
these mythically intertwined stories is the same: to have traveled far,
seen all, even the supreme grace of the Hyperboreans across the sea,
and to return disgusted nevertheless, nauseated at how little separates
the highest from the lowest, nauseated at the sight of the wretched-
ness of even the most kingly among men, retching up gold like the
foolish King Midas.[21]

The young Nietzsche fancies that he knows the difference between Being and Nothingness, between life and death, etc. He is impressed with both Schopenhauer's pessimism and his epistemology;
and he has not yet seen the connection between the two—namely,
that the faith in a True World of Being behind the veil of Becoming
degrades that veil to Nothingness. As Hegel saw very clearly, the concept of appearance, illusion, *Maya*, presupposes the projection of a
true world *behind* the appearances. Thus the Kantian thing-in-itself is
appearance *qua appearance*.[22] The hypostatization of Being *behind*
Becoming is nothing but an interpretation of Becoming *qua delusion*,
a degrading of the phenomena, a denial of the day to day, a nay-saying to *this* life. This connection between pessimism and Kantian epistemology the young Nietzsche had not made. Consequently he prefers
Apollo and Aphrodite to Hermes. Beauty as illusion *covering* a horri-

ble truth obviates hermeneutics as interpretation *approaching* truth, beautiful or horrible.

Nietzsche found himself knotted between his admiration for the transport he experienced in tragedy and music on the one hand and his certainty of the nullity of it all, the merely illusory character of all beauty on the other. He was unwilling to accept Aphrodite, whom he regarded like Hesiod as "bane in place of a blessing," as "the sheer delusion inescapable for man."[23] The young Nietzsche was unwilling to accept Aphrodite for fear of losing her.

In his conscientiousness, in his residual scientific positivism, he preferred to know little rather than half-know much—to have very little rather than risk losing all. In this he was like Thales, whom Solon questioned for his not taking a wife and having children. Thales—like Hamlet and the young Nietzsche—fancied that he had seen to the depths of things and discovered the misery that lay in store for him who bought into the delusion of domestic bliss. Thales answered Solon by tricking him into thinking that during his absence Solon's own son had died—this little jest to illustrate to Solon why Thales had not had children.

Plutarch has little sympathy for the jest and says as much in words that describe Nietzsche as well as Thales. He remarks that it is irrational not to seek conveniences for fear of losing them. People who attempt to do so, say, by adopting the ascetic mode that follows the disappointing return from ecstasy to quotidian reality,[24] will themselves be further deceived, "for the soul," according to Plutarch, "having a principle of kindness in itself, and being born to love, as well as perceive, think, or remember, inclines and fixes upon some stranger, when a man has none of his own to embrace." Quite as Nietzsche warned himself against the stranger, Lou Andreas Salome, about whom he fabricated fantasies forged from his self-denials,[25] Plutarch continues in a mode that anticipates Freudian and Nietzschean insights into transferred cathexes: "And alien or illegitimate objects insinuate themselves into his affections, as into some estate that lacks lawful heirs; and with affection come anxiety and care";

this anxiety and care reaching to the extent of Nietzsche's final crisis, his pity at the sight of a horse being beaten. Or, as Plutarch describes it: "insomuch that you may see men that use the strongest language against the marriage-bed and the fruit of it, when some servant's or concubine's child is sick or dies, almost killed with grief, and abjectly lamenting. Some have given way to shameful and desperate sorrow at the loss of a dog or horse."[26]

The story is the same, the syndrome in perfect symmetry that binds the young Nietzsche and Hamlet and Thales to a positivistic certainty in the nullity of all things, a certainty that is the pessimist's defense, his epistemological comfort that finds metaphysical solace in art both because it beautifies and more importantly because its *patent* illusoriness leaves the proud man of knowledge *certain* of his insight into the nothingness of all that lies beneath the veil of illusion. He who at once loves and despises Aphrodite remains secure in his knowledge of a determinate difference between Being and Nothingness, Beauty and Ugliness, Good and Evil, Life and Death. He who allows himself to love without the reserve of such knowledge risks all.

The young Nietzsche was not ready to risk all. Precisely in his praise of the ascetic Thales he recommends the ideal philosopher as one who, "even while he feels himself swelling into a macrocosm, all the while retains a certain self-possession, a way of viewing himself coldly as a mirror of the world."[27] A vision of homoeomereity to be sure, but a vision that praises Thales precisely for his cold caution.

The syndrome is the same as that quietism born of the unassimilated vision. Hamlet's quietism, in which Nietzsche reads not only the wisdom of Silenus but also Ophelia's fate, is a quietism accused by Ophelia as the "sovereign reason" of "blown youth blasted with ecstasy." This is the quietism of one who, having *seen* into the heart of things, beyond the petty cares of quotidian reality, now "regards as laughable or humiliating the suggestion that it should devolve upon him to set to rights a world that is out of joint."[28] Having seen beyond the differences with which the rest of us are concerned he is altogether confident that "his actions can change nothing of the eternal essence of things." This unassimilated vision of eternity, this syndrome of pessimistic quietism, this blasted ecstasy is quite the same as what Aldous Huxley reports from his mescaline trip.

While in the heights of his hallucinogenic rapture Huxley becomes preoccupied with the pure Apollonian form of the folds in his flannel trousers. He recalls that preoccupation later in his trip when he has occasion to glance at some works of art. He comes to understand "the luxuriant development of drapery as a major theme of all the plastic arts."[29] In the folds of those nonrepresentational forms the artist is set free as in a playground where he can give sensuous form to his intense if ineffable vision of the sheer *is-ness* of things—here Huxley finds it helpful to turn to the mystic tradition to borrow Meister Eckhart's term *Istigkeit* to convey the abstract because undifferentiated, yet concrete because experientially intense, impression of bare Being. Of course the sensuous folds of the drapery represent the is-ness of all things only to those who have already found entry to their playground, to the vision that perceives more than mere clothing in the paintings of Bernini and Botticelli, El Greco and Watteau. To the extent that those draperies presuppose for their communicative powers a release from literal vision, they are an inadequate medium for provoking that release in the first place. Like dialectic, "it is a sad means; basically a metaphoric and entirely unfaithful translation into a totally different sphere and speech. Thus Thales had seen the unity of all that is, but when he went to communicate it, he found himself talking about water!"[30] Similarly, Huxley finds himself talking about a pair of flannel trousers.

Like Thales, Hamlet and especially the young Nietzsche, Huxley too finds it difficult to join his homoeomerous vision of Being in a bit of folded flannel on the one hand with the bonds of fidelity to family on the other. "This is how one ought to see, how things really are," he tells himself. "And yet there were reservations. For if one always saw like this, one would never want to do anything else. Just looking, just being the divine Not-self of flower, of book, of chair, of flannel. That would be enough. But in that case what about other people? What about human relations?" Huxley finds himself blissed out, blasted. "This participation in the manifest glory of things left no room, so to speak, for the ordinary, the necessary concerns of human existence, above all for concerns involving persons."[31] One finds precious little politics in Castaneda's teachings from Don Juan.[32]

Mescaline trippers, mystics, madmen, artists, philosophers of the Vision of the One—all have the same disquieting habit of turning toward quietism. All who are confident in their access to pure Being find it loathsome to return to the cave of becoming. Having transcended even the differentiation of good and evil, "Now consolation is of no avail," viz. Ophelia's failure with Hamlet; "longing transcends the worldly toward the dead, transcends the gods themselves; human Being (*Dasein*), together with its beguiling reflection in the gods or an immortal beyond, is denied."[33] Hence the naked fear of mysticism in sober moralists like Arthur Danto.[34] Hence Huxley's disquiet: "How could one reconcile this timeless bliss of seeing as one ought to see with the temporal duties of doing what one ought to do and feeling as one ought to feel?"[35] Or as the bard puts it best of all:

> Whether 'tis nobler in the mind to suffer
> The slings and arrows of outrageous fortune,
> Or to take arms against a sea of trouble,
> And by opposing end them? To die; to sleep;
> No more; and by a sleep to say we end
> The heart-ache and the thousand natural shocks
> That flesh is heir to, 'tis a consummation
> Devoutly to be wish'd . . .[36]

This, then, is the context in which Zarathustra's further wanderings will address the ambiguities left by the Buddha's exhortations to the bodhisattva, Plato's persuasion to return to the cave and Hegel's "transition" from pure Being to Becoming. The first two—or at least their disciples—represent liberation from becoming in so clear a light that it is difficult to see what could ever motivate a return from pure Being. Their praise of transcendence may have been necessary to offset the attachments to immanence experienced by their hearers. Hegel completes the Christian tradition and marks a turn or return toward immanence, but the residual Christianity in his language leads many of his readers to intepret him as preaching the end of history, yet another consummation devoutly to be wished rather than a confession of perpetual becoming. Not until Nietzsche—and the mature Nietzsche at that—does the deathly sleep of rapture receive its due as offering not escape but instead an insight into the eternal return of the same; not only a divine release from the commonplace but a repetition of the divinity of the commonplace. Not until Nietzsche's formulation of *amor fati*—the love of fate—does the rapture of release explicitly connote a return to *this* world with all its ills, to *this* life with its actions, its commitments, its undergoings and its overcomings.

After the revelation

How do Zarathustra's further wanderings speak to the questions that have been posed in the context that has been described? How is his appropriation of ecstasy an answer to Hamlet's question and a comment on Plato's and Hegel's answers—to say nothing of hosts of lesser figures?

After his ecstasy at noon, late in the afternoon of the same day, Zarathustra returns to his cave. There he hears once again the cry of distress whose signal had led him about the mountains a good part of the morning as he sought the higher men. "Astounding!—this time the very same cry came from his own cavern. But it was a longer, stranger, more manifold cry, and Zarathustra clearly discerned many voices so combined that, were they heard from a distance, they might sound like a single voice crying out from a single mouth."[37] Both the unity and the exteriority of the cry of distress are delusions, auditory illusions introduced by distortions of distance—for as it has several times been said, that which is closest is farthest away.[38] The cry comes from none other than Nietzsche's own most inferior voices, that "society of souls" he so rightly ascribes to himself.[39] The question now: what difference does it make to each of those voices, how does it change their speeches now that the society of which they are members has undergone a sort of revolution, a Platonic *periagoge*, a turning around if so we might construe the psychic wheelie experienced by Zarathustra at noon?[40]

The King on the right—might he be King Midas?—begins. He claims to speak for all, but who's to tell? He says that the hearts of the higher men are open and delighted at how Zarathustra has humbled himself, yet with pride. In short his (or Nietzsche's) tactic of self-deprecation has secreted a yet more delightful self precisely as it is written.[41] The higher men are delighted by Zarathustra but still confused. Like followers who are enchanted yet bewildered by a guru whose *way* is obviously right yet curiously ambiguous, they would wish for once, would the *real* Zarathustra please stand up. A standard complaint: the objective correlative of the call to authenticity or the quest for identity.[42]

The King assures Zarathustra that he may now enter the intimacy of self-exposure; for even golden solitude cloys. Sooner or later one must share one's riches to enjoy them, and now it is high time, the "final remainder of God among men" is on its way to his height to seek him out and share his bounty. These are divine remnants, these citizens of the society of his soul. And even they, these divine inner selves, these higher men who are finding themselves turned around in the self-reflection of the revolutionary *periagoge* toward the realization that they are as gods and might as well get good at it, even they are still plagued by the voice of the soothsayer who *continues* to say (or so the King on the right *continues* to hear him say[43]): "—it don't pay. Life don't mean shit."[44]

In short, nothing has changed. Not for the King on the right anyway. He is the same old nihilistic critic of power. He would still declare the presidency dead.[45] But he would betray still a certain hypocrisy, a less than liberated pessimism that experiences the death of god politically but somehow fails to understand its implications for the death of politics and therefore continues to speak in the political manner: by speaking for everyone, by speaking in historical, apocalyptic, class-conscious categories, by making his cry of distress a cry for hope, a call to the *real* Zarathustra to come forward as a political leader and lead them toward "the *great* hope," perhaps for the end of history.[46]

Zarathustra is understandably shocked. He reels momentarily, then returns to his company and reports what he has found on his instantaneous distant travels—a report of some importance since it is Zarathustra's first reaction to the discovery that insight into eternity does not *cure* the temporal as the Apollonian ideal might suggest.[47] Zarathustra bluntly announces that the higher men are not all he had hoped them to be. He finds them insufficient to his needs, poor mirrors for his self-reflection, crooked and misshapen—mere bridges. Surely this is a disappointment considering there had been talk of perfection and completion. One would have hoped that after the revelation (or revolution) everything would have changed. The higher men would have somehow proven to be each perfect in his own kind—or so goes the Thomistic eschatology that places (or displaces) evil by allowing imperfection its own perfect representations.[48] But no. Zarathustra disdains the easy way out via the principle of plenitude—a place for everything and each in its place, even the strange and odd—and instead opts for the harder route of an overplenitude, an overfullness of selves who therefore conflict and call one another evil.

There will be no easy peace, no easy pluralism, but a truthful pluralism among laughing lions who sometimes growl at one another as some voice or other in Zarathustra growls at the King on the right. Perhaps it is the voice of Hermes the trickster, or Pan, or some other prankish god that will not have such heaviness; that wills more cheerful selves to rise up from the morass of day to day decisions, the shuffling of power, the sheer seriousness of politics. Perhaps it is Dionysus himself who cries out, "Speak to me of my gardens, of my blessed isles, of my beautiful discovery—why do you not speak to me of that?"[49] Why indeed! What more important concern could there be to the man who has returned from eternity itself than to discover what difference that discovery may have made? And what a disappointment to discover that it seems to have made little or none.

Is this a prelude to the dark night of the soul, that stage often advertised as the penultimate on the mystic Way?[50] Or is it not an illustration of a different ultimatum? Zarathustra utters the cry of the passionate pluralist, "I am a law only for my own kind, I am no law for All!"[51] But for his own kind he is careful to utter also an order of rank that distinguishes him from whoever vapidly allows whatever: "But whosoever hears my drummer must have strong bones and light feet,—joyous in both fighting and feasting, no melancholic, no John-a-dreams." Here Nietzsche uses the same archetype from the brothers Grimm that he used in differentiating the real Hamlet from the one we sometimes hear about, the *Hans dem Träumer* who cannot act.[52] Zarathustra continues his call to his own kind: "as ready for the heaviest as for the festive; healthy and whole." Thus does Zarathustra differentiate his pluralism from the camel's indifference, from that leveling nihilism of the worst kind.[53]

His ultimatum is not toward a single standard of perfection, not to some perfect bliss in the blinding light of pure Being, not to some standard that finally cannot even maintain itself as single. Nietzsche eschews perfect Being as a limbo indistinguishable from Nothingness, a lie about truth, a Many as well as a One and thus not a single standard at all but no standard. His ultimatum is not toward some ultimate perfection prior to which one suffers a penultimate dark night of the soul whose depths and deaths are to be left behind with the onset of perpetual peace. Rather Zarathustra's disappointments with the higher men are the enactment of a perpetual becoming that is as much the so-called ultimate as becoming is so-called Being.

Zarathustra's further travels are an enactment of the return into the cave. Of course there will be quarrels, misunderstandings, even bitter fights in which he who returns risks his life quite as Plato said.[54] The magician announces the night and the dew that antici-

pates those mists that James finds worth saving.⁵⁵ The magician
thinks himself Zarathustra's enemy when in reality he speaks only for
the left-handed half of his whole society of personalities, from his
"darker half" with its invitation to the shadows, its critique of what it
regards as an irrational rationality, a "truth-madness" (*Wahrheits-
Wahnsinne*) of "daylight-longings" (*Tager-Sehnsuchten*).⁵⁶

The right-handed (left-hemisphered) half answers back right
away. The conscientious spirit of science picks the harp from the magician and delivers his own speech, a speech that is true to form: his
fears are unchanged by the revolutionary revelation. He not only still
fears the risks toward which the magician would tempt him, not only
still craves the security of certainty, but now acknowledges in a
concession from the universalism that is science's prejudice: "We *are*
different. We *seek* different things up here, you and I," says the scientist to the dissembler, the one seeking certainty, the other its opposite. Yet both continue to speak their speeches in this ultimate phase
of Zarathustra's soul.

Zarathustra "himself" enters and intervenes in the dispute on
the side of fearlessness and courage. But the speech is, as the magician notes, a trifle too bright, perhaps even smug in its fearlessness.
The magician, whose melancholy was banned by Zarathustra when he
called to his own kind, now makes a prophecy: "Before the night is
over he will learn to love me and laud me. He cannot live long without
committing such foolishness."⁵⁷

And so does it come to pass. After an odd sojourn among the
daughters of the wilderness where Zarathustra flirts with the allure-
ments of the Orient but in the end acknowledges his constancy with
Europe, and in Luther's very own language—"Here I stand; I can do
no other."⁵⁸—after taking part in the foolishness of the ass-festival
with its ambiguous playfulness toward divinity; after even the most
remarkable event of that remarkable day—the ugliest man's profession of *amor fati*, his will to live his life once more; after what had
seemed to be some definite change for the better and not a simple
regression to the same, a conversion rather than a reversion, after the

ugliest man's revelation of eternal recurrence and after the convalescence of the other higher men as well,[59] finally Zarathustra falls into
a trance that fulfills the magician's dire prophecy.

To introduce the darkest night Nietzsche deploys every trick
of the storyteller's art, all the devices of prolongation to heighten ex-
pectation for the denouement. He prepares a musical climax for the
message of midnight, a long-phrased cadenza to follow the festive Ta-
rantella of the Last Supper, the Scherzo of the Ass-Festival, the Di-
vertimento for Sitar that sounded among the Oriental daughters of the
wilderness; to conclude the lyric-epic saga whose musically experienced earlier movements included the Largo of the Magician's
song of melancholy, its answering Presto "On Science," and the long
Allegro "On the Higher Men," Nietzsche the storyteller prepares for
his final counsel by silencing the orchestra to a triple pianissimo;
once he says, hush! Midnight approacheth; he turns long moments of
anticipation into longer moments of suspense by asking his animals to
listen ever more closely. Quieter, a second time quiet: "Still! Still!
Here one hears what cannot be heard by day." And yet a third whis-
per to a still quieter note of caution, "O Man, take care!" Finally complete silence, a pause, "Sooner would I die than relate what weighs on
my midnight heart right now."

In this stone-silence certainty is the mood of the moment, or
more than a mood. This silent enthusiasm for horror, this broaching
of the bark of his soul into blackness, is announced in words that call
out to the unspeakable. Why unspeakable? Why unheard by day? Because, like noon's epiphany, transcending the differences from which
words derive their meaning? Or perhaps because the most horrible to
each of us is something slightly different and Nietzsche, knowing
this, exploits his art as a storyteller to drag from each reader an
awareness of his own most peculiar horror, the reader's own most un-
mentionable fear? No mean trick for Nietzsche's written word to reproduce the achievement of the living presence of a Socratic or Oriental guru. No mean trick to spin with words the web of certainty without content so that the most ambiguous connotations create the mood

of certainty while leaving the reader sufficient leeway to fill in the blanks with needs that leave him sighing, "Finally I have found an author able to articulate the nameless fears." No mean feat on Nietzsche's part to create in print the analogue of those rare meetings when one looks into the eyes of the other and finds oneself truly met, not necessarily by a sheer steadiness of gaze, sometimes even by a certain deviousness of gaze, perhaps the effect of a plurality of selves peeping alternately through the body's eyes, but *met* nonetheless! No mean feat on Nietzsche's part to achieve such a wordless meeting using words.

Zarathustra speaks: "Now I have died." The Adagio floats on, and in this midnight hour the bass violins and cellos chant out a question: "Who shall be lord of the earth? Who shall say: so shall ye run, ye mainstream and little rivelets!" No sooner is the question posed than it is dismissed as day's work. Nietzsche's nighttime response to the problems of daytime social science contains as one of its most distinct components the syndrome of The Beautiful Soul. To the question "Who shall govern?" the seventh stroke of the midnight bell answers, in effect, Don't bother me. "Don't touch me! Did my world not become perfect just now? My skin is too pure for your hands. Leave me alone you stupid, clumsy, stifling day! Is the midnight not clearer?"

Yet the clock strikes on, eight and nine. Nietzsche mourns mortality, yet finds in the clarity of the midnight hour the joy of the lost noon. Here in the occasional incoherence of his drunken song Nietzsche moves beyond Hamlet's black certainty. The difference between being and not being becomes not obscured, for the midnight is nothing if not clear. The existential significance of Hegel's truth is rendered unambiguous: just as pure Being and pure Nothing are indistinguishable and hence the same, so "midnight too is noon, pain too a joy, curses also a blessing."

How to interpret what seems so obviously nonsense? After all, Bertrand Russell once said, if you allow me to give up the principle of noncontradiction then I may say anything I wish to say . . . and anything *else* I wish to say besides. Has anything meaningful been maintained if its opposite too be affirmed?

A determinate and eminently falsifiable assertion emerges from Zarathustra's drunken utterances when their significance is measured against the mystic tradition and the context of philosophies of transcendence. The equivalence of midnight and noon declares the mystic's misunderstanding in taking the "dark night of the soul" as penultimate—as if once endured then light will be everlasting. To philosophies of transcendence the drunken Zarathustra announces: "If you ever said yes to a single joy then my friends you said yes to *all* woe. All things are entangled, ensnared, enamored." There is no breaking free, no transcending to another world.

Yet clearly Zarathustra's soul has taken flight after a fashion. At the second stroke of midnight, in the second of the twelve sections of the drunken song, "His soul took flight toward great distances where it perched 'on a high ridge,' as it is written, 'between two seas, between past and future wandering like a heavy cloud.'" The *experience* is undeniable, the uninterrupted sobriety of some notwithstanding. The question remains, however, what is the *significance* of the Moment? Has it not been mystified by a mystic tradition for the most part all too otherworldly? And to the extent that the tradition tempts its aspirants toward a transcendence of this world does it not prohibit precisely those mystical experiences whose assimilation carries one more fully *into* this world?

The will to transcendence draws one away from the shadows, away from the painful dreams of the midnight hour. Yet it is precisely the unacknowledged and unrecognized dreams and shadows that prohibit liberation. They—and for each of us their identification is slightly different—determine the shape of the enemy of freedom, the jailer. To ignore the shadow in a premature transcendence to a purified identity is then to remain imprisoned . . . or so goes one plausible interpretation of Zarathustra's midnight ecstasy. Surely there are others.

A single glib reading would be ill-advised for several reasons. First, the fourth and final part of Zarathustra finds more than one glib reading of Zarathustra's significance to be ridiculous. Premature closure is just the problem. Second, the *counsel* of Zarathustra's story is not to be explained and thereby reduced to information.[60] The wisdom of Nietzsche's choice of the medium of *storytelling* lies in the possibility of using words to produce an experience whose thickness is not captured by any simple conclusion. Third, the very nature of the issue at hand prohibits glib articulations for the issue at hand is none other than the proper assimilation of the ineffable—what to say about the unsayable? How to appropriate into the whole of experience those experiences that defy articulation? Slippery ice!

The context of Zarathustra's utterances proves crucial because their meaning must derive from a determination by negation, and even that by a showing rather than a saying. Nietzsche is walking on the thin ice of negative theology where any simple affirmation, any declaration that life is one way and not another, any differentiation at all will sound a resounding crack in the momentary perfection of the pond's surface. Any sudden lurch toward determinate meaning sends one plummeting into the chill of one-sidedness in favor of whatever single determination one attempted to place on life—whether one lurches toward Meaning or Meaninglessness, Joy or Sorrow, Being or Nothing. So Nietzsche's strategy, like that of the negative theologian, must be to *show* without *saying*, and to show in such a way that the one-sidedness of previous sayings will be negated without an equally one-sided affirmation of their opposites. Just as Zarathustra invites into his cave each member of the paired opposites of higher men so now he shows the one-sidedness of a tradition that claims a purely ecstatic epiphany as the culmination of overcoming all oppositions. To Oriental advertisements for final enlightenment, to Platonic promises of transcendence, to even the Hegelian intimation of *resolution* of contradictions (whether permanent or not), Zarathustra's midnight hour declares: No, these images of completion are incomplete. The great noon must have *its* opposite as well. Joy is entangled with woe, even the woes of days' work.

The seventh stroke of midnight, the ascendency of The Beautiful Soul whose purity would prefer ineffable and beautiful pain to mundane pleasure, art and especially tragedy to the tedium of daily human relations, Nietzsche's own earlier preference for the finality of pain beneath a saving veneer of art now finds *its* opposite in the eleventh and twelfth strokes of midnight: "All joy wants all things eternally," even the most strange, even the most questionable in existence.

But in saying 'all things' one *says* very little, for to *say* one thing is to deny others. We are back to Bertrand Russell's quandary about denying the principle of noncontradiction. If nothing be denied, then anything goes. Even the spiritual torpor of the ugliest man? Even the smug atheism of a Bertrand Russell? No. Here lies the significance of the *experiences* of both the great noon and the midnight despite the fact that in their balance they seem to cancel out whatever finite significance either might have as redeeming or damning all of existence. The experience of noon's ecstasy bears witness to the liberation that attends *wholeness;* the experience of the midnight testifies to the *assimilation* of that liberation *into* the whole of life. Nietzsche has freed himself from the demonic freedom that would transport him beyond the dreadful quotidian reality Hamlet so abhorred.

Smug secularism withholds itself from wholeness in dozens of ways that usually amount to some version of the right hand's denying the left.[61] But spiritualism has its own dangers for moderns who have lost a firm footing on this earth. Whether as the storyteller's distant heaven or as the sage's internal transcendence toward desirelessness, otherworldliness is a barrier to the assimilation of liberation into *this* world . . . whatever form this world may take from each of our various and partly shared perspectives. The immanence of midnight offsets the transcendence at noon, just as the myths of transcendence offset an earthbound immanence among earlier peoples. This pair too, immanent/transcendent, has its dialectic that remains ever prone to one-sidedness. Nietzsche by no means settled or completed its dialectic. His exhortation to remain true to the earth is no simple and unambiguous call to immanence, for the meaning of 'earth' is as ever open to reinterpretation as the meaning of 'body'.[62] After all it was the tradition of "the Word made *flesh*," Christianity itself, that had become too otherworldly. Nietzsche's own words sacrificing god for the sake of man are themselves just as susceptible to an interpretation that might imprison his readers in some narrow and hard doctrine.

So much for the meaning of affirming 'all things' as it is spoken in the context of Nietzsche's answer to a particular set of questions posed by Plato, Hegel and the mystic tradition. Further explication might mislead one into the conclusion—pressed upon Hegel by his interpreters—that Nietzsche had found The Answer, the Total Speech, the Ultimate Essence of things whereas his story is if anything a showing of the errors in such one-sided pretensions.

Eternal recurrence and quietism

Absolved of the destination of One Truth, the task of interpretation is never done. The "same" that eternally recurs also differs. Here the Anaxagorean logic of homoeomereity gives meaning to Nietzsche's revelation that he himself could not find to his satisfaction as long as he superimposed an Eleatic logic of space and time onto his intuition of eternal recurrence. The existential meaning of eternal recurrence concerns the redemption of all that is and was by *amor fati*, a love of fate, an affirmation of this earth in which all woes are entangled and ensnared with all joys. Nietzsche toys with a *proof* of eternal recurrence in terms of the necessary repetition of finite patterns of behavior in a finite universe—much as frictionless billiard balls on a frictionless table would, once set in motion, endlessly repeat the same patterns.[63] Nietzsche never published this so-called proof. Perhaps he sensed its inappropriateness to the meaning of eternal recurrence however much he wished to ground the intuitive certainty of his revelation of eternal recurrence. Even in his published accounts his certainty is such that he clearly intends no recurrence of general forms whose specific contents might vary. The recurrence specifies every detail—"this spider in this moonlight"[64]—both the smallest and the greatest. He would allow no fudge factor for novelty within some large-scale Spenglerian recurrence; and an airtight Newtonian determinism, or what he sometimes called his Russian fatalism, was his only paradigm for a law that ruled the smallest as well as the greatest.

Anaxagorean logic allows the recurrence of the great in the small because there is neither a smallest nor a greatest, no first and no last, but a perpetual re-presentation of the larger in the smaller; yet, by virtue of a perspectivism, a *differance* of the larger from the perspective of *each* smaller. Thus *to* each perspective "the same" recurs endlessly, yet *from* each perspective "the same" is different. The appearance of novelty is a shift of perspectives. From either perspective "the same" recurs without beginning or end, yet a shift in perspectives reflects "the same" differently. There is no perspective from which 'the same' can be uttered neutrally or absolutely. So Einstein discovered with respect to utterances of 'the same time' or 'simultaneous'. Similarly there is no perspective from which one can refer to what will be from all perspectives the same Space, the same order of distances among the great and the small. To each great there is ever greater, to each small ever smaller, so that the meanings of 'great' and 'small' do not derive from a reference to polar opposites but from a dimension of *differance* whose axis, like the great circle of eternal recurrence, bends back upon itself.

The Anaxagorean logic of space and time demands a transcendence of the visual-tactile perceptions of larger boxes that will not fit into smaller boxes. This perceptual spatiality as a whole is a *small* part of experience. Because information does not have a "size" in the dimensions of visual-tactile spatiality, a glance through the lens of a microscope can reveal as much *information* as a glance through the lens of a telescope.

Zarathustra voices the existential correlate to the cosmology of Anaxagorean space and time when he chides himself at noon: "'Happiness—how little there is that suffices for happiness!' So I spoke once and thought myself clever. But that was a blasphemy: *that* I have learned now." The cosmic blues of the *Birth of Tragedy* were the blasphemy. "Precisely the least, the lightest, the littlest, a lizard's rustling, a breath, a breeze, a moment's glance—*little* makes the greatest happiness. Still!"[65] The cosmic blues, the patent meaninglessness of vast depths of Newtonian space, the apparently absolute insignificance of this tiny speck of earth in the great cavern of the galaxies, follow from an *ontology* of experience that would give greater *being* to empty space than to, say, the sufferings of a little child. But what is the appeal of the Newtonian ontology of space and time apart from its limited ability to account for certain physical behavior coherently? Both at its outer limits of relativistic space-time cosmology and at its inner limits of human interpretation the logic of Newtonian common sense would seem to give way to an Anaxagorean logic of homoeomereity. In the context of that Anaxagorean logic Nietzsche's Newtonian proofs of eternal recurrence are unnecessary.

The truth of eternal recurrence is manifest among small details because the moment of vision reveals the littlest, say a fold of flannel, as a representation of the greatest, the is-ness of all things. This flannel, this spider, this moonlight *must* be as they are because each is entangled, enamored and ensnared with all beauty, all ugliness. Zarathustra comes up gasping from his immersion at midnight, "Joy is deeper than woe," for the experience of that entanglement with an ugliness equal to beauty, the experience of the *inevitability* of ugliness, of the mortality of the gods as less than the least parts of the human self, is itself an experience of liberation: one is free of the need to *deny* evil for one knows denial itself as evil.

This interpretation of eternal recurrence in the context of

Anaxagorean logic brings us back around to the question of quietism. If evil is not to be denied is that the same as to say that good is not to be affirmed? Are we still to regard as ludicrous and humiliating the suggestion that it devolves upon us to set right the times that are out of joint? Not quite. For the homoeomereity of the human and the divine, the large and the small, likewise means that the "eternal course of things" the quietist would not alter now appears not as some Newtonian duration outreaching the distance of a single life and the dint of its effort; rather, eternity itself ever so occasionally appears in the least moment, an epiphany, a cusp whose reflection of the whole is radically ambivalent and not at all fixed. In those moments it is precisely the choice between good and evil that recurs eternally, when troths are forged, when one's whole past is drawn up and hurled toward a chosen future. Such moments are the bones in the body of human time—history. Calcified in ritual, their hardness gives shape—and hence order and meaning—to what otherwise lacks order and meaning. If the rituals themselves come to lack meaning that is likely the result of a sense of time unpunctuated by epiphanies in which meaning occurs. The recurrence of such moments—and hence the perpetual possibility of oaths—is the condition for the possibility of a recollection of meaning in ritual. Because the recurrence of such decisive moments also invites the possibility of evil, because evil is not to be denied once and for all in perpetual peace, quietism is impossible—at least for one to whom time still presents such decisive moments, for one who yet lives.

Here again the ambiguity of affirming 'all things' is manifest. The quietist accuses the activist of ignoring the great order of things that will not be swayed by the activist's labor on this speck of earth. Yet it remains open to the activist to point out that the quietist's "great order of things" includes the very forces that lead one to act. The quietist does not quietly *accept* all things when he *denies*, say, the sufferings of a small child at his feet. Nor of course does the activist *change* the cycle of good and evil when he takes revenge.

The choices of good and evil we make in moments of choice—

and they may or may not be many—are not such that one person can tell *all* others a great deal that is very useful for determining precisely what to choose. Nietzsche shows us only that there *are* such moments, that their logic accords with the concept of eternal recurrence, that quietism is not the necessary outcome of *amor fati*. Like the Delphic oracle's exhortation to self-knowledge, Nietzsche's counsel remains ever to be worked out by oneself. Yet the process is not utterly solipsistic, for after all it is *we* who must know *ourselves* in order to choose intelligently how to hurl shared pasts toward shared futures. So in the remainder of this chapter and throughout the next, the specificity of day to day life in the cave will come to infect the formal sterility of the empty phrase: There are choices between good and evil.

Methodology and the sacred

Opposed to the distinction between deep "essences" and surface "accidents" structuralism teaches that all the accidents are to be included in an interpretation.[66] Like Hegel's phenomenology in finding order *among* the phenomena rather than in *noumena* behind the phenomena, like hermeneutic psychoanalysis in taking each "accidental" slip of the tongue as a tool for interpretation,[67] a structuralist reading of contemporary spiritual phenomena would dismiss nothing as merely "superficial," merely "accidental." Nor need a structuralist reading fall into some single profundity whose power, however secular and this-worldly in appearance, would betray in its neat clarity its heritage as a transform of monotheism.

The advantages and disadvantages of different methodologies are hardly new to seekers among the various spiritual traditions. Hermeneutics has its home in readings of the Holy Word, which is itself a reading of the soul. So it is hardly surprising to discover that the method employed here—variously described as structuralism, relational thinking, dialectics—is also Taoist. The very first of the eighty-one sayings of the Tao Te Ching teaches: "Existence is beyond the power of words to define. Terms may be used but none of them are absolute."[68] If not absolute, then relative? Is each opposite only relative to its own opposite? Is each term denoting an opposite meaningful only by virtue of a syntactic and grammatical contrariety though *not* by semantic reference to a "real" "class" of "entities" "different" from another "class" "denoted" by another term?

The Tao says: "whether a man dispassionately sees to the core of life or passionately sees the surface are essentially the same, words making them seem different only to express appearances." In other words *appearance* contains these contradictions so we need these contrary words to express appearance. But then appearence is the surface. And the surface and the core are themselves essentially the same, so the same words that ostensibly express only appearance must, by virtue of these words denying words, express also the essence of things. Appearance is not *mere* appearance—a most Hegelian teaching. What appears of the divine are its masks or its names. Yet if the masks and names are all that appears in articulate form, then even the experience of ineffable unity does not justify the claim that the many masks are the masks of one god, the many names different articulations of the One. Granted the overwhelming sense of Unity in the Moment, still we cannot have our ineffability and eat it too. Either the unity is unspeakable and when we come to speak we may speak of many gods as well as of many masks of the same god; or the experience of the Moment is not ineffable, one claims to have heard the determinate speech of one god who forbids the worship of others.

Perhaps religious revelation, like madness, has a history.[69] Perhaps there are times when a single god speaks to many with the same words of vengeance for other gods. But as one listens for intimations of the sacred these days, as one searches among one's contemporaries for suggestions, for even remnants of religious experience, one hears precious little of specific words from some single voice on high. Rather one hears the babble of many voices, the birth-cries of many babies in the sacred nursery.

Some are inclined to baptize these new gods—and to our culture these gods *are* new—with the names of some very old gods. This business of naming the gods is very difficult. The problematic nature of naming the gods will emerge from deliberations upon a few pros and cons drawn from the many shadows on the wall of contemporary spirituality.

First, we cannot avoid naming gods if we are to speak at all. The advantage of using the names of gods rather than some other names—e.g., 'the death instinct', 'tendency toward equilibrium', 'entropy'—lies in the likelihood that as long as we speak about gods we will not claim to know as much about them as we might think we knew if we used their more scientific-sounding transforms.

Second, a disadvantage of devotion to any particular set of names lies in the likelihood that we will be unable to recognize the gods of other pantheons. E.g., the Homeric pantheon is part of a cycle of projection and introjection in which Homeric souls participated. Ours are not Homeric souls. Even as we take the Homeric soul as a model of the polytheistic possibility in general it must remain open to us to grant among more specific possibilities gods and goddesses who would be strangers on Olympus. Particularly as our culture finds more of value in the religions of the East it *may* make sense to grant the domains of Shiva, Vishnu, Brahma and hosts of others.

The choice of 'may' rather than 'will' is made advisedly. The cycle of subjectivity including gods, persons and parts of persons changes its basic inventory only very slowly. Many generations attend the birth of a god and still more its death. One cannot choose gods like clothes. The gods that fit best are those whose roots are deepest in the sedimentary layers left by generations. Nonetheless those roots may dry up and die in a prolonged drought. If the soil is right, as it seemed to be in California, gods may be transplanted from other cultures. Yet a disadvantage of naming new gods lies in the likelihood that they represent a hybrid strain not to be confused with the very old gods of the Orient who bear the same names.

Third, and again a disadvantage in naming the gods: we are liable to literalize even the gods by linking them with a specific set of discontinuous traits. A finite set of names encourages a belief in a fixed inventory of sharply differentiated talents and weaknesses where in fact the unity of the virtues precludes sharp differentiation. Naming need not encourage sharp differentiation. That it does so with us only testifies to the difficulty of transplantation from the circle of Anaxagorean thought and experience to the circle of Eleatic thought and experience, viz. the amazing phenomenon of current interest in astrology and the *I Ching*.

Astrology and the I Ching

Astrology rests on a strong claim for the homoeomereity of the heavenly and the human. To be "an Aquarius" is to have a certain type of personality *and* to have one's birthday when the heavens are situated in a precisely specifiable pantheon of archetypes. Yet most contemporary adherents to astrology are subtly and thoroughly imbued with a sense of the scientific as strictly Newtonian, as narrowly causal and necessarily predictive. Consequently the data of astrology are misused to attempt causal explanations and precise predictions where nothing more than an acausal hermeneutic is appropriate.

Astrology provides a preeminently polytheistic pantheon in terms of which human life can be interpreted pluralistically. Whether or not the astrological tradition provides the best code for decoding our current experience—and one is hard pressed to provide criteria for 'best' in this context—clearly the depth and breadth of interest in astrology testifies to the *need* for a pluralistic mode of interpretation. Polytheism, in the guise of astrology, is with us. The sense that pluralistic structures of thought necessarily represent a *regression* in human consciousness is itself a reflection of the tyranny of unity in residual monotheism. The delta is different from the primitive tributaries that had to be unified to form the river's mainstream, just as the branches of a tree are different from its roots in function however much they may mirror one another in the form of their structural proliferation from the unity of the trunk. The pluralism of a contemporary astrology *could* be different from a regression to prescientific proliferation of causes that are nothing but ad hoc redescriptions of phenomena to be explained. But the depth of Newtonian consciousness among even the devotees of astrology develops into a handling of the various data of astrology as if they describe unconnected, externally related constituents of a chemical reaction in the lab of the Newtonian scientist. An Aquarian component is treated as if it were as fully determinate and fixed in its qualities as an inert gas. Consequently the *context* of the Aquarian is then discounted in efforts at causal inference whose failure is then cited as evidence of the unscientific character of astrology.

Jung came closer to an appropriate approach to the astrological data in his essay "Synchronicity: An Acausal Connecting Principle."[70] For Jung the naming of the archetypes need not necessarily lead to a prescientific proliferation of causes. Only when their baptism takes place in the church of monotheistic consciousness is there an overwhelming tendency to treat the nominata as simple Newtonian causes rather than as complex keys for a hermeneutic of homoeomerous experience.

Yet astrology and the *I Ching* claim more than a post hoc hermeneutic. These disciplines always have and now continue to play a role in decision procedures for the present and future. If precise prediction is too much to expect of these hermeneutics, total irrelevance to the future is too little. One cannot write off the role of one's date of birth in astrology, or the casting of the coins for the use of the *I*

Ching. Both traditions make the claim that the secrets of the universe can be read however darkly through the glass of spatiotemporal signs and that these signs—the shape of the constellations at one's birth, the toss of the coins or yarrow sticks or Tarot cards—render *some* interpretive keys more appropriate than others to specific individuals at specific times. How to confirm or refute these claims, thereby rendering them at least meaningful if not immediately true or false?

Take, for example, the use of the *I Ching.* Even the most antisuperstitious child of the Enlightenment can make some sense of its use in the following way: once upon a time a group of very wise people hit upon the insight that the most important thing about human action is not so much *what* is done but rather the consciousness and intentions with which actions are performed—a very Kantian insight. They then broke down the psychic components of human decision making into six dimensions corresponding to the six lines of the hexagram. They knew, first, that the awareness of the intentions and import of an action render any piece of behavior a truly human *action* rather than a reactive response. Second, they knew that the necessary awareness would follow from having analyzed and resynthesized one's act according to how it might be located on six different dimensions defining the motivational space of experience. Third, the originators of the *I Ching* knew that men being the egocentric creatures they are would not be content with believing that the specific results of their deliberations made little difference; they knew that hardly any would attain that odd tension between intense care, marvelous wonder and sublime indifference to the *what*-to-do of decision making. Consequently they built into their very wise handbook of hermeneutics a procedure that would satisfy its users' desires to believe that they were consulting the coins in order to achieve the *correct* answer to the question of what to do—as if it made a great difference whether one went to Wyoming or remained in the city, wedded the woman or left her, lingered by the fountain or led oneself toward the desert.

These wise men knew that in these and similar cases in which men are wont to emphasize the what rather than the how of the decision, it would be necessary to give the impression that the decision procedure spoke not only to the how but also, by the very multiplicity of its possible answers, to the what as well. They knew that no matter how the coins came up, a reflection on the six dimensions of each decision would necessitate a richer self-consciousness and hence a deeper truth—a creation of meaning no matter what specific course of action was eventually taken. Consequently the casting of the coins could not help but "verify" itself. Retrospectively each would agree that the *I Ching* and the coins had come up with the "correct" decision. Of course the real cause for this agreement has to do *not* with the magical capacity of the coins for decoding the cosmos by falling in precisely the "right" ways to be appropriate to the particular situation. Rather, the "correctness" of the decision is to be interpreted according to the Socratic-Kantian teaching that the self-knowing man is the most virtuous man and that the good man can suffer no evil. The use of the *I Ching* as an overt decision procedure would then be self-validating as a result of its covert function as a self-imposed hermeneutic. The validation of the procedure would be virtually guaranteed yet in no sense trivial. Because the role of the covert hermeneutic is so beneficial, the final judgment of the use of the *I Ching* would be as difficult as a final judgment on the use of psychoanalysis (whose true functioning is probably equally as distant from the self-understanding of its practitioners as is the functioning of the *I Ching* from the self-understanding of its users).

So goes a demystification of the *I Ching*. One can easily find or imagine comparable demystifications of astrology, tarot, tea-leaf readings and any number of other methods of divination.[71] The question remains, however, why *must* one seek out the demystified explanation before taking such phenomena seriously?—a slippery question on which one's pride may break its leg. For if one fancies oneself a fully rational modern mind free of silly superstitions, if one has "outgrown" ghost stories and the childish need to believe in magical and wondrous spirits that populate a hidden world only to pop into *this* world whenever and only when one has a need for them, if one fancies that he can recognize a wooden nickel when he sees one, then he will be disinclined to deal with the question when put in such terms as, Why *must* one seek out the demystified explanation before taking such phenomena seriously. His pride will prefer to believe that modern rationality simply *does* deal with arcane phenomena in their demystified form, not that it *must*. For the latter formulation carries a taint of involuntary compulsion, a suggestion of need that arises not from the well-founded strength of one's rationality but rather from its weakness.

The suggestion that the Enlightenment rationality *must* deal with superstition in its demystified form carries with it the insight developed by Hegel and Nietzsche in the nineteenth century and revived by Horkheimer and Adorno in the twentieth, [72] namely that the rationality of the Enlightenment is but one of several equally coherent manifestations of the will to power. This rationality *needs* to debunk its rivals, not simply from a noble devotion to truths that are violated by superstition. Rather, the need stems from a desire for *control*, a desire that is thwarted by the picture of a universe in which man is ever at the mercy of alien spirits of which he has very little and perhaps cannot have more knowledge. Ever since Bacon and Descartes the ideal of Enlightenment rationality has been knowledge as *mastery* over the environment, a much higher and more demanding ideal than the supposedly primitive will to adapt or accommodate oneself to the environment by honoring or placating a plurality of partly unknowable gods.

Because the intellect of the Enlightenment accepts this higher demand to know and thereby control itself as well as its environment, it is disinclined to entertain the possibility that its desire to know is itself the function of some unknown need—a weakness rather than a strength. Hence it is likely to blind itself to its own most pressing needs for control as it presses on toward a supposedly "disinterested" knowledge. So did Oedipus blind himself as if to literalize too late the justice of Jocasta's cries: "Don't seek it! I am sick, and that's enough. . . . Wretch, what thou art O might thou never know." Both

Oedipus and the pride of the Enlightenment respond: "I will not harken—not to know the whole, Break out what will, I shall not hesitate. . . ." Like heroes hurling ourselves into battle against blindness and ignorance we are disinclined to imagine that our very heroism is a function of our own blindness and ignorance. Hence we are uneasy when someone innocently suggests that we *must* demystify the arcane.

So to both Newtonian mystics and to their enlightened detractors, a plague on both your houses: on the first for misconstruing an acausal hermeneutic as a causal science, on the second for seeing in the first the absurdities of its own limitations, to wit its incapacity for imagining that the influence of the stars upon the psyche could be anything other than mechanically causal—and surely it is absurd to imagine that one's love life is causally influenced by the *gravitational* attractions exerted by the stars at the moment of one's birth. Less absurd but nonetheless beyond the inventory of conceivable thoughts for the Enlightenment mind is the following: both the heavens and the human are transforms of an order that is successfully symbolized if not fully "known" or mastered by the hermeneutic systems of the several esoteric traditions both psychical and physical. Why must one be the *cause* of the other, one the mere *appearance* of a "deeper" reality?

Some sort of complementarity principle between the scientific and the divine might appeal to minds freed of the reductionist impulse by the logic of homoeomereity. The thought is not utterly wild. As sober a mind as John Wisdom's finds support in Freud's discoveries for his own appropriation of the gods. He describes the facts discovered by psychoanalysis as "patterns in human reactions which are well described by saying that we are as if there were hidden within us powers, persons, not ourselves and stronger than ourselves." While the discoveries of psychoanalysis have often been restricted to the pathological, "one thing not sufficiently realized is that some of the things shut within us are not bad but good." Likewise, "the gods, good and evil and mixed, have always been mysterious powers outside us rather than within. But they have also been within." The names change, and the pretensions to knowledge, but the fundamental dynamics remain very similar: "The Greeks did not speak of the dangers of repressing instincts but they did speak of the dangers of thrwarting Dionysus, of neglecting Cypris for Diana, of forgetting Poseidon for Athena."[73]

If some now speak of the dangers of thwarting Yin, of neglecting Pisces for Aquarius, doubtless the reason lies in a human wisdom that finds itself somehow misled when it is asked to analyze itself not in terms of homoeomerous personalities but in terms of analytic elements. The same human wisdom that spurns both the guilt culture of Christianity and the hubris of atheism also rejects the promises of presidents and the anger of anarchists. Lacking respectable academic articulation for the voice of its wisdom, the contemporary spirit turns often toward the bizarre to find names for its psychology, its spirituality and its politics.

Following the critique of Newtonian political theory in chapter one, chapters three through six made a sojourn into the polytheistic psychology of the many dimensional soul. This chapter turned toward the spiritual and the next returns to politics. By now the rationality of a pluralized paraconsciousness may have acquired enough thickness, enough content from mutually supporting contexts, to make a claim for coherence that can stand up to the entrenched certainty of the academically respectable paradigms. The data of cultural disintegration introduced in chapter one may now reveal a pattern that is not simply irrational but rather the manifestation of a rationality different from the Eleatic tradition of hylomorphic metaphysics. Let us return with this psychologically and spiritually enriched rationality to the topics of conversation among the pundits in the cave. Let us examine the fourth transform in the chain of parallels that led from Zarathustra's critique and reconciliation with the ugliest man to Nietzsche's critique and reconciliation with his own earlier ugliness, next to the critique and reconciliation with atheism, and now finally to a critique and reconciliation with anarchism.

VIII Into the Cave

Like those who have looked too long straight into the sun, those who see the golden round ball, the golden ring of the return of all things, are as Plato noted often blinded; and if not totally blinded then at least unaccustomed to the murk of the cave. Thales, the first philosopher, fell down a well in his upward-gazing distraction. Philosophers, it is said, do not know the way to the marketplace.[1] The marketplace, economy, home of modernity—what use is a vision if it has no application, or worse, if it finds its refutation in economic reality?

Or is usefulness a useful criterion for visions? Zarathustra spake: "Verily I love you for this, that you do not know how to live today, you higher men."[2] Good arguments are to be found for *not* returning to the cave.[3] Nor need pluralism of all philosophies claim to have The Answer that will *work* for *everyone*.

Yet what appeal is there in a philosophy that works for no one? And has not Nietzsche in his own artful way shown his shadow to warn that the sociopolitical dimension of his thought is manifestly its weakest? A brief look at the sociopolitical possibilities for many dimensional man may not be altogether out of order even if the need for grossly utilitarian certainty remains questionable. After all among the habitués of the marketplace the hope of certainty is so dim that even the candle of philosophical musings can hardly be cursed in the darkness.

It is said of decentralist schemes that they cannot work in the modern world because (a) advances in technology necessitate the centralization of resources; (b) especially the technologically advanced but also the less sophisticated branches of production function most efficiently according to "economies of scale"; (c) the decentralized individual, the jack of all trades, the "renaissance man" is an archaic throwback to simpler days, an object of nostalgia. In a world like ours one must specialize. One must profess one thing, professionalize or die like a dumb beast whose species has failed to adapt to the changing environment. Finally, (d) the central State is now more necessary than ever: the vast economies of scale required by advanced technological industrialization require planning for their stabilization. Further, since the nature of professionalization is for the most part a specialization whose progressive myopia forbids a vision of the whole, some must specialize in managing the whole: professional politicians.

These four objections—let us call them the argument from technology, the argument from economics, the argument from professionalism, and the argument from politics—all point toward the centralized State with its bureaucracy, its myths of power, its Eleatic logic of control of form over matter. Let us look at each argument in turn.

Paratechnology

The case for a decentralized technology is in some ways the easiest to make of any for what is technology if not a tool that allows a few men to do what otherwise would take many? If the first "machine" was, as Mumford argues,[4] the marshaled masses who built the pyramids, then is it not obvious that the will to mastery over nature is not simply the *product* of technology but a *motive* as well, and one that were better carried out by machines than by the muscles of toiling masses? Technology has liberatory potential.

Yet the case is not as simple as a causal analysis would suggest. No chicken or egg debate can settle the question of blame in the ecological mess by placing the burden on *either* technology *or* the will to mastery that spawned technology; for now a circle of mutual reinforcement feeds both. At this point, the question of origins is academic. Now we want a way to deal with this beast that has, most will agree, gotten out of control—that is to say, suffered an *enantiodromia:* the spirit of control has gotten out of control. Which creates a difficult situation, for like the insomniac who does not easily solve his problem by *trying* to go to sleep, one runs into obvious difficulties in setting out to *control* the spirit of control.

Yet the apparent paradox is not as tight as antitechnologists would lead us to think. Hephaestus the toolmaker is not as wily as the other gods. Turning his own techniques upon him is not like the Enlightenment's defeat of superstition by its choice of weapons—the rationality of reductive explanation in whose air no god could survive even his own defense. Control over technology does not lead toward a Pyhrrhic victory in which winning means losing. For technology does have a liberatory potential by which the little group can expand its real power, its ability to carry out its intentions, its capacity to inform its own future. Technology is not *necessarily* the author of a neo-nature that is a new alien environment of noise and dirty air and death at a distance.[5] However necessary it may be that more of our *present* technology will produce more uncontrolled and ultimately demoniacal spin-offs, technology is not the *necessary* enemy of man any more than any other wildly one-sided exploitation of one part of man against the rest. For technology *is* a part of man, just like sexuality and aggression and all those other *existentialia*[6] that have no original, determinate, distinct essences but appear always, like each of the gods, clothed in all the virtues and vices of all the rest. Trite as it is to repeat, man is among other things the toolmaking animal, *homo faber*.

Hephaestus has metaphysics in his favor. The distinction that gives sense to an opposition between man and nature when man is so obviously *part of* nature is the *différance* between human time and natural time. The latter—in the vanishing moment of its fictional pole—has no history.[7] Human time has a plot, a story line that makes history: discernible beginnings, middles and ends that were humanly meant to be. Instead of one damn thing after another, in place of a causality that pushes ever from behind without a care of what the morrow may bring, the *structuring* of history whatever its terms is always a tampering with time, a molding of the present on the basis of a symbolically envisioned future.

"Genes do as much," one may say. "They carry a code for the future organism." Quite true, and here the difference between *différance* and polar distinction is once again apposite: no gulf, no sharp line separates man from nature. Biological life exhibits teleological structures, tropisms that seem to approach choice. And some men are as dumb as beasts. But one is hard pressed to find among other organisms evidence of the capacity to code not one future but several and then, on the basis of further symbolic representation of probable environments, choose one among those several possibilities to enact. With the *willful* enactment of *one future among many*, technology enters to enable man to *tamper with time* and differentiate himself from nature. Here Hephaestus gains his metaphysical defense for his place in the pantheon.

But if Hephaestus has run amok, if like Zeus and Apollo he has claimed more than his share, if Demeter and Rhea be defiled, earth and organic life destroyed, then how can we honor him? Hephaestus himself, the gods' blacksmith, welds the link that binds the argument back to the point from which it began, the *para*digm of the *para*professional as a model for something called *para*technology.

The little prefix 'para-' connotes a structural intervention of a particular kind. Its etymological origins point in two directions. The Greek preposition $\pi\ddot{\alpha}\rho\acute{\alpha}$ appears with the genitive denoting motion from the side of, from beside, from; with dative denoting rest by the side of; with accusative in three main senses: first, beside, near or by; second, along; third, past or beyond. If the prepositional appearances of $\pi\ddot{\alpha}\rho\acute{\alpha}$ cluster around *beside* then several of its appearances as a prefix suggest a second direction in its etymological origins, another clustering around *against.* Paradox is *doxa* (speech or opinion) that is contrary to expectations. A parachute protects against "going down the chute." In some contexts the seemingly contrary meanings of beside and against appear at once, as in paradigm: a model or standard one places *beside* a given instance in order to measure or judge the latter *against* the former. Also in $\pi\alpha\rho o \upsilon \sigma \acute{\iota} \alpha$ the contrary sources mix to generate an ontological connotation suggesting a *substance* $o \upsilon \sigma \acute{\iota} \alpha$ that is not the substratum of the hylomorphic tradition but a *presence:* a *being* whose Being is, as it were, not a dead-center identity but a temporal structuring that is somehow *beside itself,* present to itself, sometimes even rent by contrarieties rendering it *against* itself.[8*]

So with paratechnology: the point is not to obliterate the technical impulse or paint technique as intrinsically demonic. Rather the point is to stand both beside and occasionally against technology; to stand beside its uses and protest against its abuses. Nothing very novel in the intention of paratechnology when so expressed, but one hears so much nonsense about technology nowadays that a few old nostrums may shine like old silver when polished with a little erudition and placed in a sensible context.

The most pernicious nonsense about technology takes the form of demonology: thou shalt not let the devil help thee in thy work else thou shalt lose thy soul to him. Again, Hephaestus is not as clever as Hades. And besides, we do the devil's work unwittingly when we refuse to look him in the eye and grant him his place in the pantheon. But Hephaestus is not Hades despite their common bond with red-hot coals.

Less symbolically: the nonsense about technology stems from an overreaction to the naiveté of those who do not see the very real dangers of technology. Yes, technology does have *its own* logic; this tool made by men is quite capable of turning upon man and using men toward *its own* ends of sterile order and efficiency. All this is quite true, but not grounds for hysterical flight into the hills to flee a demon over which we have no control. In the hills as well we find a natural order that is no more man's order than is technological order man's order. The "natural order of things" includes a creature called man whose nature is ever to bend that natural order to his own order. The presence, the *parousia*, of so-called nature is not a fixed self-identical *place* like a wilderness preserve, not a set of laws, but a structuring of time that remains *beside* itself when one of its parts, man, works *against* itself.[9]

To place technology in a more sensible context than demonology recall the sense in which the technological environment is a *transform* of the natural environment. We can no more take flight into nature from the technological environment than we could escape nature with technology. Both projects are one-sided, the one flight a transform of the other. To adapt the eminently structuralist logic of the transference relationship from psychotherapy, it is as if the antitechnologists had projected onto nature what the analysand projects onto the therapist: the dependence on technology is now transferred to a dependence on nature. Paratechnology seeks to complete the process by recognizing this transference of dependency on technology to a regressive dependency on nature. As in the psychoanalytic relationship, the successful handling of transference depends largely on a successful handling of countertransference—the therapist's own projection of his unresolved conflicts onto his perceptions of the analysand.

Ivan Illich has coined the term *counterfoil research*, which he describes as, "the dimensional analysis of the relationship of man to his tools."[10] As an example he suggests research into transportation that takes into account more than the simple dimension of speed, more even than the two dimensions of speed and economic cost. For a many dimensional analysis of cost one must consider the richer context of social and cultural costs paid for the advantage of high speed transportation whatever the price of the ticket. Illich claims, "Once the barrier of bicycle velocity is broken at any point in the system, the total per capita monthly time spent at the service of the travel industry increases."[11] Of course the practice of counterfoil research in technology, like countertransference in therapy, is fraught with the peril of imposing one's values on those who are to be liberated. Precisely because the analyst's task is to liberate his patient from himself, on whom neurotic patterns of behavior and attitude have been transferred in order to be dealt with and transcended, the analyst must know himself and his own needs very well in order to be able to make this final move: the graceful release of the analysand from his neurotic attachment to the therapist. In order to be able to accomplish the final step of overcoming a transference relationship that has outlived its therapeutic function, the analyst must have been through analysis himself, not simply to know what it is like, but to know *himself*, his innermost needs and prejudices, that shadowy realm whose *projections* will influence his relationship with the analysand and their mutual abilities to let each other go free.

It is not altogether obvious that Illich has accomplished a corresponding analysis sufficient to render his counterfoil research a paratechnology capable of achieving the necessary cultural overcoming of transference. It is not clear that Illich has acknowledged a transform of countertransference. There may be some justice in William Irwin Thompson's charge: "Illich's neofeudal world view is a vision of elites bound together in a culture of voluntary poverty."[12] There may be something to the even harsher charge that Illich is "a Tolstoyan aristocrat in search of his long-lost peasants,"[13] or to Florman's complaint about the vision of freedom in the writings of Mumford, Dubos, Roszak, Reich and Ellul: "It is a strangely restricted freedom . . . the freedom to plant barley or corn, but not to use a bulldozer or buy a new electric hair dryer. It is the half-freedom, the false freedom of the benevolent despot."[14]

To place the import of these charges into the context of the analogy between paratechnology and a sensitivity to countertransference that presupposes the analyst's own analysis, it is unclear whether Illich and others who protest the ills of technology have given sufficient attention to the role of their own likes and dislikes as they are projected into their visions of what a liberatory technology would look like. Even granting a Rousseauvian pedagogy according to which one may need to be "forced to be free,"[15] one's eventual freedom is suspect if it conforms too closely to the specific contents of the analyst's fantasy of freedom's outer marks. Surely the analyst must *manipulate* the experience of the analysand, the teacher must impose some order on the experience of the student; the liberator does not liberate by letting the slave of technology go free on his own with all his dependencies on technology still intact else he will fall straight back into precisely the patterns that enslaved him in the first place. Something must replace the patterns of neurotic dependency on technology, the pathology of dial-twiddling dissociation from sensuous immediacy, the self-defeating fantasies of better living through chemistry, bigger orgasms through pharmacology, quicker communication through electronics. Our bodies make love better than mechanical brides. Yet our bodies too are ambiguous, more now than bags of skin and bones.

Here in the cave of day to day and night to night practice all the theoretical hair-splittings have their application: the lessons of the body, decadence, the structure rather than the contents of freedom. In the single question of what devices a couple may bring to bed more than a few issues overlap. A pathological dependence on technology is possible. Yet the antitechnologists replace that dependence with no more than a romanticism for the natural.[16] No real *human* freedom results from such content dogmatism. Fixation on the natural, fear of decadence and the flight from technology all reflect a denial of the human art of tampering with time and human nature itself.

Mistakes are possible. But who is so weary he would wish a life in which mistakes were not possible?

A discernible *differance* if not a polar distinction separates paratechnology from a counterfoil research whose romanticism for the natural remains unexamined. Let us grant the insanity of allowing a laissez-faire technology. One cannot choose to keep the sonic boom of an SST out of one's bed. Still paratechnology cannot take the direction of a counterfoil research that would restrict the proliferation of less pernicious products.

One has reason to fear, for example, the very oddly totalitarian tendency in anarchist Murray Bookchin's important work towards a liberatory technology. He suggests the advertising pages of the *Ladies' Home Journal* and *Good Housekeeping* as containing an inventory of the range of products he has in mind when he makes the following suggestion: "If we single out of this odious garbage one or two goods of high quality in the more useful categories and if we eliminate the money economy, the state power, the credit system, the paperwork and policework required to hold society in an enforced state of want, insecurity, and domination, society would not only become reasonably human but also fairly simple."[17] Perhaps. But what about those of us who neither are nor wish to be simple? It will not do to revile us as having caused all human suffering for, true as that may be, we have also brought about the artful and complex structures that render both our sufferings and our joys truly human.

The problem is structurally the same as ever: some wish to remain in what Plato called the city of pigs, the land of simple souls. Others, like the more erotically inclined Glaucon, will not settle for less than a little luxury.[18] And once the eminently human desire for the fortuitous has begun its course, the wheel of commerce will roll even further. Only a fool would wish to stop it forever.

Discernibly different from Illich and Bookchin, though obviously similar in many ways, the people of the Portola Institute, publishers of *The Whole Earth Catalog*, support a paratechnology by providing access to tools. Rather than directly limiting the products available, the Portola Institute provides a People's Home Journal as it were, a Good Earthkeeping, whose pages are packed with yet more "advertising." True, they have selected out what they regard to be the "goods of high quality in the more useful categories," as Bookchin put it. But one hears nothing about eliminating the money economy, the credit system, etc. Rather the intention is to demystify technology, to render access to sometimes arcane tools that otherwise remain in the hands of specialists and professionals only too eager to turn their knowledge into a saleable commodity. Granted, the commodity system has its alienating aspects.[19] But the way out lies not in the direction of directly decreasing the number of commodities. Rather the point is to enable people to make their own, not in the isolated independence of the do-it-yourself rugged individual but in the human interdependence of a community that chooses to make and consume: H-bombs and SSTs no, hairdryers perhaps (though the thousand-watt plus variety seems a frightful extravagance when considered from the point of view of energy consumption), other harmless if silly extravagances certainly, as long as enough people in that community value them.

Of course the bounds of 'harmless' are difficult to determine and we should be ever thankful to ecologists for their scrutiny of the long-range effects and outermost ripples of each pebble tossed into the technological pool. But precisely on this logic we should beware of the boulder of the totally managed economy. The tidal wave of total revolution is not likely to be harmless however noble its immediate goals. Therefore paratechnology stresses a decentralization of technology rather than its totalitarian limitation. The point is to return man's tools to the men and women who now see only their products. Fight the alienating aspects of the commodity structure not by *limiting* production but by decentralizing it so that when mistakes are made—and there will *always* be mistakes—their effects will not be as disastrous as the long-range effects of well-intentioned but sometimes mistaken centralized decisions.

Here the aspect of the technological environment as a transform of nature becomes most important. For it is precisely from our experience with nature that we should now know that we cannot make *major changes* in the neonature of the technological environment without unforeseen secondary and tertiary traces. In the complex ecology of our technological environment we do better to carve out modest enclaves that reclaim parts of this neonature from the transferred neuroses of a nature-romanticism whose impulse to rip off large chunks of the technological environment is a strip-mining of human achievement, a hidden technologism at its most hubristic.

As an example of such a neonatural reclamation project one thinks of John Muir's magnificent manual on Volkswagen mechanics, a paradigm case of paratechnology.[20] The book is designed "for the compleat idiot," the better to overcome the progressive mystification of the internal combustion engine by the priesthood of professional auto mechanics and the Vatican in Detroit. Muir leads his readers step by step behind the altar of the holy of holies in mobile society until its innermost mysteries are revealed. Like a Luther of the machine age he leaves his flock neither outcast as heretic hitchhikers nor risking their souls riding the freeways on Illich's bicycles. Instead he translates the mysteries into the language of the people so that they too can read a compression gauge knowingly, adjust a valve, or perhaps if sufficiently brave accomplish the religious conversion of a total overhaul. The metaphor is not frivolous. For many of us the experience of riding a machine we have mended with our own hands is an existential introduction to the statement of purpose of *The Whole Earth Catalog:* "We are as gods and might as well get good at it."

The rest of that statement of purpose goes a long way toward summarizing the meaning of paratechnology: "So far remotely done power and glory—as via government, big business, formal education, church—has succeeded to point where gross defects obscure actual gains. In response to this dilemma and to these gains a realm of intimate, personal power is developing—power of the individual to conduct his own education, find his own inspiration, shape his own environment, and share his adventure with whoever is interested. Tools that aid this process are sought and promoted by *The Whole Earth Catalog.*" Paratechnology facilitates real power, the forming of alternative futures according to alternative intentions.

The rape of technology is no answer to the rape of nature by technology misused. To transcend one-sided dependence on either nature or technology a paratechnology is necessary (a) to work *beside* technology in order to make use of its real gains and (b) to work *against* the gross defects that obscure those gains. Working both beside and against technology in a way that liberates a plurality of futures requires of the counterfoil researcher that he work through the countertransference of his own projections of a shadow technologism. He cannot simply assume that the decentralized use of tools will in every case facilitate his own Arcadian vision.

Economics in scale

Against the future of many dimensional man the argument from economy speaks as follows: "The productive capacity of modern society is built upon economies of scale. Making jet planes takes *more* than making shoes. The former demands vast outlays of capital and a centralization of technological resources for efficient production. Further, the need for size presupposes the centralization and political stabilization of economic planning. If we are to accomplish something on the scale of the space program or the Interstate Highway system or standardized communications technology we cannot mount our horses and ride off in all directions. The costs of the comforts of modern life include centralized planning for economies of scale, for production facilities that obey the dictum, the bigger the better." So goes the argument of economic "realists" who find cause for alarm in what they regard as the dreadful disintegration of the political-economic edifice.

The standard speech for the necessity of vast size uncritically conflates different and distinguishable arguments. Though economics may follow the leading strings of technology in some ways it need not be so led in all. The more narrowly technological argument for economies of scale applies only to certain products for which vast capital and commensurate planning are required. Quite another argument calls for economies of scale in industries whose technology requires smaller concentrations of capital. The former argues that the nature of a specific product or the specific technology of its production requires size; the latter argues that the logic of *any* production points toward some optimal size of plant or business such that the centralization of even technologically primitive resources leads to more efficient expenditures of time and energy.

Paratechnology will help to combat the former demand for centralization: e.g., new developments in steel production allow for the efficient operation of much smaller mills than the gigantic Bessemer converters. Yet paratechnology alone is not adequate to combat the more narrowly *economic* argument that claims greater efficiency with size no matter what the means of production. The conflation of the two arguments gives the appearance of a need to surrender science, technology and efficiency in one fell swoop with a move toward smaller means of production. The "realist" points toward the demands of new technology as support for economies of scale, and, further, assumes the virtues of economies of scale as a rationale for research into still more bizarre technology rather than toward paratechnology. When the two arguments are separated, however, the *realities* prove to be otherwise than the "realist" suggests.

As early as 1947 Percival and Paul Goodman pointed out the possibilities of diseconomies of scale in modern production. Like Illich after them they emphasized the social costs and inefficiency of transporting workers to a single factory rather than locating smaller

factories closer to those who work in them.[21] Since that time a growing number of increasingly sophisticated studies has begun to undermine what Galbraith would call—while in this case contributing to—
the conventional wisdom that regards bigger as better. Though the
best known of these studies is probably E. F. Schumacher's aptly titled *Small is Beautiful,* the case can be made better than by Schumacher, who, like Illich, provides an example of useful counterfoil
research marred by unexamined assumptions that are fundamentally
nostalgic and regressive. Schumacher undoubtedly exerts a salutary
influence by stressing the need for a sensitivity to the human costs of
centralized production. But his metaphysics of the human turns out to
be a heavy-handed lament for the loss of "our great classical-Chris-
tian heritage . . . Who knows anything today of the Seven Deadly
Sins or the Four Cardinal Virtues? Who could even name them?"[22]
Let us applaud his program for returning economic research to the
larger context of ethics and metaphysics but turn to others for the actual execution of that program.

Recent works by John Blair, Jacob Schmookler, Charles Silberman and Barry Stein paint an increasingly detailed picture of possibilities for economic decentralization following from discoveries of
dysfunction in economies of scale.[23] Earlier intuitions about the in-
efficiencies of vast size find their proofs in studies that attempt to
measure the costs of anomie in dollars and cents terms that even the
most socially purblind econometrician cannot ignore: mental illness,
absenteeism and wildcat strikes now show up as part of the data of
economic theory, not as negligible friction factors to be discounted in
order to find the "true" formulas for optimal plant size.[24]

The original ideal of bureaucratic organization—to eliminate
personal idiosyncracies from standardized decision-making procedures—has given way to a growing body of theory and practice with
precisely the opposite emphasis: experts in organizational behavior,
"administrative science" and so on increasingly devote themselves to
the creation of atmospheres of mutual trust and "interpersonal competence."[25] The turn toward the human dimension, the "soft" side of

business schools offering T-groups and sensitivity sessions, vindicates the notion that a full science can lead back toward man even if a half-science takes one away from man.[26] Though "human management" surely has demonic potential—one's fantasies leap toward scenes depicting invasions of privacy for the sake of profit[27]—the fact remains that visions of reintroducing human scale to the cycle of production and consumption require proof of possibility before those in the cave will listen. However lovely the visions with which utopians return from their sojourns in the sun, however genuinely important the role of utopian thought may be in the total ecolocy of social life,[28] the point remains well put by Hegel: "The laurels of mere willing are dry leaves that never were green."[29]

While many content themselves with a reassuring pessimism that absolves them of the need to set right a world that is hopelessly out of joint, while many bask in the comfort of a certainty that nothing short of a total dismantling of the economy is worth one's effort, a few have both tasted of the vision of a better life and sought ways to begin building it here and now. Among the most mundane and therefore ultimately most hopeful studies is Barry Stein's *Size, Efficiency, and Community Enterprise* whose argument descends to the discovery that toilet paper and toothpaste are ideal products for community enterprise. The economy of such basics takes place in a "saturated market." People are pretty much bound to buy as much and not more than they need. Consequently a significant portion of the current cost of these products can be attributed to advertising, packaging and distribution—costs that are almost eliminable given a local product. Consumer loyalty need not be wooed by national advertising for name brands whose quality is virtually indistinguishable. Nor is the technology for the production of saturated market goods such that size generates greater production efficiency (to say nothing of the more nebulous but increasingly recognized *social* efficiency). "This is not a matter of cottage industries; significant enterprises can be generated in these and similar areas, employing anywhere up to a hundred or so, taking full advantage of modern technology and industrial organization, and producing for the community's needs."[30]

From the cavernous depths of technological and economic realities, the report begins to sound other than pundits observing the shadows on the wall had led us to believe. Even in technologically advanced society economic concentration is not as necessary as the conventional wisdom would have it. Further, if it is true as chapter I suggested that the great projects of unification have passed their historical peaks, then great projects have less appeal. Space programs, Interstate Highway systems and so on had their time and have now left us a neonature whose bounty is as plain as its corresponding adversities. Despite the centralization of the projects that generated this neonature, planting and harvesting in its fields can be a local endeavor. The same sun shone upon all early farmers; the same communication system may link the local users of paratechnological information. Just as early farmers had to discover which crops would grow best in a given locale so current economic and paratechnological research might discover which industries will yield not the highest cash price on some international market but rather the best combination of local employment, use of local resources and low-cost satisfaction of local needs.

The appeal of cash crops is seductive since the satisfaction of social needs is so much harder to quantify than dollars and cents; profits seem more determinate than something as nebulous as simple happiness. But the lessons are plain, the story has been rehearsed, its moral obvious to any who care to see. Among the more salient rehearsals is the sad story of cocoa, one of the best cash crops in terms of monetary yield for energy input. "One might therefore expect the cocoa villagers to be well off, well fed happy and gay," say some researchers. "We found exactly the reverse. The people were dull, apathetic and unhappy. Their villages were run down, dirty and dilapidated and their children naked, pot-bellied and sickly."[31] Nor is the reason simply the rapacious greed of Yankee imperialists. Rather the report claims that the high price paid for cocoa leads the villagers to use all their land for cocoa production leaving none for growing food. When the money runs out months before the next cocoa harvest everybody goes hungry. The researchers conclude with a condescension the next section finds inappropriate: "It is not enough to introduce a highly paying cash crop to an illiterate peasantry and expect them to profit by it."[32]

Professionalism

Professional specialization is the cash cropping of human resources. One might expect professionals to be well off, happy and gay. In fact one finds the reverse, or so it seems from William Irwin Thompson's description of "the aerospace syndrome" as observed during his safari through the jungles of M.I.T. He found dedicated men leading one-sided lives whose collectively reinforced concentration led them to leave their wives and chidren if not naked and pot-bellied then certainly neglected and bug-eyed before the TV. Or if the students themselves be regarded as the children: "to adopt William Hazlitt's metaphor, M.I.T. training fits its students for their future like beggars who maim their children so that they can become successful beggars."[33]

We are as ignorant peasants, fooled not by cash but by the all too evident lures of professionalism. The virtues of professionalism are manifest: no one can know it all. No one can do everything. And virtually everything, from the oldest profession to the newest, can be done better or worse. It makes sense to specialize in order to become better. "How do you get to Carnegie Hall?" repeated the wizened old Jew when asked for directions by a chauffeur lost on the lower east side. "Young man, you must practice, practice, practice."

The concentration exercised by professional musicians, athletes, scholars, medical personnel and countless others generates an ethos of total devotion. The professions exude a mystique of excellence. And who is to gainsay the beauty of what is best? Is it not selfish to refuse the heroism of self-sacrifice for the sake of excellence? We admire the extraordinary to the point that its emulation becomes ordinary. Everyone must find something at which he or she can be best.[34] But at some point one begins to wonder: a few heroes are fine but a whole army of heroes is liable to hurl itself into a holocaust without pausing to measure the cost. If the professional is a kind of hero or heroine then the holocaust is the hell of training and the cost is much greater than the tuition for medical school.

Can there be too much professionalism? The question is difficult to entertain not only because the professional is the modern hero and the mythology of heroism runs deep. Also, as more and more authority is vested in professionals, as each of us becomes an expert in something, all of us have an increased stake in professionalism. We must uphold standards. Of course. A challenge to the concept of expertise in general will be taken as a challenge to each particular domain of expertise, and since we all have a stake in some expertise or other we cannot afford to have our hard-won turf challenged. Self-sacrifice turns over into its opposite: self-defense. One of the most important and universally recognized features of professions as distinct from mere occupations is the role of institutions for meting out credentials.[35] Once the sacrifice has been made the hero gets his purple heart. But now that we wear our hearts on our sleeves the romance of heroism is less appealing.

The dialectical reversal from virtue to vice is destined by the very essence of the professional mythology. Just as his hubris leads the tragic hero to a dramatic reversal, so the professional hero's strength is his weakness: precisely because it is part of the professional ethos that one *cannot* practice too much, there *can* be too much professionalism. The injunction to practice, practice, practice leads to a forgetfulness of the fact that one practices in order to play. Beautiful music is the end goal, not perfectly performed scales. The performers must bring more than technical expertise to the concert hall. But this point is almost too banal to deserve restating. The more interesting consequences of total devotion to practicing have to do with subtle social effects of professionalization.

Individual cases of overspecialization yield to individual cures: the fight trainer learns to pace his boxer so that he peaks neither before nor after the date of the title bout. He learns that it is possible to do too much running six months before the match or too much sparring the day before. The good professional knows about timing, even when to take a vacation. Many doctors are good tennis players. But the good professional cannot by himself combat the *social* effects of professionalization on its mass modern scale. The doctor cannot, nor does he wish to, ask biochemistry to take a vacation. Yet advances on the part of professionals in the laboratories of pharmaceutical companies require the doctor to command an even greater arsenal of weapons against disease. The modern medical hero can no more venture forth with a little black bag than our literal warriors can go into battle with spears. The choice of weapons is not his to make. Other professionals have settled that issue for him and to such a degree that he must further specialize, further professionalize in a more restricted theatre of operations.[36]

As areas of expertise become more and more restricted, as the different professions both feed one another and fight one another in the battle for funds and brains, the final result is a phenomenon of ecological complexity. The individual professional is no more able to combat the potential ills of professionalization than the individual landowner is able to determine the air he breathes. When professionalism is all around us we can no longer depend on the prudence of individual measures taken against the dangers of overspecialization. And like other issues of ecology, the dimensions of the problem are likely to remain unnoticed until too late. Like the natural ecosystem the highly structured web of artificially created professional interconnections is so vast and so complex that local phenomena conceal their interconnectedness with the whole until things go awry.

Like the first few hours of practice, the first textile mill brings about an obvious improvement. The dehumanizing aspects of factory work may be more than counteracted by the individual good professional. When the Lowell family employed women they took care to set up a good Christian community for the "Lowell girls" of nineteenth-century Massachusetts. So manifest was their virtue, they did not need to think about dumping dye into the river. Only as more mills opened, only as more engines spewed forth noxious fumes in the name of increased production and greater output, only as all individual efforts were dwarfed by collective advance into industrial society did it even begin to become apparent that there was an ecological balance that could be upset. To the individual industrialist ecology is not an issue. Similarly, to the individual professional creeping professionalism is not an issue, not until it comes home to him through devious and almost unrecognizable routes, e.g., when the management of his everyday practice is taken over by specialists in related fields. Precisely to the extent that the ethos of professionalism demands myopic specialization, to just that extent the ecological boomerang effects of professionalism are bound to come as a surprise to each hard-working professional. How hard it is to meet the enemy and, with Pogo, discover he is us.

Like Aesop's grasshopper, we squandered our resources in the summer of our training for the future, and all the while we thought that we were the virtuous ants since the psychological security of professional training is nothing if not an exercise in delayed gratification. Like an illiterate peasantry that sacrifices its fields to the lure of cash we sacrifice several dimensions of selfhood for the laurels of recognition by the guild or, more subtly, for the delights of heroism. Nor are our motives totally to be despised. Often are the sacrifices genuinely selfless and the heroic acts genuinely useful. But as professionalism itself approaches Illich's second watershed, as the synchronous pattern of its most extravagant practices pushes us toward the recognition of its increasingly counterproductive secondary and tertiary traces, we cannot help but wonder whether the ideal of specialization has not outlived the time of its greatest usefulness.

The synchronous pattern of overprofessionalization resembles parallel loops of power amplification. The screech of the high school auditorium speaker system is our first introduction to the cybernetic phenomenon of *positive feedback:* sound from the speeches enters the microphone, becomes amplified and returns through the speakers to the microphone again in a circular chase whose resonances send our hands to our ears. Given a single feedback system one can turn down the amplification, break the resonance pattern and start over. Similarly the occasional excesses of isolated but overzealous professionals yield to discrete corrections. But when many professionals generate resonances not only in their own inward spirals of specialization but also *among* their several feedback loops, then it is as if we had several speaker systems and several microphones each sending the others into high-frequency madness. It is not enough to break the resonance pattern in one feedback loop for the noise generated by others will send it once again to caterwauling as soon as power is restored. Break the pattern of resonance between lawyers and insurance companies with no-fault auto insurance and the next thing you know the same lawyers are generating malpractice suits against doctors whose own specializations have led to such godlike pretensions that their own standards make "malpractice" virtually inevitable.

Another example: according to Illich, "the commodity called 'education' and the institution called 'school' make each other necessary. The circle can come to be broken only by a widely shared insight that the institution has come to define the purpose."[37] Yet even if one breaks the circle whose most specialized arcs train teachers to train students to become teachers and so on; even if one introduces some outside demands, as long as those demands are those of the several professions they will call for the same narrow commodity. When the society that breaks into the circle of education is not the society of

Illich's sometimes Arcadian vision but a society hooked on technological delights, then someone is going to have to be educated to twiddle
knobs and watch dials. Illich turns to the politicians as the only hope
for "cutting the power" from all the parallel feedback loops. But politics itself is another of the noise generators. By creating more problems than it solves, national politics generates signals that fail to inform our future. Its signals are, in the vocabulary of cybernetics,
noise, not information.

Parapolitics

How to reduce the screech? Wanted is a reducing valve, a
filter, in short, mind—for that is what mind is: an interpretive decod-
er that shuts out noise in order to process information. Kant discovered that mind is not a transparent medium through which signals
pass unaltered. Kant stressed the role of mind as synthesizing, as
constitutive, as working up in imagination what we thought had been
simply given. C. D. Broad and William James agree that experience
is not simply *given*, but they stress the nature of consciousness as
eliminative rather than constitutive.[38] Mind as a filter for separating
the noise from the information—that is what we need now: not the
earmuffs of the isolationist, not the sand pile of the ostrich, for then
we would deafen ourselves to information as well as noise, but mind
as an interpretive filter. Again *The Whole Earth Catalog* comes to
mind as a paradigm of mind in action, as a filter separating information about some genuinely useful tools from the noise one hears from
television advertising.

But what is the *political* significance of the mental filter? What
forms of *political* organization will reduce the screech? So goes the li-
tany. Nor can we ignore the question however mistaken its presuppo-

sitions may be, namely the vain hope that any single solution conceived along traditional *political* lines can begin to alleviate whatever
problems of modern existence one wishes to name. To ignore even the
ill-conceived question is to take the anarchist's way out, to throw up
one's hands at the impossibility of political solutions and secede from
society to become an outlaw. Recall the etymologically literal sense of
anarchism: without *archai*, without law or principle. Those among
anarchists who take the tongue-twisting trouble to call themselves
anarcho-syndicalists might be described more accurately as pluralists
to the extent that they stress the *group*, the syndicate, Some as the
fundamental locus of social theory rather than the outlaw individual,
the One. Some anarchists are more accurately pluralists but spurn the
name for fear of allying themselves with the likes of liberal pluralists
like Robert Dahl. To orient parapolitics where it belongs in the neighborhood between pluralism and anarchism, the following discussion
will follow the opposite strategy: first a spurning of anarchism, then a
more accurate differentiation of parapolitics from the usual varieties
of pluralism.

Some of the reasons for spurning anarchism are already clear:
the anarchist is the political atheist, the true believer in disbelief, the
bitter harbinger of a barren existence predicated upon the ultimate
meaninglessness of human existence. Clutching onto the certainty of
his individuality alone, even his efforts at human association are destined to the defensiveness of the "protective association."[39] Even
where his visions of mankind project gorgeous freedom once the stric-
tures of historical associations have been thrown off, even when his
eagerness to destroy the State gives him the appearance of a heroic
and death-defying radical, he is at precisely those moments his most
reactionary. In his essay, "Poetry and Revolution: The Anarchist as
Reactionary," Benjamin Barber has said what needs to be said on the
subject, e.g.: "The anarchist remains, however, a proselytizing aristocrat who, possessed by a *noblesse oblige* of the apocalyptic, is driven
to share his own transfiguration with the people. He is an egalitarian
elitist dedicated to the notion that all men can be made superi-

or. . . . He is the *Uebermensch* of the underdogs."[40] So spurned let us now turn from anarchism to a more careful effort at holding the ills of pluralism at arm's length.

Traditional pluralistic theories posit the so-called intermediate group as a link between the individual and the State. Just as the family plays a role in socializing the individual to some of the codes and customs one must master to become a member of human society, so the intermediate group, one's face to face Others, plays the role of mediating one's participation in the life of the nation as a whole. According to pluralistic theory the intermediate group is often an interest group or pressure group whose power assists the individual in making himself heard on issues of public policy.

Recent American pluralisms—from the participationist theories of Bachrach, Pateman and Thompson to mass-society liberal pluralists like Dahl and Kornhauser—reproduce the same ambivalences evident in the English pluralists, Laski and Cole.[41] The problem in both American and English pluralisms boils down to an unjustified presumption that participation in the intermediate group will prove somehow *functional* in facilitating the larger political process—whether 'facilitation' means stabilization and equilibrium (Kornhauser) or radical change (participationists and English Guild Socialists).[42]

By extending the range of 'politics' from governmental processes to corporate and social involvements, the participationists wish to have it both ways: on the one hand virtually every human activity becomes political, hence a preservation of political concern analogous to the preservation of religious concern by a liberal Tillichian theology; on the other hand this watered-down politics is purported to be sufficient to deal with the questions of a more orthodox variety, e.g., the public policies of the State. For the English pluralists the same conflict took the form of a conflation of Lockean libertarianism with a curious and often unacknowledged idealism whose emphasis upon the *social* genesis of individual rights formed the tacit background of the concern for intermediate *groups* rather than individuals.

In sum, previous pluralisms seek compromises between the primacy of the collective All and the primacy of the individual One without ever satisfactorily determining the ontological status of the intermediate Some.

Parapolitics differs from previous pluralisms precisely on their problematic point, namely the presumption that beneath the differences that separate all situses and statuspheres from one another there lies some common purpose or some common rationality that must be assumed as the condition for the possibility of politics. Unlike other pluralisms parapolitics makes no presumption of a unified purposive rationality in the State. Having seen that the mechanisms of mass politics now exhibit the ecological structure of nature, many dimensional man is in a position analogous to that of the first non-Aristotelian scientists, those who broke away from the habit of attributing rational purposes and intentions to nature. Now we have discovered the same lack of purposive structure in the neonature of politics and technology. However rational the State may have been in the days of political Kapellmeisters, its current structure more closely resembles the complex ecology of nonpurposive nature. Once this insight has been appreciated then such phrases as 'public policy' come to have the hollow ring of 'the will of god': such phrases connote efforts to find a single volition where many wills either offset one another or combine in patterns unpredictable and quite possibly unintended by anyone.

Situses and statuspheres have little to do with mediating the individual's relation to so-called public policy. So to conceive them is to ignore the political Reformation. Traditional pluralisms place the intermediate group in the role enjoyed by the priesthood in the Catholic hierarchy of the Holy Roman Empire. The priesthood mediated the peasant's relationship with the One True World. But the Reformation ended all that for the religious world over which God presided. The further sundering of Church and State paved the way for politics to replace religion as a unifying principle. God died. Now the nation-state repeats a similar process of death and reformation. Just as politics sundered itself from religion, now situses sunder themselves from the political order. Unlike traditional pluralisms, parapolitics does not presume to mediate between the individual and a "center" where only the echo of power remains to delude the superstitious.

If the transpersonal Some is in any way functional (as the residual optimism of traditional pluralism would have it) its functionality has little to do with resolving differences for the sake of unity. Rather the Anaxagorean rationality of parapolitics calls for an ever more artful articulation of *differences*—between ethnic group and ethnic group, between generations, between sexes, between signs of the zodiac, between gods, between parapolitical communities. The point of such articulation of difference has nothing to do with expropriation or oppression. The point of articulating differences is rather just the opposite; to remove us from the oppressive mantle of monotheism, to liberate us from the *Normalgott* and single vision, to make us free. Precisely the difference from the socializing other is a concomitant of the social differences whose trace is the *resistance* characteristic of the structure of freedom. The "function" of the Some differs from the function of the so-called intermediate group whose intermediary status mediates the difference between the many and the one with an experience in sameness and solidarity conceived as a sort of rehearsal for the brotherhood of all mankind.

Indeed we are brothers, but not of the romanticized family of the family-hour comedy. Our lived brotherhood pits us in struggles more intense than those pale conflicts of contemporary political campaigns. The parapolitical Some is in a sense an *interest group*, namely in the sense that some have interests that *differ* from the interests of others (along with other interests they of course share). But the parapolitical interest group differs from the conventionally defined political interest group in the sense that whatever pressures may be brought to bear by the parapolitical Some do *not* have as their strategy the indirect method of making a change in some central controlling mechanism so that intended results may eventually accrue from altered priorities in a hierarchy of values guiding "public policy."

The pluralism of parapolitics represents an historical evolu-tion of religious freedom: the wish to worship as one pleased without fear of political repression was one of the primary motives for many in their quest for the promised land of early America.[43] Once politics replaces religion as an axial principle for legitimating authority in modern society, the investment of value in *religious* freedom trans-forms into a need for *political* freedom, now understood not in terms of a bill of rights guaranteed by a fixed and universal political order but in terms of a freedom to support any of several alternative politi-cal orders. Just as liberal-democratic politics came on the scene in answer to a need for protecting religious freedom against the en-croachments of a monolithic unification of Church and State, so para-politics comes on the scene in answer to the encroachments of a mo-notheistic, overcentralized politics.

Just as this country was founded partially on the premise that one should be allowed to worship as Catholic or Protestant, Puritan or Jew, so parapolitics responds to the historical shift in the role played by politics—from tool to alien environment—by suggesting the possi-bility of a plurality of political persuasions: let a hundred parapoliti-cal systems bloom. Let the Birchers have their enclaves, let the Marx-ists have their communes, let the moderates have their modest com-munities and the utopians their experiments in living. The only sin is then the aspiration toward legislating one order for all. The only sin is centralized politics, that outmoded medium for universal order. Poli-tics itself must go the way of the Holy Roman Empire: hardly unto oblivion, nor even into the dustbin of history, but toward the reduced status of institutions that have outlived the heyday of their useful-ness. Like the Holy Roman Empire, the politics of advanced industri-al nation-states has reached a point at which it obstructs rather than facilitates human freedom.

Epilogue

The journey toward many dimensional man does not have parapolitics as its singular destination. 'Parapolitics' is no more than a name for a social praxis appropriate to many dimensional man; a concomitant symptom of his arrival, not a cause or effect. These concluding pages therefore employ parapolitics as a prism through which to view the whole. The point is not to see "what it all adds up to"—as if the case for many dimensional man were to be judged entirely by taking parapolitics as its outcome; instead the test case of social philosophy shows how the equally important psychological and theological transforms join social philosophy in the cave of contemporary politics.

These final pages therefore summarize several themes in order to show how the case for many dimensional man constitutes a systematic whole that differs point for point with the metaphysics of monism, the theology of monotheism, the psychology of purified identity and the politics of the universal, homogenous state. Though only one aspect of the whole story, parapolitical pluralism provides as good a point as any for seeing the differences between the monism of our monotheistic tradition and many dimensional existence. The issue of social justice provides a focus on which many other issues converge.

The prospect of legitimating pernicious interests is the specter that ever haunts pluralism. Any defense of the clan as a less barbarous, more Apollonian variant of the Dionysian tribe must countenance the reality of the Ku Klux Klan. But the will toward Uniform Justice For All must countenance the equally pernicious possibility that the United States of America might turn with a like shift of letter into Amerika, the land of an oppressive and unjust "justice." Murder by lawmen may be construed as legal but it left Black Panther leader Fred Hampton every bit as brutally dead as if he had been burned on a cross in some backwater bayou.

But a single martyr does not a revolution make, nor do even several justify the wholesale dismantling of the American legal system, as imperfect as it may be. For the vast network of interlocking legal and political institutions (neonature) now provides a dialectical moment of uniformity needed to complement the equally real and necessary impulse toward decentralization. Like the nature of old this neonature sets constraints on what a given community can do. At its best this neonature would allow the proliferation of clans, but not the Klan. Can we ensure that this neonature will function at its best? For at its worst we are reduced to tribal warfare.

These issues are as old as politics itself. Nothing new is likely to arise at this late date from abstract debates over whether power *ought to be* centralized for the sake of more uniform justice—the first watershed debate among those living on the tributaries in earlier political highlands; nor is there likely to be much of interest learned from second watershed debates about the factual concentration of power as long as the *ontology* of power remains unexamined. This book has little to do with ethics or political philosophy as these disciplines traditionally have been conceived, namely as quests after timeless truths about the structure of the ideal society. The realities of recent history provide occasions for this redescription of the *proper* bearers of such terms as *'self'*, *'nature'*, *'power'* and *'freedom'*.

Let the banks of the Charles River ring with talk of "rights" and "justice." Doubtless there remains work to be done in drafting the terms of an eternal contract that would relate the rights of the self to some vision of justice. But until we gain some sensitivity to the historical dimension of social philosophy, until we see that the *bearers* of these rights and the *mechanisms* of justice are named by floating signifiers whose proper referrents undergo historical transformations, then our political philosophy is so much outmoded mythology. All talk of individual rights is so much silliness when the locus of subjectivity to which those rights would pertain is found in animals rather than in human communities. All talk of justice is of marginal interest to *historically specific* concerns when theoreticians draw a veil of ignorance between the elegance of their timeless concerns and the exigencies of the particular historical situation.

The social philosophy of Some has little to do with the abstract question of whether anytime or anywhere the rights of a few may be abrogated for the sake of the greatest happiness for the greatest number (that problem of the utilitarian calculus whose very posing already endorses the satisfaction of some with the sufferings of others else how could that "greatest number" remain "happy"). The social philosophy of Some follows from a different question: even if we grant either an intuitively obvious or meticulously articulated doctrine of justice as fairness, the question remains: *at this point in our several histories* is the positive enactment of justice likely to derive from the mechanisms erected to facilitate its enactment? So posed the question might seem to be an issue for political scientists and historians rather than political philosophers. Yet mere empiricism is not sufficient to its answer because only an ontological investigation will unlock the riddles of reference for the floating signifiers, 'self', 'freedom', 'nature' and 'power'. To see how the rational enactment of justice is no longer the forte of our government is to see how our political institutions have passed beyond the watershed of their usefulness as intention-facilitating tools. Similarly, the parapolitician may agree with the proposition that individual rights are inalienable but find it to be either meaningless or mistaken until we tack down the reference of 'individual' in a way that locates the structure of subjectivity in some more discerning manner than by searching for soft brown eyes.

Following Chapter I's critique of national politics and the presidency as a viable structure of agency, Chapters II and III defined the criteria that structures of agency must fulfill. In place of the usual assumption of persons and national political authorities, Chapters II and III found intrapersonal selves and transpersonal (though nonuniveral) assemblages of persons satisfying the conditions for agency. The problem for psychology and social theory is no longer, "How shall persons relate to centralized, hierarchical systems of authority?" Instead the problem becomes: "In the absence of singular authority, how will intrapersonal selves and intrasocial Somes relate to one another without madness or bloodshed?"

The sojourn into the self in Chapters III and following found heterarchy satisfying the structure of freedom in both the psychological and mythological dimensions. Both the parts of the person and the gods of the polytheistic pantheon relate to one another without hierarchy or anarchy. Parapolitics reproduces the structure of subjectivity in the social dimension. Because parapolitics is the social transform of intrapersonal heterarchy, the lessons of the body and the lessons of Zarathustra's wanderings in the wilderness have import for social issues.

For example, it is sometimes said that diversification of values and social systems would be fine were it not for the likelihood that on one's way from one community to another one is liable to be met with a hail of machinegun bullets. This vivid image of decentralization is devastating for abstract, ahistorical theories of utopian politics. If isolated and diverse communities were somehow dropped from the sky, travelers between them might expect the worst. But the social philosophy of many dimensional man is neither ahistorical nor abstract nor utopian. Instead it reinterprets current realities and reappraises common sense's legacies from obsolete theories. (Chapters I and II). Rather than approaching social theory as a logical puzzle that must have a clear and noncontradictory solution, the social philosophy of many dimensional man acknowledges the reality of tragedy, madness and warfare. (Chapters III and V). But it is precisely by that acknowledgment, and through the sojourn into the self to seek the sources of violence, that the social philosophy of many dimensional man would hope to prevent the hail of machinegun bullets (Chapter VI).

By situating social philosophy within both historical, psychological and metaphysical horizons, the preceding chapters attempt to point out the motives and mistaken beliefs that would lead to the manning of machineguns. Beliefs about power, selfhood, mastery, control, nature and history set the context for social philosophy. As long as those beliefs are cast in the frame of Eleatic metaphysics and monotheistic theology, machinegun bullets will continue to slay the "heathen." Relational thought guarantees no solutions because the acknowledgment of tragedy and contradiction is a denial of the view that the human condition is a quasi-mathematical puzzle admitting of a clearly logical solution. But relational thought may, by attention to the contextual roots of our motives, minimize the machinegun fire.

Relational thought situates each Some within both historical and neonatural environments.

Parapolitics countenances different communites but each is homoeomerous with the whole in the sense that, like each self in an embodied person, each Some represents the "same" environment differently. The parapolitical stance within each group demands a mediation with others, a critique and reconciliation achieved by virtue of a social confrontation with the shadow. That is, each group, whether socialist or individualist, progressive or conservative, comes to recognize the others not only as Other but also as a projection of what has been repressed. The parapolitical task therefore involves the attempt to confront and acknowledge what each group is most eager to deny as part of itself.

Strategies of ritual confrontation will vary widely depending on the nature of the community and the nature of the shadow to be incorporated into a more integrated whole. It is easy enough to say that *in general* the parapolitical stance calls for strategies that demonstrate the diminution of being that results from a refusal to recognize the other in oneself. Yet those strategies will differ depending on particular historical circumstances and different human natures. Therefore it is not only difficult but misleading to be specific about the how-to of parapolitical strategies. The lack of specific imperatives is not a sign of theoretical poverty but rather a theoretical imperative toward historically specific interpretations.

The strategic stance of parapolitics follows from the systematic distinction between nature and history, not form a denial of system or a transcendence of ideology. Parapolitics is not a shallow empiricism that would shun theoretical considerations for the sake of tactical efficiency. To the contrary, the key to the concept of parapolitics is the eminently theoretical discipline, ontology: the *logos* or speech of Being. What is? The key to parapolitics is a hermeneutic ontology that discloses beings, not Being; worlds, not The World; gods, not God; histories, not History; therefore Somes, not All. Consequently parapolitics, while universalist in the sense of appealing to a theory about all theories, turns out to be antiuniversalist in the sense that the theory about all theories is itself a pluralistic theory.

Parapolitics reproduces the structure of subjectivity in the local environment while at the same time seeing to it that local efforts neither ignore the benefits nor exploit the bounty of the larger environment. We have found that man can neither ignore nor exploit nature in his attempt to carve out political-technological environments. Now that parapolitics finds the political environment potentially and—to its martyrs—actually hostile, there is a temptation to treat liberal-democratic politics as a tool that might be cast into the dustbin in favor of some other political tool, say socialism or good old Republican politics. Yet the theoretical context in which the term 'parapolitics' finds its meaning shows that the political environment of advanced industrial society is no longer a tool following the intentions of any specific group of men. Rather it plays the role of that wider environment that like the nature of old poses similar but not identical problems for all who would gain their livelihoods by harvesting its resources.

The role of parapolitics resembles the original role of politics as a man-made tool for mediating the relationship with an alien environments. Yet the difference between the relevant alien environment necessitates differences among mediating tools, not only between politics and parapolitics but also between different species of a generic parapolitics. The differences among species of parapolitics follows from the difference between the historically evolved neonature and the earlier natural environment. The reader may have noticed that the concept of nature figured differently in Chapters I and II. In Chapter I nature was the alien environment whose transforms are politics and technology. In Chapter II nature was contrasted with historical products of reason like politics and technology. The uniformity and consequent universality of natural laws contrasted with the freedom and consequent diversity of different histories. Because the neonature of politics and technology lacks the uniformity of nature, the tool that would mediate our relationship with that neonature can no longer aspire to the universality of a politics ostensibly dealing with an environment whose laws are uniform. Whatever salutary purposes it may have served in mediating relations with nature, further missionary perpetuation of the monotheistic tradition of universal politics fails to respect the historical diversity of our new environments.

The wish to legislate a universal political solution to the issues of injustice is redolent of the wish to cast some simple spell that would end the infelicities of nature. 'Tis a consummation devoutly to be wished. But only the blasted vision of those weary of all the shocks that flesh is heir to will fall for a final solution (Chapter VII).

Earlier the betrayal of life took the form of a demonic idolatry that forswore the day's work of farming, technology and politics in favor of a faith that God would take care of everything. Now that politics and technology themselves form the alien environment, unquestioning faith in politics and technology is the transform of demonic idolatry. Parapolitics and paratechnology are the day's work for a paraconsciousness that retains a laborious wakefulness quite different from Descartes's (Chapter VII).

A transform relates the old idolatry to the new. The same transform relates the old turn from faith toward works to a new secularism. Now the faith in universalist politics gives way to the necessity of local works. The transform that dictates the form for parapolitics maps the same function mediating man's relation with an alien environment onto a different environment. Because the new environment is filled with the historical products of free reason, it lacks the uniformity of the laws of that original nature. Consequently the generic parapolitics that would mediate relationships with the new environment is necessarily pluralized into many species.

Past political systems, whatever their particular persuasions, often aspired to the universal homogeneous state, partly for the purpose of overcoming war by grand alliances, partly out of a conviction that politics deals with human nature as technology deals with physical nature. Since human nature was thought to be a universal, therefore the appropriate politics seemed to be universal. Yet political systems proliferated. So too did ideologies whose interpretations of the human condition differ. In his sixth thesis on Feuerbach, Marx noted that human nature is not some bare abstraction inhering in particular individuals, but rather, "the ensemble of social relationships." As those ensembles change and proliferate so does human nature (Chapter II). Human natures are the historical results of different patterns of projection and introjection in different structures of free subjectivity. The historicity of human nature combined with the freedom of reason generates a plurality of human natures, each essential to a different circle of subjectivity. Consequently it is no longer possible to retain faith in politics as a universal tool for mediating among the instances of some universal human nature.

So far this summary has stressed the inevitability of plurality among parapolitical enclaves carved from the political-technological neonature. Unlike nature, reason is free to vary not only its products but its means of production. The social philosophy of Some appeals to that freedom and its consequent variety. Because the appeal is to freedom, however, there remains a choice for selective uniformity. The following section develops the analogy between nature and neonature. The point is to appreciate those products of reason whose reach not only rivals nature's uniformity, but whose rewards rival nature's bounty. The social philosophy of Some need not settle for a sense of justice that is capricious. The structure of freedom avoids the arbitrary (Chapter II).

Neonatural ecology

The transform from politics to parapolitics does not dictate the total destruction of traditional political and legal institutions. Instead a sensitivity to their current status as neonature suggests the relearning of an ecological consciousness transformed onto the new environment. What have we already learned in our relationship with nature?

The first human harvesters were hunters. Anthropological research indicates that around ten thousand years ago paleolithic hunters had a hand in "the unusual incidence of large-animal extinctions throughout the world." The relative ease with which large animals could be herded over cliffs enhances the hypothesis that paleolithic hunters often indulged in overkill. "The absence of appropriation provided incentives for the wastage killing evident in some kill sites, while the slow growth, long lives, and long maturation of large animals increased their vulnerability to extinction."[2] And so it might be said of some human institutions and traditions whose slow growth, long life and long maturation renders them similarly vulnerable to extinction when ripped off with the revolutionary zeal of the institutional hunter. Not until later, not until "sometime after the extinction of the megafauna," did human culture acquire "a sensitivity to the need to prevent overharvesting."[3] And so it might be said that as our politics takes on the role of environment rather than tool its relegation to the role of alien environment brings with it the danger of an overharvesting. As we herd the dumb beasts of our overgrown institutions over the cliffs of our civilized discontents we run the risk of raping this neonature in return for its bounty.

Parapolitics pauses before acting out its radical impiety and restrains the arrogance of the anarchist. Recognizing the role of the political-institutional environment as a neonatural environment demanding ecological sensitivities, the parapolitician stands to the revolutionary as farmer to hunter. Faced with the imminent extinction of fat resources—say, the bounty of the Third World on which we have preyed as if there were no tomorrow—the parapolitician learns to forego the quick kill in favor of cultivating the soil, planting seeds and waiting until his crop is grown.

How does this fundamental transformation of archetypes— from hunter to harvester—transform onto the historical shift from the power politics of predatory nation-states to the parapolitics of the postcolonial era? Aside from economic and cultural decentralization the transformation has import for attitudes toward those institutions that are less easily decentralized, e.g., communications systems and law courts. Most important: the move from "hunting" to "farming" in the neonature of the political-technological environment is precisely the move required to salvage the best of second watershed institutions and ward off the worst of the shadow of injustice that always haunts pluralism. For unlike the revolutionary hunter out for the quick kill, the parapolitical farmer works both against and beside existent institutions: *against* them in so far as he finds them as the farmer finds nature—an alien environment and not a field of first watershed tools ready to serve his will; *beside* them in so far as, like the farmer rather than the hunter, he realizes first that he cannot poach on this neonatural bounty indefinitely, and second, that he must choose wisely where to plant his crops. For not all soil is equally rich. Some soil is more difficult to farm than other. River basins are best. Where is the institutional river basin? Where in the world of human artifacts are those bottoms in which the stream of history has dumped layer upon layer of rich sedimentary soil, the silt that has passed down from high mountain streams and ages ago?

Interpretation and closure

The definition of a new problem does not determine all its solutions. The description of the transformed parameters of many dimensional existence leaves considerable doubt about how to plot a lifeline that will satisfy the several conditions for freedom. Nor would freedom follow from a set of questions that allowed but one answer, some pretentiously didactic claim for "what we in this time of crisis must do." True to the usual formality of philosophy, this account concludes leaving considerable latitude for further interpretations of the general structures so far described.

We live our lives in terms of our interpretations whose linguistic inventories name the entities we take to be real. No one lays down his life for an abstraction. In laying down his life for his nation the patriot would prove that 'nation' names a reality. Likewise the unwillingness of many to lay down their lives in the defense of some cause is proof in itself that the cause is less than unequivocally real. We construct our realities not only through our interpretations but also through actions on the basis of our interpretations. Our actions themselves sometimes constitute interpretations, as when a spontaneous gesture of affection not only declares but helps create a "friendship" from what had been a mere "acquaintance." The structures of our realities are thus sustained by mutual reinforcements among different behaviors and their theoretical interpretations as historical actions. The paradigms governing those interpretations are pervasive.

The sojourn into the self that began with the structure of subjectivity assumed and explored a homoeomereity of structure among parts of the self, selves and assemblages of selves. The basic premise of structural isomorphism has the reassuring ring of banality: social structure reflects character structure, character structure reflects social structure. From Plato to Gerth and Mills the same story.[4] Religious structure reflects political structure—Weber.[5] The relationship of a member of the technostructure to the technostructure is the same as that of the technostructure of a mature corporation to the state—Galbraith.[6] In a total consciousness or false consciousness, certain syndromes of beliefs, preferences and patterns of behavior prove to hang together in coherent and predictable patterns—Adorno et al on fascism,[7] Rokeach,[8] both Wilhelm and Charles Reich,[9] Charles Hampden-Turner,[10] the list could continue. In the context of these demonstrations of systematic continuity between forms of thought and forms of life both private and social, the question quite naturally arises: What is the pattern of continuities, what is the structure of interrelationships between the structure of selfhood and the structure of society for many dimensional man? The major premises of structural continuity is as old as social theory but the minor premise of multidimensional personality has yet to be adequately included in the syllogism of social theory.

This book combines a theory of the decentralized self with a theory of decentralized society in order to seek within the self those paradigms of interpretation necessary to sustain pluralism within society. Contemporary culture reflects a quickened pace of fragmentation. Common sense strains to keep pace. Protean changes reflect the strain (Chapter IV). But common sense, even in its Protean acrobatics, retains monistic paradigms of interpretation that misconstrue pluralistic structures. To seek more adequate paradigms within a self we must appeal to a self somehow immune to the molding influences of monistic social structures. We find that self in Nietzsche's Zarathustra. Yet Nietzsche has little to say about transforming the structure of decentralized selfhood onto a decentralized society. The syllogism of social theory calls for a move from paraconsciousness to parapolitics and paratechnology. Yet Chapter VIII's first steps in that direction remain so formal, so tentative.

To some the end of this book will therefore seem to be unsatisfactory. One could wish for a stronger resolution, a louder cadence. But for a book that praises decadence, closure is inappropriate. A clear conclusion would compromise a sense of time that denies eschatology. A final solution is not forthcoming. Instead the wish for unambiguous direction must turn back upon itself to interpret its own direction from contradictions in its own origin.

Who are the Some from which the wish for direction takes its counsel? Which collective defines the order of rank that would judge any proposed answers to the wish? We are all parts of one collective or another, and none of us is a citizen of The World. Each of us is represented by processes of collective bargaining by parties who do not always *represent* us as much as they *define* the terms of the language we speak, e.g., 'poverty,' 'success,' 'happiness', 'sin', 'evil' and 'integrity'. The terms and their local meanings define the order of rank that would test any answer to the wish for directions.

The return to an interpretation of one's own origins remains difficult to the extent that we remain trapped in a hermeneutic circle seeking a single origin. The vision that sees singular sources for political power as well as individual volition seems to forbid an incremental gathering of evidence for an alternative hermeneutic. Yet the depth and breadth of the many dimensional experience, the pluralism of the polytheistic experience, can be neither restored nor invented piecemeal. Despite increasing evidence of the decline of monotheistic power, despite increasing manifestations of pluralizing pressures in advanced industrial society, the full circle of many dimensional life and thought cannot replace the monotheism of more than two millenia as long as the potentially enriching process of pluralization continues to be experienced as dissonant, decadent and deadly—each of these terms retaining only its most negative connotations. Evidence in favor of both the fact and the desirability of many dimensional experiece will be felt as the pain of unwanted crisis, prelude to apocalypse. The conversion of consciousness called for is so thoroughgoing and subtle, however, no revolutionary accomplishment by apocalypse could hope to complete each of its mutually supporting arcs. Only by fits and starts, by the gradual enrichments that insight can add to the annual rings of the soul, by the bark of defenses shed in the most clement of seasons, only with the happiest circumstances of growth and life-giving decay have we any hope of matching our overwrought achievements with an appropriate consciousness.

To see the opportunity is not to be sanguine, for the vision needed to transform "crisis" into creativity is unpracticed. From the Athens that exiled Anaxagoras to the logical atomism of Bertrand Russell, the lenses of Western sight have been ground according to a prescription that compensates for just those blind spots we can no longer ignore, namely the molecular structure of relational existence and the differing valencies of our lives. A self-perpetuating pattern of Eleatic consciousness has so far compensated for the lazy eyes and selective blindnesses of our culture that it is now doubtful whether we can reach up and remove the spectacles through which we perceive what we take to be evidence for the perfect clarity of our vision.

Notes

Prologue

1. 'Alienist' was the word used in the nineteenth century for those who are now called psychiatrists or psychologists. For contemporary studies of the social or interpersonal roots of alienation see Kenneth Keniston, *The Uncommitted* (New York, 1965), and *Young Radicals* (New York, 1968), also R. D. Laing, *The Politics of Experience* (New York, 1967), though Chap. III below provides a critique of some of Laing's categories.

2. G.W.F. Hegel, *The Phenomenology of Mind*, trans. Baillie (orig. pub. 1807; New York, 1949), pp. 263–64.

Chapter I

1. Hegel, *Phenomenology of Mind*, p. 753.

2. Talcott Parsons, *The Social System* (Glencoe, Ill., 1951), p. 126.

3. Daniel Bell, *The Coming of Post-Industrial Society* (New York, 1973), p. 364.

4. Ibid., p. 360; see also p. 43 and chap. 6 passim.

5. For early twentieth-century American social theory see Richard Hofstadter, *The American Political Tradition* (New York, 1948); and Robert Wiebe, *The Search for Order, 1877–1920* (New York, 1967). For the most recent retrospect, see Richard King, *The Party of Eros* (Chapel Hill, N.C., 1972; New York, 1973), chap. 1.

6. William E. Connaly, "The Challenge to Pluralist Theory," in *The Bias of Pluralism*, ed. Connaly (New York, 1971), p. 15.

7. Henry Kariel, *The Decline of American Pluralism* (Stanford, 1961).

8. On Mills and his critics see not only the classic C. Wright Mills, *The Power Elite* (New York, 1956); but also the very useful volume of essays *C. Wright Mills and The Power Elite*, ed. Domhoff and ballard (Boston, 1968).

9. Hannah Arendt follows p. D'Entreves in returning to Cicero's *Potestas in populo* to support the idea that power "corresponds to the human ability not just to act but to act in concert. . . . In current usage, when we speak of a 'powerful man' or a 'powerful personality,' we already use the word 'power' metaphorically." (Arendt, "On Violence," in idem, *Crisis of the Republic* (New York, 1972), rpt. in *Self and World*, ed. Ogilvy (New York, 1973), p. 424. D' Entreves, *The Notion of the State: An Introduction to Political Theory* [New York, 1967], pp. 7, 171). The same could doubtless be said against Stanley Benn when, in order to refute the notion that power is always a relationship among people, he cites "a tenor's power to smash a tumbler with a high C." (S. I. Benn, "Power," *The Encyclopedia of Philosophy*, ed. Edwards [New York, 1967], 6:425).

10. Charles Reich, *The Greening of America* (New York, 1970), p. 88. Like the Domhoff and Ballard book on Mills (n. 8 above), *The Con III Controversy*, ed. Philip Nobile (New York, 1971), is useful. More precisely, the critics' polemics are proofs in themselves that both Mills and Reich were onto things important. Neither was cautious, both were criticized, more often than not with at least some justice, both advanced the dialectic of social thought significantly.

11. The reference here is of course to David Halberstam's works, which provide Tolstoyan thickness to the decision-making processes whose thin surface we call politics. See Halberstam, *The Making of a Quagmire* (New York, 1965), and his brilliant *The Best and the Brightest* (New York, 1972).

12. Robert Dahl, "Power," *International Encyclopedia of Social*

Science (New York, 1968), 12:405; see also idem, "The Concept of Power," *Behavioral Science* 2 (1957): 201–15.

13. Having listed as "power terms" both 'power' and 'force' (along with "influence, authority, persuasion, dissuasion, inducement, coercion, compulsion") Dahl then offers as a "broad definition": "At the most general level, power terms in modern social science refer to subsets of relations among social units such that the behaviors of one or more units (the responsive units, R) depend in some circumstances on the behavior of other units (the controlling unit, C)" (Dahl, "Power," p. 407). According to this definition the mere correlation of behaviors is then sufficient to prove a power relation.

14. Ibid., p. 410. On p. 413 Dahl takes up the issue of intention only to reduce its use to what he regards as absurdity: "What is it, then, that distinguishes having power from exercising power? The distinction could hinge upon the presence or absence of a manifest intention. We could define the *exercise* of power in such a way as to require C to manifest an intention to act in some way in the future, his action to be contingent on R's behavior. By contrast, C might be said to *have* power when, though he does not manifest an intention, R imputes an intention to him and shapes his behavior to meet the imputed intention. If one were to accept this distinction, then in studying the exercise of power, one would have to examine not only R's perceptions and responses but also C's intentions and actions. In studying relationships in which C is thought to have power, even though he does not exercise it, one would in principle need only to study R's perceptions, the intentions R imputes to C, and the bearing of these on R's behavior. Carried to the extreme, then, this kind of analysis could lead to the discovery of as many different power structures in a political system as there are individuals who impute different intentions to other individuals, groups, or strata in the system." But of course the analysis of power relations in terms of intentions need not be carried to this not altogether ridiculous extreme if one retains the distinction between manifest intentions behind real power and merely imputed intentions behind mythological power, on which more below.

15. Ibid., p. 410.

16. Ibid., p. 414: Their sublime indifference toward "the somewhat rarified philosophical and definitional questions, which many social scientists are prepared to abandon to metaphysics or philosophers of science" will, in the not very long run, cost the social scientists more time than it saves in getting around to the problems of the social sciences. As proponents of this view of measuring power Dahl lists Simon, March, Cartwright, Oppenheim and himself.

17. Among psychologists one thinks of Watson, Skinner and the be-

haviorist school; among physicists, those who resist the Copenhagen interpretation of quantum theory in favor of a quest for hidden variables whose discovery will save mechanism albeit in probabilistic rather than deterministic form. See, for example, David Bohm, *Causality and Chance in Modern Physics*, (New York, 1957), esp. pp. 94–129. Louis de Broglie appears to have moved from the second realm to the third by finally giving up the quest for hidden parameters after being convinced by von Neumann's mathematical proof that the data of microphysics are such as to be in principle inexplicable by some hidden level of strictly causal interactions. See Louis de Broglie, *Physics and Microphysics*, trans. Davidson (New York, 1955), pp. 202 ff.

18. Gregory Bateson, "Cybernetic Explanation," in idem, *Steps to an Ecology of Mind* (New York, 1972).

19. The primacy of substance to the rest of the categories is a central tenet of Aristotle's *Metaphysics*. The secondary status of relations is so obvious to Aristotle that he can add as an unargued aside in his *Nicomachean Ethics*: "i.e. substance, is prior in nature to the relative (for the latter is like an offshoot and accident of being)" (1096a21–22).

20. See J. K. Galbraith, *The New Industrial State* (New York, 1967), chaps. 6, 8, 11–13.

21. On the staging of pseudoevents see Daniel J. Boorstin, *The Image* (New York, 1962), pp. 9–12; Murray B. Levin, *Kennedy Campaigning* (Boston, 1966); Dan Nimmo, *The Political Persuaders* (Englewood Cliffs, N.J., 1970), pp. 26–29.

22. Galbraith, *New Industrial State*, p. 69 et passim.

23. This point has become vividly clear in Fireman's Mutual advertisements that televise the virtues of independent agents' carrying their competitors' policies in order to urge the more important message of the need for insurance generally.

24. Tom Wolfe, "Why They Aren't Writing the Great American Novel Anymore," *Esquire*, December 1972, p. 153.

Cf. Ferdinand Tönnies, *Community and Society*, trans. Loomis (orig. pub. 1887; New York, 1963). Tönnies's categories form the backbone of Fritz Pappenheim, *The Alienation of Modern Man* (New York, 1959). Though Tönnies's categories are much out of favor today, not only with the likes of Tom Wolfe but also among social theorists like Christopher Lasch (cf. his series on the history of the family in the *New York Review of Books* 22, nos. 18–20), one could still do worse than return to Tönnies's own formulations of these categories, which have, to be sure, fallen on some fallow ground.

25. Tom Wolfe, *The Pump House Gang* (New York, 1968), Introduction, rpt. in *Self and World*, ed. Ogilvy, p. 29.

26. Ibid., p. 26.

27. Ibid., p. 30.

28. Bell, *Post-Industrial Society*, p. 366.

29. Ibid., p. 376.

30. Ibid., p. 377.

31. Ibid., p. 373; also p. 376 et passim.

32. Instead Bell's analysis tends to support the thesis that politics has migrated from the role of tool to the role of environment. For example: "For most of human history, *reality was nature*, and in poetry and imagination men sought to relate the self to the natural world. Then *reality became technics*, tools and things made by men yet given an independent existence outside himself, the reified world. Now *reality is primarily the social world*—neither nature nor things, only men—experienced through the reciprocal consciousness of self and other. Society itself becomes a web of consciousness, a form of imagination to be realized as a social construction" (Ibid., p. 488).

33. See, for example, Nathan Glazer and Daniel Moynihan, *Beyond the Melting Pot* (Cambridge, Mass., 1963); Andrew Greeley, *Why Can't They Be Like Us?* (New York, 1971); Richard Scammon and Ben Wattenberg, *The Real Majority* (New York, 1970); Michael Novak, *The Rise of the Unmeltable Ethnics* (New York, 1973).

34. Novak, *Unmeltable Ethnics*, p. 125.

35. Ibid., p. xxviii.

36. The best source for substantiating this claim is, of course, travel. If one turns off network TV, takes to the road, and once on the road turns off the interstate highway, one finds realities so separate as to be ill-described as parts of the same Reality. For a literary hint of the cultural diversity in these United States see Bill Moyers, *Listening to America* (New York, 1971); and Calvin Trillin's series of travel diaries in the *New Yorker*.

37. Chadwick Alger, "'Foreign' Policies of United States Publics," mimeographed, (Columbus, Ohio: Mershon Center at Ohio State University, 1975), and *Your City in the World: The World in Your City* (Columbus, Ohio, 1975).

38. Wolfe, in *Self and World* , ed. Ogilvy, p. 28.

39. See Robert Heilbroner's review in the *New York Review of Books*, 20 March 1975, p. 8.

40. Ronnie Dugger, *Our Invaded Universities* (New York, 1974), p. 101. Dugger's book is a prime example of a regional literature that takes its

own locale (in this case Texas) seriously as an origin of its own way of doing things.

41. The popularity of Michael Korda's *Power* (New York, 1975) derives from more than the limited merits of the book.

42. For the two watersheds see Ivan Illich, *Tools for Conviviality* (New York, 1973), pp. 1–9. For his case on health care see his *Medical Nemesis: The Expropriation of Health* (London, 1975). For evidence of an abiding faith in politics see *Tools for Conviviality*, pp. 12–17, 47, 83, 92, 108–09, 116–17.

43. Giovanni Sartori, "L'Avenir des Parlements," *Bulletin S.E.D.E.I.S.*, 1964, quoted by Jacques Ellul in *The Political Illusion*, trans. Kellen, (orig. pub. 1965; New York, 1972), p. 162.

44. A. Böhm, "Kapituliert der Staat?" *Politische Meinung*, 1962.

45. Ellul, *Political Illusion*, p. 20.

46. Robert Nisbet, "The Decline of Academic Nationalism," *Change* 6 (1974–75): 26.

47. Ibid., p. 29. Nisbet's work is more accessible in his *Twilight of Authority* (New York, 1975).

48. Nimmo, *Political Persuaders*, pp. 198–99.

49. See Murray Edelman, *The Symbolic Uses of Politics* (Urbana, Ill., 1964), and *Politics as Symbolic Action* (Chicago, 1971).

50. Here a single reference, e.g., to Lester W. Bilbrath, *Political Participation* (Chicago, 1965), even ten references, will not serve as well as the direction to observe in any large library card catalogue the dozens of sources listed under the heading "Politics, Participation."

51. Bateson, *Ecology of Mind*, p. 452.

52. Emile Benveniste, *Problems in General Linguistics*, trans. Meeck (Coral Gables, Fla. 1971), p. 20.

53. Jacques Derrida, "Differance," in idem, *Speech and Phenomena*, trans. Allison (orig. pub. 1968; Evanston, Ill. 1973), p. 130.

54. Jean Piaget, *Structuralism* (New York, 1970), p. 36.

55. Bateson, *Ecology of Mind*, p. 401.

56. If p and q be a forty-five degree rotation of axes x and y, then just as p on the x/y coordinates is the line $x = y$ and q, $x = -y$, so x on p/q is $p = -q$ and y, $p = q$.

57. Cf. Jacques Ellul, *The Technological Society*, trans. Wilkinson (New York, 1964); Theodore Roszak, *Where the Wasteland Ends* (Garden City, N.Y., 1972), pp. 3–25, 202–54; Reich, *Greening of America*.

58. Samuel C. Florman, "In Praise of Technology," *Harper's*, November 1975, p. 57.

59. *The progressive humanization of nature was already clear to Engels: "There is devilishly little left of 'nature' as it was in Germany at the time when the Germanic peoples immigrated into it. The earth's surface, climate, vegetation, fauna, and the human beings themselves have infinitely changed, and all this owing to human activity, while the changes of nature in Germany which have occurred in this period of time without human interference are incalculably small" *(The Dialectics of Nature* [Moscow, 1954], p. 306). Similar views are developed by Marx in his *Economic and Philosophic Manuscripts of 1844* and by Marx and Engels together in the *German Ideology;* e.g., "The kind of nature that preceded human history is by no means the nature in which Feuerbach lives, the nature which no longer exists anywhere, except perhaps on a few Australian coral islands of recent origin, and which does not exist for Feuerbach either" (in *Writings of the Young Marx on Philosophy and Society,* ed. Easton and Guddat [Garden City, N.Y., 1967], p. 418).

Though of course sharply critical of Hegel's handling of the concept of nature, Marxists must confess Marx's debt to Hegel for his dialectical development of the concept of nature, if not for his allusions in the *Philosophy of Right* to the State as a second nature. For Marxists wish on the one hand to develop the concept of nature as a dialectical correlative to the historical human species while on the other they wish to criticize bourgeois social scientists for regarding descriptive generalizations about current political-economic conditions as ahistorical laws of nature. For a detailed treatment of a very complex subject see Alfred Schmidt, *The Concept of Nature in Marx,* trans. Fowkes (orig. pub. 1962; London, 1971). For a Marxist critique of Hegel on nature see Heinz Kimmerle, *Das Problem der Abgeschlossenheit des Denkens, Hegel-Studien* Beiheft 8 (Bonn, 1970), esp. pp. 35–38, 135–54, 198–200, 292–95. For a treatment more sympathetic to Hegel see R. G. Collingwood, *The Idea of Nature* (Oxford, 1945), esp. pp. 121–32.

60. Charles Merriam, *Political Power* (Glencoe, Ill., 1950), p. 8.

61. Kant's philosophy represents perhaps the apotheosis of this tendency. Thus the categories are rules of unity for appearances, the transcendental unity of apperception a subjective unity necessary for cognition. Finally in the third *Critique* Kant finds it necessary to posit a ground of unity between the laws of nature and the principles of the realm of freedom and, further, to affirm beneath the plurality of empirical laws "a principle, unknown though it be to us, of the unity of the manifold" (*Kant's Critique of Judgement,* trans. Meredith [Oxford, 1952], p. 18; cf. p. 14). Each of these unities in the Kantian system is deduced; none is observed.

62. Bateson, *Ecology of Mind,* pp. 486–87.

Chapter II

1. Cf. Ludwig Wittgenstein, *Philosophical Investigations*, trans. Anscombe (Oxford, 1963), p. 49, #124: "Philosophy may in no way interfere with the actual use of language; it can in the end only describe it. . . . It leaves everything as it is." For criticisms of the conservative bias among Wittgenstein and his followers see David Pole, *The Later Philosophy of Wittgenstein* (London, 1958); Perry Anderson, "Components of the National Culture," in *Student Power*, ed. Cockburn and Blackburn (Baltimore, 1969), pp. 214–84, esp. pp. 235–38.

2. Cf. Erik Erikson, *Identity, Youth and Crisis* (New York, 1968), pp. 15–43, for a sensitive account of the career of his concept from modest hypothesis to media darling devoid of precise meaning.

3. Examples abound: from the concept of property to the concept of progress, even unto the concept of man. For antidotes to historical amnesia regarding property, see Karl Marx, *The Poverty of Philosophy* (orig. pub. 1847; New York, 1963); regarding progress, J. B. Bury, *The Idea of Progress* (London, 1920); regarding man, Michel Foucault, *Les Mots et les Choses* (Paris, 1966).

4. *See Thomas S. Kuhn, *The Structure of Scientific Revolutions* (Chicago, 1962). The stir caused by Kuhn's book is an index of our insularity. To readers of Hegel and Marx there should be nothing surprising in the idea that the history of science presents us with sharp discontinuities as well as cumulative advances. Where Kuhn talks of "paradigm shifts," Hegel describes "conversions of consciousness" *(Umkehrung des Bewusstseins)*. Where Kuhn depicts a difference between pre- and post-paradigm approaches to a given problem, Marxists use the category of "false consciousness." Both Kuhn and his precursors are concerned to show how a given mind set can systematically avoid or distort evidence that does not conform to its preconceptions about the way things are supposed to be. Kuhn's work could cause a stir only because its use of the history of *natural* sciences could penetrate empiricist ears. To convert an empiricist consciousness whose preconceptions deny the importance of preconceptions, similar though less empirically oriented efforts at the sociology of knowledge in the *social* sciences prove inadequate, e.g., Karl Mannheim's *Ideology and Utopia*.

5. Alexandre Kojève, *Introduction to the Reading of Hegel*, ed. Bloom, tr. Nichols (New York, 1969), p. 6.

6. *Kant distinguished reason *(Vernunft)* from understanding *(Ver-*

stand) roughly as follows: understanding achieves *knowledge* by subsuming particular sense data under given categories; reason *thinks ideas,* but its speculations contribute nothing to knowledge. Hegel appreciated the importance of Kant's distinction between understanding and reason but differed from Kant over the role of reason. Where Kant found reason at fault for extending the finite categories of understanding beyond their proper employment—thereby generating "antinomies" or contradictions—Hegel found fault not with reason but with its tools: the categories of understanding. For Hegel the dialectical employment of reason was not idle speculation or, as Kant called it, "the logic of illusion." Rather the dialectical development of contradictory antinomies stood as proof that the concepts of understanding represent one-sided, finitized abstractions from the infinite play of opposites involved in every truth. By arguing reason's legitimacy, Hegel extends the import of the Kantian distinction between reason and understanding: more than Rousseau or Kant, Hegel sees the potency of reason as constitutive of human possibilities not given to simple understanding. Since the determinants of thought are not limited to the already given, reason can generate human history according to *purposes* rather than simply submitting to the *causes* known by understanding. As Marx put it in his *1844 Manuscripts,* "The great thing in Hegel's Phenomenology . . . is simply that Hegel grasps the self-development of man as a process" (in *Young Marx,* ed. Easton and Guddat, p. 321). In short, reason is man's capacity for purposeful self-creation. Contemporary skepticism's questioning of our ability to act rather than behavioristically react may be, at least in part, the result of a neo-Kantian tendency to view understanding as the only legitimate function of mind. For an excellent introduction to Hegel's critique of Kant, see Ivan Soll, *An Introduction to Hegel's Metaphysics* (Chicago, 1969), esp. chap. 4, "Infinity," pp. 111–50.

7. Jean-Paul Sartre, *Being and Nothingness,* trans. Barnes (New York, 1956), p. 38. For a critique of Sartre's radical freedom see Herbert Marcuse, "Sartre's Existentialism," in Marcuse, *Studies in Critical Philosophy,* trans. de Pres (orig. pub. 1948; Boston, 1972), pp. 157–90.

8. Plato *Phaedo* 96a ff., esp. 98e, 99a; *Crito* passim.

9. Hegel, *Phenomenology of Mind,* Preface.

10. *This remark derives no support from Karl Popper's hysterical attack against Marx and Hegel in *The Open Society and its Enemies* (London, 1945). Rather, the proximity to Popper's conclusions is cause for embarrassment and calls for a careful dissociation. Popper's conflation of Hegel with fascism has been definitively refuted by Marcuse in *Reason and Revolution* (New York, 1941) 'and by Walter Kaufmann in *Hegel* (Garden City, N.Y.,

1965). For more judicious accounts of incipient totalitarianism within the Hegelian-Marxist tradition see Kojève, *Introduction to Hegel*, and Jean-Paul Sartre, *Search for a Method*, trans. Barnes (New York, 1963).

11. Cf. Jacques Lacan, *The Language of the Self*, ed. and trans. Wilden (Baltimore, 1968), p. 26. Lacan asks us to understand "the celebrated maxim in which La Rochefoucauld tells us that *'il y a gens qui n'auraient jamais été amoureux, s'ils n'avaient jamais entendu parler l'amour,'* not in the Romantic sense of an entirely imaginary 'bringing to realization' of love which would make of this remark a bitter objection on his part, but as an authentic recognition of what love owes to the symbol and of what the Word entails of love."

12. *If the distinction between different parts of our language be denied, then one can fall back on stronger claims that *all* languages are presentational rather than representational. Here one would appeal to the studies of Benjamin Lee Whorf, *Language, Thought, and Reality*, ed. Caroll (New York, 1956); and to work in the philosophy of science that denies a clear distinction between a revisable language of theory and a fixed, universal language of observation. See the writings of Norwood Russell Hanson and P. K. Feyerabend. While the work of these neoidealists in the philosophy of science may be ultimately persuasive, one needs only a weaker claim to make the point that the language of human intentions is presentational rather than representational. Since there are ample critics of even this more modest claim, it seems strategically wiser to grant the possibility of a universal grammar for physical descriptions in the natural sciences while denying the possibility of a universal grammar of intentions in the social sciences.

A fuller account of the distinction between presentational and representational parts of our language could follow from the distinction between reason and understanding discussed in n. 6 above. Lacking that fuller account, the most we can maintain at present is a quasi-Kierkegaardian protest against promises by proponents of the System of a universal grammar. They insist that the discovery of the universal grammar is "just around the corner" because they conflate reason and understanding. The freedom of reason, its capacity to proliferate histories, not History, can frustrate every positivistic attempt to tie the final knot in the macramé of languages. The defense of freedom against the System of a universal grammar must be *quasi*-Kierkegaardian in the sense that the locus of freedom is not the solitary individual but a community, a Some sufficient to support a language among languages.

Of course there remains a possibility that we could become convinced by the positivists. In that case the brash experiment called man, which as Foucault argues has only just begun, would end with the submission of many subjects to the single vision of scientific objectivity. A self-fulfilling methodology would reduce freedom to the status of an aberration. These are the stakes ultimately at issue in the ongoing debate in linguistics. The outcome is hardly to be trusted to dispassionate objectivity—a begging of the question. Nor can the passionate Dane be depended upon since his subjectivity is so solipsistic.

13. See for example, R. W. Burnham and J. R. Clark, "A Test of Hue Memory," *Journal of Applied Psychology* 39 (1955): 164–72; Eric H. Lenneberg, "Color Naming, Color Recognition, Color Discrimination: A Re-Appraisal," *Perceptual and Motor Skills* 12 (1961): 375–82; and Herbert Landar, *Language and Culture* (New York, 1966), pp. 225–31.

14. Cf. Wittgenstein, *Philosophical Investigations,* *256 ff.*

15. Ibid., and, in addition, Plato *Theaetetus.*

16. Ludwig Binswanger's attempt to combat the reductionistic tendency in Freud provides an example of antireductionism risking defeat by accepting the language of levels: "Spirit (in its widest sense, by which is not meant the strictly religious, ethical and aesthetic) and instinct are limiting concepts in the sense that 'the instincts' remain as residue when man is taken as stripped of spirit and spirit remains when man is totally devitalized. But human existence never goes forth exclusively as spirit or instinct, it is always both. Only theoretically and abstractly can instinct and spirit be sundered. . . . If Nietzsche and psychoanalysis have shown that instinctuality, especially in the form of sexuality, extends its reach up to the highest pinnacles of human spirituality, then we have attempted to show the degree to which spirituality extends its reach down to the deepest valleys of 'vitality'" (Ludwig Binswanger, "Über Ideenflucht," *Schweizer Archiv für Neurologie und Psychiatrie* 30 [1932–33]: 75–76, cited by Joseph Needleman, *Being-in-the-World* [New York, 1963], p. 3).

17. See D. S. Schwayder, *The Stratification of Behavior* (New York, 1965). Some support can be derived from the work of Wilfrid Sellars, who explicitly objects to the language of levels as well as to the notion that language describes The World. Sellars sees that 'The World' is a piece within the language game, that one can no more support the claim that a language describes The World (referring to an extralinguistic totality) than Kant could claim that empirical knowledge of phenomena represents noumena. Yet even Sellars sees correspondence rules as directions for eventual reduction ("The Language of Theories," chap. 4 in *Science, Perception and Reality* [New York, 1963], p. 126) and regards only the language of science as the "measure of all things, of what is, that it is, and of what is not, that it is not." (Ibid., p. 173). For Sellars's doubts about the use of 'the World', see his

"Realism and the New Way of Words," in *Readings in Philosophical Analysis*, ed. Feigl and Sellars (New York, 1949). For an elaboration of Sellars's semantics, particularly his critique of Tarski-Carnap ideal language semantics and its reliance on reference to a univocal "extra-linguistic reality" as objective referrent of a universal grammar, see his *Science and Metaphysics* (New York, 1968).

18. *This skeptical point differentiates each community of interpreters from C. S. Peirce's "ultimate community of inquirers" whose cumulative efforts purportedly generate a continuous asymptotic approach to The Truth. Peirce's logic of inquiry accords with the cumulative character observed within the history of particular sciences and thus finds favor with contemporary philosophers of science who accept the so-called deductive model of scientific progress in which older theories are deducible from more comprehensive, newer theories. The *continuity* of deductive regress accounting for inductive progress contrasts sharply with the *discontinuity* of revolutionary, dialectical development. Peirce's optimism regarding the ultimate findings of the community of inquirers cannot be sustained in the face of a history of science that goes beyond the cumulative progress observed *within* particular sciences. When Kuhn and Feyerabend direct us to the conversions and revolutions that mark discontinuous leaps from one paradigm to another, we see a history of science calling for communities of interpreters rather than a single Peircean community of inquirers. Cf. Kuhn, *op. cit. Scientific Revolutions;* P. K. Feyerabend, "Explanation, Reduction and Empiricism," in *Minnesota Studies in the Philosophy of Science III*, ed. Feigl and Maxwell (Minneapolis, 1962), pp. 28–97. On the need for a proliferation of communities of inquirers see Feyerabend, *How to be a Good Empiricist*, vol. 2 of the *Delaware Seminar in Philosophy of Science* (New York, 1963). See also the papers by J. J. C. Smart, Wilfrid Sellars, Hilary Putnam, and Feyerabend in the *Boston Studies in the Philosophy of Science*, ed. Cohen and Wartofsky (New York, 1965), 2:157–262.

19. Hegel, *Philosophy of Right*, trans. Knox (Oxford, 1952), Preface. Hegel's slogan is as dangerous as it is important. The effort to ground rationality in the actual has the advantage of avoiding speculative, utopian excess. As Nietzsche would put it, one betrays *this world* when one condemns it by applying otherworldly standards. Nevertheless, faithfulness to this world risks a reactionary naturalism, the smug certainty that things already *are* as they *ought* to be. Hegel's maxim need not condone all that is currently actual because among the things that *are* one cannot help seeing tensions and contradictions prompting reason's inventions of what *might be*. Temporality, too, is actual, therefore rational. This world contains contradictions suggesting a better if not an other world.

Chapter III

1. Herodotus *The History* 7. 111.
2. Plato *Phaedrus* 265a.
3. Plato *Republic* 7. 517a; cf. 6. 509 ff. for the divided line and the rest of the cave myth. For the blinding power of the sun and the need to "study its reflection in water or some other medium," See *Phaedo* 99d.
4. Cf. R. D. Laing, *The Divided Self* (Tavistock, 1959), and esp. *Politics of Experience*. Also Michel Foucault, *Madness and Civilization*, trans. Howard (New York, 1965).
5. Erwin Rohde, *Psyche*, trans. 2 vols. Hillis, (orig. pub. 1893; New York, 1966), 2:257–59.
6. Ibid., 1: xiv.
7. John C. Lilly, *Programming and Metaprogramming in the Human Biocomputer* (New York, 1972), Preface to the Second Edition, p. x.
8. James Hillman, "Psychology: Monotheistic or Polytheistic," *Spring*, 1971, pp. 197 ff.
9. Theologians have recently rediscovered the importance of stories as a medium for the messages they wish to convey. See, for example, Sam Keen, *To a Dancing God* (New York, 1970), esp. pp. 70–74, 82 ff.
10. Bruno Snell, *The Discovery of the Mind*, trans. Rosemeyer (New York, 1960), p. 7.
11. Ibid., p. 6.
12. J. Needham, *Chemical Embryology*, 2d ed. (Cambridge, 1959), quoted by James Hillman in *The Myth of Analysis* (Evanston, Ill., 1972), p. 221.
13. Hillman, *Myth of Analysis*, pp. 273–74.
14. Ibid., pp. 223–24.
15. *The Birth of Tragedy*, sec. 1, in Friedrich Nietzsche, *Werke in drei Bänden*, ed. Karl Schlechta (Munich, 1966), 1:24 (hereafter cited as Schlechta).
16. Robert E. Ornstein, *The Psychology of Consciousness* (San Francisco, 1972), p. 67.
17. Warren S. McCulloch, *Embodiments of Mind* (Cambridge, Mass., 1965), p. 43.
18. Ibid.
19. Robert Paul Wolff, *In Defense of Anarchism* (New York, 1970), p. 61. For a further discussion of the paradox and the beginnings of a bibliography of the literature pertaining to it—Wolff is hardly the first to have dealt with the issue since Arrow's book pressed its importance—see Bell, *Post-Industrial Society*, pp. 305 ff.

20. Wolff cut his philosophical teeth with a commentary on Kant's first critique, *Kant's Theory of Mental Activity* (Cambridge, Mass., 1963). His Kantianism shows up in *The Poverty of Liberalism*, (Boston, 1968) in his predilection for approaching the problems with a 'deduction'. His disappointment shows up in the poignant preface to *In Defense of Anarchism* where he admits that after having boldly announced at the beginning of his political philosophy course at Columbia that he was going to formulate and solve the major problems of political philosophy, "midway through the semester, I was forced to go before my class, crestfallen and very embarrassed, to announce that I had failed to discover the grand solution" (p. vii).

21. *The very last page of McCulloch's book, which concludes a paper given in 1964, bears quoting in this regard: "The details of its neurons and their specific connections need not concern us here. In general, you may think of it as a computer to any part of which come signals from many parts of the body and from other parts of the brain and spinal cord. It is only one cell deep on the path from input to output, but it can set the filters on all of its inputs and can control the behavior of the programmed activity, the half-centers, and the reflexes. It gets a substitute for depth by its intrinsic fore-and-aft connections. Its business, given its knowledge of the state of the whole organism and of the world impingent upon it, is to decide whether the given fact is a case under one or another rule. It must decide for the whole organism whether the rule is one requiring fighting, fleeing, eating, sleeping, etc. It must do it with millisecond component action and conduction velocities of usually less than 100 meters per second, and do it in real time, say, in a third of a second. That it has worked so well throughout evolution, without itself evolving, points to its structure as the natural solution of the organization of appropriate behavior. We know much experimentally of the behavior of the components, but still have no theory worthy of the name to explain its circuit action" (*Embodiments of Mind*, p. 397).

22. This is just the familiar doctrine known as phenomenalism. Its original proponents are the British empiricists, Locke, Berkeley and Hume. It persists into the twentieth century in the form of "sense data" theory, trenchantly criticized by Wilfrid Sellars, "Empiricism and the Philosophy of Mind," chap. 5 in *Science, Perception and Reality*.

23. *The appeal to "clarity and distinctness" is a hallmark of Descartes's method of verifying truth. The appeal to certainty he shares with the romantics, who are less worried about clarity and distinctness but just as eager to found truth through introspection. For a critique of Cartesian introspectionism see Charles Sanders Peirce, "Questions Concerning Certain Faculties Claimed for Man," in *Values in a Universe of Chance, Selected*

Writings of Charles S. Peirce, ed. P. Wiener (Garden City, N.Y., 1958), pp 15-38. Whether derived from Cartesian clarity and distinctness or romantic epiphany, *certainty* as a criterion of truth is criticized time and again by Hegel, for whom truth emerges only from successive negations of one-sided certainties. So develops the "highway of despair" whose road map is *The Phenomenology of Mind*. Wittgenstein's critique of private evidence is hardly the first attack on introspective certainty as some Wittgensteinians seem to believe; rather he gives a final tap to an already reeling defense of private certainty.

24. Laing, *Politics of Experience*, p. 18.

25. Ibid., p. 28.

26. *Laing's debt to Sartre is most obvious in *Reason and Violence* (Tavistock, 1964), in which, together with David Cooper, he gives an exposition of Sartre's *Critique de la raison dialectique;* see pp. 93–176. More important to his interpretation of private experience, however, is his internalization of Sartrian thinking that goes back to *Being and Nothingness*, pt. 2, chap. 3, pp. 361 ff., esp. p. 363. For Hegel's description of the dialectic of master and slave see *Phenomenology of Mind*, pp. 229–40.

27. Walter Benjamin, *Illuminations*, ed. Arendt, trans. Zohn (New York, 1969), p. 86.

28. Ibid., p. 87.

29. Ibid.

30. In *The Review of Metaphysics* 25 (1971), 3–51. The several quotations below are all from pp. 26–32, 38–50.

31. Cf. John R. Searle, *Speech Acts* (London, 1969).

32. Earlier in the essay Taylor argues the need for a method of identifying the object of interpretation by some method other than the interpretation itself. The availability of another method of identification does not presuppose such an "objective" method that the interpretation itself would be rendered superfluous, simply some observational arraignment as it were, a "taking" of what is not necessarily "given" in order to discern more closely what it is "alleged" to be.

Chapter IV

1. *Iliad* 16. 459–60.

2. It is arguable, and has been so argued by Adam Parry of the

classics department at Yale, that the text of the *Iliad* indicates the Trojans preferred less centralized, more pluralistic modes of organization than the Greeks.

3. Sigmund Freud, *New Introductory Lectures on Psychoanalysis*, trans. Strachey (New York, 1964), p. 64.

4. Cf. the *Magna Moralia* 1208b30, quoted by E. R. Dodds, *The Greeks and the Irrational* (Berkeley and Los Angeles, 1964), p. 35.

5. Dodds, *Greeks and the Irrational*, p. 32.

6. Nietzsche, *Joyful Wisdom*, bk. 3, #143, Schlechta 2:135; see also *Birth of Tragedy*, sec. 3 Schlechta 1:30, where Nietzsche remarks, "The Gods justified human life by living it themselves—the only satisfactory theodicy."

7. Richard Sennett, *The Uses of Disorder; Personal Identity and City Life* (New York, 1970), chap. 1.

8. Philip Slater, *The Pursuit of Loneliness* (Boston, 1970), p. 9, n.

9. For the arbitrariness of the designation "weed," see Bateson, *Ecology of Mind*, p. 431.

10. Cf. Nathan Rotenstreich, "On Shame," *The Review of Metaphysics* 19 (1965): 55–86, esp. pp. 60 ff. Also H. M. Lynd, *On Shame and the Search for Identity* (New York, 1961); Gerhart Piers and Milton Singer, *Shame and Guilt* (orig. pub. 1953; New York, 1971); David P. Ausubel, "Relationships Between Shame and Guilt in the Socializing Process," *The Psychological Review* 62 (1955): 378–90.

11. As is usual with quick references to Heidegger, the issue is complex. He more than many others sees the nonsubstantiality of self. Yet his preoccupation with guilt *(Schuld)*, his claim that it is inescapable, may say more about moderns than about man in general. Granted that the realization of any particular possibility precludes the realization of others and thus serves as a reminder of human finitude (of what one is not and cannot be), why should this experience be one of such angst as that described by Kierkegaard and Heidegger? The negativity of the experience of finitude may be a mirror image of the positivity of monotheism. Only after the infinite God had been invented could finite man look so bad by comparison.

12. Slater, *Pursuit of Loneliness*, p. 9.

13. Ibid.

14. See Robert Jay Lifton, "Protean Man," in the *Futeribles* series, (Paris, January 1967); *Partisan Review*, Winter 1968, pp. 13–27; *Yale Alumni Review*, 1968; in idem, *History and Human Survival* (New York, 1971), pp. 316–31; slightly revised in idem, *Boundaries* (New York, 1970). Since the essay is both short and so variously printed (in several anthologies

as well as the above), page references seem both unnecessary and virtually useless until the "standard edition" is available. In introducing the essay in *History and Human Survival* Lifton comments: "Protean man continues to inhabit every facet of my work."

15. Cf. Philip Slater, *Earthwalk* (Garden City, N.Y., 1974), for an attack on Toffler's defense of transiency.

16. Cf. Hegel, *Phenomenology of Mind*, p. 164: "To supersede *(aufheben)* is at once to negate and to preserve."

17. According to *Robert's Rules of Order* a vote to call the question is a vote to end debate and come immediately to a vote on the issue at hand. If the vote to call the question does not pass, then debate may continue; if it does pass, then debate ceases and a second vote follows immediately, deciding the outcome of the issue at hand.

18. On the implicit universality of truth see above. pp. 76–77.

19. Cf. Kant, *Groundwork of the Metaphysics of Morals*, Prussian Academy Edition, pp. 429–30, 419, 422. The *reductio ad absurdum* of Kant's rationalistic rigidity with respect to promises and truths comes in his essay "On a Supposed Right to Tell Lies from Benevolent Motives" where he claims one could not deceive a murderer seeking one's own friend in one's own house.

20. And recall that Kant's precisely timed afternoon walks served as a clock for the good citizens of Königsberg.

21. See Kierkegaard's *Philosophical Fragments*, trans. Swenson and Hong (Princeton, 1962), esp. pp. 24–25, 64–65, and the "Interlude."

22. P. D. Ouspensky, *In Search of the Miraculous* (New York, 1949), p. 60.

23. Cf. sources in n. 19 above. The primacy of promising is paradigmatic of Kant's ahistorical ethics.

24. Nietzsche, *Genealogy of Morals*, II, 2, Schlechta 2:801.

25. Nietzsche, *The Will To Power* #490, Schlecta 3: 473.

26. Ibid.

27. Ibid.

28. *Genealogy of Morals*, II, 2, Schlechta 2: 801.

29. Ibid., II, 1, Schlechta 2:800.

30. Aristotle *Nicomachean Ethics* 1. 9–10. 1100c1–b10.

31. See Jakob Johann von Uexküll, "A Stroll Through the Worlds of Animals and Men," in *Instinctive Behavior*, ed. Schiller (New York, 1957); John N. Bleibtreu, *The Parable of the Beast* (New York, 1968), pp. 3 ff.

32. Robert Ornstein, *On the Experience of Time* (Baltimore, 1970), p. 41.

33. For an incisive treatment of the notion that Nows may be nested and that the monolinear line of time makes less sense than a multilinear model see Nathaniel Lawrence, "Time Represented as Space," in *Basic Issues in the Philosophy of Time,* ed. Freeman and Sellars, (LaSalle, Ill., 1971), pp. 123–32.

Chapter V

1. Hegel, *Phenomenology of Mind*, p. 666.
2. G. W. F. Hegel, *Lectures on the Philosophy of Fine Art*, trans. Osmaston, 4 vols., (London, 1920), 1:78–79.
3. See James Hillman, *Re-Visioning Psychology* (New York, 1975), chap. 2, for a superb defense of this thesis.
4. See the concluding sentence of Descartes's first *Meditation*.
5. Sören Kierkegaard, *Either/Or*, trans. Swenson and Swenson, 2 vols. (New York, 1959), "Diapsalmata," 1:20–21.
6. See the section *Zarathustra* III, "On Involuntary Bliss." See also "Noon" in part IV and Nietzsche's description of his experience of inspiration in the section on Zarathustra in *Ecce Homo*, both of which will be discussed below. Then there was the experience of August 1881 near Sils Maria, the revelation of eternal recurrence.
7. Jaye Miller, "Reflections on Decadence," *Soundings* 57 (1974): 384.
8. Theador Adorno, *Philosophie der Neuen Musik* (Frankfurt, 1949). For a fascinating, if idiosyncratic, discussion of Adorno on Schoenberg see Jean-Francois Lyotard, "Adorno as the Devil," *Telos* 19 (1974): 127–37; the essay is translated by Robert Hurley from Lyotard's book of essays, *Des Dispositifs Pulsionnels* (Paris, 1973).
9. Miller, "Reflections on Decadence," p. 373.
10. Ibid.
11. Cf. *Ecce Homo* on *Zarathustra*, sec. 4, where Nietzsche refers to the "third and last" part after "finding" which he was "finished" *(fertig)* (Schlechta 2:1133).
12. Ibid., sec. 1, Schlecta 2:1129: *"es überfiel mich."* See also sec. 3, Schlecta 2:1131–32, for Nietzsche's remarkable description of his experience of inspiration: "One hears, one does not seek; one accepts, one

does not ask who gives; like lightning a thought flashes out without any hesitation as to its form, with necessity—I've never had a choice," and so on in more physiological detail than bears repeating despite its importance as testimony to the genuineness of Nietzsche's revelations.

13. See *Will to Power* #1038 where Nietzsche records how "the religious, that is to say god-forming, instinct occasionally becomes active at impossible times—how differently, how variously the divine has revealed itself to me each time!" There he recalls Zarathustra's confession, "I would believe only in a God who could dance," but condemns him nonetheless: "Zarathustra himself, to be sure, is merely an old atheist; he believes neither in old nor in new gods. Zarathustra says he *would;* but Zarathustra *will* not—Do not misunderstand him."

14. Nietzsche, *Beyond Good and Evil* #40; Schlechta 2:603.

15. For nihilism is not only a sign of exhaustion but also a sign in some instances of strength. Cf. *Will to Power* #22: "Nihilism: It is *ambiguous:* A. Nihilism as a sign of increased power of the spirit: as *active* nihilism. B. Nihilism as decline and recession of the power of the spirit: as *passive* nihilism." The ambiguity of nihilism parallels Nietzsche's ambivalence toward decadence and his distinction between active and passive, of which more below.

16. *Ecce Homo* on *Zarathustra*, sec. 6; Schlechta 2:1136.

17. *Zarathustra* I, "On Reading and Writing," Schlechta 2:305.

18. Foucault, *Les Mots et les choses* chap. 1.

19. See Nietzsche's letter to Carl von Gersdorff, 12 February 1885: "Today I want to tell you, not without hesitation, something that carries with it a request. There is a fourth (last) part for *Zarathustra,* a kind of sublime finale for which publication is absolutely out of the question (the word 'publication' and 'public' strike me in relation to my entire Zarathustra somewhat the same way as 'cat house' and 'public cunt'—Pardon!). But this part should and must be printed now: in twenty copies for distribution among me and my friends, and with the utmost discretion" (Schlechta 3:1228–29). For a typical instance of commentators' downgrading and/or neglect of *Zarathustra* IV see Hollingdale's introduction to his edition of *Zarathustra.*

20. *Ecce Homo* on *Zarathustra*, sec. 5, Schlechta 2:1133–34; for the following quotation, see sec. 6, Schlechta 2:1135.

21. *"Erbärmliches Behagen,"* an often repeated phrase, e.g., *Zarathustra,* Prologue, 3, Schlechta 2:280–81; "On the Pale Criminal," Schlechta 2: 305; "On Child and Marriage," Schlechta 2:332.

22. Hegel, *Phenomenology of Mind,* p. 510.

23. *Will to Power* #46, Schlechta 3:696, emphasis added. In his superior edition of this work Kaufmann correctly leaves this aphorism in the context of Nietzsche's most concentrated remarks on decadence.

24. This and all other unreferenced passages from the preceding paragraph from *Beyond Good and Evil* #19, Schlechta 2:581–83, Nietzsche's definitive statement on volition. For further support see *Will to Power* ##66–68 et passim.

25. *Beyond Good and Evil* #19, Schlechta 2:583.

26. *Jürgen Habermas, "Toward a Theory of Communicative Competence," in *Recent Sociology no. 2*, ed. Dreitzel (New York, 1970), pp. 114–50. Habermas's argument is only part, if a large and influential part, of a movement in contemporary German thought toward a "communicative ethics." Among the most significant contributions to this movement are Karl-Otto Apel's works, collected in his *Transformation der Philosophie*: vol. 1, *Sprachanalytik, Semiotik, Hermeneutik*; vol. 2, *Das Apriori der Kommunikationsgemeinschaft* (Frankfurt, 1973). Communicative ethics marks a distinct advance over earlier attempts at ethics in several important respects: (1) It inherits from Marx a will to ascend from earth rather than descend from heaven with ahistorical transcendent ideals. (2) It is therefore historically and immanently based. (3) At the same time, it is not naturalistic—that is, whatever *is* is not necessarily what ought to be. (4) Communicative ethics is not *so* immanent as to endorse as ethical any and all injunctions to "act as I do," as is the tendency in, for example, Charles Stevenson, *Ethics and Language* (New Haven, 1944), and *Facts and Values* (New Haven, 1963). The latter title alone suggests the source of difficulty: a distinction between emotive and descriptive components of language that reflects the vestiges of an overly sharp positivistic distinction between facts and values. (5) Communicative ethics forswears hard facts in its admission of "quasi-transcendental" conditions for experience that are themselves both interest laden and historical (hence the 'quasi-'), e.g., economic history (Marx), technological development of symbolic interaction (Habermas), and "the *a priori* of bodily engagement" (Apel).

All this said and done, and all due respect paid to the staggering scholarly competence of its teutonic practitioners, the point remains to be made that communicative ethics cannot have it both ways: Kantian a priorism cannot be rendered incarnate in history without acknowledging an empirical plurality of conditions that splinters the Kantian claim to universality for the conditions of understanding both objects and one another. Communicative ethics takes back with the right hand what it gives with the left when it grants the importance of historical conditions separating Some from

Some and then fixes on an a priori supposedly necessary for All. If communicative ethics is a series of extremely sophisticated footnotes to Kant (as all philosophy is, according to Whitehead, a series of footnotes to Plato), then the social philosophy of Some is a manifestly less sophisticated series of footnotes to Hegel and Nietzsche, and depends for its fuller sophistication on a fuller working out of how the nineteenth-century critique of Kant would perform as an operator on communicative ethics to render a Hegelian-Nietzschean transform of this twentieth-century Kantianism.

27. To Philip Slater's lasting credit he makes this simple point many times in *Earthwalk*. It is one of the motifs of his work and distinguishes him from figures like Herbert Marcuse. Referring to Marcuse's most utopian *Essay on Liberation*, Slater writes: "As humanists so often do, Marcuse tries to devise a conceptual system in which all the things one likes fall into one category and all those things one dislikes into another. But 'good' and 'bad' are always orthogonal to important distinctions" (*Pursuit of Loneliness*, p. 154, n. 1).

28. *Will to Power* #585 (A), Schlechta 3: 548–49. Also the following two quotations.

29. *Wittgenstein comes to mind here, partly for his using, though in a context quite different from the question of truth, the image of stripping the leaves of an artichoke to find the real artichoke (see *Philosophical Investigations*, #164); partly for his *On Certainty* which in many ways bears comparison with Nietzsche's attack on the will to truth. Unfortunately the over-professionalized rules of tidy Anglo-American philosophizing are liable to lead to an effort at becoming certain about *On Certainty* rather than to an appreciation for its pluralistic implications. So we will be treated to such dull conclusions as: in a true statement, "It is said, '*This* is how things are.' *If* this *is* how things are, that is, if this is a fact, then what is said is true; *if* this *is not* how things are, that is, if it is not a fact, then what is said is false" (Alan R. White, *Truth* [Garden City, N.Y., 1970], pp. 128–29). Which all goes to show that never once in his entire book on truth has White really questioned, as Wittgenstein surely did, the monistic implications of the phrase 'how things are'. The guiding assumption throughout has it that while we may not be in possession of all the facts, while even the concept of a *fact* may remain fuzzy around the edges, still there is only *one* way things are. The problem of truth is then one of examining the complex relation between our language and The World of the One Way. Cf. D. W. Hamlyn, *The Theory of Knowledge* (Garden City, N.Y., 1970), pp. 136–42, for another example of the attempt to salvage correspondence to The One World as the essence of truth, despite an acknowledgment of the fuzziness of facts.

30. Again, *Will to Power* #585 (A).

31. True, Nietzsche states, "There is neither 'spirit', nor reason, nor thought, nor consciousness, nor soul, nor will, nor truth: all fictions that are of no use" (*Will to Power* #480; Schlechta 3: 751). But here the grouping together with will is useful precisely in showing the similarity of his arguments against each: that in both cases we have simplified complex phenomena by imputing a unity not to be found upon closer examination. See *Will to Power* ##12, 448–64, 489, 523, 529–44 for further corroboration.

32. Cf. *Genealogy of Morals*, I, 13, Schlechta 2:789–90: "A quantum of force is the same as a quantum of urge, will, or activity itself and only the seduction of language (and the fundamental errors of reason petrified in language), which misrepresent all activity as conditioned by an agent, a single subject, can make it appear otherwise. Just as popular belief separates the lightning from its flash and takes the latter as the activity of a subject called the lightning so popular morality distinguishes strength from its manifestations, as if behind those manifestations there were an indifferent substratum free to manifest its strength or not. But there is no such substrate; there is no 'being' behind the doing, acting, becoming; the 'doer' is simply added to the doing in thought—the doing is everything."

33. William James, *The Principles of Psychology* (New York, 1891), rpt. in Great Books of the Western World, vol. 53 (Chicago, 1952), pp. 638 f.

34. An affinity which, if not already obvious, has been explored by, among others, John Wild, *Existence and the World of Freedom*, (Englewood Cliffs, N.J., 1963), esp. pp. 28–34; and Herbert Spiegelberg, *The Phenomenological Movement*, 2 vols. (The Hague, 1960) 1:66–69, 111–17.

35. James, *Principles of Psychology*, pp. 641–42.

36. John Langshaw Austin, *Sense and Sensibilia* (New York, 1964), chap. 7.

37. *Birth of Tragedy*, secs. 12–15. Also Hegel, *Phenomenology of Mind*, Preface, p. 94, where in explicit comparison to the Greek achievement of learning to universalize he comments: "Nowadays the task before us consists not so much in getting the individual clear of the stage of sensuous immediacy, and making him a substance that thinks and is grasped in terms of thought, but rather the very opposite: it consists in actualizing the universal, and giving it spiritual vitality, by the process of breaking down and superseding fixed and determinate thoughts."

38. For an exposition of the legacy of the Platonic emphasis on unity in the history of Western thought see Anton C. Pegis, "The Dilemma of Be-

ing and Unity," in *Essays in Thomism*, ed. Brennan (New York, 1942), pp. 149–83.

39. James, *Principles of Psychology*, p. 888, n.

40. Hillman, "Psychology: Monotheistic or Polytheistic?" pp. 193–208. For Jung's monotheism see chiefly *Aion, Researches into the Phenomenology of the Self*; vol. 9, pt. 2 of the *Collected Works* (Princeton, 1959); for his pluralistic instincts see his development of the theory of archetypes, passim, as well as the typology of *Psychological Types*, vol. 6 of the *Collected Works*.

41. On the early growth of mental institutions as repositories for the culturally deviant see Foucault, *Madness and Civilization*. On more recent uses of the categories of mental illness for purposes of condemnation and confinement see Thomas Szasz, *Law, Liberty, and Psychiatry* (New York, 1963), and *The Manufacture of Madness: A Comparative Study on the Inquisition and the Mental Health Movement* (New York, 1970). For an examination of the latest institutional apologetics for enforced therapy, that is, the legal implications of the mental health movement, see Nicholas N. Kittrie, *The Right to be Different* (Baltimore and London, 1971).

42. *Peirce's claim, "There is, then, to every question a true answer, a final conclusion, to which the opinion of every man is constantly gravitating," must not be confused with a positivist dependence on a univocal Reality (C. S. Peirce, *Collected Papers*, ed. Hartshorne and Weiss, 8 vols. [Cambridge, Mass., 1931–35, 1958], 8:12). Peirce's logic of inquiry and pragmatic theory of truth are importantly different from the positivism of Compte. The destination of truth claims is not a Reality independent of human experience but a final consensus that is very much a part of human experience. Thus is the concept of Reality relocated from the impossible status of the Kantian thing-in-itself to the projected consensus among a community of inquirers: "To assert that there are external things which can be known only as exerting a power on our sense, is nothing different from asserting that there is a general drift in the history of human thought which will lead it to one general agreement, one catholic consent" (Ibid.).

What Habermas calls Peirce's "hidden objectivism" is already evident in his postulation of ultimate catholic consensus, for objectivity in Kantian transcendental idealism is ultimately equivalent to universal intersubjectivity: to be an *object* is to conform to the conditions of cognition shared by *all* rational beings. Because Habermas is in fundamental agreement with both Kant and Peirce on this important point he cannot locate Peirce's objectivism where it belongs—in the relocation of univocal reality in the catholic

consensus of the community of inquirers—but must develop his own scholastic commentary to find it elaborately hidden in what he calls Peirce's scholastic realism of concepts. (See Jürgen Habermas, *Knowledge and Human
Interests*, trans. Shapiro [Boston, 1971], chaps. 5–6.)

Habermas's own, not so hidden, objectivism becomes evident when
he turns to Nietzsche, whose perspectivism is precisely the denial of the
need for ultimate consensus to make sense of truth. (Ibid., chap. 12; see also
his introduction to the Suhrkamp volume of Nietzsche's writings representing
his epistemology.) Habermas's rejection of Nietzsche, though less well
grounded than Marx's rejection of Stirner, is similarly fascinating as an example of a first-rate thinker recoiling before the implications of his own
thought. Just as Marx saw—as Lobkowicz puts it in his excellent study—
"what, historically speaking, Stirner was first of all, namely, the man who
had carried the profanization of all Hegelian ideas further than any other
Left Hegelian" and therefore had to address himself at length to Stirner's position; just as the justice of much of Marx's criticism nonetheless fails to de-
tract from what Lobkowicz finds "the interesting point . . . that it avoids
touching upon the real issue, which obviously also was the reason why Marx
had at all undertaken the effort of writing hundreds of pages against this nihilistic individualism, namely, that Stirner had called in question the very
motives of Marx's own position" (Nikolaus Lobkowicz, *Theory and Practice*
[Notre Dame and London, 1967], pp. 395 ff.); just as Marx had thus both
seen and not seen the dangerousness of Stirner to his own position, so similarly, but with the difference that his criticisms are less well justified than
Marx's against Stirner, the "interesting point" about Habermas's argument
with Nietzsche lies in the extent to which Nietzsche (along with Hegel whom
Habermas also attacks and for similar reasons) calls into question the very
motive of Habermas's own position, namely, his neo-neo-Kantian epistemology of the social world with its universalist assumptions. Habermas
must insist on making Nietzsche look absurd in ways that he is not. E.g.,
"The basis of knowledge in interest effects the possibility of knowledge as
such." So far Habermas and Nietzsche are in perfect agreement—hence Habermas's anxiety and the need to continue as follows: "Since the gratification
of *all* needs is congruent with the interest in self-preservation, *any illusion at
random can put forth the same claim to validity*, as long as some need interprets the world through it" (Habermas, *Knowledge and Human Interest*, p.
297, emphasis added). Of course any illusion based on any need *can* put
forth such a claim, but if the knowledge-constitutive role of interest shared
by Nietzsche and Habermas be thought through to its end (as it has been by
Nietzsche but not by Habermas), it will be seen that the interests of each per-

spective will set up orders of rank according to which some needs are demoted and others exalted so that the "illusions" put forth by various needs will by no means maintain "the same claim to validity." Nietzsche cannot be reduced to the negative nihilism of the willy-nilly so easily. Since each of us always maintains some perspective or other, we always have an order of rank (call it Care—*Sorge*—if you like the Heideggerean version) that keeps us from granting the same claim to validity to any and all "illusions." Habermas's leveling of all illusions to equal validity manifests *his* illusion, namely that one can attain the kind of stance outside all perspectives from which such a leveling statement could be made. Such a *stance*, rather than being a *perspective*, would be the stance of objectivity free of perspective. The illusion that he can attain such a stance, the illusion manifest in his anxious critique of Nietzsche, is precisely Habermas's hidden objectivism.

43. See the first speeches of "The Honey Sacrifice" opening *Zarathustra* IV.

44. Erving Goffman, *Frame Analysis* (New York, 1974), p. 521. On p. 519 Goffman takes off from Wittgenstein's *Philosophical Investigations*, pt. 1, sec. 403–10 (Goffman's note mistakenly directs the reader to "pt. 2, sec. 403–10"): "Although certainly the pronoun, 'I,' refers to the speaker, and although certainly the speaker is a specific biographical entity, that does not mean that the whole of this entity in all of its facets is to be included on each occasion of its being cited. For he who is a speaker might be considered a whole set of somewhat different things, bound together in part because of our cultural beliefs regarding identity. Thus, the referent of 'I' in the statements: 'I feel a chill,' 'I will take responsibility,' and 'I was born on a Tuesday' shifts, although in no easily describable way." Goffman has probed far enough into the difficulties of describing this shifting (e.g., in his "A Simultaneous Multiplicity of Selves," in idem, *Encounters: Two Studies in the Sociology of Interaction* [Indianapolis, 1961], pp. 132–43) to find it important to record in *Frame Analysis* (p. 521, n.): "The semantic and syntactic issues of multiple selfing illustrated here have been very little explored."

45. William Blake, Letter to Butts, 22 November, 1802:
Now I a fourfold vision see,
And a fourfold vision is given to me;
'Tis fourfold in my supreme delight
And threefold in soft Beulah's night
And twofold Always. May God us keep
From Single vision and Newton's sleep!
For comments on the final couplet see Norman O. Brown, *Love's Body* (New York, 1966), p. 193; and Roszak, *Where The Wasteland Ends*, pp. 272–89.

Chapter VI

1. *See again the text and references (Chap. V, nn. 1–2 above) from which the last chapter took its departure. Before departing from *la belle âme* yet again we should note at least parenthetically that this paradigmatic syndrome of internalized single subjectivity is the subject of some of Jacques Lacan's impenetrably interiorized essays (*Language of the Self*). One suspects that Lacan's obscurity is his own means to the invisibility characteristic of the beautiful soul. Perhaps his following remarks are as much about himself as about their more visible subjects: "The *moi* of modern man, as I have indicated elsewhere, has taken on its form in the dialectical impasse of the *belle âme* who does not recognize his very own *raison d'être* is the disorder that he denounces in the world" ("Symbol and Language," in *Language of the Self*, p. 44). Elsewhere in "La Chose freudienne," Lacan notes: "One might . . . remark that every verbal denunciation of a disorder participates in the disorder against which it protests, in the sense that the disorder has been set up by its discourse" (Quoted by Wilden, *Language of the Self*, p. 134, n. 111). This typically French deployment of teutonic dialectic, deployed also by Lyotard against Adorno (see Chap. V, n. 8 above), cannot help but rebound upon the deployer in the form of a doubly reinforced *tu quoque*.

2. Homer, *Odyssey* 8. 266–67.

3. For an intensely intelligent discussion of the problems raised by the unity of the virtues see Stanley Rosen, "*Sophrosyne* and *Selbstbewusstsein*," *The Review of Metaphysics* 26 (1973): 617–42.

4. G. S. Kirk and J. E. Raven, *The Presocratic Philosophers* (Cambridge, 1957), frag. 499, p. 370.

5. Ibid., frag. 501, p. 371.

6. *Consider for example the use of $\xi\nu\,\kappa\,\acute{\nu}\,\kappa\,\lambda\,o\,\nu$ (well-rounded) as paradigmatic of a passage that describes the plenum ("the full") in terms symptomatic of a visual-tactile imagination: "But since there is a furthest limit" (precisely the point denied in Anaxagoras's more thorough transcendence of the senses), "it is bounded on every side, like the bulk of a well-rounded sphere, from the center equally balanced in every direction" (Ibid., frag. 8, ll. 42–43, p. 276). One can almost see Parmenides mediating upon a ball of clay as he rounds it in his hands.

Of course the majority of scholars begin from within the overintellectualized tradition whose origin is Parmenides's end point. Consequently they remain ever insensitive to Parmenides's own beginning point. E.g., Kirk and Raven write: "Starting from the premise $\check{\epsilon}\sigma\tau\iota$ 'it is',—in much the same way as Descartes started from the premise 'cogito'—Parmenides proceeds, by the sole use of reason unaided by the senses, to deduce all that can be known about Being" (Ibid., p. 266; cf. also p. 279). Nor would it seem that Kirk and Raven recall the importance of Descartes's meditations upon an eminently sensible ball of wax. (Descartes, "*Meditation II*," in *The Philosophical Works of Descartes*, trans. Haldane and Ross, 2 vols. [Cambridge, 1911], 1:156–57).

"Reason unaided by the senses" is the product of an abstraction whose process is inevitably influenced by the peculiarities of one's experience of the senses. This process of abstraction is the epistemological analogue of the characterological denial of the shadow, the opposite of the dominant personality, about which Whitmont observes: "It becomes pathological only when we assume that we do not have it; because then it has us" (Edward C. Whitmont, *The Symbolic Quest* [New York, 1969], p. 168). For proof of the fact that philosophers in the Eleatic tradition have been had in different ways by their different experiences of the sensibility they suppose themselves to have transcended, compare the above passages from Parmenides and Descartes with two other *loci classici* in the hylomorphic tradition's attempt to expose an intelligible substratum by stripping off its sensible attributes: Kant, *The Critique of Pure Reason*, A 20, 21/B 34, 35; Aristotle *Metaphysics* Z 3, esp. 1029a10–26.

Having fixed on the intellectualized end point of Parmenides's process of abstraction, Kirk and Raven virtually ignore the "Proem" where the shadow of sensibility cries out for recognition from the symbolism of the very first line: "The steeds that carry me took me as far as my heart could desire" (*Presocratic Philosophers*, p. 266). E. Zeller, in his *Outlines of the History of Greek Philosophy* (trans. Palmer [New York, 1955], p. 65), recognizes that Parmenides "understood by Being not the abstract concept of pure being but the 'full', the space-filling mass without any further specifications: Not-being is empty space." Zeller regards "the attempt to make a pure logician out of the metaphysician Parmenides" as "misguided" (ibid., p. 67). Nevertheless he reneges on his own insight when he concludes with a description of Parmenides's "untenable rejection of the world of sense in favor of an abstract being only apprehended by thought" (ibid.).

7. Quoted by Jaghit Singh in his *Great Ideas and Theories of Modern Cosmology* (New York, 1961), p. 134. On the cosmological principle see also D. W. Sciama, *The Unity of the Universe* (Garden City, N.Y., 1961), pt.

2, pp. 69–180, though Sciama's use of his "presbyope," or all-seeing observer, would seem to be in direct violation of the most rudimentary demands of relativistic perspectivism.

8. Gustav Bergmann, *Meaning and Existence*, (Madison, Wis., 1960), p. 8.

9. *The connection between Anaxagoras's philosophy and the structure of Periclean Athens seems to have been well understood by Hegel, who begins his discussion of Anaxagoras with a comparison between the Lacedaemonian subordination of the individual to the collectivity and the Athenian elevation of subjectivity to the principle of the State. "In Lacedaemon personality proper was so much disregarded that the individual could not have free development or expression; individuality was not recognized, and hence not brought into harmony with the common end of the State. This abrogation of the rights of subjectivity, which, expressed in his own way, is also found in Plato's *Republic*, was carried very far with the Lacedaemonians. But the universal is living spirit only in so far as the individual consciousness finds itself as such within it" (*Hegel's Lectures on the History of Philosophy*, ed. and trans. Haldane, 3 vols. [London, 1892], 1: 323). Hegel repeatedly notes the importance of Anaxagoras's close friendship with Pericles. Further, he claims: "Under Pericles the highest culture of the moral commonwealth is to be found, the juncture where individuality is still under and also in the universal" (ibid., p. 325).

From these and several other remarks we may conclude that Anaxagoras and Pericles belong close to the beginning of a line of relationships that have fascinated modern readers of Hegel. See: (1) Leo Strauss's commentary on Xenophon's dialogue between a philosopher and a tyrant in *On Tyranny* (Ithaca, N.Y., 1968); (2) Alexandre Kojève's comments on Aristotle and Alexander as well as (3) Hegel and Napoleon to be found scattered throughout both his *Introduction to Hegel* (e.g., pp. 35, 59, 81, 89–90, 95) and his hardly disinterested review of Strauss (*On Tyranny*, which review is included in the 1968 edition, pp. 143–88). Just as Nietzsche later admits he was writing about himself in his eulogy, "Schopenhauer as Educator," (the third of the *Untimely Meditations*; for the admission, see *Ecce Homo* III, 3, Schlechta 2: 1116) so it is probable that Kojève's reflections on philosophers and tyrants are enriched by (4) his own close relationship with Charles DeGaulle. Nor is it surprising to find Anaxagoras's invocation of *Nous* (roughly translatable as Mind or Reason) regarded by Hegel as a pale reflection in the earliest dawn of *Geist* (roughly translated as both Mind and Spirit). Nonetheless it does seem worth noting the *affinity* between Hegel and Anaxagoras with respect to (a) the role of the philosopher in the life of the state, (b) the location of the structure of subjectivity in the universal, be it *Geist* or *Nous*, and (c) a principle of homoeomereity, one of whose manifestations was the relationship between the individual and the state in Periclean Athens.

10. *Zarathustra*, Schlechta 2: 499–500.

11. *Zarathustra*, Prologue, 10, Schlechta 2: 290, is the first of many instances of what comes to be an epithet.

12. *Letter to Overbeck, 8 June 1879, not included in Schlechta. For this letter and the most thorough description of this most difficult time in Nietzsche's life see "Das Leben Friedrich Nietzsches in den Jahren 1875–1879. Chronik," in *Nietzsche Werke, Kritische Gesamtausgabe*, ed. Colli and Montinari (Berlin, 1969), Vol. IV/4, pp. 7–90. For Nietzsche's description of his pursuit of natural science see *Ecce Homo* on *Human, All Too Human*, Sec. 3. A closer look at Nietzsche's reading will show that even in his romance with natural science he never succumbed to a belief in the sensuous substratum of positivistic materialism, viz. his intrigue with the works of Roger Boscovich. (In his "*Zeit- und Lebenstafel*," Schlechta notes that in March 1873, Nietzsche borrowed from the Basel library a copy of Boscovich's *Philosophia Naturalis*. Cf. Schlechta 3: 1365.) Boscovich's atomism is remarkable in that it posits atoms as unextended "puncta" or point-centers in a field of forces. In his contribution to the book he edited, *Roger Joseph Boscovich* (London, 1961), Lancelot Law Whyte recalls Kant's argument "that forces between point-centres yielding equilibrium positions at finite distances rendered superfluous the conception of extended matter" (p. 118; Whyte cites Kant's *Monadologia physica* of 1756 and the *Metaphysische Anfangsgrunde der Naturwissenschaft* of 1886). Thus Boscovich's atomism is the very opposite of the usual physicalism that attempts to extend into scientific concepts the common sense notion that something must be related to wood as wood is related to the bed. (Cf. Aristotle *Physics* 1. 7. 191a7–11.) So Whyte concludes, "Thus with Boscovich, Michell, and Kant a new concept of matter came into existence. Matter is no longer an essentially inert substance which occupies space and in a paradoxical manner exerts an apparent action at a distance; it is now simply the localized centres of extended interactions." How close to Nietzsche's image of the self, especially as developed by Deleuze (cf. n. 21 below). To continue: "Of these three Boscovich alone used this new conception of matter to construct a mathematical cosmogony. As Nietzsche, Mendeleeff and Cassirer recognized, the *Theoria* marks one of the greatest steps in the emancipation of the human mind from the spell of appearances. Matter is not what it seems" (Whyte, *Roger Joseph Boscovich*, p. 118).

Nietzsche's so-called positivism, his intrigue with natural science, turns out to be relational thinking turned toward the natural sciences. For further corroboration see Christopher Middleton, *Selected Letters of Friedrich Nietzsche* (Chicago, 1969), p. 182, n. 47. Middleton cites several sources germane to an Anaxagorean materialism, e.g., *Joyful Wisdom*, bk. 3, #109: "Matter is an error, like the God of the Eleatic philosophers. . . . When will all these shadows of God cease to obscure us?" See also Schlechta 3: 777–78: "One translation of this world of effect into a visible world—a world for the eye—is the concept 'motion.' Here it is always assumed that *something* is moved—which means that a *thing* is envisaged, whether in the fiction of a molecule-atom or even of its abstract version, the dynamic atom: a thing which causes effects—that is, we have not freed ourselves from the habits imposed by the senses and by language. Subject, object, a doer to do what is done, the doing itself and what it does—these are considered in separation; let us not forget that this is mere semeiotics and does not designate anything real. Mechanics as a doctrine of motion is already a translation into the sense language of men. . . . The mechanistic world is imagined in terms of a world as presented to eye and touch (as a world 'in motion'), in such a way that it can be calculated, in such a way that causating units are supposed, 'things,' 'atoms,' whose effect remains constant (the false concept of the subject carried across into the concept of the atom). . . . If we eliminate all these trimmings, no things remain but dynamic quanta, in a relation of tension to other dynamic quanta, whose essence consists in their being related to all other quanta, in their 'effect' on these" (same as *Will to Power* #635).

13. Kaufmann and his cohorts have perhaps wisely avoided the task of updating the ungainly translations by Zimmern and Cohn in vols. 6–7 of the *Complete Works of Friedrich Nietzsche*, ed. Levy (New York, 1909–11; reissued, New York, 1964).

14. *Ecce Homo*, Schlechta 2: 1118–19.

15. Ibid., I, 1, Schlechta 2: 1071: "A long, all too long series of years signifies recovery for me—signifies unfortunately relapse, decay, a kind of periodic decadence as well. Need I say after all this that in questions of decadence I am experienced. . . . Looking with the eyes of the sick toward *healthier* concepts and values and, conversely, looking again from the fullness and self-confidence of a *rich* life down into the secret work of the instinct of decadence—in this I have had the longest training, my truest experience; there if anywhere I am a *master*. I now know how, I have the know-how, for reversing perspectives: first reasons for which for me alone perhaps a 'revaluation of values' is possible."

16. *Human, All Too Human* #46, Schlechta 1: 484.

17. Ibid. #50, Schlechta 1:486. Somewhere Nietzsche speaks of his

lifelong failing of constantly imagining that the sufferings of others are greater than his own.

18. See in *Human, All Too Human* I, ##50, 103; II, ##63, 133, 142; in *Joyful Wisdom* ##338, 377; in *Zarathustra* IV; in *Beyond Good and Evil* ##30, 82, 171, 202, 206, 222, 260; in *Ecce Homo*, "Why I Am So Wise," sec. 4; in *Will To Power* ##365–68, 388.

19. See the passage in *Zarathustra*'s Prologue in which Zarathustra says, "I give no alms. I am not poor enough for that" (Schlechta 2: 278). Its mirror opposite is to be found in the speech of the ugliest man: "Everyone else would have thrown me his alms, his pity, with his glance and his speech. But I am not beggar enough for that, as you guessed. I am too rich for that, rich in what is great, in what is most frightful, most hateful, most inexpressible. Your *shame*, O Zarathustra, honors me." In a sensitive study exploring Nietzsche's symbolism Harold Alderman writes: "In the difference between giving gifts and giving alms one can see Nietzsche's whole critique of religion; for with a gift one also gives responsibility, but with alms one takes it away. Giving alms preempts responsibility for a man's existence but the giving of a gift celebrates it" ("Nietzsche's Masks," *International Philosophical Quarterly* 11 [1971]: 372).

20. *Zarathustra* IV, "The Cry of Distress," Schlechta 2: 481: "My final sin," asks Zarathustra of the Soothsayer. "Do you know what it is?" "Pity," comes the answer. "I have come to seduce you to your final sin."

21. *The difference between active and reactive impulses or emotions is central to the critique of *ressentiment,* which is itself an expression of the will to power but a reactive rather than an active expression. (See, for example, *Genealogy of Morals* I, 11; II, 12.) For Nietzsche's fundamentally fatalistic metaphysics, for an ontology that denies (with Spinoza) the fiction of an utterly autonomous source of agency, for a metaphysics that sees all agents and patients equally as intersects of forces, the difference between the agent and the patient boils down to the difference of "directions" or structure in the forces that most aptly characterize a given locus of intersects. The criteria for aptness of description are not unlike those of interest to contemporary philosophers of mind. E.g., without assuming the presence or absence of some substantial entity called a mind, one distinguishes certain trains of behavior from others as more characteristically 'mental' by virtue of overt evidence for reasons as distinct from causes guiding. The former trains of behavior are deemed intentional (active), the latter unintentional (passive or reactive). See G. E. M. Anscombe, *Intention* (Ithaca, N.Y., 1963); Stuart Hampshire, *Thought and Action* (New York, 1959); Charles Taylor, *The Explanation of Behaviour* (New York, 1964).

For an excellent treatment of Nietzsche that takes no cognizance whatever of the Anglo-American tradition in the philosophy of mind but nonetheless draws some of its central insights out of Nietzsche's works see Gilles Deleuze, *Nietzsche et la philosophie*, 2d ed. (Paris, 1970) esp. chap. 2, "Actif et reactif," pp. 44–82. Deleuze's work merits mention in two other respects pertinent to the present approach: first, Deleuze stresses the *differences* between Nietzsche and Hegel (esp. pp. 9–12, 180–83); second, he performs a precise if brief interpretation of the higher men as representing not parts of Zarathustra's interiority but rather such exterior forces as—in the case of the ugliest man—*le nihilisme reactif*; or various aspects and products of modern Western culture: the leech as the scientific quest for certitude, preferring to know nothing rather than to half-know much; the retired pope as the product of culture as religion; the shadow as the movement that is culture in its compulsion toward movement (pp. 189–91).

Both these points of Deleuze's interpretation call for comment under the rubric of the dynamic just discussed in the text: the most precise and pointed differences arise in the context of the greatest agreement, not only between Zarathustra and the ugliest man but also—to address the first point—between Nietzsche and Hegel, and to address both points, between the present reading and Deleuze's. Doubtless Deleuze is correct to differentiate Hegel and Nietzsche and he does so most concisely: *"Le 'oui' de Nietzsche s'oppose au 'non' dialectique; l'affirmation, à la negation dialectique; la différance, à la contradiction dialectique; la joie, la joissance, au travail dialectique; la légèrèté, la danse, à la pesanteur dialectique; la belle irresponsabilité, aux responsabilités dialectiques"* (p. 10). Yet this very concision is rendered possible by the problematic they share. Deleuze is among the few who see the point of even discussing Hegel and Nietzsche in the same breath. Regarding point two: Deleuze's entire interpretation of the higher men can be heartily embraced in the spirit of homoeomereity. His classifications of the exterior constitute a whole that is harmonious with the classification of the interior.

To extend the series of parallels, continuous with Nietzsche's preference for French culture as opposed to Hegel's for German, Deleuze's brief two hundred-odd pages of French probably contain as many insights as its rival in Nietzsche interpretation, Heidegger's eleven hundred-odd pages of German (Nietzsche, 2 vols. [Pfullingen, 1961]).

22. *Ecce Homo* on *Birth of Tragedy*, sec. 2, Schlechta 2: 1109–1110.

23. As opposed to the usual picture that pits Hegel as a camel of resignation against Kierkegaard as a lion of discrimination, note the closing paragraphs of Hegel's preface to the *Philosophy of Right*, where he explicitly

calls for a reconciliation with reality that is "less cool" that the "cold despair that submits to the view that in this earthly life things are truly bad or at best only tolerable . . . and that this is the only consideration that can keep us at peace with the world." For an interpretation of the Hegelian absolute as comprehending the finitude of the lion on its own terms and not as the pale shadow of subjectivity that was the subject of Kierkegaard's attack, see J. Ogilvy, "Reflections on the Absolute," *Review of Metaphysics* 28 (1975): 520–46.

24. See the very final pages of part IV, "The Sign," that is none other than the laughter of a lion, a yes from the throat of denial, from which Zarathustra concludes: *"Mitleiden! Das Mitleiden mit dem höheren Menschen! . . .Wohlan! Das—hatte seine Zeit?"* Even that which had been the last temptation, even pity had its time.

25. *In *Birth of Tragedy* Nietzsche toyed with the idea of a purely aesthetic justification for human existence. See, for example, sec. 17, written around 1870, and sec. 5 of the "Critical Backward Glance" (1886) that forms the introduction to later editions of Nietzsche's extraordinary *Jugendschrift*. These early longings for "metaphysical solace" in some sort of aesthetic justification for existence figure as the last vestigial species of a genus utterly extinct in Nietzsche's later writings, namely the genus titled Justifications for Existence. Art may remain on Nietzsche's order of rank as the highest form of human existence, but that is not to say that existence can or should be *justified* aesthetically or otherwise. Part of the significance of Nietzsche's so-called positivistic period is its success in subjecting all attempted justifications to the test of the tuning fork of Nietzsche's doubt, not simply for the sake of judging each species of justification but further for the sake of learning to live without the entire genus of justifications—including art if it be so unlucky as to appear unnecessarily under that rubric.

26. *Genealogy of Morals*, Preface, sec. 7, Schlechta 2: 769.

27. Though there is a place for remarkable ascetics too, as Nietzsche shows in *Genealogy of Morals*, III. Pericles is said to have never so much as smiled. Was his Anaxagorean comprehension of frames so vast as to render nothing surprising? Was that the source of his genius as the craftsman of a homoeomerous Athens?

28. The irony of Socrates was so characterized: as like the gadfly in *Apology* 30e, as stingray in *Meno* 80c.

29. At his sentencing after the protracted Chicago Eight trial Abbie Hoffman commented: "It wasn't funny last night sitting in a prison cell, a 5 × 8 room, with no light in the room. . . . There's no light. It's not a nice place for a Jewish boy to be, with a college education. I'm sure my mother

would say that" (*The Tales of Hoffman*, ed. from the official transcript by Levine [New York, 1970], p. 284).

30. Hillman, *Re-Visioning Psychology*, p. 168.

31. In *Essays on a Science of Mythology* (Princeton, 1969), written in part by Carl Kerenyi, Jung writes: "Psychology, as one of the many expressions of psychic life, operates with ideas which in their turn are derived from archetypal structures and thus generate a somewhat more abstract kind of myth. Psychology therefore translates the archaic speech of myth into a modern mythologem—not yet, of course, recognized as such—which constitutes one element of the myth 'science.' This seemingly hopeless undertaking is a *living and lived myth*, satisfying to persons of a corresponding temperament, indeed beneficial in so far as they have been cut off from their psychic origins by neurotic dissociation" (pp. 98–99). Jung's essay "The Psychology of the Child Archetype" is also available in vol. 9, pt. 1 of the *Collected Works*.

32. *Human, All Too Human* I, #483, Schlechta 1: 693.

33. Ibid., see ##629–30, Schlechta 1: 723–25 for a further and far subtler elaboration.

34. "With you," says the shadow to Zarathustra, "I destroyed whatever my heart had honored, all boundary stones and idols I hurled to the ground" (Schlechta 2: 511). For the importance of the image of the boundary stone and its breaking see the second of "The Seven Seals" (part III, Schlechta 2: 474), "If ever my anger burst tombs, moved boundary stones . . . ," as an answer to the riddle of redemption posed in part II ("On Redemption," Schlechta 2: 394): "That time does not run backwards, that is (the will's) rage; 'that which was' is etched on the stone it cannot roll."

35. Brown, *Love's Body*, p. 15.

36. Whitmont, *Symbolic Quest*, p. 163.

37. Schlechta 1: 871.

38. Schlechta 2: 403.

39. Jung, *Collected Works*, vol. 9, pt. 2, p. 9, par. 17.

40. Hans Georg Gadamer, *Wahrheit und Methode*, 2d ed. (Tubingen, 1965) esp. pt. 2, sec. 2, "Grundzüge einer Teorie der hermeneutischen Erfahrung."

41. Whitmont, *Symbolic Quest*, p. 168.

42. Schlechta 2: 312, 486.

43. See Gary Snyder, "Why Tribe," reprinted in *Self and World*, ed. Ogilvy, p. 387: "For one to 'follow the grain' it is necessary to look exhaustively into the negative and demonic potentials of the Unconscious, and by recognizing these powers—symbolically acting them out—one releases him-

self from these forces. By this profound exorcism and ritual drama, the Great Subculture destroys the one credible claim of Church and State to a necessary function."

44. *In *Gandhi's Truth* (New York, 1969), Erik Erikson emphasizes the possibility of ritual as a means of avoiding violence (pp. 423 ff.). He cites the highly ritualized behavior of Damstags who parade in parallel before turning toward "a full mutual confrontation and a powerful but harmless wrestling" (p. 426). Cf. Konrad Lorenz, *On Aggression*, trans. Wilson (New York, 1966), and *King Solomon's Ring* (New York, 1952). Erikson's further reflections on ritual carry him in a direction similar to his reflections on character, namely toward overcoming what he regards as the historical process of human "pseudo-speciation": "History provides, however, a way by which the pseudo-species mentality of warring groups can become disarmed, as it were, within a *wider identity*. This can come about by territorial unification: the *Pax Romana* embraced races, nations, and classes. Technological advances in universal 'traffic,' too, unite: seafaring, mechanized locomotion, and wireless communication each has helped to spread changes eventually contained in a sense of widening identity which helps to overcome economic fear, the anxiety of culture change, and the dread of a spiritual vacuum" (*Gandhi's Truth*, p. 433). As sympathetic as one must be to the peaceful intent and graceful detail of Erikson's work, here again his subservience to the ideal of unification places him among the theorists of the mainstream prior to its pluralization in the delta. Rather than regard our speciation into situses and statuspheres as "pseudo," we might do better to grant that once man's tampering with time generates cultural determinations more significant to history than biological determinisms, then man's species are more significantly described culturally than biologically. Only from the perspective of a biological reductionism could these cultural differentiations be regarded as pseudo. Nor is it clear that the ritualized sublimation of violence should serve "the *anticipatory development of more inclusive identities*" (p. 433). Granted the potentially destructive defensiveness of particularly paranoid groups and the ugliness of the smug indifference of others, still the route through ritual toward decreased violence need not presume the *overcoming* of difference toward more inclusive identity but rather the *recognition* of difference. Once recognized, differences may articulate a mutually enriching ecology in place of a win-lose struggle on a common hierarchy.

45. Running throughout Bateson's essays one finds traces of the cybernetic-ecological insight that total conquest over any adversary is a modern and intrinsically self-defeating fantasy. Because the unit of survival is always organism-plus-environment, any significant alteration of the environ-

ment is bound to affect the viability of the organism enacting pretensions of control. See, for example, *Ecology of Mind*, p. 438: "We do not live in the sort of universe in which simple lineal control is possible. Life is not like that."

46. See, for example, Philip Slater's account of the dominant society's hatred of hippies in *Pursuit of Loneliness*. Though he does not mention the dynamic of the shadow explicitly, the essence of his argument has it that the fathers despise in the sons what they have denied for themselves.

47. To be sure, his lack of a political program is no oversight. From his scattered reflections on politics, on Bismarck, on Europe and on the Greek polis one can reconstruct his reasons for claiming that the progress of nihilistic decadence and slave morality has as one of its more important results the removal of the conditions for the possibility of politics. This reconstruction has been compactly performed by Tracy Strong, "Nietzsche and Politics: Parables of the Shepherd and the Herd," in *Nietzsche*, ed. Solomon (Garden City, N.Y., 1973), pp. 258–92.

48. *To vindicate Nietzsche from the obvious similarities between some of his pronouncements and the cult of *Blut und Boden* a more careful consideration of fascism is called for. In *The Fascist Persuasion in Modern Politics*, A. James Gregor argues that "fascism is the form that efforts to be pure and clear minded again are most likely to take as they respond to the demand for a unanimous definition of evil" (quoted by John P. Sisk in "Losing Big," *Harper's*, November 1975, p. 85). Surely Nietzsche's philosophy is no effort to be "pure and clear minded again," nor does it "respond to the demand for a unanimous definition of evil." Instead Nietzsche deflates that demand by a frontal attack on the false unities of Good and Evil alike. Further vindication would follow from a close comparison, not to be attempted here, between Nietzsche's views and those of Giovanni Gentile, perhaps the most philosophically articulate of fascism's apologists. See H. S. Harris, *The Social Philosophy of Giovanni Gentile* (Urbana, Ill., 1960), for a useful aid in making the necessary comparison.

49. There is, for example, something a trifle too pat about Charles Hampden-Turner's admirably concise portrait of Radical Man. A paradox infects the neat contrast between the structures describing anomic man and radical man for, given such a contrast together with a description of radical man as, "periodically SUSPENDING his cognitive structures and RISKING himself in trying to BRIDGE THE DISTANCE to the other(s)," then precisely the plunge into the character of anomie confronts radical man as his truest risk. Hampden-Turner, *Radical Man*, pp. 37, 79, et passim.

50. Cf. Heraclitus, frag. 60, in Kirk and Raven, *Presocratic Philosophers* p. 189.

51. On the difference between the Platonic preoccupation with forms of unity and the Fichtean-Hegelian preoccupation with processes of formation see Stanley Rosen, *G. W. F. Hegel* (New Haven, 1974), pp. 92 ff.

Chapter VII

1. *Zarathustra* IV, "The Shadow," Schlechta 2: 512.

2. Ibid., I, "On the Despisers of the Body"; see also *Will to Power* ##226, 314, 392, 461, 485, 492, 547, 549, 659, 676, 820, 1016, 1046, 1047, rpt. together in *Self and World*, ed. Ogilvy, pp. 172–78.

3. Nietzsche suffered much of his life from vaguely diagnosed stomach troubles and migraine headaches for which he took countless medicines, some in the morphine family. Though his sister is notoriously unreliable on most matters relating to her idolized brother we have no reason to doubt her candor in describing the time just after completing pt. 1 of *Zarathustra* as a difficult period during which "he was striving just then to give up the practice of taking hydrate of chloral—a drug he had begun to take while ill with influenza . . ." (see her introduction to *Zarathustra*, trans. and rpt. in the Modern Library edition of *The Philosophy of Nietzsche* [New York, 1927], p. xxvii).

4. For Zarathustra's own love on the contrary, see the magician's enigmatic speech toward the close of *Zarathustra* IV, "On Science": ". . . before the night is over he will learn to love me and praise me once again; he cannot live long without such foolishness. *He* loves his enemies: this art he understands the best of all I've seen. But he takes revenge for it on his friends" (Schlechta 2: 538).

5. This conversion event of the Chicago-Eight-Great received wide coverage in the media from *Win* to *Time*. The only one to make any sense of it was Michael Rossman in a beautifully reverent piece irreverently entitled, "Show us your lotus ass, Rennie!" *Social Policy*, 1973.

6. Chögyam Trungpa, *Cutting Through Spiritual Materialism* (Berkeley, 1973), is a better book than most being churned from the burgeoning spiritual-consciousness mill.

7. The quoted phrase is the closest the clear-minded common sense of British philosophy can approach the dark intricacies of dialectic. Austin uses it somewhere in *Sense and Sensibilia*.

8. See Hegel, *Phenomenology of Mind*, p. 143.

9. See, for example, Alexandre Kojève's famous series of lectures

attended from 1933 to 1939 by so many of France's subsequent leading intellectuals, collected by Raymond Queneau and published as *Introduction to the Reading of Hegel* (see Chap. II, n. 5 above).

10. Qualifications are required. While the exoteric Plato extols a preparation for death and departure from the body, the esoteric Plato holds a healthy respect for the reality and importance of art and eros. On the distinction between the two Platos as well as an introduction to the esoteric see Stanley Rosen's excellent *Plato's Symposium* (New Haven, 1968); also James Ogilvy, "Socratic Method, Platonic Method and Authority," *Educational Theory* 21 (1971): 3–16. On the link between the Western tradition's abhorrence of mere appearance and the Eastern tradition's doctrine of *maya*, doubtless Schopenhauer's philosophy is the most important to consult in considering Nietzsche's appropriation of these issues. Schopenhauer regarded his philosophy as a synthesis of Buddhism with Kant's philosophy of phenomena and noumena.

11. For a sampling of different readings of the Hegelian Absolute see Ogilvy, "Reflections on the Absolute."

12. Recall again Plato's description in *Phaedrus* 265a of a second kind of madness that "comes not from mortal weakness or disease, but from a divine banishment of the commonplace."

13. See, for example, the many accounts of mystic experiences recorded in Evelyn Underhill's classic *Mysticism* (orig. pub. 1910; New York, 1955). On the specific issue of the similarity between what the mystic tradition regards as religious ecstasy and the Western rationalist tradition regards as pathology see Rune E. A. Johansson, *The Psychology of Nirvana* (Garden City, N.Y., 1970), esp. pp. 83, 135–36. Also Erich Fromm, D. T. Suzuki and Richard DeMartino, *Zen Buddhism and Psychoanalysis* (New York, 1970).

14. Laing, *Divided Self*, esp. chaps. 4–7.

15. Baba Ram Dass, *Be Here Now* (Lama Foundation: San Cristobal, N. Mex., 1971), pp. 107–08.

16. The first was probably Schelling but his criticisms were taken up and expanded by Feuerbach, Ruge, Marx, Kierkegaard and Trendelenburg. On these early misunderstandings of Hegel the best history in English is surely Karl Löwith, *From Hegel to Nietzsche*, trans. Green (New York, 1964), esp. pp. 116 ff., though the lack of a rich enough English subjunctive lends misleading support to Löwith's report of the criticisms of Hegel.

17. On the affinity between the categories of Life and Infinitude see Hegel, *Phenomenology*, chap. 4, sec. 1, "The Truth of Self-Certainty," and *The Science of Logic*, vol. 2, sec. 3, chap. 1, "Life."

18. See Marx and Engels, *The German Ideology* in *Writings of the Young Marx*, ed. Easton and Guddat, p. 415.

19. For the modern continuation of the debate begun by Schelling (see Chap. VII, n. 16 above) as it relates to the relation between the *Logic* and the *Phenomenology* and the problem of beginning, see Otto Pöggeler, "Zur Deutung der Phänomenologie des Geistes," *Hegel-Studien* 1 (1961): 255–94; Hans-Friedrich Fulda, *Das Problem einer Einleitung in Hegels Wissenschaft der Logik* (Frankfurt, 1965); and the final pair of essays in *Materialien zu Hegels "Phänomenologie des Geistes,"* ed. Fulda and Henrich (Frankfurt, 1973): Pöggeler, "Die Komposition der Phänomenologie des Geistes," pp. 329–90; Fulda, "Zur Logik der Phänomenologie," pp. 391–425; see also Dieter Henrich, "Anfang und Methode der Logik," in his *Hegel im Kontext* (Frankfurt, 1967), pp. 73–94.

20. *Birth of Tragedy*, sec. 7, Schlechta 1: 48; this passage, often referred to in what follows, should be read in its entirety. It can be found on pp. 51–52 of the Francis Golffing translation (Garden City, N.Y., 1956).

21. Robert Graves, *The Greek Myths*, 2 vols. (Baltimore, 1955), Vol. I, sec. 83, pp. 281–85.

22. Hegel, *Phenomenology*, p. 193.

23. See Hesiod *Theogony* 11. 585 ff., on the introduction of Aphrodite: "Now when he had fashioned the beautiful bane in the place of a blessing, he led her forth where were the other gods and men, glorying in the bravery of the grey-eyed daughter of a mighty sire. And amazement held immortal gods and mortal men, when they beheld the sheer delusion inescapable for men." For another early Greek expression of similar sentiments see Homer, *Iliad* 3. 156–60.

24. *Birth of Tragedy*, sec. 7, Schlechta 1: 48.

25. See Rudolph Binion's excellent book *Frau Lou* (Princeton, 1968), for an unparalleled portrait of Nietzsche the man.

26. Plutarch, "Solon" in *The Lives of the Noble Grecians and Romans*, trans. Dryden, vol. 14 of Great Books of the Western World, ed. Hutchins (Chicago, 1952), p. 66.

27. Nietzsche, *Philosophy in the Tragic Age of the Greeks*, Schlechta 3: 364.

28. *Birth of Tragedy*, sec. 7, Schlechta 1: 48.

29. Aldous Huxley, *The Doors of Perception* (orig. pub. 1954; New York, 1963), p. 31.

30. *Philosophy of the Greeks*, Schlechta 3: 365.

31. Huxley, *Doors of Perception*, pp. 34–35.

32. See Carlos Castaneda, *The Teachings of Don Juan: A Yaqui*

Way of Knowledge (New York, 1969); *A Separate Reality* (New York, 1971); *Journey to Ixtlan* (New York, 1972); *Tales of Power* (New York, 1974).

33. *Birth of Tragedy*, Sec. 7, Schlechta 1: 48.

34. Arthur C. Danto, *Mysticism and Morality* (New York, 1972). As in his book on Nietzsche so in this fundamentally unsympathetic exposition of mysticism Danto demonstrates the maxim that acute analysis is no substitute for a synthesis of life and thought. Danto's whole approach to the problems he addresses—e.g., the first chapter's distinction between facts and values—places him at such a distance from the consciousness he would investigate that one hardly knows where to start in objecting to his conclusions. Though there are some simple errors, e.g., "Meditation requires concentration, or, perhaps, is concentration" (p. 59)—true of some forms of meditation but not of others—the more serious problem is one of a kind of spiritual false consciousness, a self-certainty in the robust reality of facts, a mind set redolent of the true disbeliever to whom nothing is more delightful than an occasional condescension from crisp scholastic professionalism to the bizarre, viz. the confession of intellectual slumming: "It is only when the price for crudeness becomes small that philosophy can afford the sort of logical shoddiness we find, say, in nineteenth century Western thought, when men did not need to be sharp for extra-worldly reasons, and philosophy as a discipline had not yet attained professionalization" (p. 24). On professionalization as vice rather than virtue see Chap. VIII below.

35. Huxley, *Doors of Perception*, p. 35.

36. Shakespeare, *Hamlet*, act 3, scene 2.

37. *Zarathustra* IV, "The Welcome," Schlechta 2: 515.

38. See for example Heidegger, *Sein und Zeit*, sec. 5, pars. 2–3. On auditory and optical illusions making what is nearest appear to be what is farthest and vice versa see Kierkegaard on what he calls the "acoustic illusion" according to which evidence of the Paradox appears to emanate from the offended consciousness: *Philosophical Fragments*, pp. 61–67. This passage is profitably read as an answer to the *Critique of Pure Reason*, A644/B672 ff., where Kant comments on the optical illusion creating a *"focus imaginarius*, from which, since it lies quite outside the bounds of possible experience, the concepts of the understanding do not in reality proceed. . . . Hence arises the illusion that the lines have their source in a real object lying outside the field of empirically possible knowledge."

39. Recall again Nietzsche's description of the complexity of volition in *Beyond Good and Evil*, sec. 19; cf. *supra* pp. 181–3.

40. For the Platonic *periagoge*, see *Republic* 7, first few pages, for the picture of the soul's liberation from the cave by its release from its chains

and its *turning around* away from the images on the wall; and cf. above pp. 95–96.

41. Goffman, *Frame Analysis*, p. 521; see Chap. V, n. 44, and pp. xxxx above.

42. Here the language connotes not Erikson's but Heidegger's and Allen Wheelis's versions of the dynamic described by Erikson as an identity crisis. See Heidegger, *Sein und Zeit*, div. 2, chap. 2; and Allen Wheelis's excellent book for its time, *The Quest for Identity* (New York, 1958).

43. Cf. the King on the right's first speech and the speech of the soothsayer.

44. This is and is not a close translation: not exactly Nietzsche's words but more equivalent in literary vulgarity than the literal translation, "It doesn't pay," etc., whose idiomatic original sounded as coarse to Nietzsche's first German readers as the looser translation to later American readers. Why else would the King on the left, who was the first time around as well something of a Mrs. Grundy, be so upset about Zarathustra's manner of speech?

45. Both speeches of the King on the right must be read in their entirety to support this interpretation, but see especially the despair of his first speech, Schlechta 2: 485: "What do we kings matter anymore!"

46. *Zarathustra* IV, "The Welcome," Schlechta 2: 517–18.

47. Apollo is the god of healing. Thus Zarathustra's discovery vindicates Hillman and Illich who argue the one-sidedness of our fantasies of sickness as something to be healed and done away with rather than lived and understood as an articulation of the embodied soul.

48. Cf. Aquinas, *Summa Theologica*, 1st pt., questions 5, 48, 49, 65; pt. 1 of 2d pt., questions 18, 29, 79–81; 3d pt. supp., questions 69, 74.

49. *Zarathustra* IV, "The Welcome," Schlechta 2: 519.

50. Cf. Underhill, *Mysticism*, pt. 2, chap. 9.

51. *Zarathustra* IV, "The Last Supper" (another bad joke, more *lila*), Schlechta 2: 521.

52. Compare Schlechta 2: 521 with Schlechta 1: 48, sec. 7 of *Birth of Tragedy*.

53. On the camel see *Zarathustra* I, "The Three Metamorphoses," and above, pp. 190 ff.

54. Plato *Republic* 7. 517a.

55. James, *Principles of Psychology*, p. 888 n.; and above, p. 187 f.

56. *Zarathustra* IV, "Song of Melancholy," Schlechta 2: 536.

57. *Zarathustra* IV, "On Science," Schlechta 2: 538.

58. *Zarathustra* IV, "Among the Daughters of the Wilderness," Schlechta 2: 544.

59. Since Zarathustra's convalescence includes his solution to the riddle of eternal recurrence (see III, "The Convalescent"—*Der Genesende*) the convalescence of the higher men may be assumed to betoken their solution as well. Cf. the end of pt. 1 of "The Awakening," Schlechta 2: 546: *"Es sind Genesende!"* And pt. 1 of the "Drunken Song", Schlechta 2: 552: *". . . wurden sie sich mit einem Male ihrer Verwandlung und Genesung bewusst. . . ."*

60. Cf. *supra* pp. 123–125.

61. Cf. *supra* pp. 109–112.

62. Cf. *supra* pp. 108–109.

63. Cf. *Will to Power* #1066.

64. What is one to make of the recurrent mention of the moon in describing those moments of revelation? Cf. *Joyful Wisdom*, #341, *Will to Power*, #1038; *Zarathustra* "The Drunken Song," sec. 5; and sec. 4 recalls also the spider mentioned in *Joyful Wisdom*, #341.

65. *Zarathustra* IV, "At Noon," Schlechta 2: 514.

66. See, for example, Claude Levi-Strauss, "The Structural Study of Myth," in *Structural Anthropology*, trans. Jacobson and Schoepf (New York, 1963), pp. 216–17: "Our method thus eliminates a problem which has, so far, been one of the main obstacles to the progress of mythological studies, namely, the quest for the *true* version, or the *earlier* one. On the contrary, we define the myth as consisting of all its versions."

67. Here one thinks of the so-called Freudian slip that is of great moment in Lacan's and Ricouer's returns to Freud.

68. Lao Tzu, *The Way of Life*, trans. Bynner (New York, 1962), p. 25.

69. For a sensitive study of the changing face of madness see Edgar A. Levenson, *The Fallacy of Understanding* (New York, 1972), esp. chap. 7, "The Changing Model of the Psychoanalytic Patient." See also the works of Hillman, Foucault and Lifton cited above.

70. In *The Structure and Dynamics of the Psyche*, vol. 8 of the *Collected Works*, pp. 417–531.

71. Hegel, for example, devotes many pages to a discussion of phrenology and finally evinces greater respect for the consciousness that leaves to the luck of the lot decisions about such contingent matters as would derive only the appearance of universal rationality from the attentions of a particular intellect. "If the individual, by his understanding, determines on a certain course, and selects, after consideration, what is useful for him, it is the specific nature of his particular character which is the ground of this self-determination. This basis is just what is contingent; and that knowledge

which his understanding supplies as to what is useful for the individual, is hence just such a knowledge as that of 'oracles' or of the 'lot'; only that he who questions the oracle or lot, thereby shows the ethical sentiment of indifference to what is accidental, while the former, on the contrary, treats the inherently contingent as an essential concern of his thought and knowledge" (*Phenomenology of Mind*, p. 710).

72. See Max Horkheimer and Theador Adorno, *Dialectic of Enlightenment*, trans. Cumming, (orig. pub. 1947; New York, 1972).

73. John Wisdom, *Gods, Proceedings of the Aristotelian Society*, 1944; rpt. in idem, *Philosophy and Psychoanalysis* (Oxford, 1957), and in *Self and World*, ed. Ogilvy, pp. 574–75.

Chapter VIII

1. Plato *Theaetetus* 173c.

2. *Zarathustra* IV, "The Higher Men," Schlechta 2: 524.

3. See, for example, Eric Voegelin, *Plato* (Baton Rouge, 1966), pp. 54, 90 ff., 116 ff. For an answer to Voegelin's arguments as to his explicit adversary, Leo Strauss, see Kojève's remarks in Strauss, *On Tyranny*, pp. 143 ff.

4. Lewis Mumford, "Utopia, The City and The Machine," in *Utopias and Utopian Thought*, ed. Manuel (Boston, 1967).

5. Technologically facilitated death at a distance is the subject of chap. 2 of Philip Slater's *Pursuit of Loneliness*. His attack on technology becomes more virulent in *Earthwalk*, even to the extent that one begins to wonder whether Slater wishes to deny the technical impulse altogether and exile Hephaestus from the pantheon.

6. Cf. Heidegger, *Being and Time*, Introduction, II sec. 4; also pt. I, 1, sec. 9.

7. On the difference between a plot and a history of one thing after another see Aristotle *Poetics* 8–9.

8. *In the distinction between *ousia* and *parousia* an entire ontology for relational thought lies hidden. To uncover that relational ontology in a scholarly way one would want to begin with Heidegger's *Being and Time* and, for some explicit remarks on *ousia* and *parousia*, his *An Introduction to Metaphysics*, trans. Manheim (Garden City, N.Y., 1961), pp. 50–51, 162–63, 169–70. Nor once launched on such a project would one want to neglect the

closing paragraphs of Hegel's *Encyclopedia* together with a commentary discussing both the prefix *para-* and *parousia*: cf. Michael Theunissen, *Hegels Lehre vom absoluten Geist als theologischpolitischer Traktat* (Berlin, 1970).

9. On the dialectics of nature see the sources cited in Chap. I, n. 59 above.

10. Illich, *Tools for Conviviality*, p. 84.

11. Ibid., p. 86.

12. William Irwin Thompson, *Passages About Earth* (New York, 1974), p. 44.

13. Ibid., p. 54.

14. Florman, "In Praise of Technology," p. 70. Florman's following lines are more temperate: "The antitechnologists are not preaching totalitarianism. They are good and gentle men, humanists at heart. But their cry for 'something like a spontaneous religious conversion' (Mumford), 'a common faith' (Dubos), 'Consciousness III . . . an attempt to gain transcendence' (Reich), 'the visionary commonwealth' (Roszak) is a cry for a new 'movement', and each new mass movement carries within itself the seeds of a new totalitarianism."

15. See Jean-Jacques Rousseau, *The Social Contract*, and Benjamin R. Barber, "Forced to be Free: An Illiberal Defense of Liberty," in Barber, *Superman and Common Men* (New York, 1971), pp. 37–80.

16. Cf. John J. McDermott, "Nature Nostalgia and the City: An American Dilemma," *Soundings* 55 (1972): 1–20.

17. Murray Bookchin, "A Technology for Life," in *Sources*, ed. Roszak (New York, 1972), p. 256. The incipient totalitarianism of Bookchin's remark is especially odd since Bookchin is among the most acute of contemporary thinkers on both anarchism and ecology. See his *Post-Scarcity Anarchism* (Berkeley, 1971).

18. Cf. Plato *Republic* 2. 372d; and Stanley Rosen, "The Role of Eros in Plato's Republic," *The Review of Metaphysics* 18 (1965): 452–75.

19. For the meaning of 'commodity' in this context see Marx, *Capital*, chap. 1; on the much studied topic of alienation probably the best account is István Mészáros, *Marx's Theory of Alienation* (London 1970).

20. John Muir, *How to Keep Your Volkswagen Alive* (Santa Fe, N. Mex., 1969).

21. Percival and Paul Goodman, *Communitas* (New York, 1947), pp. 82–85.

22. E. F. Schumacher, *Small is Beautiful* (New York, 1973), p. 93. Cf. pp. 13, 100, 107 for a metaphysics of nature that risks romantic countertransference.

23. John M. Blair, *Economic Concentration* (New York, 1972); Jacob Schmookler, *Invention and Economic Growth* (Cambridge, Mass., 1966); Charles E. Silberman, "Identity Crisis in the Consumer Markets," *Fortune*, March 1971, and "The U.S. Economy in an Age of Uncertainty," *Fortune*, January 1971; Barry Stein, *Size, Efficiency, and Community Enterprise* (Cambridge, Mass., 1974).

24. See Hampden-Turner, *Radical Man*; idem, "The Factory as an Oppressive and non-Emancipatory Environment," in *Workers' Control*, ed. Hunnius, Garson and Case (New York, 1973), pp. 30–45.

25. C. Argyris, *Interpersonal Competence and Organizational Effectiveness* (Homewood, Ill., 1962), and *Personality and Organization* (New York, 1957). Much of the work in small group dynamics (e.g., at National Training Labs in Bethel, Maine) could be construed as an effort toward educating organizational personnel in countertransference. To adopt the jargon: the point is to learn from the "lab" experience how to "own" tacit needs and expectations that otherwise may obstruct one's organizational efforts by decreasing one's interpersonal competence. The apparently "permissive" atmosphere of the lab experience is the result of the recognition that, quite to the contrary of the bureaucratic ideal of depersonalizing channels of communication, until one recognizes and owns highly personal idiosyncracies, their inevitable distortions of communication will remain unrecognized. Sensitivity toward countertransference and projection does not entail an *avoidance* of personal investment. Rather the permission to let out one's suppressed prejudices or desires facilitates their recognition. Seen in this light the lab or T-group is a training in hermeneutics whose first principle calls for an explication or rendering explicit of *Vorurteilen*, or prejudgments.

26. For a ground-breaking study in the application of scientific method to the subjective experience of consciousness see William R. Torbert, *Learning from Experience: Toward Consciousness* (New York, 1972). Torbert's method has nothing to do with elaborate technology but relies instead on intersubjective validation of phenomenological introspection.

27. William Irwin Thompson, *At the Edge of History* (New York, 1971).

28. For arguments showing the positive role of utopian thought despite its possible misuses see Karl Mannheim, *Ideology and Utopia*, trans. Wirth and Shils (orig. pub. 1929; New York, 1936); and Herbert Marcuse, *An Essay on Liberation* (Boston, 1969).

29. Hegel, *Philosophy of Right*, Zusätze, Ad 124.

30. Stein, *Community Enterprise*, p. 84.

31. Collis, Dema and Omololu, "The Ecology of Child Health and

Nutrition in Nigerian Villages: Part I Environment, Population and Resources"; quoted by Charles Hughes and John Hunter in "Disease and 'Development' in Africa," *The Social Organization of Health, Recent Sociology*
no. 3, ed. Dreitzel (New York, 1971), p. 176.

32. Ibid.

33. Thompson, *Edge of History*, p. 75.

34. Cf. H. L. Wilensky, "The Professionalization of Everyone?"
American Journal of Sociology 70 (1964): 137–58.

35. See C. Turner and M. N. Hodge, "Occupations and Professions," in *Professions and Professionalization*, ed. Jackson (Cambridge,
1970), pp. 17–50.

36. Ibid., pp. 38–39: "The case of medical practioners is instruc-
tive. When the occupationally related activities are examined, there is a
clear twentieth-century trend towards increasing specialization and division
of labour, but it is important to note that at the beginning of the century medical practitioners constituted a well-established occupational category. There
is no doubt that at present the development of techniques and the application
of substantive theory are dominated by medical practitioners themselves, albeit that in many new developments those medical men who are involved
work in conjunction with electronics specialists, laboratory scientists, pharmaceutical entrepreneurs, etc. The hypothesis may be advanced, however,
that the degree of control of the development of substantive theory underpin-
ning the practice of medicine exercised by medical practitioners is decreasing."

37. Illich, *Tools for Conviviality*, p. 21.

38. For Broad's ideas see Huxley, *Doors of Perception*, pp. 22 ff. For
James see *The Varieties of Religious Experience*, The Gifford Lectures,
1901–02 (New York, 1958).

39. See Robert Nozick, *Anarchy, State, and Utopia* (New York,
1974).

40. Barber, *Superman*, p. 25.

41. P. Bachrach, *The Theory of Democratic Elitism* (Boston, 1967);
C. Pateman, *Participation and Democratic Theory* (Cambridge, 1960); D. F.
Thompson, *The Democratic Citizen* (Cambridge, 1970); H. J. Laski, *Authori-
ty in the Modern State* (New Haven, 1919), and "The Personality of the
State," *The Nation*, no. 101 (1915); G. D. H. Cole, *Social Theory* (London,
1920), and "Conflicting Social Obligations," *Proceedings of the Aristotelian
Society*, n.s. 15 (1915). On Laski and Cole see the following sources: H. A.
Deane, *The Political Ideas of Harold J. Laski* (New York, 1955); K. C.

Hsiao, *Political Pluralism* (London, 1927); H. M. Magid, *English Political Pluralism*, (New York, 1941).

42. F. M. Barnard and R. A. Vernon, "Pluralism, Participation, and Politics," *Political Theory* 3 (1975): 180–97.

43. See Michael Kammen, *People of Paradox* (New York, 1972). Kammen's historiography stresses "biformity" (see his chap. 4). Kammen's history sets the stage for a contemporary analysis of the structure of pluralized American society because his method minimizes the presumptions of social and cultural uniformity. For his multidimensional analysis of the complex origins of American culture see esp. pp. 113–16.

Chapter IX

1. See again the concluding sentence of Descartes's first *Meditation*, and Chapter V, p. 173 above.

2. Vernon L. Smith, "The Primitive Hunter Culture, Pleistocene Extinction, and the Rise of Agriculture," *Journal of Political Economy* 83 (1975): p. 727.

3. Ibid., p. 742.

4. For Plato the design of the *Republic* is described as representing the structure of the just soul "writ large" (*Republic* 2. 368c–369b). The homoeomerous structuring of soul and city is given yet a third tier in the cosmology of the *Timaeus*. See more recently Hans Gerth and C. Wright Mills, *Character and Social Structure* (New York, 1953), p. 94: "Unity of self, occurring when all the images of self held by the person and by others coincide, will most likely occur when the position and the career of the person is composed of significant others who are harmonious in their appraisals and expectations.

"In a society where roles are stereotyped and each man 'knows his place,' as do others, there is not much chance for differences to arise between self-images and the images others hold of him."

5. Max Weber, *The Protestant Ethic and the Spirit of Capitalism*, trans. Parsons (New York, 1958); also idem, *The Religion of China*, trans. Gerth (Glencoe, Ill., 1951).

6. Galbraith, *New Industrial State*, p. 169: "The relationship between society at large and an organization must be consistent with the rela-

tion of the organization to the individual. There must be consistency in the goals of the society, the organization and the individual."

7. T. W. Adorno, Else Frenkel-Brunswik, Daniel J. Levinson, and R. Nevitt Sanford, *The Authoritarian Personality* (orig. pub. 1950; New York, 1969).

8. M. Rokeach, *The Open and Closed Mind* (New York, 1960), a critique of *The Authoritarian Personality* to the extent that Rokeach emphasizes the possibility of a fascism of the Left but remains nonetheless in agreement on the basic premise that character structure and social structure reflect each other.

9. Charles Reich, *The Greening of America*; Wilhelm Reich, *The Mass Psychology of Fascism*, trans. Carfagno (New York, 1970), p. xii: "It is not difficult to see that the various political and ideological groupings of human society correspond to the various layers of the structure of the human character. We, however, decline to accept the error of idealistic philosophy, namely that this human structure is immutable to all eternity. After social conditions and changes have transmuted man's original biologic demands and made them a part of his character structure, the latter reproduces the social structure of society in the form of ideologies." Two comments: first the two Reichs are right to affirm the linkage of character structure and social structure but equally wrong in their equal and opposite claims of causal sequence, Charles from consciousness to society, Wilhelm from society to consciousness. Second, Wilhelm has in mind the mythological idealism that is the object of the Marxist attack. Marx himself recognized that it was Hegel who first fully appreciated the historical character of human nature: "The outstanding thing in Hegel's Phenomenology and its final outcome—that is, the dialectic of negativity as the moving and generating principle—is thus first that Hegel conceives the self-genesis of man as a process, conceives objectification as loss of the object, as alienation and as transcendence of this alienation, that he thus grasps the essence of labour and comprehends objective man—true, because real man—as the outcome of man's own labour" (Marx, *Economic and Philosophic Manuscripts of 1844* [Moscow, 1961], p. 151). The cycle of reproduction of man by society and society by man admits of historical alteration but the very cyclical nature of the process forbids any simple causal claims concerning the origins of any particular alteration.

10. Hampden-Turner, *Radical Man*.